Hawkshaw's great crescent roof may have gone but Cannon Street still retains its two baroque towers.

PSL FIELD GUIDE

Railways of the
SOUTHERN REGION

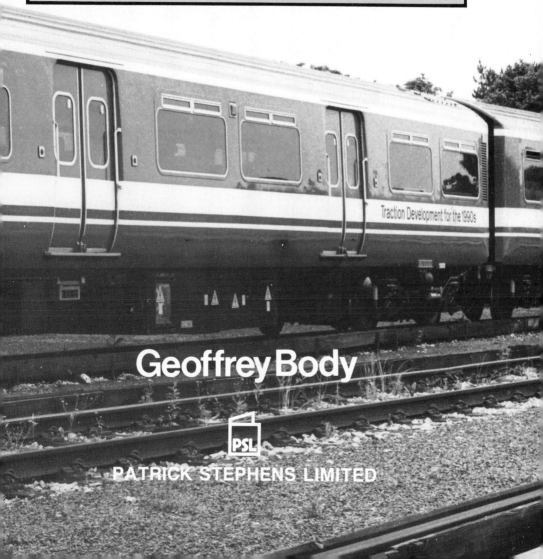

PSL FIELD GUIDE

Railways of the
SOUTHERN REGION

Traction Development for the 1990s

Geoffrey Body

PSL

PATRICK STEPHENS LIMITED

Title page *A Network South East 'traction development unit', part of the move towards replacing traditional stock with the latest developments in high-capacity, sliding-door suburban rolling stock.*

First published in 1984
Reprinted with additional material 1989

British Library Cataloguing in Publication Data

Body, Geoffrey, *1929—*
  Railways of the Southern Region. — (PSL field guide).
  Rev. ed
  1. Southern England. Railway services: British Rail.
  Southern Region
  I. Title
  385'.09422

  ISBN 0-85260-297-X

Patrick Stephens Limited is part of the Thorsons Publishing Group, Wellingborough, Northamptonshire, NN8 2RQ, England.

Printed in Great Britain by Biddles Limited, Guildford, Surrey
Typeset by MJL Limited, Hitchin, Hertfordshire

10 9 8 7 6 5 4 3 2 1

Contents

Acknowledgements
The author especially acknowledges the assistance received from the Southern Region of British Rail in the preparation of this book. Without that assistance its compilation would not have been possible. Particular thanks are due to S.B. Minks for his help in starting the project, to Peter Ellis for much of the initial groundwork, to A.M. Bath for the provision of operational information and to the many SR local managers who provided local data. Neil Sprinks made a major contribution to this work as he did to the WR volume and Ian G. Body again drew the maps. Many of the photographs were provided by British Rail (Southern and Network South East), the preservation scenes came from the lines depicted and the other illustrations came from Neil Sprinks and the author's collection.

SECTION 1

The Southern Region field guide

The character of each of the five regions into which the British Rail network is divided differs greatly. The Western Region, dealt with in the first volume in this series of field guides, is an area of great main lines, cross-country routes and holiday branch lines. The Southern Region, by contrast, compresses hundreds of stations and dozens of services into the relatively small area of Southern England from Kent to Dorset, providing an intensive service for London and a generous one for the counties south of the capital but still cherishing quite a few historic backwaters amid the impressive modern activity of its largely electrified network.

The Southern is not just concerned with the problems of bringing 76,000 people into Waterloo every working day, or of the 57,000 into Victoria or the 49,000 into London Bridge. The region also conveys thousands to the coast for their annual sunshine and forms a gateway for shipping links with Europe, the Channel Islands and the Southampton liners. The Southern carries countless shoppers on its off-peak services, caters for the early and late workers of the Kent industries and treats as routine its unique Waterloo and City line or the ex-tube train service which connects with Portsmouth steamers on the Isle of Wight.

The objective of this volume remains the same as that of its predecessor. It aims to give a complete, detailed and interesting coverage of the railway activity of the area, showing what there is, what its function is and how it evolved. It is a look at the modern railway and how it originated, designed to be sufficiently factual to be useful but at the same time to capture the best of the past and the most interesting of the present.

To provide a 'feel' of the subject the book starts with a look at the Southern as a whole and then provides a gazetteer embracing all the locations of significant interest. The heading for each entry describes its location in terms of line and distance from the London terminal or other appropriate point and the entry itself then covers the origins, main features and service or function of that location. Following the gazetteer section the threads are then drawn together again in a digest of information for each of the principal routes and there are sections on operation, preservation and similar specialist aspects for those who have particularised interests.

The sub-headings of the gazetteer section give the line on which the station or

Left *Commuters arriving at Waterloo during the morning business period.*

depot concerned stands and, where necessary, pinpoint it further by indicating a major location on either side. The distance from the relevant (London) terminal is then quoted based on the official distances recorded in the Southern Region's Sectional Appendix to the Working Timetable. These distances are given in miles and chains and refer to the signal box or other specific focal point (eg, level crossing) of the location being described. In the absence of such a feature the distance refers to the centre point of the location, the portal nearest London in the case of tunnels. In the case of branch lines the length of the line is given.

Within the gazetteer entries services, feature descriptions and similar information is usually recorded in the Down direction, eg, Waterloo–Weymouth. In railway terms Down is the direction away from London. Since this is related to the route of the originating company some lines may include a change of direction. In the case of the Strood–Paddock Wood line, for example, the two separate approaches to Maidstone West result in there being two Up directions for the line, one from Maidstone West to Charing Cross via Strood and the other from Maidstone West to Charing Cross via Paddock Wood. The changes of mileage which occur in such cases are detailed at the change of mileage point.

All significant locations have a gazetteer entry although some are grouped in a line entry because that line is better described as an entity than by its separate parts. Minor locations, like minor closed lines, are included in the appropriate major entry but can be traced there through the Supplementary Index. In the case of the train service, this is paraphrased to convey the basic off-peak weekday pattern plus any special features, since the precise details are liable to change and can be obtained from the BR public timetable. Although the coverage seeks to be as comprehensive as possible within the space available there is no standard format for entries in the interest of maintaining readability.

The reference numbers for the gazetteer entries appear again in the first of the supplementary sections which follow. Here are summary descriptions of each of the main routes of the region which allow their function and physical features to be seen as a whole. Coupled with the table of diverging routes and branches, this section can be used to add interest to a journey in the same way that the gazetteer will add interest to a location visit. Related to a good relief map the route data gives not only a picture of the railway working and hardware but also a view of the countryside traversed and some insight into the way the early railway surveyors came to terms with the countryside—not always easy in the counties of the south where the high ground tends to run east to west.

Other supplementary sections cover the principal closed lines, the preservation and non-BR locations and the main departmental activities of the modern railway in order to cater for those interested in the whole railway panorama in a particular area and in a particular railway activity over the whole of the Southern area.

Throughout the text of the book mention is made of footbridges and other good spots for viewing and photography but, however interesting a railway location may be, trespass is an offence under the bye laws as well as being dangerous and anti-social. The same applies to private property where there is a railway interest. Although a strong regard for safety is a major consideration in the railway industry, British Rail is helpful to the careful and both viewing and photography are generally permitted, at the discretion of the local BR management, wherever access is free or by platform ticket.

British Rail provides a comprehensive service for information on trains, fares and facilities and there are many reduced fare facilities which can be put to good use in the pursuit of a railway interest or study. Most of the large stations have comprehensive travel centres and details of stations able to provide passenger train information are listed in local telephone directories.

In the interests of good public relations, the railway PROs at board, region and division level will try to help with any special needs, but with limited time and resources they are not really in a position just to satisfy idle curiosity. Visits to the works of British Rail Engineering Limited should be pursued with the location concerned, but any request for special facilities tends to interfere with the full-time task of running the railway and visits are best achieved by means of the many open-day opportunities. The rail tours organised by railway societies often cover lines not normally used by passenger trains and represent another opportunity to see more of the railway network.

In preparing this book every effort has been made to ensure accuracy and account has been taken of changes known to be coming along during the interval between writing and publication. Yet the railway scene is constantly changing—new facilities being introduced, old ones abandoned and even new evidence of the past uncovered—and for the benefit of future volumes the compiler would be glad to hear from readers about any additional or altered items.

Abbreviations used

* Indicates some abnormality in calculating the distance, explained in the text which follows.
AHB   Automatic half barriers.
AOCL   Automatic open crossing, locally monitored.
CCTV   Closed circuit television monitored.
ch   Chains.
demu   Diesel electric multiple unit.
DGL   Down Goods Loop.
dmu   Diesel multiple unit.
DPL   Down Passenger Loop.
emu   Electric multiple unit.
LC   Level crossing.
m   Miles.
MP   Milepost.
RG   Miniature red/green warning lights.
TMO   Trainmen operated.
UGL   Up Goods Loop.
UPL   Up Passenger Loop.

Key to maps

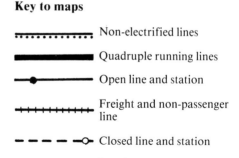

Non-electrified lines

Quadruple running lines

Open line and station

Freight and non-passenger line

Closed line and station

London Transport line

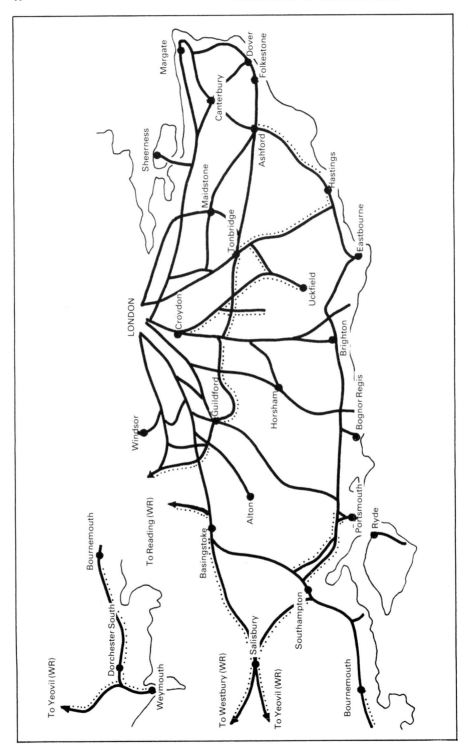

SECTION 2

The Southern

British Rail's Southern Region is the modern successor to a succession of earlier railways. Its immediate predecessor was the Southern Railway, one of the 'Big Four' main line companies created by the Railways Act 1921, although the Southern system included the main line through Devon and Cornwall to Bude and Padstow, now truncated beyond Exeter and in Western Region territory. The Southern lasted from 1923 until Britain's railways were nationalised on January 1 1948 and during that time it created a respected image of its own and turned the fragmented electrification schemes of its pre-grouping constituents into a major, efficient network of electrified lines south of London.

The Southern has always been associated with ports and resorts and it was these which originally produced its constituents. The South Eastern Railway took over the mantle of the old coaching companies serving Dover and then had to share it with the later London, Chatham & Dover Railway in the combined South Eastern & Chatham format. The London, Brighton & South Coast Railway started with a modest main line to Brighton and then threw off a host of branches including those east and west along the coast to Hastings and Portsmouth. In the same way that the LB&SC blossomed from the original London & Brighton scheme, so the London & Southampton Railway grew into the sizeable London & South Western with main lines to Portsmouth, Southampton/Weymouth and through Salisbury, Yeovil, Exeter and Plymouth right out to the Atlantic beaches of North Cornwall.

Further back in time lie four pioneers. The first was the Surrey Iron Railway, authorised by an Act of May 21 1801, opened from Wandsworth to Croydon on July 26 1803 (and subsequently extended to Merstham) and now enshrined in part of the route of the Wimbledon-West Croydon line. The second pioneer, the Canterbury & Whitstable Railway, was sanctioned in 1825 and its opening on May 3 1830 actually preceded that of the Liverpool & Manchester, although it could not claim the same impact on railway history.

The other two pioneer railways became the lynchpins for the growth of the whole Southern system. The first was the London & Greenwich Railway which obtained its Act on May 17 1833. The 3¾-mile route needed 878 brick arches to carry it from London Bridge to Deptford but that historic stretch of railway, opened on December 14 1836, is still in use today. The London & Croydon Railway followed, authorised on June 12 1835 and opened on June 1 1839 from West Croydon to Corbetts Lane with trains running via the London & Greenwich to a separate station at London Bridge.

Old and new scene as Isle of Wight steam unloads its ex-London Transport replacement.

From these beginnings emerged four substantial companies which, by a process of competition and co-operation, became three major systems and established their dominance over the three geographical sectors of the Southern Railway, labelled the 'Eastern', 'Central' and 'Western' Sections and still perpetuated in the operational divisions of the modern Southern Region. For clarity the growth of these groupings and their principal lines are best examined separately, although an overview of the relative time scale is frequently omitted or obscured in conventional histories. Here we can, at least, look at their origins collectively.

The first of the three trunk routes authorised was that of the London & Southampton Railway which satisfied Parliament in the 1834 session and had a section of line opened from Nine Elms to Woking Common on May 21 1838. The London & Brighton, authorised on July 15 1837, opened the Brighton-Shoreham portion on May 12 1840 and the main line in the following year, with the South Eastern taking from June 21 1836, when the Royal Assent was received, until February 7 1844 to reach Dover. Initially the L&S used Nine Elms, and the other two London Bridge, for their London termini.

Having opened its first section of line in 1838, the London & Southampton changed its name to London & South Western Railway in the following year and completed the last gap in its main line between Basingstoke and Winchester on May 11 1840. With work on the Outer Dock at Southampton nearing completion the line was soon to be busy with the steamer passengers and mails transferred from Falmouth and, by 1841, had a branch probing towards Portsmouth (via Gosport and the ferry).

There was much early rivalry between the LSW and its neighbour the Great Western, centred on the LSW's ambitions west of Southampton and various schemes to link that port and the Midlands. The first extension west was by acquisition of the winding route from Southampton to Dorchester via Ringwood which took its soubriquet 'Castleman's Corkscrew' from the name of the Wimborne solicitor who was its prime mover. This was opened on June 1 1847 to be followed by another set of battles with Exeter as the target. Eventually the LSW reached that city, from Salisbury and via Yeovil, on July 19 1860 by which time many of the main arteries of the network had been completed, viz: Woking to Guildford—May 5 1845; Battersea (Clapham Junction) to Richmond—July 27 1846; Bishopstoke (Eastleigh) to Salisbury (Milford)—March 1 1847; Nine Elms to Waterloo—July 11 1848; Richmond to Datchet—August 22 1848 and to Windsor December 1 1849; Fareham to Cosham (for Portsmouth)—September/October 1848; Guildford to Ash Junction—August 20 1849 (to Farnham October 8 1849; to Godalming October 15 1849); Hampton Court branch—February 1 1849; Farnham to Alton—July 28 1852; Staines to Ascot—June 4 1856, to Wokingham July 9 1856; Basingstoke to Andover—July 3 1854, to Salisbury (Milford) May 1 1857; Lymington Branch—July 12 1858.

The elements of the Somerset & Dorset system and of the LSW lines in Devon and Cornwall had started to emerge by 1860 but they are largely outside our coverage. Similarly some of the later lines have not survived to remain within it. The Portsmouth Direct route from Godalming just comes within the pre-1860 period with the Portsmouth arrival of the first train on January 24 1859 after the physical and legal fracas with the LB&SC over access via Havant. The eastern access to Bournemouth did not come until 1870 (via Sway, 1888).

The LB&SC was a well-run and well-liked little concern which had a fair amount of trouble in protecting its territory from the incursions of its neighbours. It had come into existence on July 27 1846 when the Royal Assent was given to the Act amalgamating the London & Brighton and London & Croydon. By this time its system had been extended along the coast westwards as far as Chichester (reached June 8 1846) and to St Leonards (June 27 1846) eastwards. Subsequent major extensions were: Chichester to Havant—March 15 1847;

Cab view and controls.

The Southern Railway was a leader in the signalling developments but the old signal box at Holborn Viaduct and the clumsy relays act as a reminder of how much has changed.

Croydon to Sutton/Epsom—May 10 1847; Havant to Portsmouth—May 10 1847; Lewes to Wivelsfield—October 2 1847; Keymer Junction to Lewes—December 8 1847; Three Bridges to Horsham—February 14 1848; Hailsham and Eastbourne branches—May 14 1849; Sydenham to Crystal Palace—June 10 1854; Wimbledon to Mitcham/Croydon—October 22 1855.

A group of London area lines followed between 1856 and 1860 including Crystal Palace-Wandsworth Common-Battersea Wharf and the 1860 extension over the river to Pimlico (Victoria). The local lines around East Grinstead, the Epsom/Leatherhead line and the Horsham-Pulborough/Petworth line were welded into the system in the years around the middle of the century. Again many of those which followed later have now gone with the notable exception of the Hardham Junction-Arundel Junction link (August 3 1863) and the completion of the Mid-Sussex route between Horsham and Leatherhead (1867), the Littlehampton branch (August 17 1863), the Seaford extension (June 1 1864) and various London area changes.

Parliament had encouraged the original Brighton company to operate a joint line with the South Eastern between the junction with the London & Croydon and the parting of their routes at Redhill. This led to all sorts of difficulties as the two systems grew and it culminated in the last years of the 19th century in the LB&SC building a separate pair of tracks between Purley and Earlswood to quadruple the main line capacity while reducing the problems of the joint use of Redhill.

The South Eastern itself had followed its 1844 main line and Paddock Wood-Maidstone branch with a branch from Tonbridge to Tunbridge Wells (opened September 20 1845) and others from Ashford to Margate (December 1 1846) and Minster to Deal (July 1 1847). In this period it also purchased the infant North Kent scheme and acquired the Reading, Guildford & Reigate line which was opened in sections in 1849. Other major routes followed: Ashford to Hastings—February 13 1851; Tunbridge Wells to Hastings—February 1 1852; Strood to Maidstone—June 18 1856; Lewisham to Beckenham—January 1 1857; extension to Charing Cross—January 11 1864; extension to Cannon Street—September 1 1866; Dartford Loop Line—September 1 1866; Sevenoaks cut-off route—May 1 1868.

Not a lively concern in its later years, the South Eastern was enlivened in this expansion period by the advent of a rival for the Dover traffic with a main line that was to be shorter but harder to work. The London, Chatham & Dover Railway originated in an Act of August 4 1853 granted to the East Kent Railway which opened its first section from Strood to Chatham on March 29 1858, became the LC&D in the following year and finally reached Dover on July 22 1861 (Dover Harbour, November 1). By this time the newcomer had achieved access to London independent of the SER's North Kent line by contriving a route via St Mary Cray to Victoria, following this with the City line to Ludgate Hill in 1866. After a preliminary attempt at co-operation in 1875 and a flirtation between the LC&D and the LB&SC in 1886, the sustained rivalry between the two companies serving Dover eventually ended in a working union labelled 'South Eastern & Chatham' and operative from January 1 1899.

The complex pattern of London terminal stations was established in the 19th century. After starting with London Bridge, which the London & Greenwich opened in 1836, the SER used Bricklayers Arms to avoid Greenwich tolls from 1844 to 1852. The breach was healed but 12 years later the 1.9-mile route to

Charing Cross was opened, with a triangular link into Cannon Street following two years later on September 1 1866. Three major London stations for the SER were matched by its arch rival the LC&D when it added its line to Blackfriars Bridge (Ludgate Hill) in the same year, with Snow Hill/Holborn Viaduct following in 1874 and St Pauls station (now Blackfriars) in 1886.

The LC&D had been sharing Victoria with the LB&SC since 1860, with its portion of the double station being brought into use on August 25 1862, and forsaking the approach via Crystal Palace for its own access via Herne Hill in the following year. The Brighton company had been using the line across the river to Victoria since 1860 and two years later had opened the cut-off approach from Windmill Bridge Junction via Balham. The LSW had extended from Nine Elms to Waterloo as early as 1848 and then left it until 1907 to acquire the nine-year-old Waterloo & City Electric Railway and achieve its own link to the city as opposed to that via Waterloo Junction or over other companies' metals.

Over the remainder of the 'Southern' territory the second half of the 19th century saw the building of many local and minor lines, the birth of a third route to Dover via Maidstone East and the emergence from the various East Sussex developments of a new route to Eastbourne. The four great railways became three with the formation of the SE&C partnership and the focus of activity moved away from expansion to consolidation of the network and improvements in services. Shipping activity was considerable, locomotive performance was improving, rolling stock standards were slowly being raised and operational methods had evolved to combine safety with the need to move steadily increasing levels of traffic.

As they moved into the 20th century the southern railways offered a great variety of passenger services from main line express journeys to circular routes or branch line meandering. You could leave Waterloo after a day in London and catch the 4.30 pm Restaurant Car service to Bournemouth, arriving there at

Left *One of the railway's worst enemies, snow freezing on points, signals and current supply rails.*

Right *The reconstruction of Cannon Street in progress in 1976.*

7.17 pm. If Brighton was your destination the 4.25 pm Pullman service would have you there by 5.55 pm. The 4 pm ex-Charing Cross would deliver you to Dover in exactly two hours. The companies could whisk you to Europe or the Channel Islands, take you for a day out on the steeply-graded Dyke branch, cram you into six-compartment six-wheel stock for your homeward commuter journey or find something worse for the annual excursion to the sea or the hop fields.

As the First World War ended and the Bill for the Railways Act stood before Parliament, the London & South Western Railway had grown to 1,034 miles (877 owned) on which it used 922 locomotives, 301 electric cars and 19,359 items of rolling stock. Dividends on consolidated ordinary stock were 6 per cent in 1919 and 1920 and had been around this figure for many years.

The LB&SC did not publish mileage figures in its last years but for 1915 the total was 473 (426 owned) and by 1920 the company had 609 locomotives and 12,991 wagons and coaches. It was paying 5¼ per cent.

Despite their working union, the SER and LC&D retained their separate identities and declared dividends of 4¼ per cent and 4½ per cent respectively. The SE&C Railway Companies Managing Committee operated 624 miles of railway (1913 figure) on behalf of the two constituents and by 1920 this was producing £1.84 m in net receipts of which 59 per cent went to the SER and 41 per cent to the LC&D in accordance with the 1899 agreement.

The period between the two wars, the years following grouping and of independence from direct Government control, was the period in which each of the main line companies welded its constituents together and developed its own special character. The Southern took as its first general manager Herbert (later Sir Herbert) Ashcombe Walker who was made general manager of the London & South Western on January 1 1912 and who was to lift the new larger enterprise to great stature. During Walker's 14 years at the helm the Southern was welded

into an efficient and modern system, largely electrified, conveying thousands to work each day, others to their relaxation on coast or Downs and much freight and passenger business to and from the great ports.

This period was dominated by the process of electrification which had started in the first years of the century. From the pioneer days of Magnus Volk's electric railway at Brighton, interest in electric traction had been increasing and its use for expanding the London tramway network was a great incentive to action on the part of the railways south of the Thames. Starting with 1903 powers to electrify the whole of its network, the LB&SC used a German overhead system and began public services over its first route, the South London line, on December 1 1909. Steam trains were at first retained for the early morning workings but the electric trains saved 12 minutes in journey time and were soon reversing the drift from trains to trams.

The South London line scheme was followed by Victoria to Crystal Palace via Streatham Hill (May 12 1911) and Peckham Rye-Tulse Hill-West Norwood/ Leigham Junctions (March 1 1912) with plans for completing the LB&SC's suburban network then being halted by the war years. The South Eastern, which had also obtained powers in 1903, planned to use post-war Government financial assistance to revive its electrification schemes while the L&SW had started its electric workings on October 25 1915 with a Waterloo-Wimbledon service. In the following year it extended the services to the Shepperton and Kingston lines and then to Hampton Court and the Hounslow Loop. Curiously the L&SW drew its powers from a Board of Trade Order rather than from a Parliamentary statute.

Under Walker's compulsive leadership electrification was soon a major feature of the activities of the newly-formed SR with 1925 producing the Balham-Coulsdon North and Sutton via Selhurst schemes (operational from April 1 1925) and from July 12 the extensions to Dorking North and Guildford, Victoria/Holborn Viaduct-Herne Hill-Shortlands-Orpington, Nunhead-Crystal Palace and the Catford Loop. Based on a decision to standardise on the L&SW's 600 V third-rail system the South London line was converted from June 17 1928, other conversions following and ending the LB&SC's high tension ac

Left Behind the scene changes on BR include such things as the use of microfilm display units in the maintenance process.

Right The art of firing—a little and often where the fire burns brightest.

system. The suburban electrified network was soon extended to Epsom Downs, Beckenham Junction, Herne Hill-Haydons Road-Wimbledon and the Caterham and Tattenham Corner branches. By July 6 1930 the major part of the suburban system was operational. Using the third-rail system, the large scale conversion of steam stock for suburban sets and regular interval timetables, the new services brought a steady expansion in suburban housing and a new look to the whole area.

The 1930s were dominated by main line electrification schemes prompted by the availability of Government funds for the relief of unemployment. The main ones were: Brighton main line—into public use January 1 1933; Seaford/Ore and Haywards Heath-Horsted Keynes—July 7 1935; Portsmouth, Alton and branches—July 4 1937; Portsmouth via Horsham—July 3 1938; Gillingham and Maidstone schemes: July 2 1939.

The schemes required major changes in track layout, in stations, and in the provision of new stock and accommodation for its maintenance. The distinctive style of SR architecture dates from this era and electrification also led to a revolution in train planning and control. The four-aspect colour light signalling introduced between Holborn Viaduct and Elephant & Castle on March 21 1926 was not only the first of many such developments on the SR but also the first in the world.

These changes swept away some of the traditional hardware but steam remained unchallenged for working to the Channel Ports and on the old LSW main lines to the West. Maunsell had taken over quite a mixed bag of locomotives from the constituent companies but, by 1925, Eastleigh had produced No 453 *King Arthur* with *Lord Nelson* following and giving the SR the most powerful locomotive in Britain at that time. By 1930 Eastleigh was turning out the 'Schools' 4-4-0s, a highly successful design soon at work all over the system. O.V. Bulleid became Chief Mechanical Engineer in 1937 but his Merchant Navy class, such a dramatic break with tradition, did not appear until 1941.

The SR acquired a substantial steamer fleet at grouping and paid much attention to its shipping and docks activities. A car-carrying vessel was at work on the cross-Channel services by 1931, and the 1936 Dunkerque Train Ferry

became the first through working of passenger-carrying vehicles to and from the Continent and new paddle steamers steadily appeared on the Isle of Wight services. Freight, albeit modest in total, moved in volume from places like Southampton and to/from the London markets. The busy SR giant not only built new lines from Wimbledon to Sutton and from Motspur Park to Chessington South but also found time for smaller matters, encouraging the building of the Romney, Hythe & Dymchurch Railway across the Romney Marshes, participating in the scheme to develop a resort on the Thames at All Hallows and even acquiring the tiny Lynton & Barnstaple Railway.

During the Second World War the Southern was a front line railway, undertaking thousands of special troop movements, carrying supplies to the airfields in Kent and contributing its vessels and its men to the conflict. But by October 1 1945 it had reinstated its restaurant car services and by April 15 1946 was again running the 'Golden Arrow' service to Calais, complete with cocktail bar and public address system.

In the first years of nationalisation came the double-deck trains to Dartford (1949), the exchange of territory with the WR (1950) and diesel electrification to Hastings via Tunbridge Wells (1957). Two further electrification schemes were still to come. The Kent Coast Scheme was approved by the British Transport Commission in 1956 and the first part, covering the Gillingham-Ramsgate/Dover lines over the old LC&D, plus the Sheerness branch, came into public use on June 15 1959. The full service on the ex-SER lines in Kent (excluding Ashford-Hastings) was put into operation on June 18 1962 to complete the second portion of the scheme.

The Isle of Wight maintained its non-conformist traditions when ex-London Transport stock was put to work on the surviving Ryde Pier Head to Shanklin line from March 20 1967. Then came the Bournemouth scheme involving the ex-LSW main line from Brookwood to Branksome plus the branch to Lymington Pier. When the electric services were brought into use on July 10 1967 the Southern Region got a completely new timetable and also the novelty of push and pull working beyond Bournemouth.

Since the extension of electrification to Bournemouth most of the SR changes

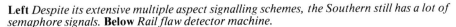

Left *Despite its extensive multiple aspect signalling schemes, the Southern still has a lot of semaphore signals.* **Below** *Rail flaw detector machine.*

have been concerned with improving the network. Major schemes of re-signalling and track layout improvement have taken place especially around the London area, with the London Bridge scheme taking in 150 miles of track and the latest scheme covering the Brighton main line with just two modern panel boxes.

When the Canterbury & Whitstable Railway opened on May 3 1830 the main line railway system of the 'Southern' counties totalled just over six miles. When the pioneer's anniversary was celebrated at Canterbury Cathedral 150 years later the Southern had grown to 3,096 miles of track (2,379 electrified) with 566 passenger stations. The system produced 320 million passenger journeys a year, 47.7 per cent of them and over half the total for BR, by season ticket. Every ordinary day 4,000 trains carried 724,000 passengers to and from the region's eight London terminals (Charing Cross, Cannon Street, Waterloo, Victoria, London Bridge, Holborn Viaduct and Blackfriars, plus Elephant & Castle), 292,000 of them during the busiest hour of the morning.

The largest station on the Southern Region is Waterloo, with 21 platforms occupying 24½ acres. From here main line routes run to Exeter via Salisbury, to Bournemouth with push-and-pull working of portions from the fast services on to Weymouth, and to Portsmouth which has an onward shipping link to the Isle of Wight. Completing the responsibilities of the South Western Division are suburban routes to Alton, Chessington, Hampton Court, Horsham, Reading, Shepperton and Windsor.

Victoria deals with rail-air passengers to and from Gatwick and those using the short sea routes via Dover, Folkstone and Newhaven, all in addition to its normal business. It has main line services to Margate/Ramsgate and Canterbury/Dover via the Medway towns, others to Brighton, Bognor and Littlehampton and along the coastal routes west via Chichester and east to Eastbourne and Hastings. It shares with London Bridge local services to Coulsdon, East Grinstead, Epsom and Reigate.

London Bridge, now thoroughly modernised, still has its through and terminating service divisions, giving it an immense volume and variety of trains and a high amount of interchange activity. Its local services are similar to those from Victoria, it is used by the Brighton line slows and such services as those on the South London line, and trains from Charing Cross via Waterloo East call at the London Bridge through platforms on their way to Dover and Margate via Ashford, Hastings via Tunbridge Wells and the routes via Dartford.

The former LC&D line into the City of London adds Holborn Viaduct and Blackfriars to the London stations and perpetuates the Southern practice of circular and loop routes with a link to and from London Bridge. Its fellow City station, Cannon Street, has a busy time in the Monday to Friday peaks dealing with trains to and from Hastings, East Kent and the Medway towns before settling for a more peaceful pattern of off-peak services to Addiscombe, Orpington and via Dartford.

The SR train pattern is full of complex services requiring highly professional operation. There are dozens of fascinating examples such as the routing of Gravesend services where the half-hourly pattern via Woolwich Arsenal is interspersed with alternative via Bexleyheath and via Sidcup trains and good connections are provided off the all-stations trains via Greenwich. Many routes have two patterns like the Uckfield and East Grinstead branches where the joining and separating of portions at Oxted is replaced by through services

A reminder of the Pullman era, one of the Golden Arrow vehicles pictured in 1969.

during the busier periods. Equally many patterns have two routes like the intertwined Victoria-Effingham Junction and Waterloo-Effingham Junction services which further alternate to serve Dorking and Horsham.

Although dwarfed by the passenger travel activity, the Southern Region's freight business is by no means unimportant. It totals around 8 m tons a year and is much in evidence on the lines serving Kent where trains of ferry vans or coal empties keep up a cracking pace to maintain their paths amid the busy passenger movements. Major traffics include the flows of petroleum products from the refineries at Fawley and the Isle of Grain, cement from Northfleet and a variety of other construction materials from outwards sand to inwards aggregates. Steel, cars and general merchandise are also carried, the latter primarily on Speedlink services or through the Freightliner terminals. Southampton has two of the latter including the sophisticated Maritime terminal which handles containers to and from the deep sea shipping routes. A great deal of GPO and newspaper traffic is also carried.

The Southern Region operates around 5,000 passenger trains a day, mostly with electric stock in permanently coupled units of two or four vehicles (plus the six-car Hastings diesel-electrics and the three-car Class 204-7 demu sets) with a driving cab at each end and combined in multiples to provide the right train size for the traffic. Broadly the emu stock falls into three categories—main line, outer suburban and suburban—with seating capacity and facilities related to the length of journey and traffic density factors. Suburban sets like the four-coach, non-corridor Class 415s (4 EPB) date from 1951 and seat 374-408 passengers whereas the four-car Class 410 (4 BEP) sets used on the Kent and Sussex Coast routes and the subject of recent refurbishing provide only 160 seats plus a further 21 in the buffet. New standards of design and comfort were heralded in

1979 with the introduction of the modern, sliding door Class 508 four-car sets which seat 320 people per set, Class 455s appearing in 1983.

For its six non-electrified routes the Southern uses diesel-electrical multiple units or diesel-electric locomotives hauling conventional coaches, as on the Waterloo-Exeter line. It also has Class 08 shunters for freight and marshalling work and Class 73 electro-diesels capable of operating from the third rail system or using the diesel engine when working in non-electrified areas. Among the other specialised traction and rolling stock equipment are the Class 485/6 ex-LT stock used on the Isle of Wight, the Class 427 sets used on the Victoria-Gatwick service, the Class 487 single coach units of the Waterloo & City line and some single coach motor luggage vans (Class 419) used for the conveyance of parcels and mail on Continental routes. To support this activity the SR has 16 maintenance depots and over 70 carriage servicing depots.

Of the total SR track, 77 per cent is electrified and 55 per cent laid with continuous welded rail. Most of it is in constant use, some is used intensively and all requires regular and effective maintenance. A feature of the SR scene in recent years has been an extensive remodelling of layouts to provide simpler and more effective working, the latest example being the alterations in the Gloucester Road triangle. Here a new section of railway has been built involving

These simple but attractive wooden station buildings at Selling probably date back to the original opening of the line in 1860.

nearly a mile of new embankment using some 200,000 tonnes of mine waste from Betteshanger Colliery, and two new bridges.

The region's civil engineers are also responsible for stations, tunnels and bridges. The former can involve major commercial development schemes such as the one at Blackfriars, complete remodelling such as that carried out at London Bridge, a new station such as that at Moulsecoomb or just repairing a small building or a sleeper platform. The picture for tunnels and bridges is equally varied. The 119 tunnels on the routes still open range in size up to the 1 m 1,693 yards of Sevenoaks Tunnel and the total of 8,790 bridges includes opening and lifting bridges, bridges of metal, brick and masonry, most owned by BR but some not, quite ordinary structures or magnificent architectural and engineering masterpieces like the 1,475 ft Ouse Viaduct on the Brighton main line.

The Southern Region still operates traditional signal boxes with absolute block working effected through block instruments and semaphore signals. It also has single lines using tokenless block or other control forms but one of the major characteristics of the region is the extent of its colour light signalling, worked from panel boxes and with many supplementary features such as the automatic operation of station announcements and the provision of train information.

The rapid electrification of the Southern stimulated a signalling revolution and, on March 21 1926, the line from Holborn to Elephant & Castle, a modest 3¾ track miles, received colour light signalling to start a chain of progress that has found its latest expression in the Brighton line scheme. The 1926 beginning involved centralising the signalling on two signal boxes with 86 and 120 miniature electric levers. Ten years later the Maldon to Vauxhall project involved covering 49½ track miles and the Waterloo box produced a concentration of 309 levers. By 1940 colour light signalling was at work on 338 miles and the miniaturisation of relays plus developments in points machines and other equipment allowed the figure to grow to 1,614½ by 1970 and 1,938¾ by 1980. In the ultra-modern installation at Three Bridges there are 715 signals and 564 points on the panel and 1,055 track circuits to show the position of trains over 280 miles of track.

All these aspects and features of the Southern make it a region of great fascination. Stand on the footbridge at Tulse Hill or on one of the countless other junction and interchange stations and it seems a miracle that the intricate pattern of services should function so well. Watch the fight to get leaves off the track in Kent or ice off the points at Slade Green carriage sidings, or try your hand at the stock balancing part of the train planning process and it is understandable that occasionally it does not.

To the rich mixture of modern and traditional railway can be added a high level of preservation activities. The pioneer Bluebell Railway scheme has been followed by the Kent & East Sussex revival of one of the Colonel Stephens lines, the Sittingbourne & Kemsley inheritance of one of the industrial lines of the Kent paper-making industry and the Winchester & Alton Railway's 'Watercress Line' with its strong SR motive power emphasis.

Several industrial lines are still at work in the area and no visit to Brighton is complete without a trip on the historic Volk's Electric Railway. The Romney, Hythe & Dymchurch line's miniature LNER Pacifics make a visit a must and a few cliff railways add further to the variety of the railways of the Southern Region.

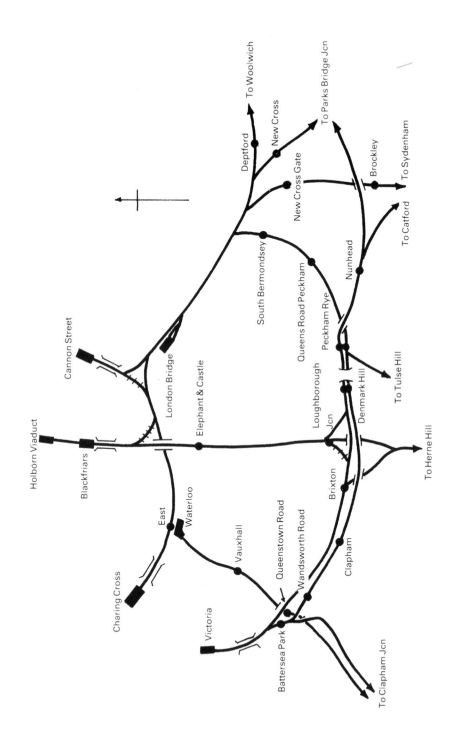

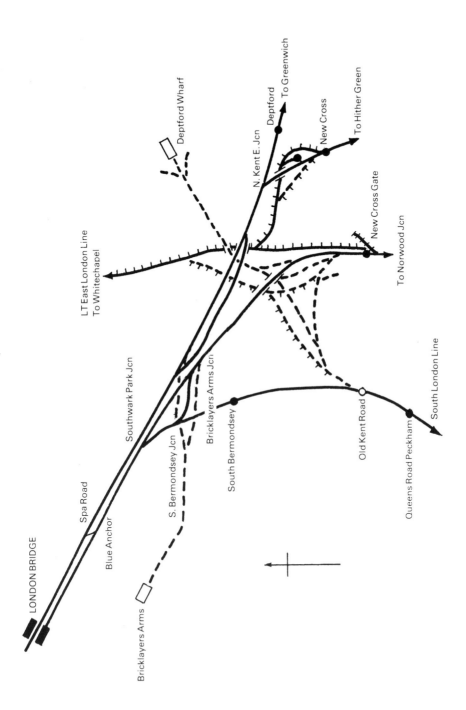

LONDON BRIDGE

Spa Road

Blue Anchor

Southwark Park Jcn

S. Bermondsey Jcn

Bricklayers Arms

Bricklayers Arms Jcn

South Bermondsey

Old Kent Road

Queens Road Peckham

South London Line

LT East London Line
To Whitechapel

Deptford Wharf

N. Kent E. Jcn

Deptford

To Greenwich

New Cross

To Hither Green

New Cross Gate

To Norwood Jcn

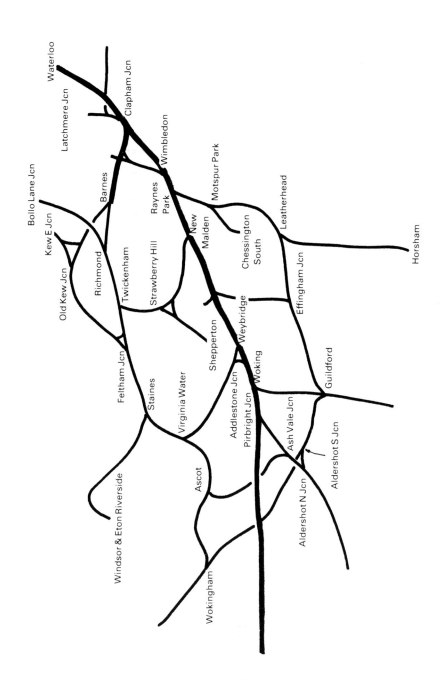

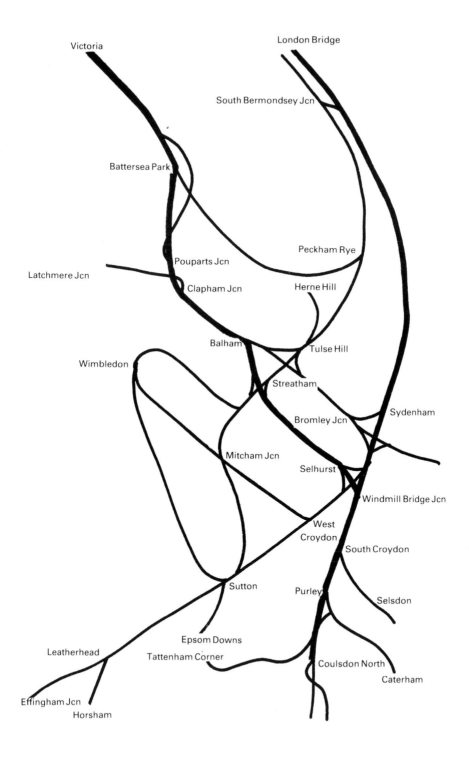

Victoria

London Bridge

South Bermondsey Jcn

Battersea Park

Peckham Rye

Latchmere Jcn

Pouparts Jcn

Clapham Jcn

Herne Hill

Balham

Tulse Hill

Wimbledon

Streatham

Sydenham

Bromley Jcn

Mitcham Jcn

Selhurst

Windmill Bridge Jcn

West
Croydon

South Croydon

Sutton

Purley

Selsdon

Epsom Downs

Leatherhead

Tattenham Corner

Coulsdon North

Caterham

Effingham Jcn

Horsham

SECTION 3

Gazetteer

Abbey Wood—see North Kent Line

A.1 Abbotscliffe Tunnel

Charing Cross-Dover line, between Folke-stone and Dover. 73 m 23 ch from Charing Cross

The 1 m 182 yd tunnel (73 m 23 ch to 74 m 31 ch) lies on the former SER route's coastal approach to Dover opened on February 7 1844. The 25 ft high tunnel had to be cut through chalk and the following section prepared by blasting the cliff face away. The tunnel contains 13 galleries, each about 5 ft wide, leading out to the cliff face and numbered from the Dover end. Above, the cliff face slopes at 45 degrees and below is the Lydden Spout, fed by water from inland sources and rising during heavy rains to be carried away by the drains in the galleries.

A.2 Addiscombe Branch

Lewisham-Hayes line, branch from Elmers End. 1 m 70 ch

The line from New Beckenham to Addis-combe, formerly Croydon (Addiscombe Road), was opened on April 1 1864 as an extension of the Mid-Kent Railway (SER) Lewisham-New Beckenham route. Today the portion from Elmers End is worked as an adjunct to the service on the later Hayes extension. In the off-peak a two-car set departs from the Down side bay at the junction following the arrival of the trains from Charing Cross/Cannon Street to Hayes and then provides three return Up services each hour from Addiscombe.

At Elmers End (11 m 7 ch) the two double lines separate at the country end of the station and the single line from the bay platform joins the route to Woodside (12 m 10 ch) where the station opened in 1871 and has its main buildings, in tradi-

tional style, on the overbridge at the London end. The small signal box retains a name sign in SR green.

Immediately beyond Woodside comes a further double line junction where the line to Sanderstead diverges from the one to Addiscombe. The former was opened on August 10 1885 and runs via Bingham Road (12 m 67 ch), three tunnels (13 m 18 ch to 13 m 43 ch)—the 266 yd Woodside Tunnel, the 122 yd Park Hill Tunnel and the 157 yd Coombe Lane Tunnel—Coombe Road (13 m 67 ch) and Selsdon (14 m 40 ch). After getting a new lease of life from electrification in 1935 these stations were down to a limited emu shuttle service in the Monday to Friday peaks by 1983 and lost even this from the May time-table.

The other route, to Addiscombe (12 m 77 ch), ends at the simple terminal station where passenger trains use the two faces of the single platform. Beyond are the single-storey, 19th century station buildings. There is a wooden signal box at the London end of the station, controlling the local workings with semaphore signalling, and on the Down side are carriage sidings and a four-bay shed.

A.3 Addlestone

Virgina Water-Weybridge line. 20 m 71 ch from Waterloo*

Addlestone, served by the half-hourly Staines-Weybridge service, was opened on February 14 1848 as part of the branch from Weybridge to Chertsey. The opening of the route from this end is still marked by the reckoning of the distances via Wey-bridge.

The station comprises Up and Down platforms with brick buildings, canopies, a footbridge and a CCTV barrier crossing.

The main buildings are on the Down side, single storey and with two gable ends towards the main road. Towards Weybridge the line crosses the River Wey Navigation before the double track freight route veers off west at Addlestone Junction (19 m 74 ch).

The lines between Addlestone and Weybridge are controlled from the Surbiton box and those in the other direction by Feltham.

A.4 Adisham

Victoria-Dover line, between Canterbury East and Dover Priory. 67 m 60 ch from Victoria

The station dates from the opening of the LC&D's line from Faversham to Dover on July 22 1861 and is preceded by a high viaduct. Although the three-storey signal box has gone, the station still has its traditional buildings on the Down side and the brick goods shed remains, now in private hands and with an extension. The Up side has only a wooden shelter.

There is a basic hourly service to Victoria in one direction and to Dover Priory in the other.

Albany Park—see Dartford Loop Line

A.5 Aldershot

Waterloo-Alton line. 35 m from Waterloo

Aldershot town and station both owe their existence to the military camps which came into being nearby in 1855. Initially these were served by Farnborough on the

Aldershot, seen from the country end of the Down platform. The 1870 station buildings are receiving a face lift.

LSW main line and Ash and North Camp on the SER's route to Reading, but Aldershot got a station as part of its growth from village to town when the main line at Pirbright Junction was connected to Farnham on the Guildford-Tongham-Farnham route on May 2 1870.

The main buildings of today's station, located on the Up side and including ticket, information, parcels and refreshment facilities, largely date from 1870. Two-storey and constructed in brick they are pleasantly solid in appearance with gabled sections each side of the main entrance and tall chimneys above. From beneath the flat canopy with decorated supports a subway leads to the Down island platform and its passenger loop. Beyond this are the coal sidings.

Aldershot derives its service from the Waterloo-Woking-Alton trains and from those Ascot services which reverse to pass via the Aldershot North (33 m 40 ch) and Aldershot South Junction (50 m 1 ch) connections with the SER route to Guildford. The remaining military sidings, including ground frame access (33 m 76 ch) and accommodation for special trains, are on the Up side near Aldershot North Junction but the old signal box there has gone and its work is now done by the Aldershot box. The 76 yd Aldershot Tunnel lies between 34 m 46 ch and 34 m 50 ch.

A.6 Aldrington

Brighton-Littlehampton/Portsmouth line, between Brighton and Shoreham. 1 m 74 ch from Brighton

Opened as Dyke Junction Halt on September 15 1905, Aldrington consists of two platforms with corrugated shelters plus a

ticket office on the Up side which is reached by a footpath from the adjacent road.

From just west of the station a single line branch used to climb 3½ miles to serve the still popular beauty spot of Devil's Dyke, high up on the Downs. Opened on September 1 1887, the trains from Brighton took 14 minutes on the steep climb via Rowan Halt (opened 1933) to the Dyke but once at the top visitors had the choice of many diversions including, for a time, the opportunity to cross the ravine by cableway or descend to Poynings by the 3 ft gauge Devil's Dyke Steep Grade Railway. The branch from, and worked by, the LB&SC climbed to a height of 501 ft above sea level but it became little used except at holiday times. After being closed from 1917 to 1920 services finally ended on the last day of 1938.

Aldrington is served by the Brighton-Littlehampton/Portsmouth slow services.

Aldrington, once the junction for the branch to Devil's Dyke, and now just a typical example of a small SR station.

A.7   Alton

Waterloo-Alton line. 49 m 13 ch from Waterloo

Alton's first railway arrived from Farnham on July 28 1852 and the town got a new station, slightly nearer Alresford, when the Alton, Alresford & Winchester Railway was opened on October 2 1865. The link between Pirbright Junction and Farnham was authorised in that year (and opened in 1870) and the addition of two other routes from Butts Junction, just west of Alton, increased the station's importance even further. The first of

A nice example of a footbridge, at Alton station.

At Alton a terminating Down train waits to start its Up working.

these was the Basingstoke & Alton Light Railway, dating from June 1 1901, closed in 1917 for seven years and then cut in 1933. The Meon Valley route followed in 1903, giving Alton through trains to Portsmouth and Gosport and even a Deal-Bournemouth service (via Alresford).

Today Alton is a terminus for the half-hourly service to and from Waterloo, the main line westward being closed in 1973 and now in the hands of the Mid-Hants Railway preservation scheme as far as Alresford. SR trains use the Up platform where the main buildings—modest, single-storey and of brick—are sited. The Up bay is out of use, the signal box is derelict and its work taken over by Farnham, but semaphore signals were still in existence in 1983 at the country end of the station where a rusting connection is continued

on to the Mid-Hants Railway section. The Down island platform has been allocated for use by Mid-Hants trains from 1984.

A.8 Amberley

Victoria-Portsmouth line, between Horsham and Arundel Junction. 54 m 62 ch from London Bridge

Dating from the opening between Pulborough and Ford on August 3 1863, Amberley station has the River Arun on one side and the Chalk Pits Museum on the other. It lies on its own mini-summit with gradients of 1 in 151 on either side and the 83 yd North Stoke Tunnel (55 m 30 ch to 55 m 33 ch) preceding the flat stretch to Arundel.

The original buildings on the Down side, now minus station house and goods

Amberley station with a typical LB&SC shelter on the Up side.

shed, still include a combined booking office plus 14 lever frame housed in a bay projecting on to the platform. The Up side has just a shelter and there is a footbridge and emergency crossover. The service derives from the hourly Victoria-Bognor Regis trains.

Ampress Works—see Lymington Branch

A.9   Andover

Waterloo-Exeter line, between Basing-stoke and Salisbury. 66 m 19 ch from Waterloo

Andover's railway history is steeped in the LSW/GWR feuding. The former's main line arrived from Basingstoke on July 3 1854 as a modest single track and pushed on to Salisbury on May 1 1857. Just a year later the GWR-backed Andover & Redbridge scheme obtained its authorising Act although capital and construction difficulties later brought it into the LSWR fold with opening taking place on March 6 1865.

The Midland & South Western Junction line, opened from Red Post Junction to Swindon in 1882-3, was less of a worry to the LSWR, especially when the young Sam Fay moved from that company to run the cross country line. The route around the town to Andover Town station and on to Kimbridge Junction closed in 1967 (three years earlier for passenger traffic) and the only surviving branch from Andover is the former M&SW route which runs on the Up side of the main line as far as the old Red Post Junction before heading off north to Ludgershall.

From the Basingstoke direction today's line curves around the north side of the town, by way of an embankment, a cutting and over the tiny River Anton, to the former Junction station. The

platforms are staggered and linked by footbridge. The main buildings, partly original, are on the Down side where the traditional wooden goods shed still retains its loading gauge. The Up Platform has wooden buildings and a canopy and behind is the siding accommodation used for the UKF half trains together with the ground frame controlling access to the freight-only line to Ludgershall.

Both the Exeter and the Waterloo/Basingstoke-Salisbury services call.

A.10   Anerley

London Bridge-Windmill Bridge Junction line. 7 m 47 ch from London Bridge

As Anerley Bridge the station was one of the original London & Croydon Railway stations, opened on June 5 1839. Indeed, parts of the surviving Up side buildings may well date from then. A subway leads to the Down side which has a waiting shelter only. 'The Railway' public house stands beyond.

There are four lines through the station, the central pair being the Up and Down Through lines, and the service is derived mainly from the half-hourly London Bridge-Sutton trains.

Angerstein Wharf—see North Kent line

A.11   Angmering

Brighton-Littlehampton/Portsmouth line, between Worthing and Arundel Junction. 15 m 44 ch from Brighton

Served by the Victoria-Littlehampton trains and the Brighton-Portsmouth/Littlehampton slows, Angmering is one of the original 1846 locations still busy with

Arundel station looking south.

passengers although its once considerable traffic of market garden produce by freight and passenger train has now gone. The single-storey traditional station buildings are at the country end on the Up side, with the goods shed at the Brighton end providing a reminder of the goods facilities which existed until 1964. The sub-station and Up siding accommodation are also at this end, the traditional signal box and crossing at the other. Roundstone CCTV crossing (15 m) precedes the station.

Appledore—see Ashford-Hastings line

Ardingly Branch—see Haywards Heath

A.12 Arundel

Victoria-Portsmouth line, between Horsham and Arundel Junction. 58 m 28 ch from London Bridge

Arundel station, dating from August 3 1863, stands beside the A27 in a flat portion of the Arun Valley with a view of the historic town it serves. Closed since 1963 the Up side goods shed is now in private hands but the passenger station remains busy with Victoria-Portsmouth and Bognor Regis trains and a few originating and terminating Littlehampton services.

Down side passengers have two covered areas and the signal box stands on this side although the bay once used by the Littlehampton trains no longer has rails. The main buildings are on the Up side. Brick, substantial and largely original they are quite severe unless one spots such touches as the ceiling mouldings and the highly elaborate boot scraper near the front door of the station apartments.

The station is followed by Arundel Junction (59 m 75 ch) which links the

Mid-Sussex route from Victoria with the coast route from Brighton to Portsmouth at a point (19 m 1 ch) east of Ford. Arundel signal box controls this and the remainder of the triangular link with the Littlehampton line. On the Down side east of the junction are traces of the pre-1863 alignment.

A.13 Ascot

Waterloo-Reading line, junction for line to Ash Vale Junction. 28 m 79 ch from Waterloo

The 1853 Staines, Wokingham & Woking Junction Railway reached Ascot from Staines on June 4 1856 and extended on to Wokingham on July 9 of that year but the link towards Ash Vale did not come until 22 years later. The main services are still those on the Reading route with the Guildford trains connecting into and out of these although there are through peak services on the Guildford line which pass and interchange with the Reading line trains at Ascot.

Despite its woodland setting the station was looking rather sorry for itself by 1982. The mixture of old, rendered main buildings and supplementary wooden buildings on the Up side carried the scars of a fire in the latter and the old 'Southern Service' sign was looking its age. Of the four platforms the two southernmost are out of use, all trains using the Up and Down main lines and the Down Loop, the former being reversible. This facility enables Up services to depart from the single track between Platform 1 and the island platform, Down Reading services

Ascot, with a Guildford train waiting at platform 3 and with less than attractive concrete lamp standards.

The Up side at Ascot, affected by fire and showing signs of its age, in 1983.

mainly using the same line and branch trains running to and from Platform 3 on the opposite side of the island. The platforms are linked by subway and there is a covered walkway for race meeting traffic, especially heavy for Royal Ascot in June.

Once the traffic warranted a separate racecourse station and four signal boxes but by 1983 much of the Down side track plus the London end carriage sidings were out of use.

A.14   Ascot-Ash Vale Line

This link between the Reading and Aldershot lines was authorised in 1873, opened from Ascot to Sturt Lane on March 18 1878 and from Frimley Junction to Ash Vale on June 2 1879. It was electrified from January 1 1939 and now has a half-hourly off-peak service between Ascot and Guildford with through trains to and from Waterloo in the business travel periods. The double line portion to Frimley is controlled from the Feltham box and the single line thence to Ash Vale by the latter.

From Ascot (28 m 79 ch) the route turns sharply south through pleasant woodland to Bagshot (32 m 8 ch) where the single-storey main buildings—including canopied

entrance section with gabled portions each side, decorated windows and barge boards—typify the original building style. Following a bridge high above the town, the route heads across Bagshot Heath and passes through the Chobham Ridge and Surrey Hill heights via the 121 yd, brick-lined Bagshot Tunnel (33 m 60 ch to 33 m 66 ch).

Camberley (35 m 30 ch), originally on a single track doubled in 1893, was called Camberley & York Town until 1923. The station for Sandhurst, it now has a modern station building of the D70 Maze Hill type with tall glass panels and incorporating an office and showroom in the development. There is also a CCTV barrier crossing and a trailing crossover. Frimley (37 m 48 ch), however, retains the traditional style of the line although the 1878 buildings are slightly larger than those at Bagshot and have triple instead of single windows.

The landscape has now become one of marsh, marsh vegetation and gravel pit lagoons as the old connections to the main line are passed and junction is made with the route from Brookwood just before Ash Vale signal box (40 m 57 ch) and station. Opened bearing the name of the 'North Camp' it served on May 2 1870, Ash Vale comprises Up and Down platforms linked by a subway which houses the ticket office. The route crosses the Basingstoke Canal here.

A.15   Ash

Redhill-Reading line, between Guildford and Wokingham. 49 m 18 ch from Charing Cross

Preceding Ash is the former Ash Junction where the SER route to Reading and the closed LSW route to Farnham via Tongham parted company. The earthworks are still visible and the mileage changes here from 35 m 50 ch (from Waterloo via Guildford) to 48 m 34 ch (from Charing Cross via Redhill). Then comes Ash Crossing box and level crossing (49 m 15 ch) and then the 1849 station. This is served by Ascot line trains and the Tonbridge-Reading dmus and comprises the two-storey main buildings on the Up side and more modest provision on the Down. The former engine shed is now let.

A.16   Ashford (Kent)

Charing Cross-Dover line. 56 m 9 ch from Charing Cross

Ashford is a railway centre of considerable modern and historic significance. The original main line of the South Eastern Railway reached the town on December 1 1842, pushed on to Folkestone in the following year and by February 7 1844 trains were running through to Dover. The railway established its locomotive works in this modest Kent town in 1847 and although this closed in 1962 it will be remembered for a continuing contribution to Southern traction dating back to the days of James Cudworth and James Stirling. Like most 'railway' towns Ashford still reveals much evidence of its railway

Clearing points in front of Ashford box.

community and although the wagon works, kept alive by export orders until 1981, is now but a skeleton of its former self there is major emu maintenance activity at Chart Leacon to the west of the station.

Ashford became a junction with the opening of the line to Margate in 1846, the Hastings branch following five years later. The final route to arrive was the Chatham-backed tentacle from Maidstone East which was opened on July 1 1884. These lines all remain in existence and active although Ashford has lost its trains to the closed Hythe and New Romney branches.

The approach to Ashford in the Down direction is marked by the vast sheds of the Chart Leacon depot on the Up side of the main line. The depot was built on the site of a former swamp at the time of the Kent Coast electrification and now employs some 400 people. Some suburban rolling stock and the whole of the Southern's express and diesel electrical multiple unit stock comes into the repair shops for overhaul after every 100,000 miles. In addition the inspection shed carries out day to day maintenance work on electric and diesel shunting locomotives.

Prior to the junction with the Maidstone East line (55 m 53 ch) the main lines have been joined by Up and Down passenger loops, the two Down lines becoming reversible at the junction. Nearby is the site of West Yard, with its brick goods shed and coal depot activity, and that of the old LC&D terminus, closed in 1899. Ashford station, which follows, is a modern affair with island platforms separated by the main and loop lines and with Up and Down platform lines beyond. Hastings

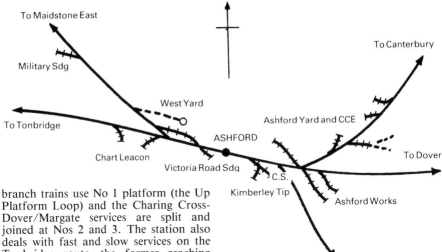

branch trains use No 1 platform (the Up Platform Loop) and the Charing Cross-Dover/Margate services are split and joined at Nos 2 and 3. The station also deals with fast and slow services on the Tonbridge route—the former reaching London in 58 minutes—and with the Victoria/Maidstone East-Ramsgate/Margate trains.

Immediately beyond the station the Hastings route veers off towards the coast under the eye of the panel box, the junction with the line to Canterbury West then following (56 m 34 ch) plus Willesborough LC (56 m 74 ch) where the route becomes double line again. The works area south of the main line is full of interest and the freight yard beside the Down Canterbury line is still active. Between the two the locomotive works and shed areas are slowly being cleared of the remnants of their former bustling activity.

Speedlink wagon in Ashford shops.

A.17   Ashford-Hastings line

Despite being threatened with closure at least twice this branch from the original SER main line at Ashford forms an important link with the eastern end of the coastway route between Hastings and Portsmouth. However, the through passengers, local traffic and summer visitors represent only modest business by economic standards and the three-car sets in use are rarely overcrowded. The basic train pattern is hourly in each direction with the journey taking 48/50 minutes and the Down trains booked five minutes at Rye to allow the Up services to cross.

The line originated as an 1845 proposal to extend the coast route of the Brighton, Lewes & Hastings company to Ashford. The project fell to the South Eastern which gave up its alternative of a branch from Headcorn to Hastings, but the rivalry resurfaced in a dispute at Bopeep Junction when the line was opened on February 13 1851.

The double line section commences at the junction immediately beyond the signal box at Ashford and then heads south via the site of the old goods siding and the surviving AHB crossing at Ruckinge (60 m 15 ch), through gentle countryside of woods and pasture, to Ham Street & Orlestone (61 m 51 ch). This is a simple station of staggered Up and Down platforms with a traditional two-storey house and ticket office extension on the former and a simple shelter opposite. Further AHB crossings follow at Warehorne (62 m 60 ch) and Kenardington (63 m 73 ch) and between these the line crosses the Royal Military Canal, built originally as a defensive measure and converting the Romney and Walland Marsh area into an island by linking the coast at Hythe with the River Rother at Rye.

The line is not electrified and Appledore (64 m 50 ch), where the double line becomes single and the freight-only line to Lydd Town departs, embodies a great many features of the traditional railway, including semaphore signalling. The wooden gates and signal box are followed by staggered platforms, the Up side with imposing two-storey station buildings and the old goods shed backing on to the platform and the Down side with just a shelter. There is an Up Refuge Siding and the facing junction for the Lydd line follows the end of the double line section from Ashford.

On to Rye the line continues its course along the edge of the fertile coastal plain where marsh drainage has brought extensive arable and sheep farming. There are AHB crossings at Becketts (66 m 47 ch), Star (69 m 20 ch) and East Guldeford (70 m 19 ch) and then a tied girder bridge for the crossing of the River Rother. The CCTV crossing at Grove Road (71 m 24 ch) is distinguished by a most appealing tiny gatehouse and marks the beginning of the station complex of passing loop, Down siding, staggered platforms and signal box. The Rye Down side station buildings were described in 1973 as 'one of the best examples of railway Italianate, well in

keeping with the gentle flavour of the old town and with a graceful triple-arched centrepiece, subtle touches in the window frames and an outstanding site at the head of an avenue of trees.' The old brick shed remains extant and the complex ends at Ferry Road CCTV crossing (71 m 44 ch) overlooked by the Gopsall Pottery windmill. The branch to Rye Harbour (1854-1962) joined the main route here and its trackbed can still be seen. Along the eastern bank of the River Rother ran the 3 ft gauge Rye & Camber Tramway (1895/1908-1939).

With the upland ridge one side and the Royal Military Road (A259) on the other the route now heads for Winchelsea (73 m 22 ch) where a 20 mph speed restriction applies on the approaches to the AOCL crossing. The Up side platform is used. It spans a small stream and has a wooden shelter, the old station house surviving on the Down side. The single line from Appledore is worked on the Tokenless Block system and there are now no further signals on the stretch to Ore. This at first continues nearly level as it keeps company with the River Brede but then has to climb steeply to the summit at the entrance to Ore Tunnel.

Along this final section of the line two of the three halts opened in 1907 still survive. The first is Doleham (77 m 43 ch) lying in a wooded setting at the foot of the bank and comprising a single Up side platform with timber shelter. The other is Three Oaks (78 m 65 ch) where the line

Three generations of luggage barrows.

remaining in use switches to the Down side leaving the Up side platform isolated. Again the station is a simple one with just a shelter. The 1,402-yard Ore Tunnel (80 m 26 ch to 81 m 10 ch) marks the beginning of the descent to Ore and the double line on to Hastings.

A.18   Ashford (Surrey)

Waterloo-Reading line, between Richmond and Staines. 17 m 40 ch from Waterloo

The quiet dignity of the Welsh School building heralds the approach to this modest station served by the Windsor line trains. The location dates from 1848 but the main buildings—house plus offices— on the Down side are of later vintage. The Up side has just a shelter.

A.19   Ashtead

Raynes Park-Leatherhead line, between Epsom and Leatherhead. 16 m 19 ch from Waterloo

Ashtead dates from the opening of the line on February 1 1859 and was a joint LSW/LBSC station. The present buildings date from a 1967-8 reconstruction and comprise a ticket office on the Down side and a shelter plus waiting room on the Up, both excellent examples of their kind. The station also has a footbridge, car park, London end CCTV crossing and some traces of the goods facility which closed at the beginning of 1962. There are alternating services on each of the station's two routes, Victoria-Horsham/Effingham Junction and Waterloo-Dorking/Effingham Junction.

Ashurst—see Uckfield Branch

Ash Vale—see Ascot-Ash Vale line

A.20   Aylesford

Strood-Maidstone West-Paddock Wood line, between Strood and Maidstone West. 38 m 74 ch from Charing Cross

Aylesford's platforms are staggered, the one on the Up side being flanked by the original (June 18 1856) station buildings. Multi-gabled and highly decorated these are of Kentish ragstone with Caen Stone dressings. They have similar leaded windows to those at Cuxton and are attributed to a bequest from Aylesford Priory. A substantial signal box of traditional design

controls the double barrier crossing and also the CCTV-monitored one at Aylesford Village (39 m 36 ch). There are crossovers at each end of the layout and reminders of busier days exist in the former siding area and old goods shed on the Down side.

The half-hourly Strood-Maidstone West/Paddock Wood trains call.

A.21   Aylesham

Victoria-Dover line, between Canterbury East and Dover Priory. 68 m 66 ch from Victoria

Aylesham was opened on July 1 1928 to cater for the considerable mining population brought by the development of the Kent coalfield. A temporary siding later used for building materials for miners' houses is still marked by earthworks at the London end of the station. Today it has modern, prefabricated buildings (the main ones on the Up side) and is served by the hourly trains to Victoria and Dover Priory.

Bagshot—see Ascot-Ash Vale Line

B.1   Balcombe

Victoria-Brighton line, between Three Bridges and Haywards Heath. 33 m 64 ch from London Bridge

Balcombe, in the midst of the Sussex Weald, lies 6 miles up the 8-mile climb north from Wivelsfield to the summit, formerly marked by Balcombe Tunnel Box. The location dates from the July 12 1841 opening of the route and the small station buildings on the Down side may well be partly original.

Preceding the station are Balcombe Tunnel Junction (31 m 28 ch) where the four tracks reduce to two and then the 1,141 yd Balcombe Tunnel (32 m 2 ch to 32 m 54 ch), a notoriously damp tunnel high amid the trees and streams of Balcombe Forest. It was also the scene of a noted murder in 1881 when a Mr Gold, travelling on the 2 pm express from London Bridge, was attacked with a gun and a knife. After a fierce struggle Gold was thrown from the train as it passed through the tunnel. The murderer, Lefroy by name, was picked up by the police at Preston Park and the victim's watch and chain were found concealed in one of his boots. He was convicted at Lewes Assizes and duly hanged.

B.2 Balham

Victoria-Brighton line, junction with line to Crystal Palace 4 m 52 ch from Victoria

In addition to the main line services passing through, Balham deals with trains on the Victoria-Horsham/Effingham Junction and Epsom Downs lines and those from Victoria to East Croydon and West Croydon and to Beckenham Junction. It was opened on December 1 1856 as part of the Crystal Palace line scheme and became a junction six years later with the addition of the route via Selhurst to Windmill Bridge Junction. A third track was added shortly after this and a fourth in the 1890s. Air raid damage in the Second World War brought further changes including the conversion of the Up local platform to an island serving both Up and Down local lines.

Reached from the combined LT/BR entrance in Balham High Road, stairs lead up to the two island platforms above, the Down side serving the local lines and having the main brick functional buildings for waiting and staff use and those on the Up side being of wood.

Beyond the country end of the station the two routes diverge at Balham Junction on either side of the Southern Region signal box building.

Banstead—see Epsom Downs Branch

B.3 Barming

Victoria-Margate line, between Otford Junction and Maidstone East. 37 m 43 ch from Victoria

This pleasant country station, served by the Victoria-Maidstone East/Ashford stopping trains, dates from the opening of the line on June 1 1874.

It is preceded by the 33 yd Preston Hall 'A' Tunnel (37 m 10 ch to 37 m 12 ch) and the 54 yd Preston Hall 'B' Tunnel (37 m 17 ch to 37 m 19 ch).

Barnehurst—see Bexleyheath line

B.4 Barnes

Waterloo-Reading line, junction with Hounslow Loop. 7 m 7 ch from Waterloo

The station location, hard by Barnes Common, dates from the opening of the line to Richmond on July 27 1846, junction status coming with the first portion of the Hounslow Loop in 1849. The signal box and junction lie west of Barnes station and mark the point at which the four tracks from the London direction separate into two pairs.

The station itself, passenger only since the goods depot closed in 1969, comprises the central island platform serving the Up and Down Through lines and used by the Hounslow Loop and via Richmond services. Two outer platforms serve the loop lines and there are crossovers at the London end of the station. The main buildings, on the Up side, are substantial and elegant with steep gables, tall chimneys and a variety of door and window styles. Rocks Lane crosses the station by a girder bridge and towards Mortlake there are CCTV crossings at Windsor Line (7 m 26 ch) and White Hart (7 m 52 ch).

Barnes Bridge—see Hounslow Loop

B.5 Barnham

Victoria-Portsmouth line, junction for Bognor Regis Branch. 22 m 29 ch from Brighton

Barnham Junction, as it was called until 1929, dates from 1864 and the opening of the Bognor Regis branch, the latter leaving the main line by a conventional double line junction at the country end of the station's two platforms. Branch trains can use the Down Passenger Loop around the outer face of the Down island platform and there are berthing sidings beyond this and trailing into the Down branch line. On the Up side a trailing connection off the Down Main leads to the Up siding terminating behind the platform. This also doubles as the second of the station's two crossovers.

The platforms at Barnham, extended to 820 ft under the 1938 electrification, are linked by subway and provided with conventional accommodation and canopies. Access to the street is via a covered arcade to the ticket office buildings fronting the B2233. The buffet is on the Down side as is the signal box whose semaphore signals control the pattern of branch, Victoria line and Brighton line trains which interconnect at Barnham. Portsmouth and Bognor train portions are separated/combined at Barnham.

B.6 Basingstoke

Waterloo-Weymouth line, junction with Reading line. 47 m 61 ch from Waterloo

Beyond Basingstoke the four tracks of the former LSW main line divide at Worting

Down Bay platform at Basingstoke.

(Battledown) Junction (50 m 21 ch) for Salisbury and the West and for Southampton and the coastal route on to Weymouth. On the London side it is joined by the line from Reading used by the Class 205 sets on the Reading-Portsmouth service and by through trains between Poole and the North. The GWR origins of this route are apparent in the dead end line and separate platform face it uses at Basingstoke and in the name *Great Western* still carried by the adjacent hostelry.

Basingstoke station proper comprises Up and Down fast lines on either side of the central island. The outer platforms serve the slow lines, the one on the Down side housing the main offices and the Up side one having the branch platform as its northern face and beyond that a freight loop from the reception road in the Up yard to the Reading line. The adjacent North Yard, formerly used for GWR goods traffic, is now a Foster Yeoman stone terminal. Beyond the junction, on the Up side of the main line, are Barton Mill carriage sidings.

There is a connection from the Reading line right across to the Down side of the station where the great water tower, plated 'LSWR Wimbledon Works 1904' contrasts strongly with the GWR traces opposite. The plain station buildings, in red brick and down to street level, are more attractive from the outside than from the platform where wooden canopies hide any grace they may have. On the country side of the station the Down Yard houses freight and engineering activity and there are extensive sidings in the Up Yard opposite. The former loco shed was here.

The London & Southampton Railway had reached Basingstoke with the extension from Winchfield (then Shapley Heath) on June 10 1839. The Winchester-Southampton section opened on the same day but coaches had to be used to bridge the gap until the difficult stretch up to Litchfield Tunnel and down another ten miles to Winchester could be completed. The through route was then opened, with the usual celebrations, on May 11 1840. Basingstoke became part of the LSW/GWR

A Class 47 heads a Freightliner train from the Reading line on to the main line at Basingstoke en route for Southampton.

battleground with a proposal for a line north to Didcot, aimed eventually at giving Southampton a link with the industrial Midlands, but the GWR won that battle and its route reached Basingstoke from Reading on November 1 1848. The poor relationship between the two companies necessitated a separate station for the GWR line, an arrangement which lasted until 1932. The main line probe west to Salisbury opened nine years after the GWR arrival and the short-lived Basingstoke & Alton Light Railway on June 1 1901.

The Bournemouth line semi-fast services call at Basingstoke, as do the all-stations trains and those on the Exeter line. In addition to the Reading-Portsmouth workings, the Liverpool/Manchester-Poole trains also call at Basingstoke. Control is in the hands of the 1966 signal box which, with the similar box at Eastleigh, replaced 26 traditional boxes between Farnborough and St Denys. The panel embraces the main line from Farnborough to Steventon and Grateley and the branch almost to Southcote Junction.

Bat & Ball—see Sevenoaks

Battersea Park—see South London line

B.7   Battle

Charing Cross-Hastings line, between Tunbridge Wells and Hastings. 55 m 46 ch from Charing Cross

As might be expected this steeply graded route was opened in stages and Battle was its southern extremity from January 1 1852 until the final section was completed on February 1 of the same year. It is a line of impressive stations and Battle is outstanding, its gables, tall chimneys and mullioned and leaded windows giving it 'a dignity in keeping with the nearby parish church and the remains of Battle Abbey'.

The station lies near the summit of the final 1 in 100 climb before the descent to the coast and is preceded by a CCTV crossing at Riverhall (52 m 36 ch) and an AHB crossing at Battle Road (52 m 52 ch), site of the former Mountfield Halt. A viaduct heralds the final approach to the signal box, sited near the Marley Lane barrier crossing, and then the staggered platforms. The main buildings are on the Up side with a brick goods shed behind and the former dock nearby. On the Down side the buildings have been demolished and the Down siding is no longer in use.

Battle has a basic hourly train service to and from Charing Cross with some faster peak period links with Cannon Street.

B.8   Bearsted

Victoria-Margate line, between Maidstone East and Ashford. 42 m 59 ch from Charing Cross

Part of the Chatham probe into South Eastern territory, the line from Maidstone to Ashford opened on July 1 1884 and with it Bearsted & Thurnham station. Served today by the hourly Victoria-Ashford/Ramsgate trains, the station retains its original buildings which include the use of oversailing for the gables. There is a signal box on the Down side on the 1 in 60 climb from Maidstone East.

B.9   Beaulieu Road

Waterloo-Weymouth line, between Southampton and Brockenhurst. 88 m 6 ch from Waterloo

Beaulieu Road, deep in the New Forest, was opened with the line in 1847. The two platforms, each with a shelter, are reached by steps from the B3056 overbridge and served by the hourly Waterloo-Bournemouth stopping trains.

Beckenham Hill—see Catford Loop

B.10   Beckenham Junction

Victoria-Ramsgate line. 8 m 53 ch from Victoria

Beckenham opened on the first day of 1857 as the terminus of the line from Lewisham and became a junction in the following year when the Bromley Junction-Bickley section was opened to give the emerging Chatham route its first access to London in 1860. Today the station handles two calling services, the Victoria-Orpington trains routed via West Dulwich and the Crystal Palace line trains which originate and terminate in the Up side bay at the station. There is also a coal concentration depot reached from the Down line of the curve from New Beckenham and with a second connection off the Down Main on the station side of the junction.

The station itself comprises two platforms, separated by the Up and Down lines and with an overbridge at the country end and the junction of the three routes at the London end. The main, period buildings are on the Up side and the signal box stands in the vee of the junction with the line from New Beckenham.

Beddington Lane—see West Croydon-Wimbledon line

Bedenham Sidings—see Fareham

Bedhampton—see Havant

Beeding Sidings—see Shoreham

B.11   Bekesbourne

Victoria-Dover line, between Canterbury East and Dover Priory. 64 m 58 ch from Victoria

Opened with the line on July 22 1861, Bekesbourne is now a simple, unmanned station serving Bekesbourne, Bishopsbourne, Littlebourne and Patrixbourne in a pleasant orchard area of Kent. It consists of footbridge linked platforms with waiting shelters, with the 64¾ milepost on the Down platform and then, on the continuing climb towards Snowdown, a viaduct over the Nail Bourne stream.

There is a basic hourly service each way with extra trains morning and evening. For about five weeks from the end of October each year this is one of the spots where the SR gets most trouble from falling leaves, crushed by the train wheels into a hard black deposit on the rails.

Bellingham—see Catford Loop

Belmont—see Epsom Downs Branch

B.12   Beltring

Paddock Wood-Maidstone West-Strood line, between Paddock Wood and Maidstone West. 36 m 50 ch from Charing Cross

Unlike the other stations on this 1844 line Beltring did not open until September 1 1909. During the Second World War there was a siding here for the forwarding of farm produce but this closed on June 5 1961 and the station now consists simply of sleeper platforms with shelters and a small ticket office near the AHB crossing. There is a tied girder bridge over the Medway to the north.

Lying in an area of sheep meadows and great oast houses, Beltring is served by the hourly Paddock Wood-Strood trains.

Belvedere—see North Kent Line

B.13   Bentley

Waterloo-Alton line. 44m 24 ch from Waterloo

Bentley station was opened two years after the Guildford-Farnham line was extended to Alton on July 28 1852. The location increased in importance from December 11 1905 when the Bentley & Bordon Light Railway was opened to serve Longmoor military camp. In its early years the 4 m 59 ch branch had a service of 12 rail motors daily (five on Sundays) plus two more from Farnham and Guildford, two goods trains from Guildford and some weekend workings to and from Waterloo. The junction, still discernible on the Down side, lay 17 ch from Bentley with the intermediate Kingsley Halt 2 m 47 ch further on.

Passenger services on the single line branch ceased on September 16 1957 and freight ended in 1966 leaving Bentley today just a simple station of Up and Down platforms served half-hourly by the Alton line trains. There is a modest, single-storey building on the Up side and a footbridge on the Down platform with its simple shelter and footpaths off into the countryside. The extra face used by the former branch trains is still obvious.

B.14   Berrylands

Waterloo-Weymouth line, between Wimbledon and Surbiton. 10 m 78 ch from Waterloo

This commuter station lies on the portion of the 1839 main line elevated for its crossing of Norbiton Common and the Hogsmill River. Increasing traffic from local housing developments gave the location its first station, served by Hampton Court trains, on October 16 1933. The present, ground level Clasp building dates from a 1969 reconstruction and has stair access to two platforms on the outer, local lines, provided with waiting shelters. The basic service is half-hourly and still provided by the Hampton Court trains.

B.15   Berwick

Victoria-Eastbourne/Hastings line, between Lewes and Eastbourne. 15 m 50 ch from Brighton

The small building on the Down side houses the ticket office and waiting room, there is a shelter on the Up platform, car parks on both sides and a double barrier crossing at the country end of the station controlled by the signal box alongside the Down line. The train service is provided by the hourly Brighton-Eastbourne slows.

Berwick opened on June 27 1846 and in the 1920s was noted for despatching more milk churns than any other SR station. Now even the goods facility has been gone since 1963, although a siding still runs to the old Down side dock. There are AHB crossings at Ripe (13 m 25 ch), Selmeston (14 m 58 ch) and Wilmington (17 m 29 ch).

B.16 Betchworth

Redhill-Reading line, between Redhill and Dorking Town. 27 m 17 ch from Charing Cross

The station buildings on the Down side are original (1849) and in the steeply gabled style found elsewhere on this line. Betchworth is served by the Tonbridge-Reading dmus and has a signal box and double barrier crossing plus the remains of a small dock and Up refuge siding with attendant ground frame. There are further crossings on either side, Brockham (28 m 8 ch) with traditional gates and Buckland (26 m 49 ch) with AHBs, and both with diminutive period crossing houses.

The 384 yd Betchworth Tunnel is on the Leatherhead-Horsham line (22 m 60 ch to 22 m 73 ch from Waterloo).

B.17 Betteshanger Colliery

Charing Cross-Margate line, between Sandwich and Deal. 89 m 11 ch from Charing Cross*

The NCB line to Betteshanger Colliery runs some 1¾ miles from the main line, south-west and under the A258, to the colliery. The connection to the main line trails into the Down line with a facing crossover to the Up, both protected by the Home signals of the adjacent box. North-wall RG crossing (90 m 9 ch) lies towards Deal.

Loading is by conveyor and grab, wagons then passing over an automatic weighbridge before their journey to BSC and CEGB destinations.

B.18 Bexhill

Victoria-Eastbourne/Hastings line. 29 m 69 ch from Brighton

Bexhill got its first station, on the present site, when the single line Brighton probe east from Lewes reached Bulverhythe, just west of Hastings, on June 27 1846. Its second was opened on the west side of the town on June 1 1902 under a scheme promoted by the Crowhurst, Sidley & Bexhill Railway, linking those three places with its 4½-mile branch from the SER main line and eventually becoming part of the SE&C empire. From a generous terminus at Bexhill (West) 'H' tanks worked the branch shuttle in its later years with dmus taking over in 1958. After freight traffic ended in 1963 the branch, which included a substantial viaduct, closed completely on June 15 1964.

Today's remaining station is served hourly by the Victoria-Eastbourne-Ore trains and by the all-stations trains to and from Brighton (and Ore). It has two long platforms with slopes leading up to the ornate buildings on the overbridge. Dating from 1901, the block has a ticket hall with a high central roof and still retains one of its former three ornate canopies. There are waiting rooms on the platforms and, on the Down side, the Bexhill signal box and the private freight terminal operated by L.J. Hydelman & Co for the reception of domestic fuel oil.

Bexley—see Dartford Loop Line

B.19 Bexleyheath Line

Lewisham to Crayford Creek Junction. 9 m 32 ch

This, the most recent of the three lines between London and Dartford, leaves the North Kent route just beyond Blackheath and serves seven stations before rejoining it at a triangular junction just east of Slade Green. The route came into being because, despite a good deal of public pressure, the South Eastern Railway declined to promote a line to serve the area lying between the North Kent line and the Dartford Loop. The Bexley Heath Railway originated a scheme to fill this gap but then took 12 years to implement it and only finally opened its line on May 1 1895. Money was too scarce to provide much of a celebration and the company's subsequent bankruptcy and absorption by the SER was no great surprise.

From Lewisham (6 m 4 ch) the route runs to Blackheath (6 m 75 ch) which is dealt with in the North Kent Line entry and where the junction in a wooded cutting is followed by the 437 yd Kidbrooke Tunnel (7 m 26 ch to 7 m 46 ch). Kidbrooke station (7 m 74 ch) is one of the original five although it now has more modern shelters and a Clasp ticket office block on the Up side to help it serve the large area of houses and flats nearby. A high embankment leads to Eltham Well Hall (9 m 2 ch), opened as Well Hall but now provided with long, low brick buildings in the Southern style on the Up side and an unusual, but attractive, shelter of lapped wood and corrugated roofing on the Down.

Eltham Park (9 m 41 ch) was called Shooters Hill when it opened on July 1 1908. Like its neighbour it has a pre-grouping milepost on the Down platform but its impressive features are the long, arcade-like ramps from the ticket office on the overbridge and the decorative valance boards and supports provided for the long canopies. A new station is to be built in Glenlea Road, Eltham, in place of the existing facilities and combining bus and rail in one complex. Falconwood (10 m 27 ch) only dates from January 1 1936 and has silver birches adorning the approach cutting. A single-storey, brick ticket office building leads down to a covered foot-bridge and canopied platforms and the station marks the point where the Dartford panel takes over from London Bridge.

The remaining stations are all original and have similar SR styles displayed in their main buildings. Welling (11 m 28 ch) has its ticket office block on the Up side and a shelter like the one at Eltham Well Hall on the Down. The pattern is similar at Bexleyheath (12 m 59 ch) but the main block is more substantial and the Down side has the 12¾ milepost as well as a brick shelter. A footbridge links the plat-forms of this station, which deals with well over two million passengers a year, and a road bridge spans it.

Barnehurst (13 m 71 ch) is approached in a cutting with overbridges, one skewed by using angled brickwork in the abut-ments. Access to this pleasant station is from the small brick ticket office above the Up platform, behind which stands the large, severe sub-station building. Barne-hurst still retains the air of a country station and it is not uncommon to see foxes while waiting on its platforms. There is a crossover here as well as at Kidbrooke and Falconwood.

The route ends with two junctions, Perry Street Fork Junction (15 m 7 ch) making a facing connection with the Erith loop to Slade Green and Crayford Creek Junction (15 m 36 ch) re-uniting it with the North Kent Line. The train service between the London-Dartford routes is interlinked, one train of the three in each hour via Bexleyheath going through to Gravesend, as on the other routes.

B.20   Bickley

Victoria-Ramsgate line, junction with Tonbridge line. 11 m 76 ch from Victoria

Bickley is part of the history of the piece-meal Chatham route between London and Dover, rails reaching the area from Brom-ley Junction on July 7 1858 and from the Rochester direction on December 3 1860. The latter link enabled trains to start running from Victoria to Faversham and on to Canterbury East with access to Dover coming in 1861. The link with the SER Tonbridge line was much later, not coming until 1902 but then representing one of the fruits of the joint management of the former rivals.

The four-track approach to Bickley is up a 1 in 95 gradient and with the Fast and Slow lines paired. There are crossovers from Fast to Slow and then Slow to Fast at Bickley Junction (12 m 38 ch) and then Up and Down loops to the SER route at Petts Wood Junction, the latter passing beneath the Tonbridge main line (see Chislehurst diagram).

Bickley station itself has island platforms between the Fast and Slow line pairs with stairs up to the ticket office on the overbridge at the country end.

Modern double barrier crossing between the traditional signal box and The Railway Hotel at Billingshurst.

B.21 Billingshurst

Victoria-Portsmouth line, between Horsham and Arundel Junction. 44 m 71 ch from London Bridge

The first section of the Mid-Sussex Railway line south from Horsham opened, through Billingshurst, to Petworth on October 10 1859. The station house part of the Up side complex dates from then but there is only a shelter on the Down side. The goods shed building is of interest for its rather attractive fan windows.

The combination of Portsmouth and Bognor Regis trains gives Billingshurst an excellent service.

Bingham Road—see Addiscombe Branch

B.22 Birchington-on-Sea

Victoria-Ramsgate line, between Herne Bay and Margate. 70 m 56 ch from Victoria

The extensive housing development at the western end of the coastal approach to Margate enjoys the same service via the 1863 station. This comprises footbridge-linked platforms plus crossover and with traditional ticket office building and tall, narrow station house (now in private hands) on the Up side and on the Down a combined waiting room and shelter with integral canopy and of LC&D origins.

B.23 Birkbeck

Victoria-Beckenham Junction line, between Crystal Palace and Beckenham Junction. 10 m 26 ch from Victoria

The route from Bromley Junction dates from 1858 but was closed from 1915 until electrification in 1929. Birkbeck was opened by the Southern Railway on March 2 1930. The route here is well above street level and the two-platform station is reached by steps from Elmers End Road. Its modest buildings are largely of wood and were showing the scars of fire damage in 1983.

The station is adjacent to Crystal Palace cemetery and is served half-hourly from Victoria. It is preceded by Bromley Junction (9 m 24 ch) where there are Up and Down side single line connections towards Norwood Junction and joining the main line from London Bridge at 9 m 75 ch/8 m 35 ch.

Bishopstone—see Seaford Branch

B.24 Bitterne

Southampton-Portsmouth line, between St Denys and Fareham. 2 m 36 ch from Southampton

Bitterne serves the Bitterne, Bitterne Park and Townhill Park areas of Southampton and has an hourly service to Portsmouth and Southampton/Salisbury. The station comprises Up and Down platforms with the ticket office included in traditional brick buildings on the Down side and a wooden shelter with integral canopy on the Up. The location dates from the opening of the line to Netley in 1866 and was a passing point of some importance until the route was doubled, crossing the local and through Cardiff trains and specials such as those to Netley Hospital.

B.25 Blackfriars

Holborn Viaduct-Herne Hill line. 30 ch from Holborn Viaduct

Blackfriars is essentially a bowler hat and brolly station, one of the Southern Region's three City terminals and open only from Monday to Friday. It stands on a site owned jointly by BR and King's College, Cambridge, and is bounded by Queen Victoria Street (where the main entrance is situated) to the north, New Bridge Street to the west, Puddle Dock and the Mermaid Theatre to the east and Blackfriars underpass and the River Thames to the south.

The present station, completely rebuilt between 1972 and 1977 and officially opened by the Lord Mayor of London, had four predecessors. The first, Blackfriars Bridge, opened on June 1 1864 as the first stage of the LC&D's extension into the City. Designed by Joseph Cubitt, it stood on the east side of the approach to a new road bridge then being built and, although apparently an impressive affair, lasted only six months as the terminus before the route moved on and it became part of the goods depot. Cubitt then took his tracks over the river on a lattice girder bridge to a small temporary station in Little Earl Street and this location had the distinction of being the first to serve the City of London proper.

Ludgate Hill permanent station opened on June 1 1865 and remained in use until March 3 1929, trains running through to Farringdon Street from the beginning of the following year. It was followed by St Pauls, reached by a parallel bridge across the Thames, opened on May 10 1886, and

serving the public for almost a century before it was closed for the building of the present station. St Pauls changed its name to Blackfriars when London Transport opened the St Pauls Underground station in 1937 and it suffered badly during the air raids of World War Two.

The rebuilding of Blackfriars presented many problems, both technical and financial. Among them were the congested nature of the site, the fact that the station was built on arches, the mixture of trains terminating with others running through to Holborn Viaduct, and the existence of London Transport lines underneath. An added complication was that the cold

Modern roofing over the Blackfriars through platforms contrasts with the older bridge behind.

store below, over a hundred years, had frozen the ground solid to a depth of 20 ft. All this plus the fact that three bridges needed either complete renewal or major repair and the need to keep trains running while the work was in progress.

Repairs to bridge decking on Blackfriars with St Pauls Cathedral in the background.

The financial problem was solved by a commercial development, incorporating the new station and funded in the long term by the income generated. The development was shared jointly by the site owners, BR using its own funds for the contribution of £7¾ m, which included £3½ m for the station part.

A feature of the station is the preservation of the original stone plaques depicting the names of the 54 cities and towns which could somehow be reached from the station opened as St Pauls in 1886. Ranging from St Petersburg to Sevenoaks, Brindisi to Beckenham and Dresden to Deal, they originally adorned the station frontage and now appear in one wall of the new concourse. Also preserved is the 19th century timber and stone screen on the eastern elevation of the station bridge where it crosses Blackfriars underpass. The station complex won a tiling award which is exhibited on one of the walls and a novel feature of the design is the use of rubber bridge bearings for the portion over the LT station in order to reduce vibration from trains.

Entrances from the street and the Underground lead to a pleasant concourse housing the ticket office with the access to the three terminal platforms nearby and then a subway link between the two through platforms. The station is used by nearly 16,000 people daily, over 9,000 of them during the morning and evening business periods. The off-peak services run to and from West Croydon, also Sevenoaks via Swanley. Peak variations include Lewisham via Nunhead and London Bridge via Sutton.

Approaching the station in the Up direction the Fast and Slow line pairs from Elephant & Castle are joined by the Blackfriars Spur from Metropolitan Junction at Blackfriars Junction, with a Down side Carriage Reception Road linking the spur with No 1 Platform and No 2 Carriage Road leading off this. The station proper is preceded by the signal gantry and line indicators and the crossovers between the Up and Down Holborn lines and links to the terminal platforms. The old bridge remains in existence upstream of the present one and the site of Blackfriars goods is still evident on the Up side approaches.

Blackheath—see North Kent Line

B.26   Blackwater

Redhill-Reading line, between Guildford and Wokingham. 55 m 58 ch from Charing Cross

Blackwater, opened on July 4 1849, now comprises Up and Down platforms with shelters, an overbridge at the Guildford end and a crossover at the Reading end. The Tonbridge-Reading dmus call.

This modest location can boast three previous names Blackwater & Sandhurst, Blackwater & York Town and Blackwater & Camberley.

Rail joint and lightweight rail flaw detector apparatus.

B.27   Bognor Regis Branch

Victoria-Portsmouth line, branch from Barnham. 3 m 46 ch

Bognor, originally just a modest village, was first served by a station on the main line from Brighton to Portsmouth located near the village of Woodgate and variously known as Woodgate or Bognor. Several early plans to improve its facilities, including one LSW scheme, came to nothing and it was left to a local project to obtain an Act in 1861 and open the branch from Barnham—which took the place of the previous main line station which then closed—on June 1 1864. The growth from village to town and resort continued and Bognor became Bognor Regis by royal decree after King George V's recovery from illness was helped by a stay there in 1928.

From a facing junction at the country end of Barnham station (22 m 29 ch from Brighton) the present double line branch heads through flat arable land to the industrial outskirts of Bognor Regis where a level crossing and sub-station precede the station area. A typical SR-style brick signal box on the Up side controls access to the four platform lines and the release road between platforms 2 and 3. An interesting feature is the survival of an LB&SC Saxby & Farmer ground frame for the release of the locomotives using platform 3.

The station buildings date from 1902 and the frontage is in red brick with two gable ends and a pretentious three-storey corner block surmounted by a cupola clock tower. They lead via the high booking hall to the concourse which has the usual station facilities, including a buffet to take over the role of the former tea room.

The train service is a mixture of through trains to Victoria (some via Dorking) and London Bridge, portions added to Portsmouth-Victoria trains, trains to Victoria going into Littlehampton and out again and also connecting with Portsmouth-Brighton slows, local shuttles making similar connections and a few through Brighton all-stations services.

B.28   Bookham

Leatherhead-Effingham Junction line. 20 m 45 ch from Waterloo

The 1885 station buildings on the Down side, very much Claygate style, identify the station as part of the New Guildford Line package, the branch from Effingham Junction to Leatherhead being opened on

February 2 1885 along with the portion of the line from Guildford. The station is preceded by the short 91 yd Bookham Tunnel (20 m 31 ch to 20 m 35 ch) and followed by the site of the goods yard (closed in 1965) where the former goods shed has now become a private dwelling. On the Up side the shelter plus canopy has a nice line in decorated spandrels.

Alternate Victoria/Waterloo-Effingham Junction services call half-hourly.

Bopeep   Tunnel   and   Junction—see Hastings

B.29   Borough Green & Wrotham

Victoria-Margate line, between Otford Junction and Maidstone East. 29 m 46 ch from Victoria

During the day the Victoria-Thanet services on this route run fast between Bromley South and Borough Green, leaving the Victoria-Maidstone East trains to serve the intermediate stations. Borough Green itself has Up and Down platforms with the latter preceded by a Down Passenger Loop and the whole controlled from the small Up side signal box which has the Up Starter right outside its windows. Part of the Down side building complex may date back to the 1874 opening of the line but the longer portion, with tall chimneys and four dormer windows, is a later addition. There are two crossovers, a concrete footbridge and a repeater on the Down platform.

B.30   Bosham

Victoria-Portsmouth line, between Chichester and Havant. 31 m 43 ch from Brighton

The station itself was one of the original 1847 stopping points but the present station buildings date from shortly after the turn of the century. The main ones, two-storey and gabled, are on the Down side with a simple but attractive pair of waiting rooms on the Up. On the same side is a traditional signal box controlling gates across the B2146 at the country end of the station which is preceded by Brook Lane LC (31 m 29 ch) and followed by an AHB crossing at Funtington (32 m 19 ch).

The basic train service is provided by the Brighton-Portsmouth slows and the Victoria-Portsmouth semi-fasts and caters for both the adjacent houses and the picturesque village of Bosham which has links with King Canute and is featured in the Bayeux Tapestry.

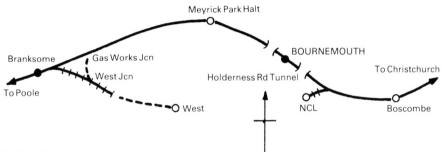

B.31 Botley

*Eastleigh-Fareham line. 78 m 72 ch from
Waterloo*

This line, and the first station at Botley,
were opened on February 7 1842 after a
false start in the previous year and hasty
modifications to Fareham Tunnel. Today
the station, served by Reading/Eastleigh-
Portsmouth trains, marks the end of the
double line section from Eastleigh and the
commencement of the Tokenless Block
section on to Fareham. It is also the site of
a stone terminal which is located on the
Up side but is conveyor-connected to a
Down siding formed from the stub of the
old branch from Bishop's Waltham.

The Bishop's Waltham line, opened on
June 1 1863, ran from a single platform
terminus, along the river via Durley Halt
to the Down island platform at Botley. It
closed to passengers as early as January 2
1933 but freight continued over the 3 m
56 ch line until April 30 1962.

Beyond Botley the route passes through
Botley Wood and the 122 yd Tapnage
Tunnel (81 m 35 ch to 81 m 40 ch). Then
comes the site of Knowle Junction where
it is still possible to see the trackbed of the
Meon Valley line from Alton and the
divergence, past the site of Knowle Halt,
of the double line avoiding the Fareham
tunnels and formerly rejoining the main
route just before the junction at Fareham.

Botley signal box remains in existence
but only for working the crossovers and
for access to the Foster Yeoman siding,
the main control lying with the Eastleigh
panel.

B.32 Bournemouth

*Waterloo-Weymouth line. 108 m 2 ch from
Waterloo*

From March 14 1870 such of Bournemouth's 2,000 inhabitants as wished to
travel to London could make the whole
journey by train instead of having to use
the horse-drawn omnibus service to Hamworthy for the Southampton & Dorchester
line or to Christchurch for the line opened
from Ringwood on November 13 1862.
They used a station, later called Bournemouth East, on the site of the NCL depot
at Holdenhurst Road.

A link from Poole to Bournemouth
West was opened on June 18 1874 and the
east and west approaches were joined on
July 20 1885 with a new through station,
called Central from 1899. Trains ran via
Sway from March 6 1888 and the splitting
of Bournemouth and Weymouth portions
was transferred from Ringwood to
Brockenhurst.

East station closed with the opening of
the central station, Meyrick Park Halt in
1917 and Bournemouth West and Boscombe on October 4 1965. The latter
continued as a coal depot but the line to
Bournemouth West has now been
truncated and provides access to the carriage servicing depot. The four-bay shed,
280 ft long was built during 1965 as part
of the Bournemouth electrification pro-

*Bournemouth station in 1982 and with an
Up slow in the bay.*

ject, the curve from Gas Works Junction being removed at the same period.

In readiness for electrification the Up and Down middle lines at Central station were removed, the Up platform lengthened to 800 ft and two sidings added at the Poole end. The first of the new electric trains arrived in 1966 with the full time-table coming into operation on July 10 of the following year and bringing the resort within 100 minutes of Waterloo.

Today Bournemouth has a basic service pattern of three trains an hour to and from Waterloo. In the Down direction the order is slow, fast, semi-fast, with the fast trains calling only at Southampton where they overtake and connect into the slows. These also convey a four-car portion which works on to Weymouth. Although the Bournemouth-Salisbury (via the now closed Fordingbridge line) and Wimborne services, plus the local workings, have long gone, the 108 miles from Waterloo now takes only 96 minutes compared with the 126 of the *Bournemouth Belle* in 1938 and 150 minutes in the later LSW days. The mantle of the services to the North over the Somerset & Dorset route is now carried by the Poole-Manchester/Liverpool/Newcastle trains.

The former freight facilities on the approach to Bournemouth are followed by the minor Holdenhurst Road Tunnel, the ornate portal of the old offices and then the station proper with its overall roof supported on tall walls and the main two-storey buildings backing the long Down platform. There is a short Up bay at the London end and parcels area, signal box and dock at the country end before the second short Cemetery Road tunnel. Then cutting gives way to embankment and a high bridge, with the former direct curve to Bournemouth West marked by a tall viaduct. The trailing connection from the carriage servicing area follows. This comprises berthing space for 14 × 4-coach sets plus the inspection shed which is equipped with pits and an overhead crane.

B.33   Boxhill & Westhumble

Leatherhead-Horsham line, between Leatherhead and Dorking. 21 m 14 ch from Waterloo

The A24 followed the example of the River Mole in looping round the North Downs hill known as The Priory but the LB&SC's railway, authorised in 1863 and opened on March 11 1867 as part of the

Mid-Sussex route to Portsmouth, went straight through the 524 yd Mickleham Tunnel (19 m 55 ch to 19 m 78 ch). Immediately after the tunnel the route crosses the Mole and then continues to Boxhill & Westhumble station via the dramatic scenery of Mickleham Downs and Box Hill to the east. Thanks to the stipulations of the original landowner the station buildings match their surroundings with the main complex on the Down side, steeply gabled in the French style and with decorative tiles and dominating tower. The Up side buildings, smaller and now boarded up, have a novel window pattern and linked canopy.

B.34   Bracknell

Waterloo-Reading line, between Ascot and Wokingham. 32 m 24 ch from Waterloo

The station for this busy Berkshire town has been the subject of a modern re-development scheme which has embodied the BR ticket and administrative offices in the ground floor of a multi-storey block backing the Up side platform. There is then a concrete footbridge link to the Down side which has a modern platform shelter. An overbridge crosses the railway at the London end of the station while the old yard area at the country end is now a car park.

The route dates from July 4 1856 and runs through woodland via Whitmoor Bog RG crossing (30 m 73 ch), the station and then AHB crossings at Waterloo (34 m 76 ch) and Star Lane (35 m 30 ch). There is a half-hourly basic service.

Brading—see Isle of Wight

B.35   Bramley

Reading-Basingstoke line. 46 m 41 ch from Paddington

Although this Berks & Hants line opened on November 1 1848, Bramley only came into existence as a goods siding in 1865 and did not start dealing with passengers until 30 years after that. Today the old yard is followed by an AHB crossing and then the two-platform station with traditional brick buildings on each. The service is provided by the three-car Reading-Basingstoke/Portsmouth workings.

At the Basingstoke end of the Down platform is the headshunt for access to the Army depot sidings.

B.36 Branksome

Waterloo-Weymouth line, between Bournemouth and Poole. 110 m 51 ch from Waterloo

The simplified, gabled station buildings date from the 1874 opening of the line from Poole to Bournemouth West. Signed 'Branksome for Eastern Poole', the station is served by the hourly four-car push-pull sets which extend the Waterloo-Bournemouth service to Weymouth. A 30 mph speed restriction applies through the station which lies in a shallow cutting with a tall signal box at the London end.

The third rails continue as far as Branksome to permit access to the Bournemouth carriage servicing depot.

Brentford—see Hounslow Loop

B.37 Brighton

Victoria-Brighton line. 50 m 49 ch from London Bridge

Brighton, always anxious to impress, managed two railway opening ceremonies within a little over a year. The first, on May 11 1840, marking the completion of what is now the beginning of the Coastway line westwards, was saluted by the Band of the Lancers and was witnessed by 'an exceedingly animated crowd'. The short line linked Brighton with Shoreham, to which the locomotives and rolling stock had been brought by sea, and the inaugural trip took a mere 11½ minutes.

Memorable as that event may have been, it paled into insignificance alongside the second railway ceremony in September 1841. The London & Brighton Railway had triumphed over four rival schemes

Brighton goods shed, still revealing a touch of flamboyance in the decorative ironwork of the canopy brackets.

and obtained its Act on July 15 1837 for a link from the London & Croydon at Norwood to Brighton with branches to Shoreham and Newhaven. By early 1841 the new tracks had reached Haywards Heath with a connection on by coach which brought Brighton within four hours of London. With encouragement from countless spectators, John Urpeth Rastrick's work was pushed on through the tunnels at Clayton and Patcham and came finally to the Queen of Watering Places and its eager, welcoming townsfolk. The line to Lewes was opened in the same decade, on June 8 1846, and the branch to Thomas Read Kemp's development at Kemp Town came into service on August 2 1869.

Rastrick was responsible for the working area at the station but the main buildings were to the designs of David Moccatta. Although there have been changes over the years (notably in 1882-3 and pre-electrification) and the platforms and concourse have been enlarged, the station remains unaltered in its essentials. It is really three terminal stations in one, linked by a concourse and topped by a 'light, chaste and elegant three-bay roof'.

The main line terminal occupies the centre portion of Brighton station and is flanked by a section for the Coastway West trains to Portsmouth and another for the Coastway East services to Lewes, Seaford and Eastbourne. Five bays serve nine platform faces, the present No 9 plat-

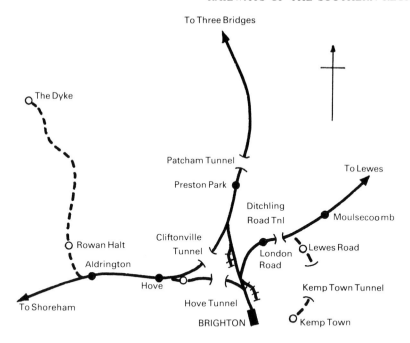

To Three Bridges

The Dyke

Patcham Tunnel

To Lewes

Preston Park

Ditchling
Road Tnl   Moulsecoomb

Cliftonville
Tunnel   London   Lewes Road
                     Road

Rowan Halt

Aldrington

Kemp Town Tunnel

Hove

To Shoreham   Hove Tunnel

BRIGHTON   Kemp Town

Some of the decorative work on one of the roof support pillars at Brighton.

form being partly wooden-decked. Trains for the Kemp Town branch went from this side until the line's closure on January 2 1933 (June 14 1971 for freight) but their platform has disappeared under the Southern Region's largest car park which has spaces for 1,000 cars.

The cab road between platforms 7 and 8 formerly gave access through a tunnel to Trafalgar Street. It later became a parcels working area for van trains in platform 7 but BR's C&D parcels activity ended in June 1981. Another tunnel, beneath platforms 5 and 6, formerly linked the Top and Lower yards but this now serves as a storage area, lecture room and even a miniature rifle range. The rail incline between the two yards is also out of use.

On this same, Down, side of the station stood the old Brighton locomotive works and the goods depot, the latter with a separate connection passing behind the works area. The multi-siding goods yard included coal, cattle and car facilities, docks, a travelling crane and banana warehouses and there were four longer sidings into the goods shed. This quite evocative building is still standing and the site of the goods connection is marked by the small, attractive Brighton Upper Goods box.

The works area dates back to London & Brighton days but locomotive building did not begin until 1852. The works continued to serve the LB&SC and later the Southern Railway but in 1971 the area became a less romantic, but more useful, car park. Under the 1933 electrification the new signal box was housed in part of the works building complex and only this has survived the changes of the years.

On the opposite side of the station and its main line approach lay a group of facilities from Brighton Shed to the old Pullman Works just south of the junction for the Hove line. Now the area is used for a combined engineering depot occupied jointly by traffic and CM&EE staff and for carriage stabling and servicing work. It is here that all routine maintenance is carried out on Central Division emus. The staff of around a hundred deals with 1,200 coaches every month and replace as many as 150,000 brake blocks a year. The old green, enamel 'Brighton' sign was still to be seen in 1983 and a 45-ton breakdown crane was allocated at that time.

Outside the station frontage the colonnades have gone and the clock gable is partially obscured by the canopy over the forecourt which leads to the tiled, modernised entrance hall, ticket office and Travel Centre area. Below are the period tiles and mosaic flooring of the low level exit to Trafalgar Street and above the administrative, TOPS and trainmens' accommodation. On the concourse the suspended clock retains a little of the grandeur of former years as does the vintage train indicator where the brasswork has been polished so often that the name of the makers, 'The Railway Indicator Co' can barely be made out.

Beyond the platform ends the Coastway West route continues the curve of Platforms 1 and 2 and disappears into the 220 yd Hove Tunnel (30 ch to 40 ch). Beyond it the route is joined by the avoiding line from Preston Park which passes through the 535 yd Cliftonville Tunnel (49 m 56 ch to 50 m) on its way to Hove Junction (50 m 56 ch). Preston Park station (49 m 21 ch), opened as Preston on November 1 1869, has a pair of subway-linked island platforms and buildings of modern design which include the ticket office in the Up side group. Beyond Preston Park the route reduces to two lines and begins its ascent to the 492 yd Patcham Tunnel (47 m 65 ch to 48 m 7 ch). The Cliftonville curve was opened on July 1 1879.

The Coastway East line veers away from the main line over a magnificent curving viaduct 400 yds long and with its

27 arches rising to a height of 67 ft above the valley floor. This brings the route to London Road station (57 ch). Opened on October 1 1877 London Road has staggered platforms linked by a subway with the stately two-storey main buildings on the Up side housing both ticket office and station apartments. The platforms are followed by the high arch of the 63 yd Ditchling Road Tunnel (63 ch to 66 ch), a short cutting and then Kemp Town Junction which formerly led to Lewes Road station and, by viaduct and tunnel, to the Kemp Town terminus.

On the Coastway West route the train service pattern from Brighton is one of semi-fast services to Portsmouth and slower services to Portsmouth and to Littlehampton plus some peak workings from/to West Worthing. On the main line there are hourly fast services from Victoria, stopping at East Croydon and taking 58 minutes and from London Bridge taking 72 minutes. The slower services are half-hourly. Eastwards the services to Ore and Seaford change pattern to Eastbourne and Seaford during the main part of the day, with the latter connecting into the semi-fast Victoria-Eastbourne/Ore services.

B.38 Brixton

Victoria-Ramsgate line. 3 m 14 ch from Victoria

Brixton station, which dates from 1862 and is served by the Victoria-Orpington trains, is preceded by Brixton Junction (3 m 8 ch) where the link to the Catford Loop departs via Canterbury Road Junction (3 m 8 ch) and Cambria Junction (3 m 70 ch). It has a shelter only on the Up platform, traditional buildings on the Down and the ticket office at Atlantic Road level below, and is crossed by the metals of the South London Line using a tied girder bridge. Nearby is the ornate clock tower of the 1880 Railway Hotel.

There are traces of the platforms used by one-time services to the City, the Midland Railway and the GNR.

B.39 Broadstairs

Victoria-Ramsgate line, between Margate and Ramsgate. 77 m 9 ch from Victoria

Broadstairs, forever associated with Charles Dickens, was the first resort on the Kent coast to label itself 'select'. Its railway dates from the opening of the Herne Bay-Ramsgate section by the

The Southern Railway's reconstruction at Broadstairs.

B.40 Brockenhurst

Waterloo-Weymouth line, junction for Lymington Branch. 92 m 66 ch from Waterloo

LC&D on October 5 1863 but the town has grown greatly from the population of less than 2,000 it had at that time.

From the direction of the Railway Tavern the station is approached by a ramp which leads to the ticket office in the Down side buildings and which date from an SR reconstruction. Behind the Up platform stands the 1859 Crampton Tower, planned to become a museum.

Broadstairs enjoys the same service as Ramsgate and Margate.

The line from Southampton Central, then Blechynden, was authorised in 1845 and opened to Dorchester via Brockenhurst, Ringwood and Wimborne on June 1 1847. Brockenhurst increased in importance with the addition of the Lymington Railway in 1858 and the Christchurch line in 1888. It remains a location of significance despite the closure of the Ringwood route, the transfer of the work of splitting Weymouth/Bournemouth trains and the loss of its goods facilities.

The station is located immediately west of the barrier crossing of the A337 road, site of the modern panel box and the old No 8 crossing house. The two island platforms are reached by footbridge from the single-storey station buildings on the Up

To transfer traffic to and from the parcels office Brockenhurst was provided with this bridge with pivots across the Up loop when released by the signalman.

side. These date from the improvements made when the Christchurch line opened in 1888 but, oddly, the supports at either end of the canopy do not match.

The Up platform has its second face to the Up Loop line and parcels access from the approach road is via a bridge which swivels across the running line after a plunger has been used to secure the release from the signal box. The second face of the Down platform is for the Lymington trains which then run parallel to the main line, past the engineers' sidings and on to Lymington Junction before heading for the coast. The old shed and offices remain on the Up side and a public footbridge provides a good viewing vantage point.

The Waterloo-Bournemouth all-stations and semi-fast trains call to give Brockenhurst two trains an hour in each direction, the branch trains connecting with the latter.

B.41   Brockley

London Bridge-Windmill Bridge Junction line. 3 m 56 ch from London Bridge

Although the route is part of the original 1839 line to Croydon, and then to Brighton, Brockley did not get its station until March 6 1871 and today has a modern, Clasp-type building. Located on the Down side this is one of the rarer, two-storey examples with the ticket office at the higher level. The two platforms serve the Up and Down slow lines and the London Bridge-Sutton trains call. At the London end the line is crossed by the Nunhead-Lewisham line, formerly the LC&D Greenwich Park branch which had a station at Brockley Lane until 1917.

B.42   Bromley North Branch

Charing Cross-Dover line, branch from Grove Park. 1 m 49 ch

This double track branch, which leaves the main line immediately beyond Grove Park station, was opened on January 1 1878. It was built by one of those numerous and now forgotten companies, the Bromley Direct Railway, after several ideas for such a line (including one which would have involved a tunnel under part of the town) had failed to materialise. The line became part of the SER empire in the year after opening. There is now one intermediate station, Sundridge Park, which may have started life as a private halt for the local landowner.

As soon as it leaves the main line the branch swings south and begins to climb,

first on an embankment. There is a good view of Sundridge Park Golf Club before the route comes to the intermediate station which sits in a cutting between two bridges. Although simplification work has taken place here recently the attractive wooden ticket office remains and there is some decorative valance work as well.

Continuing its climb the line comes to Bromley North and the crossovers which link the two platform lines at the end of the single platform. The original station had three tracks between two platforms and converging on a turntable but it was completely rebuilt in 1925, the year before electrification, to provide an example of just what the Southern could do in terms of small station design.

The new station had a lofty booking hall leading to a 2,360 sq ft concourse topped by a three-span glass roof and equipped with waiting rooms and a bookstall. From this concourse attractive iron gates led to a broad single platform 520 ft long and 30 ft wide able to accommodate a standard electric train on either side. A glazed umbrella roof extended for almost the whole length of the platform. Bromley North remains much the same today although the Up side carriage siding has been one of the casualties of the years and the goods yard closed on May 20 1968.

The Bromley North branch is controlled from the London Bridge panel and has a half-hourly shuttle service to and from Grove Park during the day, plus a few through services to and from Charing Cross in the business periods. Under the June 1981 economies the branch closed from 19.30 on Saturdays until Monday morning. Sundridge Park is at 10 m 12 ch and Bromley North at 10 m 47 ch.

B.43   Bromley South

Victoria-Ramsgate line, between Shortlands Junction and Bickley Junction. 10 m 71 ch from Victoria

Bromley South was just plain Bromley when it opened on November 22 1858 as part of the Mid-Kent Railway's Bromley Junction-Bickley line. Today it is an important interchange point on a four-track section of the Chatham main line with island platforms between the fast and slow line pairs. Access is via the ticket office building (rebuilt for the 1959 electrification which also paired the tracks by use instead of by direction as previously) on the overbridge at the London end of the station which is served by around 370 trains every 24 hours on weekdays, 148 of them in the peak. Main line services to Dover and Thanet call at Bromley South and it has an intensive local service on the Victoria-Orpington and Holborn Viaduct-Sevenoaks routes, with an interchange facility between them that is complex, fascinating and of considerable value to the traveller.

The former goods shed with its tiny goods office is still extant although now in private hands and a public footbridge provides a good vantage point.

B.44   Brookwood

Waterloo-Weymouth line, between Woking Junction and Farnborough. 27 m 79 ch from Waterloo

At Brookwood there are connections between the local and through lines allowing access to the two platforms. The main buildings, with the ground floor at street level, are on the Up side with a subway then leading to the Down side waiting rooms. Both lots date from a 1903 reconstruction, the former being in an extravagant style with impressive Dutch gables and with a cobbled forecourt reminder of the horse and carriage days.

Brookwood station owes its existence to an approach to the LSW by the London Necropolis & Mausoleum Company which had been empowered by an Act of 1852 to establish a cemetery 'in the Parish of Woking' and to contract with the railway for the 'carrying of bodies in properly constructed carriages'. The cemetery and a short branch line to it were opened in 1854 and the main line station ten years later.

A second branch was opened from Brookwood on July 14 1890 to serve the rifle ranges at Bisley and was temporarily extended to the adjacent army camps in the First World War. Special trains were worked over this line for territorials and for rifle shooting meetings while on the cemetery line specials were run from the company's private station at Waterloo at least twice a week and sometimes daily. The M7 tanks allocated for the work ran round their trains at Brookwood before completing the journey to either the North or the South station in the cemetery. The Bisley line closed on July 19 1952 but is still marked by the bay platform at the country end of Brookwood station and a bridge over the Basingstoke Canal. Only the earthworks mark the route of the cemetery line which ceased operation in May 1941.

Today's more mundane train service at Brookwood is provided by the Alton, Basingstoke and stopping Bournemouth services.

B.45   Burgess Hill

Victoria-Brighton line, between Keymer Junction and Brighton. 41 m 39 ch from London Bridge

The single-storey main buildings on the overbridge at the London end of the station date from 1877 and are in typical LB&SC style with centre section, decorated and gabled end sections and tall, solid chimneys. Happily the 1841 station buildings are still in existence on the Down side where they are used as an office for Corralls coal depot. On the Up side are wooden buildings, the station house and the old brick goods shed.

The train service is provided by the Victoria-Brighton semi-fasts.

B.46   Bursledon

Southampton-Portsmouth line. 8 m 49 ch from Southampton

The Southampton-Netley line, opened in 1866, was extended on to meet the Eastleigh-Gosport/Portsmouth route on September 2 1889. The course chosen involved the route turning inland to Bursledon in order to cross the upper reaches of the Hamble estuary and then head straight for Fareham.

Today Bursledon station is unstaffed with a bus-type waiting shelter on each platform and served by the hourly Southampton-Portsmouth trains. A marina stands behind the Up platform and the river is crossed by the Hamble Viaduct nearby.

Buxted—see Uckfield Branch

B.47   Byfleet & New Haw

Waterloo-Weymouth line, between Weybridge and Woking. 20 m 32 ch from Waterloo

This is a 1927 location on the four-track main line and with outer platforms to the Up and Down local lines. These are reached by subway from the Up side ticket office and served half-hourly by the Waterloo-Guildford/Portsmouth trains. The station is closed on Sundays.

Byfleet Junction (20 m 23 ch) lies on the London side of the station, providing a direct Up link to Addlestone Junction on the Chertsey line but with the Down con-

nection passing under the main line. The spur was formerly used for freight between Feltham and the main line, but was also available for Royal Trains between Windsor and Portsmouth.

Other transport interest in the area includes the link between the Basingstoke Canal and the River Wey Navigation near the crossing of the latter just west of the station and the old Weybridge airfield on the Down side just east of it.

Camberley—see Ascot-Ash Vale Line

C.1   Cannon Street

London terminus with triangular connection to Charing Cross-London Bridge line. 1 m 73 ch from Charing Cross

All that remains of the original station opened at Cannon Street by the South Eastern Railway on September 1 1866 are the 120 ft high twin towers at the river end of the old station walls and often described as 'standing stark against the city sky'. Indeed, the station was built to serve the City of London and is still used by some 75,000 passengers every day, mostly bound for desk or typewriter. As a consequence Cannon Street has relatively few trains in the middle of the day and none at all on Saturdays and Sundays.

That original station, built on a viaduct to carry its platforms over Upper Thames Street, was an impressive affair nearly 700 ft long. Its massive brick walls carried

Hawkshaw's great crescent roof may have gone but Cannon Street still retains its two baroque towers.

Sir John Hawkshaw's lofty single arch span of glass and iron, almost semi-circular and from beneath which the tracks emerged on to the long bridge carrying them over the River Thames. The viaduct alone consumed 27 million bricks, while the front of the station was dominated by E.M. Barry's five-storey City Terminus Hotel, soon to become the Cannon Street Hotel and later to be converted to an office block called Southern House—not, however, before it had been the venue in 1920 of a meeting which saw the birth of the Communist Party in Great Britain. Badly damaged by bombs during the war, the building finally disappeared completely during rebuilding in the 1960s.

Cannon Street takes its name from Candelwykstrete which goes back to the wax chandlers of medieval times. When Samuel Pepys met the Lord Mayor there, at the time of the Great Fire of London, he called it Canning Street and when the station was being built such a mass of human remains, piles and foundations was unearthed that it was at first thought to have been the site of the citadel of Londinium. Alas, this proved not to be so, but the location was obviously one of some importance to the Romans.

Twice in less than 50 years Cannon Street has closed down completely for the track to be remodelled. The first time was from June 5 to 28 1926 in readiness for suburban electrification and this saw the virtual end to trains from London Bridge reversing at Cannon Street to get to Charing Cross. The second was from August 2 to September 9 1974 during a vital phase of the scheme which remodelled and resignalled 150 miles of track on the approaches to London Bridge and produced the modern technological miracle of London Bridge panel.

The station produced by the rebuilding of the 1960s is on two levels. From Cannon Street, or Dowgate Hill, a short flight of steps leads to a concourse with shops, ticket office and travel centre. More steps lead to another rubber-floored concourse with buffet, bookstall and the eight platforms, each with a train indicator at the entry point. The eight platform lines combine into two pairs of lines, fast and slow, for the crossing of the river and two then diverge from the fast pair to Metropolitan Junction (1 m 31 ch from Charing Cross) while the four-track route continues to Borough Market Junction (38 ch from Cannon Street, 1 m 51 ch from Charing Cross).

The first train of the day is the 05.07 to Dartford and the last the 19.09 to Dartford. In the morning and evening business periods there are services to and from Sevenoaks, Tunbridge Wells, Hastings, the Medway towns and the Kent Coast. Off-peak Cannon Street serves Addiscombe, Orpington, Dartford and Gravesend.

C.2   Canterbury

Canterbury East station is on the Victoria-Dover (via Faversham) line, 61 m 65 ch from Victoria; Canterbury West is on the Charing Cross-Margate (via Ashford) line, 70 m 27 ch from Charing Cross

The two major routes described in the heading cross at Canterbury, within sight of the city's great cathedral, but Canterbury South on the Elham Valley line up from Folkestone closed to passengers in 1940 and to freight in 1947 after wartime use by rail-mounted guns. Five years later, on December 1 1952, came the closure of the route of the pioneer Canterbury & Whitstable Railway which had started work on May 3 1830 and was still to have a final fling with a short period of emergency use during the period of the East Coast floods early in 1953.

Today the senior surviving station is Canterbury West, reached by the South Eastern Railway from Ashford on February 6 1846 and linked to Ramsgate from April 13 of that year. A plaque outside commemorates the fact that it was the first station in the world to issue a season ticket, although the reference is to the vanished C&W station which stood just beyond the William Cory fuel sidings on the Up side. The date of this beginning of railway commuting was July 25 1834.

Canterbury West, essentially a fairly plain station, has simple single-storey buildings on each platform, the main ones on the Up side relieved by the two Doric pillars of the portico. Of the erstwhile

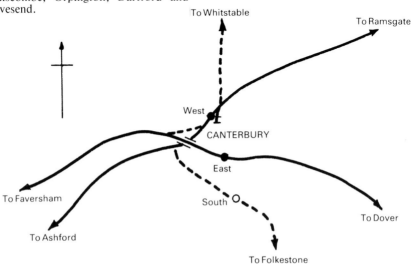

The signal finials show up well in this view of Canterbury West.

four tracks between them the middle pair have now gone but there is a goods loop behind the Down platform with two connecting sidings at the London end where the cattle dock was formerly located. At the other end was once the connection to the C&W line. The goods yard area is on the Up side and notable features of the station include the signal box mounted on a gantry and the ornamental entrance gates. There are level crossings at Whitehall RG (69 m 30 ch), St Dunstans CCTV (70 m 15 ch), St Stephens CCTV (70 m 55 ch) and Broad Oak AHB (71 m 77 ch).

Canterbury East is the more central of the two stations and the junior by 14 years. Opened on July 9 1860, it is approached by a viaduct over the River Stour which gives a fine view of the cathedral. From the viaduct approach it is also possible to spot the route of the connection to the Canterbury West line and the earthworks of the junction for the Elham Valley route, the former enjoying no less than three separate existences in connection with traffic in each of the two wars and again during the 1953 floods.

Raised above street level, Canterbury East like Canterbury West is probably original. The ticket hall and entrance are on the Down side, immediately opposite Dane John Gardens which provided a home for the pioneer C&W locomotive *Invicta* for nine years. On this side are the extended goods shed, the narrow waisted signal box and beyond the latter, the Down Goods Loop. The Up yard is out of use although one Up siding remains. A public footbridge provides a viewing vantage point.

Canterbury West has an hourly service from Charing Cross with the trains splitting at Ashford and giving a Down journey time of 91 minutes. The hourly service from Victoria via Maidstone East and Ashford, which caters for intermediate stations from Borough Green to Ramsgate, takes 22 minutes longer. Via Faversham Canterbury East can be reached in 78 minutes from Victoria.

Canterbury East as it was in 1921, still with an overall roof.

C.3   Carshalton

South Bermondsey Junction to Leatherhead line, between Mitcham Junction and Sutton. 12 m 30 ch from London Bridge

When the line from Peckham Rye to Sutton was opened by the LB&SC on October 1 1868 this station took over the name Carshalton from what is now Wallington. The route is raised at this point and stairs lead down from the platforms and waiting rooms to the Down side ticket office adjacent to the underbridge at the country end. The London Bridge-Wimbledon/Sutton loop trains call in addition to the Dorking/Horsham and Effingham Junction services.

C.4   Carshalton Beeches

Norwood Fork Junction to Sutton line, between West Croydon and Sutton. 13 m 72 ch from London Bridge

Opened in 1906, this station was Beeches Halt until it became a full station in

readiness for electrification to Sutton on April 1 1925. The main buildings, in brick, are at the end of the footbridge on the Up side and two Sutton and two Epsom Downs services call hourly.

C.5   Caterham Branch

Victoria-Brighton line, branch from Purley. 4 m 57 ch

The birth of the Caterham line had all the ingredients of trouble. The traffic potential was only modest, and the fact that the line was in SER territory but made junction with the LB&SC made it a pawn in their rivalries. Opening was delayed for nearly a year and when it did take place, on August 5 1856, the Brighton company took another three months to re-open their junction station. The problems continued until 1859 when the Caterham Railway went bankrupt and the SER took over the line.

Today this double line electric branch leaves the main line immediately beyond Purley station and then sheds the Tattenham Corner branch before heading along the valley opposite Riddles Down and the Oxted line. The route lies in an area of pleasant suburban housing as far as

Caterham, with colour light signals and traditional wooden signal box.

Kenley (16 m 29 ch from Charing Cross) where from the Up side brick ticket office stairs descend to one platform and a foot-bridge leads to the other. On the latter there is a wooden waiting room with awning and the attractive, high gabled station house.

At Whyteleafe (17 m 58 ch) there is a CCTV double barrier crossing at the country end of the platforms which house a single-storey wooden ticket office on the Up side with just a canopy and the 17¾ milepost on the Down. Serving a wooded, suburban area, Whyteleafe did not open until the first day of the century.

At Whyteleafe South (18 m 18 ch), Warlingham until 1956, the single-storey main buildings and the crossing box are on the Down side and the Up platform has just a wooden shelter and integral canopy. The narrow, gabled station house remains and there is a monument beside the Down line between these two stations.

Continuing its wooded valley course brings the branch to the terminus at Caterham (19 m 70 ch) where the two faces of a single platform are linked to the single-storey ticket office which dates from the period of doubling the line just before the turn of the century. There is a carriage siding on the Up side and a wooden signal box at the end of the plat-form controlling conventional semaphore signals.

The branch is subject to a line speed maximum of 60 mph and there are 20 mph limitations at the junction and for entering and leaving Caterham. The basic service is half-hourly from Charing Cross (London Bridge in the peak), reflecting the SER ancestry of this Central Division line. This also shows up in the mileages. The basic service is worked by six-car formations dividing at Purley and with the leading four vehicles continuing to Cater-ham and the remainder to Tattenham Corner.

C.6   Catford Bridge

Lewisham-Hayes line. 7 m 42 ch from Charing Cross

Catford Bridge was one of the original Mid-Kent stations opened with the line on

January 1 1857. It retains traditional brick buildings on both platforms and is served by the Charing Cross/Cannon Street-Hayes trains. Catford Stadium lies at the London end between the Mid-Kent and Catford Loop routes. There is a crossover at this end, an engineers' siding on the Down side and a vintage 7½ milepost sign on the Down platform.

C.7   Catford Loop

From Nunhead to Shortlands Junction. 4 m 69 ch

Incorporated in 1889 as an independent local concern, the Shortlands & Nunhead scheme became a reality with opening on July 1 1892 and grew in stature to become an accepted relief route for the LC&D main line via Penge East. Today the line is known as the Catford Loop and leaves the Nunhead-Lewisham line just beyond Nunhead station (5 m 77 ch from Victoria).

All the stations on the line date from opening and all have Up and Down platforms and a total daily service of between 80 and 90 trains running between Holborn Viaduct and Sevenoaks.

After crossing over the main line from London Bridge the route comes to Crofton Park (7 m 11 ch) where the small traditional ticket office building is at street level above the station. The ticket office position is reversed at Catford (8 m 3 ch) which was reconstructed in 1971 with more modern buildings. A lattice girder bridge takes the route over the Mid-Kent line to accompany the Ravensbourne stream to Bellingham (8 m 73 ch) which lies below the street level ticket office and still has some decorative canopy valance boards on the Up side.

Between Bellingham and Beckenham Hill there is a crossover and a group of Down side carriage sidings, laid when the Crystal Palace High Level branch closed. Beckenham Hill station (9 m 45 ch) follows with single-storey period ticket office buildings on the Up platform and then comes a wooded section through Beckenham Place Park and Summerhouse Hill Wood to Ravensbourne (10 m 34 ch). Here the station lies in a slight wooded cutting below the small brick ticket office on the Crab Hill overbridge at the London end. The section ends at Shortlands Junction (10 m 66 ch).

C.8   Charing

Victoria-Ramsgate line, between Maidstone East and Ashford. 53 m 11 ch from Victoria

This is a two-platform station served by the Victoria-Ashford all-stations trains and the Victoria-Ramsgate/Margate services. The main ticket office and station house complex is on the Down side with a small brick and wood signal box on the Up controlling crossover, Up siding and standard semaphore signals.

C.9   Charing Cross

Not only is Charing Cross important in terms of railway distances over the former South Eastern Railway lines but it is also

The original Charing Cross station, now tastefully modernised, was opened in 1864, just over one year before the erection of the Eleanor Cross to replace the 13th century original.

the point from which London distances are measured for road signposts and milestones. They are taken from the base of the Eleanor Cross in the station forecourt. The cross was erected in 1865 and is a replica of an original dating from 1292 when it was one of a series of 12 put up at each of the overnight resting places of the body of Queen Eleanor, wife of Edward I, on its journey from Harby in Nottinghamshire to Westminster Abbey.

The station originated from the Charing Cross Railway project of the SER, incorporated on August 8 1859 and designed to take the South Eastern trains on from London Bridge by a roof level route to a station in the West End. Work began in 1862 on the site of Hungerford Market and near the blacking factory where Dickens worked as a boy and mentioned by him in *David Copperfield*. Here too, but much earlier, Samuel Pepys had watched a public execution, describing the victim as 'looking as cheerful as any man could in that condition'—a description which might also be applied to the 38,000 commuters who use the station each morning.

One of the problems of the building period was the insistence of St Thomas' Hospital, then in Southwark High Street and owning a small corner of the land needed for the new railway, that the entire premises be bought at a cost of £¾ m. Lengthy arbitration ensued and settlement was eventually made on the basis of

The view from Charing Cross over the Thames, past the Royal Festival Hall and on towards Waterloo East.

£300,000. The first trains started to use Charing Cross on January 11 1864 for Greenwich and stations on the Mid-Kent line, with the North Kent and main line trains following from May 1. There were then six platforms as there are today.

This was the era of the railway hotel syndrome and, as befitted a trunk route to the Continent, the South Eastern wanted premises of substance. The wish was translated by E.M. Barry into a 250-bedroom building in the French Renaissance style, opened in 1865 and described as 'of a grandeur befitting important foreign travellers'. A later description labelled the hotel as 'more restrained than St Pancras but still having an aura of everything being larger than life'. A 90-bedroom annex, connected to the main building by a footbridge over Villiers Street, was completed in 1878.

Today the seven-storey hotel forms part of the impressive station frontage which includes an ornate ironwork balcony running at first floor level across to the other side of the building with its portico entrance to the station. The link from London Transport emerges nearby, on to a concourse which is the smallest of any London terminal but well equipped with a central block of facilities, travel centre and automatic train departure indicator. The latter was installed in 1967 to become the first of its kind at a London main line station.

The concourse leads to six platform faces which are used by some 111,560 passengers every day. Local services to Dartford, Hayes, Sevenoaks and Orpington use platforms 1-3, services to the Medway towns go from platform 4 and to the Kent Coast from platforms 5 and 6.

The last three become the fast pair of lines and the first three the slow pair although all lines are connected after the six-track section over the bridge. There is a single holding siding with access to platforms 1-3 and all working at the station is controlled from the London Bridge panel.

Charing Cross was the scene of a serious disaster on December 5 1905 when one of the tie rods on the enormous vault of the Hawkshaw roof snapped, just at a time when 30 men were working above the station. The entire roof collapsed, but slowly enough for the platforms to be cleared of passengers and a train halted outside the station. Even so two workmen were killed, together with a bookstall attendant and three people in the adjoining Avenue (now the Players) Theatre which bore the brunt of the falling girders and was totally destroyed.

Beyond the station is Charing Cross Bridge No 7 which takes the route over the River Thames. It replaced the Brunel suspension bridge which had been opened for foot passengers in 1845. The new railway bridge used the same piers and the chains of the suspension bridge went to Bristol to help in the completion of the Clifton Suspension Bridge as a memorial to Brunel's work after his death. Bridge No 7 was built to carry four tracks with a footpath either side but these were later reduced to three and the bridge widened by the addition of the two-track 'half through' bridge. A sixth line, known as the Middle Road, was obtained at the expense of the up stream footpath.

The Charing Cross Bridge had a bad time in terms of public opinion in the years immediately before and after the formation of the Southern Railway, when the proposals included one to transfer the railway activity back to the south bank of the river. It also caused a few problems in 1979 when, for six months, most of the 400 trains using platforms 1-3 had to terminate at Waterloo East or be diverted to other terminals while the original wrought iron girders were replaced with steel ones at a cost of £3 m.

Charlton—see North Kent Line

C.10   Chartham

Charing Cross-Margate line, between Ashford and Canterbury West. 67 m 14 ch from Charing Cross

The Ashford-Ramsgate line had been open for 13 years when the station at Chartham, complete with tiny 'cottage'

ticket office, was opened in 1859. Today it is still very much a traditional type of station with wooden crossing gates, wooden platform shelters and a wooden signal box with semaphore signals complete with finials. On the London side of the station the line crosses the Great Stour river and the two then continue together towards Canterbury, through an area of artificial lakes and gravel pit workings. The Victoria-Ramsgate/Margate trains call at Chartham.

Chart Leacon—see Ashford

C.11   Chatham

Victoria-Ramsgate line. 34 m 25 ch from Victoria

Chatham contributed its name to the London, Chatham & Dover Railway which started life there when the East Kent Railway opened its single line eastwards to Faversham on January 25 1858. The gap to connect with the North Kent line at Strood was filled two months later and the new enterprise, backed by such names as that of the great locomotive engineer T.R. Crampton, reached Dover in 1861.

Chatham is still the main station for the Medway towns and derives an excellent service from stops by all trains on the routes via Swanley and via Gravesend. The original entrance and booking office was replaced in 1981 by a new ticket office and travel centre from which stairs lead down to the platforms. The Ensign Buffet is located on the Up side while the Down platform is partly isolated by a former platform line used in conjunction with the parcels concentration depot and reached via a ground frame at the country end until the depot closed in June 1981.

From the Rochester direction Chatham is approached via the 428 yd Fort Pitt Tunnel (33 m 79 ch to 34 m 19 ch). After the station comes a skew road bridge and then the 297 yd Chatham Tunnel (34 m 34 ch to 34 m 48 ch). The mis-named Chatham Central was nearer to Rochester and is dealt with in that entry, along with Chatham goods sidings; the dockyard line connection is from Gillingham.

C.12   Cheam

South Bermondsey Junction to Leatherhead line, between Sutton and Epsom. 15 m 76 ch from London Bridge

The route itself opened from West Croydon to Epsom on May 10 1847 but the LB&SC built a new station at Cheam as part of its electrification plans in the period prior to the First World War. Its simple, brick main buildings are on the Down side and there are waiting rooms on the Up side.

The wide space between the Up and Down lines at Cheam used to accommodate the fast lines and there was a goods depot here until 1964. Now the station is just served half-hourly by the Victoria-Effingham Junction/Horsham trains.

C.13 Chelsfield

Charing Cross-Dover line, between Orpington and Sevenoaks. 15 m 25 ch from Charing Cross

Chelsfield lies on the difficult South Eastern route opened on March 2 1868. The route has been rising steadily for the last ten miles and the station lies on the final climb of 1 in 120, through the 597 yd Chelsfield Tunnel (15 m 67 ch to 16 m 14 ch) to the summit near Knockholt. Served hourly by the Charing Cross-Sevenoaks slower trains, Chelsfield now has a modern Up side building of the 'see-through' type with outer walls of glass enclosing a ticket office and heated waiting room.

C.14 Chertsey

Virginia Water-Weybridge line. 22 m 25 ch from Waterloo*

The LSW branch from Weybridge to Chertsey opened on February 14 1848 but Chertsey got a new station, on the opposite side of the road to the original one, with the extension of the line to Virginia Water on October 1 1866. It is not clear whether this is the present, imposing two-storey structure on the Down side where the plain brick construction is effectively relieved by the decorative window arches and rounded door pediments. The Up side buildings are simpler, but still pleasing.

Chertsey's goods facilities were withdrawn in 1964 and the former carriage sidings have been abolished but the station remains busy and its passengers include children from the many schools in the town. The basic train service is provided by the half-hourly 2x2-car Staines-Weybridge workings (with some through Waterloo services in the peak) but some trains originate and terminate at Chertsey which the public timetable acknowledges as having two alternative routes to Waterloo. Its distances are based on the original one via Weybridge.

The short platforms are linked by a footbridge and there is a CCTV-monitored double barrier crossing, both at the Weybridge end. Control is from Surbiton box. North of the station the bridge carrying the line over the M25 motorway is of concrete and of the 'cable-stay' type in which the deck is suspended by cables from central towers.

C.15 Chessington Branch

Raynes Park-Leatherhead line, branch from Motspur Park. 4 m 16 ch

This 4¼ miles of double track branch from Motspur Park was the last line to be constructed by Sir Herbert Walker's Southern Railway and, to date, remains the last passenger railway to be built as part of the surface system of Greater London. The original plan, approved by the SR board in 1929 and by Parliament in the following year, was for a loop from a point just beyond Motspur Park on the Raynes Park-Epsom line, through Chessington and rejoining the same line north of Leatherhead. The intention was to provide a railway to serve the new housing estates then springing up in the area south of Surbiton but by the time the line had reached Chessington South war was

Chessington South station showing the concrete shape in vogue in 1939. The line continues beyond the station to a coal concentration depot.

imminent and by 1961 the Green Belt put a stop to any further housing developments south of what had by then become an established terminal.

Work on the branch started at the Motspur Park end early in 1936 and the first section, to Tolworth with an intermediate station at Malden Manor, was opened on May 29 1938. It was served by three trains an hour throughout the day, seven days a week. The remaining portion came into service on May 28 of the following year.

Apart from a shallow cutting just after leaving Motspur Park (9 m 57 ch) and shorter ones between Tolworth (12 m 6 ch) and Chessington North (13 m 25 ch) and near Chessington South station (13 m 73 ch), the whole of the line is on an embankment. There are seven bridges over public roads, a road bridge over the railway at Chessington South, and a three-span, 140 ft viaduct over the Hogsmill River just beyond Malden Manor station (11 m 5 ch). The gradients are modest, eg, 1 in 100 and 1 in 160 to Tolworth.

All of the bridges are of steelplate girders, both encased in concrete and supported on concrete piers and abutments. Concrete is also the main feature of the four stations. All are of the same basic design, with more than an echo in their appearance of the cinema architecture of the 1930s, modern and even futuristic by the standards of their day but rather less appealing to modern tastes. There is a ticket hall at street level—below the line except at Chessington South—and then stairs and subway to the platforms. Chessington South is the station for Chessington Zoo.

The route was electrified at the time it was built and although there were originally signal boxes on the platforms at Tolworth and at the terminus, the whole line is now controlled from Motspur Park. The basic train service is now half-hourly with trains taking 31/2 minutes for the journey to and from Waterloo. The two original goods yards, both on the Down side, are now coal concentration depots. The Tolworth depot, at the country end of the station, is an NCB depot operated by Coal Mechanisation Ltd. It has a rotary discharge conveyor and uses its own ic locomotives to position wagons from/for the reception line which has a headshunt and trailing connection into the Down running line. The Charringtons depot at Chessington South lies beyond

the road overbridge on what would have been the continuation route to Leatherhead. Changes at the passenger station here include the abandonment of the Up platform in favour of all trains using the Down where the ticket work now takes place at platform level.

The record of useful service by the branch is marred by only one serious accident and that occurred at the Motspur Park end in dense fog on November 6 1947. A fogsignalman wrongly showed a green light to a train from Holmwood, causing it to run into the second car of a crowded evening commuter train from Waterloo to Chessington South as it moved across its path on to the branch. Four passengers were killed and 12 injured.

C.16   Chestfield & Swalecliffe

Victoria-Ramsgate line, between Faversham and Margate. 60 m 45 ch from Victoria

This is the 'junior' station of the Thanet area, only opening as a halt on July 6 1930. It has wooden waiting shelters and Up side ticket office and is an interesting example of the use of rails and sleepers in platform construction. There is an hourly service in each direction.

C.17   Chichester

Victoria-Portsmouth line. 28 m 51 ch from Brighton

The Brighton & Chichester Railway reached Chichester from the east on June 8 1846, terminating at a temporary station on the London side of the present one's level crossing. The present station dates from the extension on to Havant opened on March 15 1847, but the buildings result from a reconstruction scheme commenced before the outbreak of the Second World War but not finally completed until 1961. However, they have been worth waiting for and are both functional and attractive. The main entrance on the Up side leads to a high, airy ticket hall with four lamp clusters suspended from the decorated ceiling. There is a second entrance from the car park on the Down side, the two being linked by a covered footbridge. Wood, patterned plastics and mosaic tiles have been successfully combined to enhance the basic brick structure.

From the Barnham direction there is a succession of traditional signal boxes and level crossings—Woodgate Crossing box (23 m 53 ch), Woodhorn AHB LC (25 m

The Down side at Chichester showing its spacious and pleasing design.

20 ch), Drayton (former station) box and crossing (26 m 48 ch), Whyke Road box and crossing (27 m 70 ch), Basin Road CCTV LC (28 m 39 ch) and then Stockbridge Road CCTV LC (28 m 43 ch). There is also an extensive aggregate terminal and a siding for ferry vans on the Up side and a Cory depot on the Down. Chichester station itself then comprises the two main platforms with a Down passenger bay, water tank and coal sidings behind and, opposite, two parcels bays, offices, traditional goods shed and surviving goods yard. The latter includes dock, gantry and sidings extending west to the traditional gates at Fishbourne Crossing (29 m 27 ch) which precede the connection to another aggregate terminal at Lavant.

The freight siding towards Lavant survives from the line linking Chichester and Midhurst. Opened July 11 1881 and closed to passengers on July 8 1935, freight services continued until 1951 when a C2X 0-6-0 fell into a collapsed culvert. The line was then cut back to Cocking and subsequently to Lavant. On the other side of Chichester the West Sussex Railway, opened from Chichester to Selsey Beach in 1897-8, finally closed in 1935 after a chequered existence but is still remembered in the sign of 'The Selsey Tram' pub at Stockbridge where the light railway followed the route of the Chichester Canal.

Today Chichester is served by the hourly slow and semi-fast trains on the Brighton-Portsmouth route and by the hourly London-Portsmouth service.

C.18   Chilham

Charing Cross-Margate line, between Ashford and Canterbury West. 65 m 9 ch from Charing Cross

A station opened at Chilham when the line opened in 1846 but its original wooden buildings are now survived only by the short platforms joined by a concrete footbridge. Evidence of the past remains in the crossing houses at Chilham Mill LC (64 m 76 ch) and Chilham Road (65 m 40 ch), the former being equipped with miniature red/green warning lights.

The train service is the same as that for Chartham and Chilham, too, lies near the Great Stour river in an area of woods and ancient monuments and trackways.

C.19   Chilworth

Redhill-Reading line, between Dorking Town and Guildford. 39 m 15 ch from Charing Cross

The railway has dropped from the summit at MP 35 to pick up the course of the Tilling Bourne on this section through the unstaffed station at Chilworth. It opened on August 20 1849 as Chilworth & Albury but the original, much gabled and decorated station house is now let along with the former signalbox where it was not unknown for the signalman to discover a snake nestling under the floorboards. The barrier crossing is CCTV-monitored, the old gates having gone to the Dart Valley Railway. Tangley AHB LC lies at 39 m 48 ch.

The service is provided by the Tonbridge-Reading dmus.

Chipstead—see Tattenham Corner Branch

C.20   Chislehurst

Charing Cross-Dover line, between Hither Green and Orpington and junction with the Chatham main line. 11 m 19 ch from Charing Cross

The shortening of the original South Eastern Railway route to Dover by building the cut-off line brought the first trains to Chislehurst & Bickley Park on July 1 1865. A new station nearby came into use three years later with the extension of the

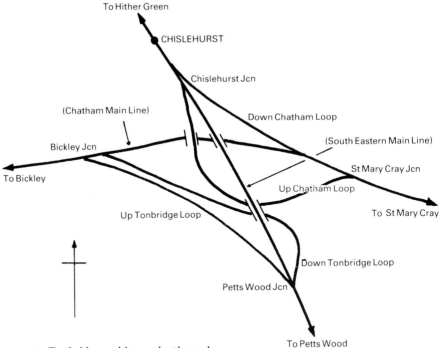

route to Tonbridge and its use by through services.

The next period of development for Chislehurst came in the early years of this century when the line was widened and brick buildings reconstructed on both platforms. Today the Down side complex is still in full use and the original decorative touches in the window arches have been enhanced by repainting of the canopy supports.

The spurs between the two main lines date from the same period, ie, that following the introduction of a managing committee for the rival SER and LC&D companies. Chislehurst Junction (11 m 55 ch) provides the link towards St Mary Cray (13 m 17 ch) while that from the Chatham line connects Bickley Junction (12 m 38 ch) with Petts Wood Junction (12 m 25 ch). The two Chislehurst tunnels are on the London side of Elmstead Woods and comprise the 649 yd North tunnel (9 m 61 ch to 10 m 10 ch) on the slow lines and the 591 yd South tunnel (9 m 63 ch to 10 m 10 ch) on the fast lines.

Chislehurst is served by the Cannon Street-Orpington and Charing Cross-Sevenoaks trains. Its former Up side goods yard is now an ARC stone terminal.

Chiswick—see Hounslow Loop

C.21   Christchurch

Waterloo-Weymouth line, between Brockenhurst and Bournemouth. 104 m 28 ch from Waterloo

Early rail travellers to and from Christchurch had to use Holmsley station on the 'Castleman's Corkscrew' route from Southampton to Dorchester via Ringwood. The growing town then got its own station on the branch from Ringwood on November 13 1862, the route pushing on to Bournemouth eight years later. In the 1880s the line to Bournemouth was doubled and Christchurch got a new station slightly further west. This was on May 30 1886, the direct route from Brockenhurst arriving on March 6 1888.

Today's station, served by the Bournemouth slow and semi-fast trains, comprises Up and Down platforms with the main (1886) single-storey brick buildings, with central gable, on the former. It is difficult to spot the junction for the winding route along the Avon to Ringwood, closed on September 30 1935, and harder still to imagine the 38-minute local journeys let alone the earlier use as the main route to London.

On either side of the station three-span bowstring bridges are required to carry the main line over the Avon and Stour rivers.

C.22   Christ's Hospital

Victoria-Portsmouth line, between Horsham and Pulborough. 40 m 7 ch from London Bridge

It is hard to believe today but at one time Christ's Hospital, West Horsham, had seven platforms and could be used as part of a route from Brighton to Guildford. The original Horsham-Pulborough (and Petworth) line opened in 1859, acquired a link from Itchingfield Junction to Shoreham in 1861, became part of the Mid-Sussex route in 1863 and then added the Stammerham Junction-Peasmarsh Junction (for Guildford) route after another two years. Both branches lost their passenger trains 100 years later.

Today the imposing Christ's Hospital station opened at Stammerham Junction when the school of that name moved from London has shrunk to just two platforms, waiting shelters and a ticket office in the Up side signal box. There are still signs of the nearby Stammerham Junction (once intended to be triangular) and of the old Itchingfield Junction further south.

The basic service is derived from the Victoria/London Bridge-Bognor trains.

C.23   Clandon

New Guildford Line, between Effingham Junction and Guildford. 25 m 26 ch from Waterloo

After a modest climb at 1 in 100 from Horsley the New Guildford Line comes to Clandon, another station in the original

1885 LSW mould and in much the same style as Claygate at the other end of the line. The main buildings and car park are on the Down side and there are half-hourly trains to Guildford and to Waterloo.

Clapham—see South London Line

C.24   Clapham Junction

Waterloo-Weymouth line, 3 m 74 ch from Waterloo and Victoria-Brighton line, 2 m 57 ch from Victoria

There have been many descriptions of Clapham Junction. 'Fulfils the old Victorian idea of a railway station'; 'the incomparable phenomenon of the Steam Age'; 'a location of its own' (true enough; look up Arding & Hobbs department store in the London Telephone Directory and you will find the address given as 'Clapham Junction SW11'); 'the busiest railway junction in the world' (again, true enough; more than 2,300 trains pass through it every 24 hours and in the peak periods this can mean 2,000 passengers every minute).

The London & Southampton opened its Wandsworth station in 1838 and extended from Nine Elms to Waterloo ten years later. The LB&SC line ran parallel through this part of Battersea from 1858, first to Pimlico and then to Victoria from 1860. Finally, on March 2 1863, the GWR arrived by means of the West London Extension Railway and connected not only with the

Clapham Junction panel, nearly ready to take control of one of the world's busiest layouts.

LSW and LB&SC lines in the Down direction but also towards Waterloo, Victoria and the LC&D main line. Clapham Junction station dates from this time, replacing Wandsworth (renamed Clapham Common in 1846).

The Clapham Junction of today still reflects its origins, although there have been many changes over the years, including reconstruction in 1904-7 and a 1969 ticket office improvement scheme, and it has become less of an interchange point and more concerned with originating and terminating traffic. Overall it has 17 platforms, numbering from the Up side, covering 11.239 hectares and with the longest measuring 721 ft. They are organised in three groups catering for the Windsor/Thames Valley lines, along the South Western main line and for Central Division trains. Most of the 2,000-plus daily trains are through services although, in 1983, there were some originating and terminating trains on the Brighton side and still services to and from Kensington Olympia in the morning and late afternoon/early evening.

The Central Division route crosses over the South Western main line from Waterloo and then approaches Clapham Junction by way of Pouparts Junction (2 m 4 ch). The approach from Waterloo is via West London Junction (3 m 17 ch) and Clapham Junction 'A' box (3 m 63 ch). From Clapham Junction 'A' it is 9 chains to the SR/LMR boundary on the West London Extension Railway route to Kensington and a further 20 chains to Latchmere Junction. From Latchmere Junction there are connections under the main line to the Down side of the station and to the ex-LC&D lines via Culvert Road and Longhedge Junctions. At the country end of Clapham Junction the vee between the routes houses Clapham Yard and major rolling stock maintenance and servicing activity.

Despite various bits of modernisation the station is still a busy but sombre place with many wooden buildings and a long subway with shops and some remaining gas lighting fitments. The former four signal boxes were reduced to two when the new power box on the Down side came into use for controlling Central side services. The work of the remaining Up side 'A' box was transferred as well in 1983.

C.25 Claygate

New Guildford Line, between Hampton Court Junction and Effingham Junction. 15 m 11 ch from Waterloo

The first of the original stations along the New Guildford Line, Claygate dates from February 2 1885 and is typical of the design and building package provided by the LSW for the whole route. In Claygate's case the main buildings are on the Down side and comprise a station house at the country end of the group with the remainder consisting of ticket office, waiting, staff and toilet facilities, all single-storey and of red brick construction. A semi-dormer arrangement for the upper windows of the station house, tall chimneys with oversailing and decorative spandrels for the canopies save the result from being too functional.

Claygate first got its electric trains in 1916, passengers then continuing onwards by steam push and pull sets. The growth of the passenger business on other routes newly electrified led to a transfer of stock away from the New Guildford Line in 1919 and reversion to steam working until the electrification throughout of 1925.

The station lost its goods facilities in 1963. It is in a pleasant setting and has a half-hourly service in each direction.

'Tunnel Cottage' atop Clayton Tunnel.

C.26 Clayton Tunnel

Victoria-Brighton line, between Keymer Junction and Brighton. 44 m 44 ch from London Bridge

From the road, near the junction of the B2036 and the B2112 south of Hassocks, there is an excellent and intriguing view of the north portal of Clayton Tunnel. Not only is the portal decorated with towers and turrets but between them, right over the tunnel mouth, is the tiny 'Tunnel Cottage', bringing vividly to mind the words of the song, 'the railroad runs through the middle of the house'.

The great tunnel, 1 m 499 yds (44 m 44 ch to 45 m 66 ch), was part of the final link in the main line to Brighton. It lies on the rising stretch of 1 in 264 used to pierce the South Downs and once trains emerge from the more modest portal at the south end the gradient becomes 1 in 264 down towards the coastal resort. After a few problems with damp had been overcome, work on the tunnel was completed in time for the opening of the final portion of the route on September 21 1841. In the early years the walls were whitewashed and the tunnel lit by gas jets, quite a contrast with the modern electric lighting in the relay box alcoves today.

The tunnel made unhappy history on Sunday August 25 1861. Three trains, two excursions and one stopping service, had been despatched from Brighton within a period of seven minutes and although the first duly cleared the tunnel the treadle mechanism which should have returned the protecting signal to danger failed to work. The signalman showed a red flag to warn the following driver but he was over the summit and well into the tunnel before he could halt his train.

Two tragic mistakes then occurred. The second train began to reverse out of the tunnel but the signalman could not have been aware of this. Uncertain about whether or not the driver had seen his warning he telegraphed the signalman to the north asking whether the train had cleared the tunnel. The affirmative answer he got actually related to the first train but, taken for the second, it was used to allow the third train a clear passage into the tunnel. There it met the reversing train in a terrible collision which killed 23 and injured 175. It might have been even worse had not one of the passengers, a Brighton grocer, run over the hill and arrived in time to stop a southbound train.

One good thing to emerge from the tragedy was a recommendation from the Board of Trade enquiry which led to the substitution of a space interval system for the time interval despatch system.

C.27 Clock House

Lewisham-Hayes line. 10 m 23 ch from Charing Cross

Although the line here opened in 1864, Clock House station was not brought into use by the SER until 1890. Today it is served by the Hayes trains and access to the two platforms is from the traditional ticket office building on the Beckenham Road overbridge at the London end of the station.

Clock House used to be a bad place for flooding, necessitating substitute steam traction as late as the '50s.

C.28 Cobham & Stoke D'Abernon

New Guildford Line, between Hampton Court Junction and Effingham Junction. 18 m 63 ch from Waterloo

The modest drop at 1 in 100/200 from the Oxshott direction levels out as the 1885 New Guildford Line route passes through Cooks CCTV LC (17 m 39 ch) and comes to Cobham. This is another station in the standard pattern of the line with main buildings, in the Claygate style, on the Up side. On the same side at the country end the goods shed, now in private hands, survives from the 1965 freight closure although the former yard now serves as a car park. The sub-station and its siding are on this side while the opposite platform carries both gradient and milepost signs. A covered footbridge links the two platforms and south of the station a two-span bridge takes the route and its half-hourly trains over the River Mole.

C.29 Collington

Victoria-Eastbourne/Hastings line, between Willingdon Junction and Bexhill. 29 m 4 ch from Brighton

Collington, which serves the western end of Bexhill, has two platforms linked by a footbridge, a waiting shelter on each and a small ticket office. It opened as Collington Wood Halt on September 3 1905, closed a year later, re-opened as West Bexhill Halt, became Collington Halt in 1929 and then plain Collington in 1969. The Brighton-Ore trains call.

Copyhold Junction—see Haywards Heath

C.30   Cooden Beach

Victoria-Eastbourne/Hastings line, between Willingdon Junction and Bexhill. 27 m 53 ch from Brighton

The location dates from September 11 1905 but the single-storey station building at street level typifies the SR building style of the 1935 electrification period. From the ticket office, waiting room and bookstall a subway leads to the raised platforms which have traditional wooden shelters.

The station is very close to the beach and is served by the hourly Victoria-Ore and Brighton/Eastbourne-Ore trains.

C.31   Cooksbridge

Victoria-Eastbourne/Hastings line, between Keymer Junction and Lewes. 47 m 31 ch from London Bridge

The cut-off route from the main line to Lewes was authorised in 1845 and purchased in the same year when the Brighton company acquired the Brighton, Lewes & Hastings concern. Under the new ownership the link from the main line to the coastal route was then opened on October 1 1847 although Cooksbridge does not appear to have obtained a station until four years later.

Today the two-platform station is served mainly by Haywards Heath-Seaford/Eastbourne trains, with some services extended in either direction and a break in service late morning and early afternoon. The former station buildings on the Down side are not now in use and tickets are issued from the signal box at the country end of the station. It also controls the double barrier crossing.

C.32   Cosham

Southampton-Portsmouth line, between Fareham and Portcreek Junction. 90 m 6 ch from Waterloo

Cosham stands on the coastal plain to the west of Portsea Island and the triangular link between the Southampton and Guildford approaches to Portsmouth. It is an area of light industry on one side and housing on the other with the Reading/Eastleigh-Portsmouth and Salisbury/Romsey/Southampton-Portsmouth trains providing an excellent level of service. The station itself was an 1848 joint LSW/LB&SC enterprise and has its main, partly original, buildings on the Down side with waiting rooms and canopy on the Up. There is a double barrier crossing and a corrugated goods shed in the remains of the Up side goods yard.

At Cosham Junction (90 m 43 ch) the route divides to Portcreek Junction (91 m 1 ch) and to Farlington Junction (91 m 9 ch/40 m 38 ch from Brighton).

C.33   Coulsdon

Victoria-Brighton line; Coulsdon North is on the Quarry Line, 14 m 66 ch from London Bridge and Coulsdon South on the Main Line, 17 m 3 ch from Charing Cross

Coulsdon North, originally Stoat's Nest, dates from the 1899 LB&SC round of alterations when the quadrupling of the main line was pushed south by means of the separate Quarry Line. The original station at Stoat's Nest, located between the present Purley and Coulsdon North stations, lasted from July 1841 to December 1856 and had the distinction of being the first to serve Epsom racegoers. Raceday trains were reported as 'well patronised' despite the eight miles still to travel from the station to the course!

Coulsdon North was a busy station while it remained the southern outpost of Central Division electrification but today only two of the four platforms are used. There are trains only during the morning and evening business periods and closure has been under consideration. The location comprises centre island and two outer platforms, one between the Up Main Line and the Down Quarry Line. Only the Down face of the island and the Up side platforms are in use and beyond them are Coulsdon North Sidings with access controlled by the adjacent shunting box. The main station buildings, original, single-storey, in red brick and with an ornamental roof line, are also on the Up side.

The junctions on the London side, formerly controlled by Coulsdon North Signal Box and now part of the Three Bridges panel area, are critical junctions in the working of Central Division services. They link the Through and Local lines and the two routes into which the main line separates to the south.

Coulsdon South station on the original L&B main line lies on the 1 in 264 climb to Merstham Tunnel and was opened on October 1 1889. It comprises Up and Down platforms linked by overbridge and with ticket office on the Up side and shelters on the Down. It is served by London Bridge-Redhill trains.

Just before this book went to press, the threatened closure of Coulsdon North was carried out and its trains were diverted to Smitham from October 3 1983.

Cowden—see Uckfield Branch

C.34   Crawley

Victoria-Portsmouth line, between Three Bridges and Horsham. 30 m 49 ch from London Bridge

Together with neighbouring Three Bridges and Ifield, Crawley station serves the vast Crawley New Town development. The route itself dates from February 14 1848 but the previous station was closed on July 28 1968 when the present complex replaced it. The station now comprises Up and Down platforms linked by a footbridge with the ticket office embodied in the ground floor of a six-storey commercial development.

The previous Crawley station lies just west of the present one. A high signal box, still signed 'Crawley' in Southern green, stands on one side of the double barrier crossing and the remains of the old platforms are on the other.

Victoria-Horsham and Victoria-Bognor Regis/Portsmouth trains provide Crawley's main service.

Crawley New Yard, formerly a public freight depot, is connected to the main line on the London side of Three Bridges. It is now used for coal traffic to the NCB coal concentration depot, for distribution by Dor-to-Dor Ltd and as private sidings for RMC sand and aggregates. Traffic passes via the reception road and the NCB exchange line.

Crayford—see Dartford Loop Line

Crofton Park—see Catford Loop

Crowborough—see Uckfield Branch

C.35   Crowhurst

Charing Cross-Hastings line, between Tunbridge Wells Central and Bopeep Junction. 57 m 50 ch from Charing Cross

Lying part way up the climb from Bopeep Junction to Battle, on a winding section of the route and some way from Crowhurst village, it seems unlikely that a station would have been built here had not the LB&SC built a new one at Bexhill Central in 1901 and the SEC responded with a new branch to Bexhill West on June 1 1902. The branch had bay

platforms on either side at the new station at Crowhurst and crossed two rivers via a 17-arch viaduct on its way to Sidley and the Bexhill terminus.

Today the Down side bay at Crowhurst has been filled in and the two-coach push and pull sets no longer have to cross the main line between trips. The Down side buildings are closed but the decorative canopy valance remains. The Up side signal box is also closed but the long main buildings with hipped roof and the former bay platform still testify to the location's erstwhile junction status.

Crowhurst is served hourly by the Charing Cross-Hastings trains. Speed restrictions of 35-60 mph apply as far as milepost 60½.

C.36   Crowthorne

Redhill-Reading line, between Guildford and Wokingham. 58 m 66 ch from Charing Cross

The station was opened in 1858 to serve Wellington College, the famous public school created to provide an education for the sons of deceased army officers and granted its charter by Queen Victoria in 1853. The name Crowthorne was taken in 1928 and the station now consists of Up and Down platforms with the main, closed buildings on the former and a shelter on the latter. The hourly Tonbridge-Reading dmus call.

C.37   Crystal Palace

Victoria-Beckenham Junction line, between West Norwood Junction and Bromley Junction. 8 m 56 ch from Victoria

The Crystal Palace continued to exert great influence on Britain and its railways even after the events of 1851 and the move from Hyde Park to Sydenham Hill. It was a major factor in the incorporation of the West End & Crystal Palace Railway and the link it created, from December 1 1856, between the LB&SC spur from Sydenham and Wandsworth Common with subsequent extensions to Norwood and Pimlico in 1857 and 1858 respectively. In the latter year a further section was opened on May 3 extending the new route to Beckenham and, by 1860, the London end had moved on to Victoria and the country end had joined up with the Rochester line to give birth to a new main line from Kent, the LC&DR.

The LB&SC had opened its station, reached from the Sydenham direction, on June 10 1854. It was a grand affair, with

French and Brighton influences, and a fitting approach to the Crystal Palace above. Not to be outdone, the LC&D built a line from Loughborough Junction to a higher level station at Crystal Palace where the station it opened on August 1 1865 was right beside the exhibition building and was even grander than the Brighton's effort. Usually known as 'High Level', the station had a patchy existence, closing from 1917 to 1919 and from 1944 to 1946 and shutting down finally on September 20 1954. Until the Crystal Palace was destroyed by fire in 1936 access from the LC&D station was by a tunnel and from the Brighton station by a 720 ft colonnade, complete with plants and statuary.

The present, former 'Low Level', station at Crystal Palace still has some original portions although the frontage dates from around 1875. Although the Roman Catholic chapel room is no longer used the station still has a cathedral-like atmosphere as one passes from the period booking hall to the vault-like station and the stairs down to the original station area. On the approach from the Balham direction the station is preceded by the 746 yd Crystal Palace Tunnel (8 m 16 ch to 8 m 49 ch) and immediately on emerging from this the spur round to Sydenham veers off to pass through the great old station, leaving the line for Beckenham Junction to continue through the more modest, but busier, two platforms used by the Victoria-Beckenham Junction, Victoria-West Croydon and London Bridge-Redhill trains.

Crystal Palace, the impressive station buildings still echo the Great Exhibition and are somewhat remote from the working platforms below.

In the larger building the central terminating lines have been lifted and the through lines passing outside the platforms but inside the retaining walls are used only for peak hour London Bridge-Crystal Palace/Streatham Hill services.

C.38 Cuxton

Strood-Maidstone West-Paddock Wood line, between Strood and Aylesford. 33 m 36 ch from Charing Cross

The line was opened on June 18 1856 and the station buildings, on the Up side, are original. Single-storey, gabled and with leaded windows believed to be influenced by Aylesford Priory, they contrast with the simplicity of the wooden shelter and tiny signal box opposite. The latter controls the semaphore signals and wooden crossing gates.

The basic train service is half-hourly to/from Maidstone West and/or Paddock Wood.

D.1 Dartford

North Kent Line. 17 m 12 ch from Charing Cross

Dartford's geographical location as the gateway between London and North Kent has made it an important commercial and residential centre with three railway lines (and four routes) from the London direction and a link on to the Medway towns and the Channel ports and resorts. The town got its first station with the opening of the North Kent Line in 1849 but its strong Italianate buildings have now surrendered their function to a modern, impressive ticket office complex using glass and metal in a functional but pleasing relationship.

A footbridge leads to the two staggered island platforms which deal with an intensive pattern of services, including many originated for or terminating from the London direction. To deal with the high volume of traffic—17 services leaving for London between 08.00 and 09.00, for example—Dartford has a reversible line between the Up and Down Main lines from Dartford Junction (16 m 65 ch) to the station where there is also an Up Loop behind platform 1 and connected to the four carriage sidings beyond. Opposite is a DPL and the panel signal box, together with the News Platform and a Down siding. There are crossovers at this end of the station, at the London end and at Dartford Junction.

D.2   Dartford Loop Line

Hither Green to Dartford Junction. 9 m 76 ch

One of the three lines and four routes linking Dartford with London, the Dartford Loop was built as an easier route than the one via Blackheath, there being no link between Greenwich and Maze Hill until 1878. Diverging from the SER's then developing main line at Hither Green it was to run south of the built-up riverside area and rejoin the earlier line just west of Dartford. Work began at the Dartford end and, with no major engineering obstacles to overcome, was completed in time for opening on September 1 1866, less than four years after the promotion of the Parliamentary Bill.

The first electric trains began operating over the route on June 6 1926 and the 12 trains a day of the line's early years has now risen to around 70 each way, three an hour off-peak and some morning/evening services running fast between London and Sidcup or originating/terminating there. The open fields of the last century have given way to suburban housing and the route's primary function now is to serve the extensive commuter business it came to generate.

The double line route commences at Hither Green (7 m 16 ch) and runs via Lee Loop Junction (7 m 43 ch) (and its connecting spur with the main line) to Lee station (7 m 66 ch) which provides the first example of the single-storey lapped wooden buildings which are typical of this line. Over an embankment and past Colfe's School it then comes to Mottingham (9 m 40 ch) which has a trailing crossover and is where the Dartford panel takes over from London Bridge. Although the ticket office building is in brick, Mottingham (called Eltham until 1927) still has its share of wooden structures, but the Down sidings are now out of use. There is a pleasant park nearby.

New Eltham (10 m 32 ch) started life in 1878 as Pope Street and reveals contrasts between traditional wooden buildings and modern shelters and between skew overbridges of different periods.

Sidcup (11 m 73 ch) is a large version of the standard pattern of station on the loop although it has a fair amount of SR concrete additions and also a Down Passenger Loop at the country end used for reversing the workings which Sidcup originates in the morning peak and which terminate there in the evening. The station footbridge is a post war addition, previously the only link between the two sides was under the line via the road bridge. The next station Albany Park (12 m 68 ch), dating only from July 7 1935 and the opening of a new housing estate, lies in a shallow cutting and is much more modest although it has a curious Up side shelter with a sort of 'lapped concrete' base. On the embankment towards Bexley (13 m 69 ch) is a set of anti-tank 'dragon's teeth' left over from Second World War invasion fears.

The lapped wooden buildings reappear at Bexley and house the ticket office on the Down side but Crayford (15 m 25 ch) has been modernised and has a set of Clasp buildings on the Up side as well as modern shelters and a footbridge. The access to the Down sidings has been severed but the old ground frame and its diagram remain near the SER 15¼ milepost sign. Beyond the station crossover at the country end comes Crayford Spur 'B' Junction (16 m 11 ch), providing a link towards Slade Green via Crayford Spur 'A' Junction (16 m 41 ch) and then Dartford Junction (16 m 65 ch) where the loop line trails into the earlier route.

Datchet—see Windsor Branch

D.3   Deal

Charing Cross-Margate line, between Dover Priory and Ramsgate. 90 m 56 ch from Charing Cross (via Canterbury West)

After the opening of the line from Ashford to Margate in 1846 the South Eastern Railway added a branch from Minster to Deal which came into use on July 7 of the following year. Deal then remained a terminus until June 15 1881 when the line to Dover was added as a result of one of the periods of SER/LC&D co-operation. The present service is via Dover but the milepost mileage still reflects the original approach via Minster and increases towards Dover.

The station at Deal is near to the sea and stands at the foot of the six-mile descent from Guston Tunnel, the original line then continuing over the flatness of the Lydden Valley. The layout is curious, with three lines between the two, footbridge-linked platforms presumably to facilitate running round although the station now deals only with through trains. The main, two-storey brick buildings are on the Up side with just shelters on the Down, behind which stand little used sidings. The signal box and Middle Crossing are at the Minster end.

Today Deal is served hourly via Ashford and Dover, with some peak services using Cannon Street. The service is adequate, regular and effective but seems just a little mundane compared with the days of Saturday through trains from the GWR system and generous Pullman facilities, including a car on the 12.5 am service which arrived and terminated at Deal at 2.34 in the morning.

D.4   Dean

Redbridge Junction-Salisbury line. 88 m 10 ch from Waterloo (via Eastleigh)

The traditional main buildings on this 1847 line station are on the Down platform and have similarities in their gabled style with neighbouring Dunbridge. On the same side the station is preceded by Dean Hill AHB crossing (86 m 57 ch) and the connection to Dean Hill MoD siding and followed by the connection to the ECC quarry. There is also an AHB crossing at the Salisbury end of the station which is served by the Portsmouth-Salisbury locals.

D.5   Deepdene

Redhill-Reading line, between Redhill and Guildford. 29 m 65 ch from Charing Cross

The station, now comprising Up and Down platforms with shelters and reached by stairs from street level, opened in 1849 and has had two previous names (Box Hill & Leatherhead Road and Box Hill) and one period of closure (January 1917 to January 1919). It lies on a short level section at the foot of a seven-mile dip from Betchworth, down to Deepdene and up again to milepost 35. The station is quite near Dorking North and the SER route crosses the Bognor line east of Deepdene station and then passes over the River Mole on a high viaduct of five brick arches.

Deepdene House (now no more) was the wartime headquarters of the SR and the D-Day build up was planned in caves in its gardens.

Denmark Hill—see South London Line

Deptford—see North Kent Line

D.6   Dinton Sidings

Waterloo-Exeter line, between Salisbury and Gillingham. 88 m 49 ch from Waterloo

Dinton station closed in 1966 but the location remains significant as the access point for the military depots served by the Baverstock, Chilmark and Down private sidings. There are two ground frames, East and West, equipped with 'Train Released' and 'Train Shut In' plungers and unlocked by Annetts Key. The former Up line on this single line section is now part of the siding complex and trainmen operate in conjunction with MoD staff. The system developed originally from the Fovant Military Railway opened during the First World War.

Doleham—see Ashford-Hastings Line

D.7   Dorchester

Dorchester South is on the Waterloo-Weymouth line, 135 m 70 ch from Waterloo; Dorchester West is on the Yeovil-Weymouth line, 161 m 63 ch from Paddington

The 'Castleman's Corkscrew' route from Southampton reached Dorchester on June 1 1847 and the broad gauge Wilts, Somerset & Weymouth line arrived ten years later, on January 20 1857. These two

Left *Up Weymouth-Waterloo portion at Dorchester South.*

Below *A Westbury-Weymouth dmu has just got the 'Right Away' at Dorchester West.*

routes still exist to serve Dorset's county town and pass via the South and West stations respectively to join at Dorchester Junction (136 m 15 ch) where the GWR mileage (162 m 14 ch) begins to apply for the rest of the journey on to Weymouth.

On the former GWR line from Yeovil the regional boundary occurs before Dorchester West station at milepost 160¼ which lies on the single line Tokenless Block section. The single line continues through the 267 yd Poundbury Tunnel (161 m 3 ch to 161 m 15 ch) and then doubles at the station. The junction of the two lines follows the two stations and the route after dipping briefly then climbs at 1 in 91 to the 819 yd Bincombe Tunnel (164 m 44 ch to 165 m 2 ch) and the derelict Bincombe Tunnel signal box.

Dorchester West station has traditional buildings, faded but with the stamp of Brunel, on the Down side and is served by the Bristol-Weymouth dmus. Dorchester South is rather more unusual. The original terminal still exists (located with extension to Exeter in mind and provided with incongruous pilasters to front the single-storey buildings) and passengers cross a 'bridge' over the erstwhile trackbed to reach the curved platforms served by the hourly Waterloo-Weymouth four-car portions.

Local movements are controlled by the box in the V of the junction and the station signal box on the LSW route is now closed. So too are the once-extensive goods yard, the loco depot and cattle pens, and the assortment of sidings including the Chalk, Brewery and Mansfield (Eddison Steam Rolling Co) Sidings. At one period Up Weymouth trains

reversed into and restarted from the Up Bay (the Up platform of the old station) and special Appendix instructions covered this operation.

Dorking provides an example of station facilities combined in a commercial development.

D.8 Dorking

Dorking is on the Leatherhead-Horsham line, 22 m 8 ch from Waterloo; Dorking Town is on the Redhill-Reading line, 30 m 42 ch from Charing Cross

By courtesy of its protege, the Reading, Guildford & Reigate Railway, the South Eastern Railway metals were the first to reach Dorking, arriving on July 4 1849 and extending on to Shalford Junction on August 20 of that same year. Today the station consists of just the two staggered platforms standing on a short level section near the foot of the four-mile climb at 1 in 100/96 from Deepdene to the route's summit near milepost 35. Tonbridge-Reading dmus call.

Deepdene serves the eastern end of Dorking and is close to the other Dorking station, once Dorking North. This was to become part of the Mid-Sussex route created by the LB&SC to shorten the distance from Portsmouth to London but the section south to Horsham was originated by the independent Horsham, Dorking & Leatherhead Railway and linking the two approaches at Dorking produced a pronounced curve in the route, partly to accommodate a link from the SER route towards Horsham. Eventually the link from Leatherhead arrived at Dorking on March 11 1867 with that on to Horsham being completed on May 1.

Some of Dorking's earlier buildings survive on the Down island platform but on the Up side a commercial development has given the station an ultra modern ticket office as part of the office block complex. The Down Platform Line and the Down Passenger Loop are reversible and station yard working is authorised on all three platform lines to enable Dorking to deal with the Waterloo services which turn round there outside the peak, the Victoria services continuing on to Horsham. At other times some of the Bognor trains run this way.

In addition to the main running lines there are five carriage sidings beyond the DPL and a short siding in the old yard area. The London end of the station complex is marked by the signal box and an overbridge and the country end by the overbridge carrying the line from nearby Deepdene.

D.9 Dorking-Horsham line

The origins of this line are given in the previous entry and today, although it carries an hourly through service from Victoria off-peak, the intermediate stations are only open during the Monday to Friday business travel hours. Then they have links to both Waterloo and Victoria and some non-stop Bognor services are routed this way.

After leaving Dorking and passing under the former SER route the line enters the 384 yd Betchworth Tunnel (22 m 60 ch

to 22 m 73 ch) which takes it under
Betchworth Park. A long, flat, gentle
curve via Lodge Farm LC (25 m 38 ch)
brings the route to Holmwood (27 m 5 ch)
where the single-storey ticket office
building on the overbridge probably dates
from the 1867 opening of the route and
the wooden shelters are excellent examples
of their kind.

Ockley (29 m 20 ch) lies in the heart of
wooded countryside and comprises two
platforms with the ticket office on the
Down side and a shelter on the Up, with a
subway linking the two. Warnham (33 m
46 ch) has another good example of the
solid type of shelter erected by the LB&SC
although its tickets are issued from the
signal box on the Up side near the
traditional crossing gates. The Sussex
Brick Company formerly had a private
siding on the Down side.

The route joins that from Three Bridges
at 35 m 38 ch (37 m 43 ch via Three
Bridges).

Dormans—see East Grinstead Branch

D.10   Dover

*Dover Priory is on the line from Victoria
via Faversham (77 m 23 ch from Victoria)
to Dover Western Docks (78 m 30 ch). It is
also served by trains on the Charing Cross-
Margate via Tonbridge line*

Its position opposite the French coast has
made Dover important right from Roman
times. It has grown in stature through the
era following the creation of the Cinque
Ports in 1271 and a development period
after the arrival of the first railway in 1844
to its present status as a major cross-

*Dover Priory station and Priory Tunnel
looking towards Buckland Junction.*

roads for traffic to and from Europe. In
the process the harbour has developed
from a small haven at the mouth of the
River Dour into today's great exchange
point for vessels and cargo—human,
vehicular and freight.

Sir Walter Raleigh is on record as
saying that 'nowhere in the whole circuit
of this famous island is there any port
more convenient . . . than Dover'. And
well over 350 years later G.A. Sekon
added, 'Dover has from the earliest days
of the discovery of Britain constituted in
some respects the most important town in
this island . . . the town in Britain nearest
to the outside world.'

Despite this recognition and the increasing effect of steamers taking over from
sailing packets, Parliament was adamant
that only one railroad outlet was needed
from London so that the SER route to
Dover had to accompany the London to
Brighton line as far as Redhill, making it
some 20 miles longer than the 68 miles of
the coaching route. The SER also had the
difficulties of the access along the coast
from Folkestone to contend with, needing
four tunnels and the blowing up of Round
Down Cliff to create a path for the new
railway.

Dover's first station, opened with the
arrival of the SER line on February 7 1844,
was Dover Town which started life with
six trains a day to and from London.
Three years later work began on the
Admiralty Pier and by the time the LC&D

route reached the port in 1861 the line from Town station had been extended and trains were running on to the pier for direct access to the ships.

What is now Dover's main station, Dover Priory which takes its name from the nearby ruins of St Martin's Priory, was opened by the LC&D on July 22 1861. By November 1 of that year LC&D trains were passing through the tunnel to Harbour station and subsequently on to the pier to accelerate the rivalry with the SER services and steamers. Harbour station was replaced by Dover Town & Harbour in 1863 in one of the cycles of rationalisation and name changing and, when the landward end of Admiralty Pier was widened, its function passed to Dover Marine (now Dover Western Docks) which opened for military traffic on January 2 1915 and to the public on January 18 1919. In this period Dover Town (SER) closed on October 14 1914 and the Harbour station on July 11 1927. The train ferry berth opened in 1936.

The senior, SER, route to Dover carries a basic hourly service from Charing Cross with trains dividing at Ashford for Margate via Canterbury West and via Dover Priory. In between a fast service leaving on the hour calls only at Ashford and Folkestone Central and reaches Dover in 88 minutes. The approach along the coast, frequently quite a spectacular journey in winter, is via the 532 yd Martello Tunnel (71 m 22 ch to 71 m 47 ch), the short, overgrown platform of Warren Staff Halt (72 m 2 ch), the 60 mph restriction through the 1 m 182 yds of Abbotscliffe Tunnel (73 m 23 ch to 74 m 31 ch), Shakespeare Staff Halt (75 m 9 ch) and the 1,387 yd Shakespeare Tunnel (75 m 14 ch to 75 m 77 ch). The first sidings commence here, with Dover Town Yard on the Up side prior to Archcliffe Junction (76 m 42 ch) where the signal box controls the routes to Dover Marine box (76 m 59 ch) and Dover Western Docks (76 m 72 ch) and the connection to Dover Priory.

The service over the former LC&D route has a similar pattern but with hourly departures from Victoria alternating slow with semi-fast and Dover Western Docks with Ramsgate, inter-linking at Faversham and with peak hour services to and from Cannon Street. The faster journey times are around 97 minutes. In this direction the approach is by way of the Buckland Junction (76 m 32 ch) with the line from Deal, the 264 yd Charlton Tunnel (76 m 65 ch to 76 m 77 ch), the 158 yd Dover Priory Tunnel (77 m 8 ch to 77 m 16 ch) and then Dover Priory station (77 m 23 ch). The station is followed by the 684 yd Dover Harbour Tunnel (77 m 32 ch to 77 m 63 ch), Hawkesbury Street Junction signal box (77 m 72 ch) where the spur towards Folkestone departs, Southern House LC (78 m 10 ch), Dover Marine box (78 m 17 ch) and, finally, Dover Western Docks (78 m 30 ch). From Hawkesbury Street Junction to Archcliffe Junction the milepost distances are 77 m

Dover Marine.

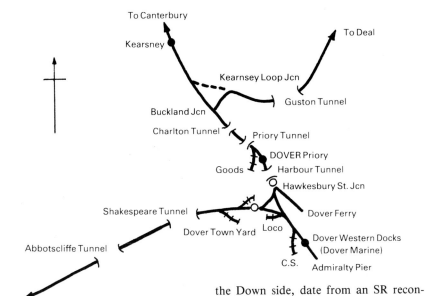

To Canterbury

Kearsney

To Deal

Kearsney Loop Jcn

Guston Tunnel

Buckland Jcn

Charlton Tunnel

Priory Tunnel

DOVER Priory

Goods   Harbour Tunnel

Hawkesbury St. Jcn

Shakespeare Tunnel

Dover Ferry

Dover Town Yard   Loco

Abbotscliffe Tunnel

Dover Western Docks
(Dover Marine)

C.S.   Admiralty Pier

To Folkestone

72 ch, 77 m 76 ch/76 m 53 ch and 76 m
42 ch.

Lying between its two tunnels, Dover
Priory is well seen from the overbridge at
the seaward end. There is a scissors crossover preceding the two platforms of which
the Up is an island with its outer face to
the Up Passenger Loop and GPO sidings
beyond that. The main buildings are on

Train ferry operation at Dover.

the Down side, date from an SR reconstruction and comprise ticket, waiting and
parcels facilities plus travel centre and
buffet, the latter with some interesting
prints to enliven the walls. The signal box
is on this platform from which there is a
special bus link to the Eastern Docks.

The double line route from Hawkesbury
Street Junction to Western Docks becomes
single just before Southern House LC.
The connection to Dover Ferry Ground
Frame is at the former point while three of
the platform lines at Western Docks con-
tinue on to Admiralty Pier. Western
Docks station comprises two island plat-

forms under an all-over roof and with ticket and parcels offices, buffet, train crew depot and police accommodation, and customs and immigration facilities. It deals mainly with passengers to and from the Continent using the sailings to and from Ostend and Dunkirk (via a long footbridge to the ferry berth) and the extra services to Calais and Boulogne in the summer. The carriage sidings deal with the cleaning and berthing of 84-120 vehicles daily.

Prior to the re-structuring of rail freight services Dover Town Yard kept its single, continuous-duty pilot locomotive fully occupied in shunting the 14 rather exposed sidings. There is an 80 tonne weighbridge here. At the Ferry Sidings up to 150 ferry wagons may need marshalling on the 12 sidings to supply or clear a day's sailings in each direction. Cars are loaded and unloaded in the Admiralty Siding and the Bulwark Street depot deals with fuel oil for ship bunkering and local distribution.

Other locations at Dover include the locked Pilot Tower LC on the double line route from Western Docks to Archcliffe Junction and the locomotive depot connection just beyond it. At Buckland Junction the opening of the Dover & Deal line on June 15 1881 included a (1882) link from the Chatham lines and the trackbed of this is still visible. At the opposite end of the Dover complex trains on the coastal route pass over the workings of two Channel Tunnel schemes, the first inspired by Edward Watkin of the SER as part of his dream of a through route from the North of England to Paris. Like the LC&D's twin-hull steamer *Castalia*, designed to reduce seasickness on the channel crossing, this inspiration has so far come to nothing but the railway has contributed much to the life and activity at Dover, a fact still evident although the grandeur of the ferry and boat trains has given way to today's intensive emu workings.

D.11   Dumpton Park

Victoria-Ramsgate line, between Margate and Ramsgate. 78 m 26 ch from Victoria

Dumpton Park comprises an island platform with stairs up to the footbridge at the Margate end and served hourly by Margate-Ramsgate and Victoria-Ramsgate trains. The station dates from the building of the 'new line' linking Margate and Ramsgate and had two openings, a

ceremonial one on July 2 1926 and a public opening 17 days later. A 30 mph restriction applies over the curves through the station.

From a point near the station the Ramsgate Tunnel Railway used to run through the former LC&D tunnel to Ramsgate Harbour.

D.12   Dunbridge

Redbridge Junction-Salisbury line. 84 m 21 ch from Waterloo*

Dunbridge, on the 1847 Eastleigh-Salisbury line and reflecting this in its milepost distances, lies just north of the former Kimbridge Junction with the Andover line. The trackbed of the latter route is still discernible just before Kimbridge AHB crossing (83 m 45 ch).

Dunbridge station comprises Up and Down platforms with traditional buildings, including ticket office, on the former and a bare platform on the Down side with the old dock and goods shed behind. There is a double barrier crossing and former signal box at the Salisbury end of the station which is served by the Portsmouth-Salisbury locals.

D.13   Dunton Green

Charing   Cross-Dover   line,   between Orpington and Sevenoaks. 20 m 46 ch from Charing Cross

There was a station at Dunton Green right from the opening of the line in 1868 and it became a junction on July 7 1881 with the opening of the 4¾-mile line via Chevening Halt and Brasted to Westerham. All services were withdrawn from the latter on October 30 1961 and although the Westerham Valley Railway Association tried hard to get a preservation scheme off the ground the route is marked today only by the trackbed visible on the Up side at the London end of Dunton Green.

Dunton Green itself was opened as Dunton Green & Riverhead and, having abandoned its single platform for the branch, now consists just of conventional Up and Down platforms with shelters, footbridge, and a mixture of concrete walling and older iron fencing. It has a basic hourly service derived from the Charing Cross-Sevenoaks trains.

D.14   Durrington-on-Sea

Brighton-Littlehampton/Portsmouth line, between Worthing and Arundel Junction. 12 m 13 ch from Brighton

Brick buildings, including a ticket office,

on the Up side reveal the 1937 origins of the station. A concrete footbridge leads to the Down platform and its waiting room and there are three services an hour in each direction.

E.1   Earley

Waterloo-Reading line, between Woking-ham and Reading. 66 m 1 ch from Charing Cross

In place of the previous separate station at Reading, SR trains on the Waterloo and Tonbridge lines now use a separate plat-form at the WR station and Earley is the first stop within the regional boundary (at MP 67) for the Tonbridge service dmus and the Waterloo emus. Although the line to Guildford dates from 1849, Earley station was brought into being 14 years after that date.

Earley has Up and Down platforms, milepost 66 standing on the latter in addition to the main station buildings which are unusual in having an overhang-ing upper storey with a spiral iron stair-case at one end. The Up platform, fronting the old yard (closed in 1969) has a wooden shelter and a footbridge link to the Down side.

There is a Shell oil terminal on the Down side at the London end, the single discharge siding being reached by a loop and headshunt immediately following milepost 65¾.

E.2   Earlsfield

Waterloo-Weymouth line, between Clap-ham Junction and Wimbledon. 5 m 46 ch from Waterloo

Earlsfield derives an excellent service from stops by Chessington South, Hampton Court and Kingston Loop trains and its traffic is increasing as a result. The station dates from April 1 1884 but only the Up and Down local line platforms are used in normal circumstances. These are reached by stairs from the ticket office below the station.

Just beyond Earlsfield there is a staff halt (6 m 28 ch) on the Up Through Line at the London end of the Wimbledon carriage servicing complex.

E.3   Earlswood

Victoria-Brighton line, between Redhill and Three Bridges. 21 m 50 ch from London Bridge

The original Brighton main line and the later Quarry route rejoin at the London end of Earlswood station making it an important junction controlled by the signal box there until Three Bridges took over. The station dates from 1868 and has its architecturally interesting main buildings (dating from the quadrupling period) on the Up side with a subway link to the complex of island platform plus two outer platforms of which only the local line plat-forms are normally used. At the London end are the rusting sidings of Redhill South Yard.

Trains call at Earlswood during the Monday to Friday business periods only.

E.4   Eastbourne

Victoria-Eastbourne/Hastings line. 23 m 73 ch from Brighton

Eastbourne was little more than a village, standing back from the coast and devoted to farming and fishing, when the single line branch from Polegate brought the first train on May 14 1849. Subsequently, developed by landowners and aided by royal patronage, the village grew into a town and resort with a high residential and holiday appeal. The LB&SC recognised this growth by providing a new, re-sited station in 1866 and the Southern Railway by providing electrifi-cation in 1935.

Eastbourne is approached via Willing-don Junction (21 m 38 ch) where the routes from Lewes and Hastings join north of Hampden Park station (21 m 75 ch) which comprises Up and Down platforms, signal box, double barrier LC and refuge siding. At Eastbourne itself the high signal box is on the Down side with a small coal concentration area nearby. Opposite are carriage sidings and the remaining freight sidings, the goods shed now being part of a market development.

The terminal has four platforms, No 4 having been shortened and a cab road lying between it and No 3. The station facilities, including a new ticket office, are grouped around the concourse allowing the frontage to be used for a travel centre, bus office and lock-up shops. Externally the station still retains some of its mixed Italianate-cum-Renaissance style with a square clock tower and flowers hanging from the awning to modify the impression of past splendour locked in time.

Eastbourne can no longer be reached via Hailsham and there are no Sunday Pullmans or Saturday links with the LMS and GWR, but it has a good hourly service to and from Victoria (the Ore

portion being added/detached at Eastbourne) and all-stations services east and
west along the coast. It is a train crew
depot, has a parcels office and dock, and
has S&T and Civil Engineer's establishments in the yard.

E.5   East Croydon

*Victoria-Brighton line. 10 m 28 ch from
London Bridge*

This is one of the SR's busiest stations,
open continuously and served by some
700 trains a day on the Charing Cross-
Caterham/Tattenham Corner, London
Bridge-Uckfield/East Grinstead, London
Bridge-Redhill and Victoria-Sussex Coast
lines. From the 1895 buildings—double-
storey, with clock gable and roof balus-
trades—on the overbridge at the country
end, ramps lead down to the three subway-
connected island platforms. Beyond platforms 1 and 2 on the Up side (and used by
Victoria line trains) the former goods
shed, an interesting example of its kind, is
now in the hands of a road haulage concern. The rest of the old goods yard,
closed in 1973, is either let or used for car
parking.

East Croydon is on the original 1841
L&B route but was first modified when
the line to Victoria was opened. The
separate platforms created then (labelled
New Croydon and used for separating
Victoria and London Bridge train
portions) were LB&SC property and part
of the constant bickering with the SER
which characterised the period. The
present station dates from the 1895-9
reconstruction period with further
changes, including platform extension,
dating from the current Gloucester Road
triangle scheme. A short branch to
Croydon Central was open from 1868 to
1871 and 1866-90 and was used by
through trains to Willesden and Liverpool
Street.

East Croydon is now the Borough's
principal station. It is directly linked with
the GPO sorting office and has travel
centre and buffet facilities.

E.6   East Dulwich

*South Bermondsey Junction-Leatherhead
line, between Peckham Rye and Tulse
Hill. 4 m 23 ch from London Bridge*

East Dulwich was opened by the LB&SC
as Champion Hill on October 1 1868.
Raised above street level, its two platforms
are served by the London Bridge-Sutton
trains.

E.7   East Farleigh

*Strood-Maidstone West-Paddock Wood
line, between Paddock Wood and Maidstone. 42 m 75 ch from Charing Cross*

East Farleigh lies on a 40 mph curve, in a
bend of the Medway's west bank, and was
opened on September 25 1844. The station
has staggered platforms with traditional
wooden buildings on the Up side, together
with a small wooden signal box which
controls the gated crossing. There is a weir
behind the station and a Civil War battle
took place near the bridge.

The hourly Paddock Wood-Strood
trains call.

E.8   East Grinstead Branch

Branch from Hurst Green. 8 m 49 ch

Four lines once radiated from East Grinstead and it dealt with services to Tunbridge Wells from London via Oxted and
from Three Bridges, trains on two routes
south to Lewes/Brighton and various local
workings. Now the town is the terminus
for a service to and from London Bridge
and also has through workings at peak
hours and three-car demu units linked
with an Uckfield portion at Oxted off-
peak.

The first railway to arrive at East Grinstead was that from Three Bridges on July
9 1855. A link on to Tunbridge Wells
came on October 1 1866 accompanied by
a new through station displacing the
former terminus. A third station was
opened on August 1 1882 when, in a two-
year period following the end of the
LB&SC v SER feuding, lines were opened
to Culver Junction, Haywards Heath and
northwards to South Croydon Junction.
Interchange was facilitated by high level
platforms on the Three Bridges-Tunbridge
Wells route where it crossed over the
Oxted-Horsted Keynes line platforms.
Goods traffic used the original passenger
terminus and there was a transfer line
from the Tunbridge Wells direction to the
Horsted Keynes route and a loop from the
high level towards Oxted.

Today the branch commences at Hurst
Green Junction (21 m 35 ch), is double
line, non-electrified throughout, and
drops in easy stages to Lingfield before
rising again, mainly at 1 in 70, to East
Grinstead. The former link from Crowhurst Junction to the Tonbridge line
preceded the overbridge carrying that line
and lay at the foot of the 2-mile descent at
1 in 100.

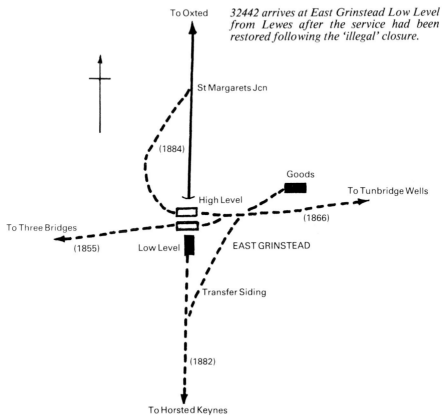

To Oxted

St Margarets Jcn

(1884)

Goods

High Level

To Tunbridge Wells

(1866)

To Three Bridges

(1855)   Low Level   EAST GRINSTEAD

Transfer Siding

(1882)

To Horsted Keynes

32442 arrives at East Grinstead Low Level from Lewes after the service had been restored following the 'illegal' closure.

Lingfield station (26 m 23 ch) lies on reverse curves subject to a 50 mph speed restriction. It dates from the opening of this part of the line on March 10 1884 and follows the old yard and dock area and the Up side brick signal box. The main buildings, in the LB&SC style for the area, are on this side as is the covered walkway link with the racecourse. The Down platform, reached by footbridge and provided with a shelter, carries the 26 MP sign and was once an island.

The other intermediate branch station, Dormans (27 m 62 ch), lies in a wooded cutting. The only platform structure is a shelter on the Up side, the main station buildings standing on top of the bank on the Down side and comprising a substantial two-storey block of original LB&SC design and with an awning over the open portion of the L configuration.

On the final part of the route the line crosses a high viaduct and passes the site of St Margarets Junction on the Up side and where the connection round to the east-west route and high level station was made. A curving cutting then heralds the surviving station at East Grinstead (30 m 4 ch) which is the low level part of the 1882 station and has Clasp-type buildings dating from the early 1970s on the Down side and a waiting shelter opposite. The former yard, closed in 1967, lies at the country end on the Down side with the signal box opposite. The route then terminates just beyond the crossover and at the southern end of the ten-arch Imberhorne Viaduct.

Repeater signal and water tower at East Grinstead.

E.9 Eastleigh

Waterloo-Weymouth line, junction for Fareham line and freight-only line to Romsey. 73 m 35 ch from Waterloo

The London & Southampton Railway opened the section between Southampton and Winchester on June 10 1839, including a station at Bishopstoke (now Eastleigh). The main line was completed in the following year and on November 29 1841 Eastleigh became a junction with the opening of the branch to Gosport (closed due to problems with Fareham Tunnel and reopened on February 7 1842). Another route was added when the line to Salisbury (Milford) via Romsey was opened on January 27 1847 (passenger traffic March 1). Local passenger services ceased on the Eastleigh-Romsey section on May 5 1969.

Bishopstoke Junction became Eastleigh & Bishopstoke in 1889 and two years later became the home of the LSW carriage works, the locomotive works transferring from Nine Elms in 1909. The name Eastleigh became known throughout the country for the Urie and Maunsell locomotives built there.

Today Eastleigh is still a busy railway centre with a considerable influence on the life of the town. On the approach from Albrook (72 m 46 ch) there are slow lines outside the Up and Down fast, producing four lines between the two platforms and a Down Passenger Loop on the outside face of the Down island and used by Fareham line trains. The Romsey line junction precedes the station, as does Eastleigh panel box which was brought into use in 1966 and, as a result of the 1981-2 Southampton area re-signalling, now controls the main line from south of Basingstoke to Millbrook and the routes to Romsey, Fareham and Totton.

Immediately following Eastleigh station the route to Fareham branches off and between the two routes lie the BREL works, the locomotive depot and the diesel maintenance depot. The latter was brought into use in 1957 to maintain the units on the newly-introduced Hampshire diesel services and was rebuilt as part of the Bournemouth electrification to grow, in 1967, to encompass a covered area of 8 × 4-car lengths.

The traditional station buildings at Eastleigh are followed by footbridge access to the platforms. Beyond these, on the Down side, is a complex of yards and carriage sidings, the former dealing with

The carriage washer at Eastleigh.

such traffics as Foster Yeoman stone from the Mendips, traffic from the Ford private siding, ICI chemicals and freight for/from road distribution by H. Young Transport Ltd.

Eastleigh is served by the Bournemouth line slows and semi-fasts and by the Reading-Portsmouth route trains.

E.10   East Malling

Victoria-Ramsgate line, between Otford Junction and Maidstone East. 35 m 64 ch from Victoria

Although the route opened in 1874, East Malling did not get a station until 1913. Its two platforms, each with wooden shelters, are reached by stairs from the road which passes under the line at the country end and are served by hourly Victoria-Maidstone East trains which connect into the Thanet services.

East Putney—see Point Pleasant Junction-Wimbledon line

E.11   East Worthing

Brighton-Littlehampton/Portsmouth line, between Shoreham and Worthing. 9 m 55 ch from Brighton

This simple 1905 station originated as Ham Bridge Halt. It consists of Up and Down platforms with shelters and ticket hut and is served by the Brighton all-stations trains.

E.12   Edenbridge

Redhill-Tonbridge line. 33 m 3 ch from Charing Cross

The SER route from Redhill was opened as far as Ashford by the end of 1842,

Edenbridge opening with the stretch to Tonbridge on May 26 of that year. It now comprises staggered platforms with shelters and a signal box controlling two crossovers, semaphore signals and the refuge siding preceding the Up platform. The Reading-Tonbridge dmus call.

Just west of Edenbridge station the route crosses over the Uckfield branch (by a bridge separating two sections of tunnel), the entry for which contains details of Edenbridge Town station.

E.13   Eden Park

Lewisham-Hayes line. 12 m 34 ch from Charing Cross

Eden Park still has its 1882 buildings, in typical SER style, on the Up side. A subway then leads to the Down platform. There are three trains an hour to and from Hayes and Charing Cross/Cannon Street.

E.14   Effingham Junction

Junction of line from Leatherhead and New Guildford Line. 21 m 10 ch from Waterloo

Although the New Guildford Line from Hampton Court Junction and the LSW's probe west from Leatherhead date from 1885, the station at Effingham Junction is three years younger. Its two platforms stand just south of the physical junction between the two routes (21 m 4 ch/22 m 15 ch) and have modest wooden buildings. Stairs lead to the footbridge and to wooden ticket office buildings perched above the Down platform at street level.

As the area is now controlled from Guildford signal panel the old station signal box at the London end of the Up platform is now used by staff reversing trains from Victoria. These move from the Down line to the carriage shed reception line and then transfer, via the crossover, to the Up line after the Down Guildford train has passed. The seven-bay shed was built when the route was electrified in 1925, a sub-station also being provided in the vee of the junction.

With services on the New Guildford Line and to Waterloo and Victoria via Epsom the station is well served.

E.15 Egham

Waterloo-Reading line, between Staines and Virginia Water. 21 m 2 ch from Waterloo

The Waterloo-Reading and Staines-Weybridge services combine to give Egham a basic pattern of four trains each way hourly. The location dates from June 4 1856 and has its main brick and wood buildings on the Up side, with a shelter, sub-station and MP 21 on the Down. A footbridge links the two at the CCTV barrier crossing end and there are further crossings either side, the AHB LC at Pooley Green (20 m 51 ch) and another at Rusham (21 m 61 ch).

Egham is the station for the teacher training centre at Holloway College which stands to the west of the line.

E.16 Elephant & Castle

Holborn Viaduct-Herne Hill line. 1 m 47 ch from Holborn Viaduct

The link from Herne Hill towards the Thames was ready for opening on October 6 1862 when a temporary station was provided at Elephant & Castle, the LC&D providing a permanent station in the following February. The line here runs on arches and from a cavern-like station entrance behind the Elephant & Castle shopping complex stairs lead up to the combination of centre island and two outer platforms serving the grouped pairs of slow and fast lines.

The station is busy during the peak periods (Mondays to Fridays) and has a half-hourly off-peak service to West Croydon and to Sevenoaks. Of the total of 192 trains a day, 97 of them are in the peak. The station has the usual facilities, plus a veteran indicator board of the lever type on the centre island platform.

E.17 Elmers End

Lewisham-Hayes line, junction for Addiscombe branch. 11 m 7 ch from Charing Cross

The 1864 New Beckenham to Addiscombe

line and the 1882 line to Hayes separate at the country end of Elmers End station, with a single line from the Up side bay connecting to the former. There is also a rusting Down bay in front of the sub-station and a crossover at the London end of the complex, which is controlled from London Bridge. The two platforms are linked by footbridge and the modern ticket office complex of glass and wood has a pleasant multi-locomotive mural over the entrance to the Up platform.

The train service pattern has varied over the years, including periods with the shuttle service being to Hayes but now that point takes the through service from Charing Cross/Cannon Street and a 2-car connecting shuttle runs to Addiscombe. A peak service on the line to Sanderstead did not re-appear in the 1983-4 timetable.

E.18 Elmstead Woods

Charing Cross-Dover line, between Hither Green and Chislehurst. 10 m 21 ch from Charing Cross

This station, preceded by the two Chislehurst tunnels, started life as Elmstead on July 1 1904 and received its suffix four years later. It still has a wooded setting on the four-track portion of the main line and derives a half-hourly basic service from the Charing Cross-Orpington/Sevenoaks trains. The main brick buildings on the Down side are sizeable but plain, although the canopy and its supports are rather more decorative.

Eltham Park—see Bexleyheath Line

Eltham Well Hall—see Bexleyheath Line

E.19 Emsworth

Victoria-Portsmouth line, between Chichester and Havant. 35 m 50 ch from Brighton

Emsworth, one of the original 1847 stations, is approached by an embankment. It has Up and Down platforms with modest accommodation and a train service derived from the hourly Victoria semi-fasts and the hourly Brighton slows.

E.20 Epsom

South Bermondsey Junction-Leatherhead line, between Sutton and Leatherhead. 18 m 73 ch from London Bridge, 14 m 18 ch from Waterloo

Epsom welcomed its first railway in 1847 with the arrival at Epsom Town of the

London & Croydon extension. The Epsom & Leatherhead was authorised in 1856 and became a joint LB&SC and LSW enterprise as a result of the latter's Wimbledon & Dorking threat. It was opened three years later and the LSW route from the main line arrived in the same year. This process gave Epsom two stations, the 1847 Epsom (Town) and the LSW station on the present site, the former being closed to passengers on March 3 1929 but continuing in a freight capacity until May 3 1965.

From Epsom's street level ticket office on the Down side a subway and stairs lead to the two island platforms (of the 1929 SR station on the site of the former LSW one), both with brick buildings and canopies. The outer face on the Up side is used for Waterloo trains and the inner one for Victoria services, similar arrangements applying on the Down side except that start-back facilities are provided to allow trains to return to their respective termini. The two routes divide at the London end of the station and are controlled by a wooden signal box elevated on a frame between the two platforms at the country end. At this end there are Up and Down electric carriage sidings plus the connections reducing the four lines to two.

Alternating half-hourly services Waterloo-Dorking (Horsham in the peak) and Effingham Junction interconnect at Epsom with the Victoria-Horsham/Effingham Junction trains.

E.21   Epsom Downs Branch

South Bermondsey Junction-Leatherhead line, branch from Sutton. 4 m 2 ch

This LB&SC branch was opened from Sutton to a terminus south-east of Epsom and about ¾-mile from the racecourse on May 22 1865. It was electrified from June 17 1928 and now enjoys a half-hourly basic service calling at the intermediate stations at Belmont and Banstead. Just beyond Sutton the former double line route has been singled by lifting the Up track and One Train Working is now in operation.

From Sutton (14 m 75 ch from London Bridge) the route heads south through suburbs to come to Belmont (16 m 1 ch) where the Down platform is used and has a modern Clasp building housing the ticket office and waiting room. The Up platform, with shelters and footbridge, is still in situ.

After passing under a skew bridge the route now curves steadily west as it climbs at 1 in 55/61/79 and enters a limestone cutting through a section of Banstead Downs to come to Banstead station (17 m 40 ch). Here the main buildings are on the overbridge at the London end with just a shelter on the Down platform and no line to serve the Up where a traditional wooden shelter and canopy remain.

The route curves south through more open countryside on the descent to Epsom Downs (18 m 77 ch) where the previous four platform lines have been reduced to one either side of the centre platform. The two outer platforms are overgrown and trains normally use the Down line only as only one set is on the branch at a time. The combined house, ticket office, waiting room, etc, block is now partially let and is showing signs of its age. It seems a far cry from the most hectic race traffic days when the station signal boxes had to be supplemented by three intermediate boxes whose signal arms and lamps were removed when not in use.

Eridge—see Uckfield Branch

Erith—see North Kent Line

E.22 Esher

*Waterloo-Weymouth line, between Sur-
biton and Weybridge. 14 m 31 ch from
Waterloo*

Esher was another of the original stations
on the 1838 Nine Elms-Woking line and
was first called Ditton Marsh, later Esher
& Hampton Court and then Esher & Clare-
mont. The present station, which serves
Sandown Park Racecourse, dates from an
1877 reconstruction minus the centre
island. The remaining outer platforms to
the Up and Down Local lines are served
half-hourly by the Guildford-Portsmouth
slow trains. The old goods building on the
Up side survives from the 1962 withdrawal
of freight facilities and the old race platforms used to be on this side (Woking
end), complete with slotted signal.

E.23 Etchingham

*Charing Cross-Hastings line, between
Tunbridge Wells Central and Robertsbridge. 47 m 34 ch from Charing Cross*

Etchingham, opened with the first section
of the Hastings line on September 1 1851,
was built on the site of an old manor
house. In the fashion of the period some
of the manor's sandstone blocks were
used to build the elegant station buildings
on the Up side, although the facings at
every corner, chimney, window and door
are a little overpowering for a modest
country station.

The two platforms are staggered and
followed at the country end by a double
barrier crossing and then the signal box,
the latter controlling semaphore signals
including the very tall Up starter. There is
a basic hourly service in each direction.

E.24 Ewell

*Ewell East is on the South Bermondsey
Junction to Leatherhead line, 17 m 27 ch
from London Bridge and Ewell West on
the Raynes Park to Leatherhead line, 12 m
78 ch from Waterloo*

Ewell East was the first station to serve
Ewell, the route opening from West
Croydon to Epsom on May 10 1847 but
the suffix not being taken until 1923. The
ticket office and waiting room buildings
are on the Up side with a footbridge to the
Down platform which has a secondary
entrance and a shelter. The half-hourly
Victoria-Effingham Junction/Horsham
trains call.

Ewell West, also known just as Ewell
until 1923, was opened with the LSW
route from Raynes Park on April 4 1859.
Part of the two-storey main building on
the Down side is original but the Up side
has just a wooden shelter. Goods traffic
ceased in 1961. The station is crossed by a
road overbridge and has a half-hourly
Waterloo-Dorking/Effingham Junction
service.

E.25 Eynsford

*Victoria-Ramsgate line, between Swanley
and Otford Junction. 20 m 32 ch from
Victoria*

The Sevenoaks Railway, worked and then
absorbed by the LC&D, promoted the
route which opened from Swanley to
Sevenoaks on June 2 1862 and is now used
by Ashford/Thanet services as far as
Otford Junction and by the Holborn
Viaduct-Sevenoaks trains which serve
Eynsford. After leaving Swanley it cuts
through a range of hills using the dead
straight, 828 yd Eynsford Tunnel (18 m 67
ch to 19 m 24 ch) and then crosses the
River Darent by means of an imposing
nine-arch viaduct to come to the modest
country station at Eynsford. Here the
complex consists of Up and Down
platforms, 1862 station buildings, ageing
wooden shelter with decorative canopy
and concrete footbridge, all serving Eynsford village and its magnificent 13th
century church and, on the opposite side
of the valley, the splendid Tudor manor
house called Lullingstone Castle.

The 'ghost station' at Lullingstone was
completed in 1939 on a site between the
tunnel and the viaduct. Although
appearing in the public timetables as 'date
of opening to be announced' it was never
brought into use and gradually became
derelict.

Falconwood—see Bexleyheath Line

F.1 Falmer

*Brighton-Lewes line. 3 m 39 ch from
Brighton*

The first Falmer station lasted from 1846
to 1865 when the station site was moved
from the Lewes side of the 490 yd Falmer
Tunnel (3 m 62 ch to 4 m 5 ch) to the
Brighton side. The present buildings date
from a reconstruction at the end of the
last century, the main ones on the Down
side comprising ticket office, staff rooms
and adjacent station house. The main
portion has a central gable and provides
another example of accommodating a
signalling frame in a bay projecting on to

the platform. There is a footbridge to the Up platform which is provided with a glass and wood shelter.

Falmer, which lost its goods facilities in 1961, serves Sussex University and enjoys a 20-minute service to and from Brighton and east to Lewes/Seaford/Eastbourne/Ore. It is superbly located high in the South Downs, some of the flint from which is incorporated in the station house. There is an excellent signal gantry example on the Down side near the sub-station.

F.2   Fareham

Southampton-Portsmouth line, junction with line from Eastleigh. 84 m 21 ch from Waterloo

Fareham's first railway was the LSW branch from Bishopstoke (Eastleigh) opened on November 29 1841 through to Gosport but then closed again because of problems with the Fareham No 2 Tunnel and not re-opened until February 7 1842. What is now the major route, that from Southampton to Portsmouth, dates from 1848 (east) and 1889 (west), the Eastleigh route joining it via the 56 yd Fareham No 1 Tunnel (83 m 17 ch to 83 m 20 ch) and the 553 yd Fareham No 2 Tunnel (83 m 21 ch to 83 m 46 ch). When the link between Alton and the Eastleigh-Fareham line was opened on June 1 1903 a second route was built from Knowle Junction to Fareham to avoid the tunnel. This was brought into use on October 2 1904; although now closed, the trackbed is still visible.

Near the signal box and stone terminal, the Tokenless Block single line from Botley meets the main line in a 20 mph junction at the west end of the station. At the other end, a second 20 mph junction occurs where the original route to Gosport and Portsmouth (by ferry) now veers off as a freight-only 25 mph single line, truncated at Bedenham Sidings (87 m 40 ch) and worked on the one train basis. Between the two the station has two platforms and four faces (two through, one bay, one dead end).

Fareham is served by trains between South Wales/Bristol, Salisbury/Romsey and Reading-Portsmouth/Brighton.

F.3   Farnborough

Farnborough (Main) is on the Waterloo-Weymouth line, between Pirbright Junction and Basingstoke and 33 m 17 ch from Waterloo; Farnborough North is on the Redhill-Reading line, between Guildford and Wokingham and 53 m 16 ch from Charing Cross

Used by royalty until the opening of Windsor, Farnborough (Main) lies on the second portion of line to be opened by the London & Southampton Railway, that from Woking Common to Shapley Heath (Winchfield) which came into use on September 24 1838. The present station consists of platforms to the Up and Down slow lines (the centre island now having gone) and dates from the 1903 reconstruction period. The main buildings are on the Down side where there is also a coal concentration depot with a ground frame controlling access from the Down Slow. There are also fast to slow and slow to fast crossovers. The basic service comes from the Basingstoke and slower Bournemouth trains, with some additions at peak times.

Farnborough North opened on July 4 1849 and now comprises Up and Down platforms with shelters. It is served by the Tonbridge-Reading dmus.

F.4   Farncombe

Waterloo-Portsmouth line, between Guildford and Haslemere. 33 m 40 ch from Waterloo

The station at Farncombe dates from May 1 1897 and the main buildings, on the Up side, comprise a long, single-storey block in red brick with end gables, much stone facing and a weak Tudor style. A more modest version appears on the staggered Down platform. A CCTV LC at Farncombe East (33 m 29 ch) precedes the station which is followed by another double barrier crossing, with the signal box adjacent. The hourly slower Portsmouth services call.

F.5   Farnham

Waterloo-Alton line, between Aldershot and Alton. 40 m 33 ch from Waterloo

LSW metals reached Farnham on October 8 1849 as part of the single line branch from Guildford via Ash Green and Tongham and went on to Alton in 1852, the route from Brookwood arriving 18 years later. Under the 1937 electrification the route from Ash Junction was closed to passengers although it can still be spotted behind the Farnham sub-station.

Farnham station is preceded by the former junction, now marked by a 30 mph curve and a change of mileage from

36 m 75 ch to 39 m 22 ch. It comprises Up
and Down platforms with a solid two-
storey brick building and a prefabricated
single-storey building on the former. The
old goods shed is now in private hands
and on the Down side are further buildings
plus the signal box and sidings for the
engineers' and coal traffic. The Up side
carriage shed at the country end of the
station still retains its wartime camouflage
paint and another novel feature is the
survival of a section of cobbles in the
station forecourt. There is also a CCTV
crossing and a tip siding.

During the business travel periods some
services originate or terminate at Farnham
but during the rest of the day it is served
half-hourly by the Alton line trains.

F.6   Farningham Road

*Victoria-Ramsgate line, between Swanley
and Rochester. 20 m 41 ch from Victoria*

Farningham Road, once signed additionally '& Sutton-at-Hone', was opened on
December 3 1860. It comprises Up and
Down platforms with typical country
station buildings on the former and a
footbridge link to the latter. At the
London end are the disused private sidings
of the steel stockholders, Miles Druce,
and beyond the station is a viaduct carrying
the line over the River Darent. The signal
box is open only on an 'as required' basis.
The Ramsgate/Dover all-stations trains
serve the station.

F.7   Faversham

*Victoria-Ramsgate line, junction for
Dover Western Docks. 51 m 77 ch from
Victoria*

Faversham is a pleasant and busy station
comprising two island platforms and
followed by the junction at which the
Ramsgate and Dover lines separate. The
islands are served by the Up and Down
Main lines and Up and Down passenger
loops, paired by direction and all authorised for station yard working. They are
used for interchange between the all-
stations service on one route and the semi-
fast service (which left Victoria 28 minutes
later) on the other, these roles reversing
half-hourly. The platform buildings and
the Down side ticket office reached by
subway are in light brick with red brick
decoration and the station has buffet
facilities.

What was to become the LC&D main
line reached Faversham on January 25

1858 and pushed on to Canterbury (and
Whitstable) two years later. The derelict
loco shed area beyond the junction is a
reminder of the bustling days of steam
and it is interesting to note the command-
ing view enjoyed by the shedmaster's
office. Beyond the four freight sidings
alongside the Down Ramsgate line are the
rusting remains of the lines of the Faversham Creek Branch. On the Up side of the
junction are carriage sidings, including the
Field Siding, and the signal box. Graveney
AHB LC lies along the Ramsgate line
(54 m 77 ch) and Clock House AHB LC
along the Dover line (53 m 51 ch).

F.8   Fawley Branch

*Waterloo-Weymouth line, branch from
Totton. 8 m 79 ch*

An Order for the Totton, Hythe & Fawley
Light Railway was confirmed by the
Board of Trade on November 10 1903.
Today, a sight of the vast Esso refinery
and of the trainloads of oil traffic originating on its private siding network makes it
difficult to credit that nothing happened
about the original Order until the 1920s.
Then, a single line was opened down the
west shore of Southampton Water and
began carrying passengers to Marchwood,
Hythe and Fawley stations. Later the
private Hardley Halt came into use on the
Hythe-Fawley section. To the passenger
traffic was added the freight of the Agwi
Petroleum Corporation at Fawley, Up
side sidings for Union Carbide Ltd and
the International Synthetic Rubber Co
and the MoD network at Marchwood.

The passenger service on the branch
continued until February 14 1966 and
public goods facilities lasted for a further
year but today the route serves only the
MoD at Marchwood and the oil and
chemical activities at Fawley.

The single line, freight-only route
commences with a 15 mph junction adjoining Totton LC (82 m 43 ch) and passes via
AHB crossings at Jacobs Gutter Lane
(84 m 12 ch), Trotts Lane (85 m 11 ch) and
Tavell's Lane (85 m 66 ch) to Marchwood
(86 m 8 ch). There is a level crossing and
crossing loop here and Marchwood signal
box takes over from Eastleigh panel, with
the remainder of the line being worked on
the 'No Signalman' Key Token system.
The route continues via more crossings—
Pumpfield Farm RG (86 m 37 ch), Veals
Lane AHB (86 m 69 ch), West Street AHB
(88 m 38 ch), School Road (88 m 68 ch)
and Frost Lane AHB (89 m 60 ch)—to the

The BR contribution to the Fawley operation has included the movement of these refinery towers.

Fawley ground frame (91 m 42 ch) controlling access to the sidings. Here trainmen place the Key Token in an auxiliary instrument while exchanging traffic in the freight sidings.

F.9   Faygate

Victoria-Portsmouth line, between Three Bridges and Horsham. 34 m 28 ch from London Bridge

This was one of the original stations, dating from the opening of the line on February 14 1848. There is a shelter on each platform and the ticket office is part of the small signal box on the Up platform. Victoria-Horsham trains call hourly.

F.10   Feltham

Waterloo-Reading line, between Twickenham and Staines. 14 m 68 ch from Waterloo

Feltham was one of the original 1848 locations and it has seen many changes since. The approach from the London direction is via Feltham Junction (13 m 35 ch) which provides a link with the Hounslow Loop and was the route taken by freight exchanged with the Southern Railway's Feltham marshalling yard. The yard has now passed into history but Feltham remains important for the new signal box which took over from 45 manual boxes in September 1974 to complete the replacement of semaphore signalling by colour lights in this area of the Southern Region. The box controls 70 miles of track from

Richmond/Chiswick to Bracknell/Frimley/Chertsey/Norbiton plus the Shepperton and Windsor branches.

The station comprises Up and Down platforms with a severe two-storey house plus later additions on the Down side and shelter plus canopy on the Up. The old goods yard site is at the London end and Feltham West CCTV crossing (14 m 74 ch) at the country end. Stops by Windsor and Reading trains provide the off-peak service and Guildford line trains call in the peak.

Near Feltham station on the Down side a few rusting sidings mark the 79 acres of Hounslow Marsh upon which the great marshalling yard and engine shed complex was built towards the end of the First World War. The yard was Sir Herbert Walker's brainchild, designed to concentrate the piecemeal operations previously carried out at Nine Elms, Woking and Willesden. It was built with reception sidings, Up and Down Humps and sorting sidings, and transfer yard and was brought into use progressively from October 3 1920.

F.11   Fishbourne

Victoria-Portsmouth line, between Chichester and Havant. 30 m 12 ch from Brighton

Not far from the remains of Britain's largest known Roman residence, this 1906 station is a modest one of raised concrete platforms with a corrugated shelter and staff hut on each and traditional gates and crossing house at the London end. It is preceded by crossings at Clay Lane (29 m 49 ch) and New Fishbourne (30 m 8 ch) and followed by one at Blackboy Lane (30 m 25 ch). There are peak links with Victoria but the main service is provided by the hourly Brighton-Portsmouth slows.

F.12   Fishersgate

*Brighton-Littlehampton/Portsmouth line,
between Brighton and Shoreham. 3 m 47 ch
from Brighton*

Fishersgate comprises Up and Down platforms with shelters, linked by footbridge
and with a small ticket office on the Up
side. The location dates from September
15 1905 and is served by the Brighton-
Littlehampton/Portsmouth trains.

F.13   Fleet

*Waterloo-Weymouth line, between Farn-
borough and Basingstoke. 36 m 38 ch
from Waterloo*

Opened in 1847 as Fleetpond, this station
was reconstructed with Clasp buildings in
1966. It has platforms to the outer Up and
Down local lines, with a ticket office on
the Down side and some notable flower
beds. The service is the same as that at
neighbouring Farnborough.

   Bramshot (Golf Club) Halt, ¾ m on
the Farnbrough side, served local golf
devotees until 1946.

F.14   Folkestone

*Charing Cross-Dover line; Folkestone
West is 69 m 22 ch and Folkestone Central
69 m 73 ch from Charing Cross*

The South Eastern Railway's line to
Dover reached the outskirts of Folkestone
on June 28 1843 and then had to wait for
the completion of the 19-arch Foord
Viaduct before a permanent station (at
what was to become Folkestone Junction)

could take over on December 18 of that
year and the route continue on to Dover in
1844. While all this was going on the SER
had purchased the near-derelict harbour
at Folkestone, put divers and dredgers to
work and begun construction of a freight
route to it. Although the railway possessed
no powers to operate steamers itself it
quickly found a contractor to operate to
Boulogne and followed this with introducing passenger trains on to the harbour
branch in 1849.

   Folkestone grew rapidly and soon
became the SER's principal packet port.
In the growth process the town spread
westwards resulting in the 1863 Folkestone
West and the 1884 Folkestone Central
growing busier than Folkestone Junction
(latterly East) which eventually closed on
September 6 1965. Folkestone West was
originally Shorncliffe Camp, Shorncliffe
Camp itself being moved slightly east and
becoming Shorncliffe. To add to the con-
fusion the present Folkestone Central was
Cheriton Arch when it opened on
September 1 1884, and Radnor Park from
1886 to 1895!

   Approaching the coast the route today
passes the overgrown cutting which once
carried the Elham Valley line with the two
tracks then becoming four at Cheriton
Junction (68 m 16 ch). There are slow to
fast and fast to slow connections either
side of Folkestone West which has its
main, single-storey buildings, in brick and
with hipped roof, on the Up side of the
two platforms to the slow lines. The
former goods yard and dock are at the
London end of the station.

   The route continues and makes its high
level approach to Folkestone Central
which has two island platforms reached by
ramp and subway from the lower complex
of ticket and enquiry office and bookstall.
The station was reconstructed in modern

*The approach to Folkestone
takes the line high above the town.*

materials at the time of electrification.

Beyond Central station the route reverts to Up and Down lines only as it continues over the Foord Viaduct with views over the town and harbour to Folkestone East Staff Halt (70 m 76 ch) comprising tiny Down platform and longer Up platform. The signal box follows (70 m 79 ch), located near the Down platform and controlling a double crossover and the connection to the three Boat Train Roads on the Up side of the main line. The route towards Dover continues with the 532 yd Martello Tunnel (71 m 22 ch to 71 m 47 ch) and Warren Staff Halt (72 m 2 ch), the latter overgrown but carrying the 72 milepost.

Trains to and from Folkestone Harbour reverse in the Boat Train Roads before dropping down the 1 in 36/30 gradient via Folly Road CCTV LC (71 m 29 ch), past the crossovers and over the swing bridge to the crossing, signal box and station at Folkestone Harbour (72 m 2 ch). The short Down and long Up platform provide direct access to the 1980 refurbished terminal building and the multi-purpose Sealink ferries sailing to Boulogne, Calais and Ostend. There are berthing, carriage and former freight siding connections off the Harbour line at the junction end and it continues on to the pier as a single line beyond the Harbour station. Motor luggage vans working on the line are limited to hauling 50 tonnes and there are specific regulations governing the use of assisting locomotives required because of the steep gradient.

For town passengers, Folkestone is served by the via Dover portion of Margate trains and the hourly fast trains which reach the town in 77 minutes. In addition to the boat trains, its special workings can include trains for conveying life-saving apparatus along the coastal section to the east 'to deal with an emergency at sea'.

F.15   Ford

Victoria-Portsmouth line, junction for the Littlehampton Branch. 19 m 55 ch from Brighton

Ford was one of the original 1846 stations and increased in importance when the completion of the Mid-Sussex line and the opening of the Littlehampton branch made it an interchange point in 1863. The branch reaches the station via a connection trailing in the Down direction at Ford Junction (19 m 31 ch). Further junctions (Littlehampton Junction on the branch and Arundel Junction on the main line)

complete the triangle and carry the Bognor-Ford-Littlehampton-Victoria, the Portsmouth-Brighton/Victoria and the Littlehampton-Brighton services.

The station comprises Up and Down platforms, linked by subway, with modest brick buildings on the Up side and waiting rooms plus LB&SC canopy on the Down (formerly an island).

A bridge over the Arun, at the junction end of the station, dates from the 1938 electrification when it replaced a drawbridge provided as part of the 1863 re-alignment of the coast line.

F.16   Forest Hill

London Bridge-Windmill Bridge Junction line. 5 m 50 ch from London Bridge

Forest Hill was one of the original London & Croydon stations, opened on June 5 1839 under the name Dartmouth Arms. Now it lies on the four-track route to Windmill Bridge Junction and has platforms to the slow lines served by London Bridge-Sutton and Charing Cross-Caterham/Tattenham Corner trains. The former LB&SC buildings have been superseded by a shelter on the Down side and Clasp ticket office, shelter and derelict brick signal box on the Up.

Typical rural station booking window.

F.17   Frant

Charing Cross-Hastings line, between Tunbridge Wells Central and Roberts-bridge. 36 m 53 ch from Charing Cross

Lying amid delightful wooded country-side, Frant opened with the first part of the Hastings route in 1851 and much of the mock Tudor main building on the Down side is original. The Up side has just a lapped wooden shelter with integral canopy. The low platforms are staggered and served by morning and evening trains only. The goods yard, closed September 3 1962, is now just a coal stacking ground. There is a story that the goods shed was never used because it was built by mistake on land the railway did not own.

Fratton—see Portsmouth

Frimley—see Ascot-Ash Vale Line

Fulwell—see Shepperton Branch

Furzebrook Sidings—see Wareham

G.1   Gatwick Airport

Victoria-Brighton line, between Redhill and Three Bridges. 26 m 47 ch from London Bridge

The first station here was opened in 1891 and called Gatwick Racecourse. Tinsley Green, a new station to serve the airport, opened on September 30 1935 and changed its name to Gatwick Airport on June 1 of the following year. Although closed in favour of the present (and former Racecourse) station on May 28 1958 platform remains can still be seen south of today's airport station and Tinsley Green Junction (27 m 34 ch) is the site of links between each of the four tracks.

Rail-air passengers, already around three million annually, could treble by the next decade and to cater for this Gatwick Airport station has been the subject of extensive reconstruction. The pairs of local and through lines are supplemented at the station by Up and Down Platform Loops and from the three island platforms there are escalator links to a wide range of concourse facilities above the station and on the same level as the BAA terminal. The lines through plat-forms 1, 2 and 3 are reversible, as is the line to platform 6 for terminating trains only.

Special services to Gatwick include those on the Reading line but 85 per cent of the rail-air passengers travel via Victoria which can be reached in 37 minutes. The £720,000 already spent there will be dwarfed by a scheme for a rail-air terminal being built on a raft over plat-forms 9 to 17. Push and pull working using Class 73 locomotives and air conditioned stock is under consideration.

G.2   Gillingham (Dorset)

Waterloo-Exeter line, between Salisbury and Regional Boundary. 105 m 23 ch from Waterloo

Gillingham has a Down Passenger Loop to enable it to function as a passing point on this 1859 route, once part of the LSWR's mainline to the South West but now single and operated under the Token-less Block system.

The main station facilities are on the Up side including the substantial brick build-ings, a coal yard, forecourt weighbridge and the ground frame access to the UKF fertiliser depot. The signal box is on the Down side and controls the passing of the Waterloo-Exeter trains which serve Gillingham. To deal with one early morning originating Up service, Down trains may start back from Gillingham when the signal box is closed.

The 742 yd Gillingham Tunnel (107 m 44 ch to 107 m 78 ch) lies just beyond the 1 in 100 mini-summit at milepost 107½.

G.3   Gillingham (Kent)

Victoria-Ramsgate line, between Chatham and Sittingbourne. 35 m 75 ch from Victoria

When the East Kent Railway opened east-wards from Chatham in 1858 the first stopping point was a country station called New Brompton. Today this is Gill-ingham, a busy commuter station with a basic service of three trains an hour each way on the main line and two more on the North Kent line for which it is an originat-ing/terminating point.

The station is approached via the 897 yd Gillingham Tunnel (35 m 7 ch to 35 m 47 ch) and comprises an Up island platform with faces to the Up Passenger Loop and the reversible Up Main Platform Line and a Down platform which accommodates the modern offices of the Area Manager. Access to the platforms is by stairs from the ticket office at the London end. At the country end an Up side signal box controls the barrier crossing and there are carriage sidings, shed and washer. The old loco shed was here too. Opposite, the line to Chatham Docks leads from the freight siding area. This 57 chain route is worked on the One Train basis and limited to 25 mph.

G.4   Gipsy Hill

Victoria-Beckenham Junction line, between West Norwood Junction and Crystal Palace. 7 m 77 ch from Victoria

This was another of the original stations opened on December 1 1856 on the West End of London & Crystal Palace Railway's line from Wandsworth Common. A gabled ticket office on the Gipsy Hill over-bridge at the country end leads to a bare Down platform and bilious green wooden buildings on the Up. Victoria-Beckenham Junction/West Croydon and London Bridge-Redhill line trains call.

G.5   Gloucester Road Junction

Victoria-Brighton line, junction with London Bridge-Windmill Bridge Junction line. 9 m 60 ch from Victoria

Gloucester Road signal box was commissioned in 1954 to control some 1,200 movements every 24 hours including the Windmill Bridge Junction with the line from London Bridge (mileage change 10 m 1 ch to 9 m 69 ch) and the movements to and from Selhurst Depot and Norwood Yard. Its function ceased with the transfer of the work to the new Brighton Line signalling scheme as part of which the track layout was altered to carry the Victoria local lines and the London Bridge fast lines over all others by means of a new piece of railway.

G.6   Glynde

Victoria-Eastbourne/Hastings line, between Lewes and Willingdon Junction. 11 m 14 ch from Brighton

The station for Glyndebourne, Glynde, lies between the coastal Downland and the inland plain and dates from the opening of the line in 1846 although the attractive, single-storey main buildings on the Down side are probably slightly later than this. The Up side has just a wooden shelter and the two are linked by footbridge.

The approach is via Beddingham AHB LC (10 m 8 ch) and a Down siding, with the AHB crossing at Ripe (13 m 25 ch) following. The hourly Brighton-Eastbourne trains serve Glynde.

G.7   Godalming

Waterloo-Portsmouth line, between Guildford and Haselmere. 34 m 37 ch from Waterloo

The first railway scheme for Godalming was intended to use a system of flangeless wheels kept on their wooden rails by guide wheels but the route became part of the LSW's bid for more direct access to Portsmouth and the line opened to Godalming on October 15 1849 was of conventional construction. A new station was opened, on the present site further south, on January 1 1859 as part of a line from a junction on the original branch, to Havant. The original station continued in use until its passenger function was taken over by Farncombe, the passenger service ending on May 1 1897 but freight continuing until January 6 1969.

Godalming today comprises Up and Down platforms with the main buildings on the Down side and a modern shelter-cum-windbreak on the Up. The former are in the same style as Petersfield with a central station house portion, but are in a form of rubble construction. Portsmouth trains call half-hourly.

G.8   Godstone

Redhill-Tonbridge line, between Redhill and Edenbridge. 28 m 13 ch from Charing Cross

Both route and station date from 1842. The latter, which follows the 1,327 yd Bletchingley Tunnel (26 m 25 ch to 27 m 5 ch), comprises staggered platforms with crossovers, overgrown Down siding, bridge over the A22 and Up side wooden signal box. The Tonbridge-Reading line dmus provide an hourly service in each direction.

G.9   Gomshall

Redhill-Reading line, between Dorking Town and Guildford. 35 m 21 ch from Charing Cross

Tonbridge-Reading dmus serve this minimum facilities station, opened on August 20 1849 and lying in a beautiful setting below the 700 ft Hackhurst Downs. This whole section of line runs along the foot of the North Downs, via the site of Westcott Rifle Range Halt closed in 1928, through the staggered platforms of Gomshall station and on past Burrows Lane AHB LC (35 m 60 ch) and Brook AHB LC (37 m 19 ch). The summit of the route, with gradients of 1 in 96 either side, lies about a mile before the station and provides a clear view of Leith Hill, the highest point in Surrey. The station still retains its old brick signal box building.

G.10   Goring-by-Sea

Brighton-Littlehampton/Portsmouth line, between Worthing and Arundel Junction. 13 m 7 ch from Brighton

The 1846 station lies on the A259 about a mile from the coast and comprises Up and Down platforms with traditional signal box and crossing at the country end. The single-storey brick buildings on the Up side are almost overwhelmed by the canopy; on the Down side there is only a shelter and cycle shed. The train service is the same as that at Angmering.

G.11   Grateley

Waterloo-Exeter line, between Andover and Salisbury. 72 m 49 ch from Waterloo

Dating from the opening of this section on May 1 1857, Grateley is now an unstaffed station served by the Waterloo-Salisbury trains. The Down platform can accommodate seven cars but is lit and maintained only for four; the Up is only long enough for four. Both sides have shelters.

Immediately west of Grateley there is evidence of the trackbed of the route that ran beside the Up line and then headed on to Salisbury Plain via Newton Tony Junction and Amesbury to Bulford and a link with the military camp there. The line was opened in stages as a light railway between 1901 and 1906 and continued at work until 1963. The separate line from the junction to Grateley and a burrowing junction (Amesbury Junction) towards Salisbury date from 1904. Pre-war seven trains each way ran between Salisbury and Bulford on weekdays and included a call at Porton (closed September 9 1968) on

the main line. Porton is still discernible on the descent to Laverstock and still furnished with SR 'Catch Point' notices.

Gravesend—see North Kent Line

Greenhithe—see North Kent Line

G.12   Greenwich Line

North Kent East Junction to Charlton Junction. 3 m 12 ch

The London end of this route was opened as a line between Spa Road and Deptford by the pioneer London & Greenwich Railway on February 8 1836, the line being extended to London Bridge from December 14 1836 and to a temporary station at Greenwich on December 24 1838 with a permanent station being provided there two years later. The existence of Greenwich Observatory and the attitude of the Admiralty precluded extension eastward and the next part of the route to be opened was the Charlton-Maze Hill section (1873) with the final Greenwich-Maze Hill gap not being closed until 1878.

The route leaves the main line at North Kent East Junction (4 m 25 ch from London Bridge) and the two tracks then run on arches, through the 40 mph restriction applying to the staggered platforms above the High Street at Deptford (4 m 76 ch) and on to the wide 20 mph curve at Greenwich (5 m 36 ch) where the spacious 1878 buildings of the third Greenwich station are at the street level below. The 450 yd Greenwich College Tunnel (5 m 65 ch to 6 m 5 ch) lies on the modest rise which takes the route under the National

The D70-type of station at Maze Hill includes this new design of access barrier.

Maritime Museum to Maze Hill (6 m 27 ch).

When the 1873 station at Maze Hill was burnt down 98 years later it was replaced by one incorporating a completely new idea in ticket control derived from pilot studies at Meopham and an extensive dialogue between traffic staff and SR architects. Using modern materials a new Up side building was constructed at Maze Hill known as the 'D70' type and now being used elsewhere on the region. Within the ticket office and waiting room complex double gates are provided, electrically-operated by push button from the ticket office and during the off-peak periods, when the access/exit point is not manned, these are used to admit passengers after ticket purchase or release them after ticket surrender.

From Maze Hill, signed as the station for the National Maritime Museum, the route continues to Westcombe Park (6 m 76 ch) with its typical SER turn-of-the-century buildings on the Up side, and then to the junction (7 m 37 ch) with the North Kent Line just before Charlton station.

The basic service consists of trains every 20 minutes to Cannon Street and Dartford.

G.13   Groombridge

Tunbridge Wells Central-Eridge line. 46 m 46 ch from London Bridge *

Groombridge dates from the opening of the East Grinstead, Groombridge & Tunbridge Wells Railway's line on October 1 1866 and its mileposts still reflect this and its former pattern of services via East Grinstead. The more recent hourly Tonbridge-Eridge service is under threat of withdrawal from the two-platform station which has its ticket office and waiting area on the Up side, with just a waiting room on the Down.

Above *Groombridge station box, an old LB&SC design which once had signal posts at the corners!*

Below *Groombridge Junction signal box. Groombridge station used to be a busy interchange point.*

G.14   Grove Park

Charing Cross-Dover line, between Hither Green and Chislehurst. 8 m 78 ch from Charing Cross

Grove Park station was opened by the SER on November 1 1871, six years after the opening of the line and seven years before the branch to Bromley North was added. The four tracks on this section are grouped with the fast pair on the south side and the station is preceded by fast and slow facing crossovers and trailing links between the Down Fast and Up Slow.

From the brick and wood ticket office complex on Baring Road overbridge stairs

lead down to Grove Park's two island platform and to the separate No 1 Platform from which the branch shuttle normally works (although there is also a connection from the Down Fast). A footbridge links all three platforms and there is a link between the two lines of the branch and between the Down Fast/Up Slow/Down Slow at this country end of the junction station. The Chislehurst Tunnels follow, while at the London end Grove Park Sheds are part of the Hither Green complex.

Cannon Street/Charing Cross-Orpington and Charing Cross-Sevenoaks trains, all with a branch connection, give Grove Park a basic service of three trains an hour in each direction.

A view of Guildford from the London end. Note the very long footbridge.

G.15 Guildford

Waterloo-Portsmouth line, junction with Redhill-Reading line. 30 m 27 ch from Waterloo

Guildford has routes radiating to Waterloo (via Woking and via Effingham Junction), to Redhill/Gatwick Airport/Tonbridge, to Portsmouth, to Aldershot/Ascot and to Reading, and provides extensive interchange facilities between them. The station lies on the west side of

The Guildford panel box in 1966.

the town with the junction of the lines to Ash, Woking and Effingham Junction to the north and Shalford Junction, where the Redhill and Portsmouth lines separate, following (at 31 m 24 ch) the 845 yd Chalk Tunnel (30 m 43 ch to 31 m 1 ch) and the 132 yd St Catherine's Tunnel (31 m 13 ch to 31 m 19 ch).

The station dates from a reconstruction in the 1880s and presents a better appearance to the world than it does internally. The substantial main buildings are on the Down side platform adjoining the Down Main line. There is a bay at the London end of this for the New Guildford Line trains and then three island platforms linked by footbridge and subway, the former providing a long exit connection to the developments west of the town centre. The Up Main line uses platform 4 and three UPLs and two DPLs use the other platform faces, all platform lines being authorised for station yard

working and all but No 2 being reversible. Station car park, forecourt information office, bookstall and buffets complete the facilities.

Surrounding the platform area there is a freight and engineers' yard on the Down side, with the old goods shed standing immediately opposite the passenger station (and a good example of its kind) and a former 'Wholesale Corn Merchants' warehouse nearby. On the opposite side are carriage sidings and, nearer the junction, the Guildford panel box. Brought into operation in April 1966, this controls 50 miles of track from Worplesden to the north to Farncombe to the south and to Shalford, Aldershot Junction/North Camp and Effingham Junction on the other routes.

The first railway to reach Guildford was the Guildford Junction company's single, soon to become double, track from Woking. Its first train left Guildford at 7.30 am on May 5 1845 to complete the journey in 12 minutes. Despite the hour free beer was issued to the workmen who had built the line. Four years later came the link to Farnham and this was extended

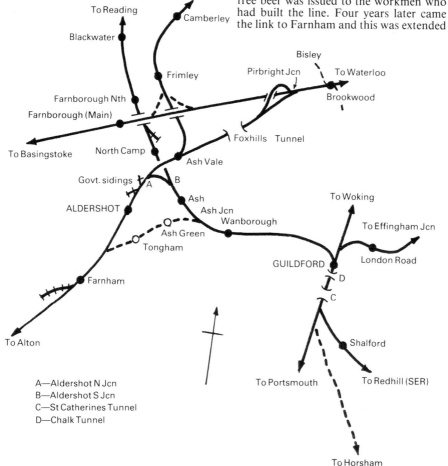

A—Aldershot N Jcn
B—Aldershot S Jcn
C—St Catherines Tunnel
D—Chalk Tunnel

in 1852 to become the Alton line. Other events of 1849 were the opening to Godalming and from Shalford Junction to Dorking, the former destined to become part of a new main line to Portsmouth ten years later and the latter completing the South Eastern's probe west to Reading. Guildford's status as a railway junction increased further when the LB&SC route from Horsham arrived in 1865 and when the New Guildford line opened on February 2 1885. The other major event in Guildford's railway history was proclaimed by the Town Crier on July 9 1925 when the new electric service was announced in historic fashion.

London Road station (28 m 47 ch from Waterloo) lies over on the other side of town, adjacent to the A3 from which it takes its name. It is in typical New Guildford Line pattern, similar to Claygate and with the main buildings on the Down side. The Up side differs in having a bookstall and a repeating signal to cope with the curve on which the station is situated. The route round the town to Guildford box and the junction (29 m 70 ch) is largely elevated with one of the high bridges effecting the crossing of the River Wey.

The services on all the routes stop at Guildford and they include the Waterloo-Portsmouth buffet car services and the Manchester-Portsmouth trains.

H.1   Hackbridge

South Bermondsey Junction-Leatherhead line, between Mitcham Junction and Sutton. 11 m 41 ch from London Bridge

The main station buildings are on the Up side, similar to those at Mitcham Junction and in the LB&SC style of the opening period—October 1 1868. They comprise a gabled two-storey house, ticket office section and single-storey, gabled end section. The Down side has a substantial and attractive brick shelter, again to a traditional design. The London Bridge-Sutton loop services call in addition to those to Horsham and Effingham Junction.

H.2   Halling

Strood-Maidstone West-Paddock Wood line, between Strood and Aylesford. 35 m 18 ch from Charing Cross

Halling opened 34 years after the line itself, which dates from June 18 1856. Served by the half-hourly Strood-Maidstone West/Paddock Wood trains, the station comprises Up and Down plat-

forms with plain, single-storey brick buildings on the former and just a tiny wooden shelter on the latter. Preceding the station is the Down line connection, released by Cuxton, giving access to the extensive Rugby Portland Cement Company's works where internal shunting is done by the firm's own power.

H.3   Hamble

Southampton-Portsmouth line, between St Denys and Fareham. 7 m 19 ch from Southampton

Although the link between Netley and Fareham was completed in 1889, Hamble itself dates only from 1942 when passenger facilities were added to the Hamble Road Siding. The two platforms are linked by footbridge and have only simple building block shelters. The station is unstaffed and open only on weekdays when the Salisbury/Romsey-Portsmouth trains call. The connection from the BP oil terminal trails into the Up line on the Southampton side of the location.

H.4   Hampden Park

Victoria-Eastbourne/Hastings line, on the approach to Eastbourne. 21 m 75 ch from Brighton

Hampden Park was called Willingdon when it opened on New Year's Day 1888. By that time the line into Eastbourne from the 1846 Brighton-St Leonards route had been open 39 years and the link from Willingdon Junction (21 m 38 ch) to Stone Cross Junction to complete the inverted triangle since 1871. Lying at the apex of this, along the flat route taken by the railway around Willingdon Hill, Hampden Park has two platforms with a ticket office on each and a Down side signal box controlling semaphore signals, the junction and a double barrier crossing. There is a refuge siding and dock at the country end of the station.

Hampden Park has some morning and evening London trains but the basic service is provided by the all-stations Brighton-Eastbourne-Ore workings.

Hampton—see Shepperton Branch

H.5   Hampton Court Branch

Waterloo-Weymouth line, branch from Hampton Court Junction. 1 m 49 ch

It is a far cry from the horse traction used after opening on February 1 1849 to the Class 508 sets which now work between

1971 signal box and relay room at Hampton Court.

Waterloo and this short double line branch to the south bank of the Thames near Hampton Court Palace. The basic service is half-hourly with a journey time of 30 minutes to the intermediate station at Thames Ditton (14 m 1 ch) and 34 minutes to Hampton Court, at one time advertised as the station 'For East and West Molesey (1½ miles)'.

From Hampton Court Junction (13 m 27 ch), which has 30 mph speed limitations to and from the branch, the Down line passes over the main route by means of a skew bridge and two sets of brick arches, and then joins the Up to head north to Thames Ditton. Raised above street level, the station here has its main brick buildings on the Up side, complete with tiny ticket office window.

A double barrier crossing, CCTV-controlled (14 m 51 ch), precedes the bridge over the River Ember and arrival at the terminal (14 m 76 ch) where the former Down platform has been abandoned in favour of using the two faces of the Up. The station buildings, in semi-Jacobean style, continue the line of the platforms and present an ornate face to the street with decorated windows, doors and corners and extravagant gable ends.

The line speeds for the branch are 40 mph on the Up line and 45 mph on the Down. It is controlled from Surbiton box, train guards giving the 'Train Ready to Start' signal from Hampton Court.

H.6 Hampton Wick

New Malden-Twickenham line, between Kingston and Teddington. 12 m 44 ch from Waterloo

The first Hampton Wick was opened by the LSW on July 1 1863 but the present station dates from a 1969 reconstruction and is raised above the street level ticket office to prepare for the route's crossing of the Thames. Kingston loop and Shepperton branch trains serve Hampton Wick to give the station a total of eight trains an hour.

Ham Street—see Ashford-Hastings Line

H.7 Hamworthy

Waterloo-Weymouth line, between Poole and Wareham. 115 m 77 ch from Waterloo

The opening of the Southampton & Dorchester line on June 1 1847 produced the present Hamworthy location (then Poole Junction) and a station, then called Poole, at the end of the present line to the freight and coal depot lying on the western side of the narrow entrance to Holes Bay. The line across the causeway to Poole proper dates from June 1 1893 and now forms part of the main line from Waterloo, the old 'Poole' branch closing to passengers three years later.

Hamworthy station's two platforms are linked by a subway and the small, red brick, main buildings are on the Up side. The outer face of the Down island platform is fenced off and the DPL is not used for picking up or setting down. The signal box, of wood on a brick base, is on this platform beyond which the goods depot line curves off seawards. The latter, single and worked on the No Signalman Key Token basis, is 2 m 8 ch long. In the opposite direction the trackbed of the original main line to Broadstone Junction is still visible at the London end of the Up platform. Westwards towards Wareham lies the bridge which carries the line over the entrance to Lychett Bay.

The hourly push-pull Weymouth portions link Hamworthy with Bournemouth and Waterloo.

H.8   Harrietsham

Victoria-Ramsgate line, between Maid-stone East and Ashford. 47 m 36 ch from Victoria

The hourly Ramsgate trains call at Harriet-sham which comprises Up and Down platforms, with main buildings on the former in the solid 1884 LC&D style and just a brick shelter with canopy on the latter. In the old goods yard, closed in 1961, a traditional goods shed remains and is now used by a builders merchant.

H.9   Haslemere

Waterloo-Portsmouth line, between Shal-ford Junction and Petersfield. 42 m 79 ch from Waterloo

The station was opened with the line in 1859 and now comprises Down, and Up island platforms, the former accommo-dating the signal box and long station buildings block and the latter an Up Passenger Loop at its outer face. Over three miles of 1 in 80 rising gradient precede Haslemere in the Down direction but this once formidable challenge to LSW steam power does not trouble the three hourly Portsmouth trains which now provide the station's Down service.

H.10   Hassocks

Victoria-Brighton line, between Keymer Junction and Brighton. 43 m 42 ch from London Bridge

Hassocks stands below the lofty South Downs on the LB&SC main line's final climb to conquer the heights by means of Clayton Tunnel. Opened as Hassocks Gate on September 21 1841, it was for many years the station used by excursions to the Downs and its platforms were widened for this purpose. The Up side

today has fairly modern Clasp-type buildings and there is a second ticket office in the long, shelter-type structure on the Down side. The old wooden signal box stands at the country end of the platform on this side and the former goods shed and an engineers' siding lie on the Up side.

The station is served by the Victoria/London Bridge semi-fasts.

H.11   Hastings

Charing Cross-Hastings line. 62 m 33 ch from Charing Cross

The Victoria via Eastbourne and Brighton-Hastings routes approach this noted Sussex resort along the coast via St Leonards West Marina (32 m 56 ch from Brighton). They join the later route via Tunbridge Wells at Bopeep Junction which follows the station at West St Leonards (60 m 59 ch from Charing Cross) and marks a mileage change from 32 m 76 ch to 60 m 69 ch. After the junction comes the 1,318 yd Bopeep Tunnel (60 m 71 ch to 61 m 51 ch) and then St Leonards Warrior Square station (61 m 55 ch). The 788 yd Hastings Tunnel (61 m 59 ch to 62 m 15 ch) precedes Hastings station where the mileage again changes from 62 m 33 ch to 82 m 34 ch which represents the distance from Charing Cross via Ash-ford. The 230 yd Mount Pleasant Tunnel (81 m 60 ch to 81 m 50 ch) then takes the west-east progression to Ore (81 m 42 ch).

The LB&SC and SER companies came into hot conflict in their desire to secure the Hastings business. The former reached the area by means of the Brighton,

West St Leonards looking towards Bopeep Junction and Bopeep Tunnel.

Lewes & Hastings company's 1846 route to Bulverhythe/West Marina and the latter by the line from Ashford to Bopeep Junction which became the scene of a direct confrontation on the chosen opening day, February 13 1851. Obstructive tactics by the SER prevented the Brighton trains using the section from the junction to Hastings until the following day, a Saturday, and after the weekend matters got even worse. The SER blocked the LB&SC stock in at Hastings, removed track at Bopeep and even put barriers in the way of the coach link organised by the latter. But all the fun ended with an LB&SC injunction against the SER and normal working duly commenced, the link from Tonbridge reaching Bopeep in the following year.

These days the station that all the fuss was about is a modest enough affair (rebuilt 1931) of two island platforms and a footbridge to the typical SR corner complex of ticket hall, ticket office and period buffet. From here the six-car Class 201 dmu sets provide an hourly link to and from Charing Cross, basic hourly services also operating on the route to Ashford and from Ore to Brighton and Victoria. St Leonards Warrior Square is situated at the eastern end of Bopeep Tunnel and has a substantial block of original buildings, in red brick, on the Up side and a modern shelter on the Down. West St Leonards is on the sharp 20 mph curve from Bopeep and reached from a brick ticket office above the station, while St Leonards West Marina now comprises carriage washing, shed, fuelling and berthing facilities where the station which replaced the original LB&SC Bulverhythe was itself replaced in 1882 and then finally closed in 1967. The signal box in the V of Bopeep Junction controls the junction and its approaches

while the box at Hastings controls the working on the main lines and UPL and DPL there plus access to Park Sidings, Brighton Siding and the line eastwards.

The constraints of space and the three tunnels at Hastings make it less than easy to work. Bopeep Tunnel was cut through something of a geographical phenomenon, a variable series of clays, silts and sands in widely differing degrees of compactness. It is lined throughout with brickwork in the form of an elliptical arch nearly 3 ft thick.

H.12   Havant

Waterloo-Portsmouth line, junction with route from Brighton. 37 m 41 ch from Brighton

Serving both this Hampshire town and, since the closure of its branch on November 4 1963, the residential and holiday population of Hayling Island, Havant, is a substantial station with platforms served by Up and Down loops, extensive single-storey buildings on the Down side and waiting rooms on the Up. The original station was opened when the LB&SC reached Havant from Chichester on March 15 1847, but it was resited in 1863 and then rebuilt during the Southern era. There is a double barrier crossing between the station and the junction of the Guildford and Brighton lines where there is a large brick signal box on the Down side and the Brighton distance of 37 m 24 ch takes over from the Waterloo distance of 66 m 18 ch. The two routes give Havant a basic service of six trains

An attractive view of the now-closed Hayling Island branch with a train on Langstone Bridge.

per hour in each direction with one or two originating and terminating services.

Havant was the scene of a nasty wrangle between the LSW and LB&SC companies starting on December 28 1858 when the former, as lessees of the new route to Portsmouth, tried to enforce their right of passage over the Brighton metals west of the junction. There were skirmishes between the staff of the two companies and a horse bus service had to be used by LSW passengers until the matter was resolved at law, with trains then running freely from January 24 1859.

Opened on July 16 1867, the Hayling Island branch just failed to reach its century. It was leased to the LB&SC from the end of 1881 and at one time had a service of 17 trains each way over the 4½-mile route. Despite the scheme for a link with Southsea and more recent preservation proposals, the 'Hayling Billy' is now just a memory. The piers of the former railway bridge to the island and the terminal goods shed at West Town were still visible in 1983.

Bedhampton (38 m 14 ch) is a 1906 station on the 1847 joint line on towards Farlington Junction (40 m 38 ch). It has a CCTV crossing with a large finial atop the former crossing box and is served by Guildford and Brighton line slows.

H.13   Haydons Road

Streatham South Junction-Wimbledon line. 2 m 18 ch from Streatham South Junction

Once Haydens Lane, this joint LSW/LB&SC (Tooting, Merton & Wimbledon Railway) station opened on October 1 1868. It now comprises Up and Down platforms with wooden buildings and a canopy on each plus a small ticket office on the Up side. The line is controlled by Victoria panel and served by the half-hourly London Bridge-Wimbledon/Sutton-London Bridge trains.

H.14   Hayes (Kent)

Lewisham-Hayes line. 14 m 32 ch from Charing Cross

The original West Wickham & Hayes Railway was sold to the SER prior to the opening of the branch from Elmers End on May 29 1882. Today Hayes station has lost its goods yard (closed April 19 1965), signal box and engine turntable and consists simply of a single platform, two platform lines, and a carriage siding on the Down side (once the engine release

line). The station buildings at the top of the slope beyond are typical of the SR's smaller reconstruction schemes (rebuilt again after wartime bombing) with shops either side of the entrance and panelled display cases beside the ticket office window. The basic service provides a train every 20 minutes to and from Charing Cross/Cannon Street.

H.15   Haywards Heath

Victoria-Brighton line, between Three Bridges and Keymer Junction. 37 m 59 ch from London Bridge

From July 12 to September 21 1841 Haywards Heath was the southern terminus of the London & Brighton Railway, passengers for and from the weekday service of four daily trains bridging the gap to Brighton by coach. Since those days Haywards Heath has grown to a sizeable township with a busy station served by the Eastbourne and Brighton line trains and comprising two island platforms providing faces to the Up and Down through lines and to the outer local lines from Copyhold Junction (37 m). At street level on the Up side are the station buildings including ticket office, travel centre and bookstall, all dating from the 1932 reconstruction.

From September 3 1883 to October 28 1963 there was a link from Horsted Keynes to Copyhold Junction and a remnant of this survives as a 70 ch freight-only single line, worked on the One Train basis and subject to a 25 mph speed limitation, to Ardingly and the ARC stone terminal there. South of Haywards Heath is the 249 yd Haywards Heath Tunnel (38 m 5 ch to 38 m 17 ch), brick-lined and with stone-topped brick portals.

H.16   Headcorn

Charing Cross-Dover line, between Paddock Wood and Ashford. 45 m 20 ch from Charing Cross

The original SER main line reached Headcorn on August 31 1842 and pushed on to Ashford on December 1 of that year. There were subsequent proposals for a line from Headcorn to Hastings but it had to wait until 1905 to become a junction, and then only a modest one with the Kent & East Sussex Railway. The Headcorn-Tenterden section of the latter was closed on January 4 1954 and trees have almost overgrown the evidence of its trackbed at Headcorn.

Today Headcorn comprises Up and

Kent & East Sussex platform at Headcorn, not exactly a hive of industry.

Down platforms served by loops which were added to the two main lines in 1924. The main, timber buildings are on the Down side and the service is provided by the hourly Charing Cross-Ashford trains.

H.17 Herne Bay

Victoria-Ramsgate line, between Whitstable and Margate. 62 m 58 ch from Victoria

The Herne Bay & Faversham Railway, renamed the Margate Railway, opened its line on July 13 1861 despite SER opposition. Then, as the Kent Coast Railway, the route was extended eastwards on October 5 1863 and duly became part of the LC&D Thanet main line. Today the station comprises a Down platform with red brick main buildings (including a buffet in the booking hall) and connected by subway to the Up platform which was

formerly an island. The old goods shed, with its steeply pitched roof, is still there.

Herne Bay enjoys the same service to and from Victoria as Margate and has a regular commuter business in addition to its summer traffic.

H.18 Herne Hill

Victoria-Ramsgate line, between Brixton Junction and Beckenham Junction. 3 m 76 ch from Victoria

Herne Hill station opened on August 25 1862 as part of the LC&D's direct access to Stewarts Lane (for Victoria), the City line north as far as Elephant & Castle following on October 6 of the same year. Today's station still has the original, substantial brick buildings with raised end and rear sections and typical LC&D window arch decoration. Stairs then lead up to more modern buildings on the two island platforms which provide faces to

An early view of Herne Hill.

the main lines and the Up and Down passenger loops and interchange between the Holborn Viaduct-West Croydon and Victoria-Orpington trains.

For many years the name Herne Hill was well known for its sorting sidings and the station also divided/joined Victoria and City train portions.

The route from Holborn Viaduct via Loughborough Junction joins that from Victoria via Brixton at Herne Hill North Junction (4 m 31 ch/3 m 71 ch) and the link to Tulse Hill departs at South Junction. Now displaced by the Victoria panel, the former Herne Hill signal box precedes the station on the Up side.

H.19   Hersham

Waterloo-Weymouth line, between Surbiton and Weybridge. 15 m 73 ch from Waterloo

A 1936 station on the four-track embankment section, with outer platforms to the slow lines and a basic half-hourly service to Waterloo and Guildford/Portsmouth.

Hever—see Uckfield Branch

Higham—see North Kent Line

H.20   High Brooms

Charing Cross-Hastings line, between Tonbridge and Tunbridge Wells Central. 32 m 70 ch from Charing Cross

Opened in 1893 as Southborough, High Brooms acquired its present name in 1925. It lies on the 5-mile climb from Tonbridge and serves a growing suburb of Tunbridge Wells by means of the hourly Hastings and Eridge services. The station itself comprises Up and Down platforms with the original single-storey main buildings, gabled over the ticket office entrance, on the Up side. On this side at the London end there is a trailing connection, controlled by ground frame, from the Shell/Cory oil terminal which is fed from the Isle of Grain. Further on is Southborough Viaduct and a winding section of the route restricted to 40 mph between milepost 31¼ and milepost 32½.

H.21   Hildenborough

Charing Cross-Dover line, between Sevenoaks and Tonbridge. 27 m 2 ch from Charing Cross

The station, opened on May 1 1868, has Up and Down platforms, linked by a footbridge, which were lengthened as part of the Kent Coast electrification scheme. There are lapped wooden main buildings on the Up side and the service is derived from the hourly Charing Cross-Ashford trains. An SER milepost stands on the Down platform and the 6-mile 1 in 122/144 bank from Tonbridge up to Sevenoaks takes its name from the station.

Hilsea—see Portsmouth

H.22   Hinchley Wood

New Guildford Line, between Hampton Court Junction and Effingham Junction. 14 m 4 ch from Waterloo

Although the New Guildford Line dates from 1885, Hinchley Wood did not come into existence until 1930. It is now the first station after leaving the main line and stands in the vee where the Down line from Hampton Court Junction (13 m 27 ch) meets the Up line before it begins a wide arc under the main line to join it on the Up side. The station platforms are shaped to reflect the diverging lines and there is a shelter plus small ticket office near the stairs to the footbridge at the country end. The service is half-hourly between Waterloo and Guildford.

H.23   Hinton Admiral

Waterloo-Weymouth line, between Brockenhurst and Christchurch. 101 m 5 ch from Waterloo

Served by the Waterloo-Bournemouth all-stations trains, Hinton Admiral lies 1½ miles inland from Christchurch Bay and consists of Up and Down platforms with 1888 main brick buildings, typical of the Sway cut-off route, on the Up side. There is a sizeable wooden shelter on the Down platform and the former goods shed lies behind.

H.24   Hither Green

Charing Cross-Dover line, junction with Dartford Loop Line. 7 m 16 ch from Charing Cross

Despite the junction status of Hither Green passenger station, opened by the South Eastern on June 1 1895, Hither Green is better known for the marshalling yard which was opened four years later and given a link from the Dartford Loop via the Lee Spur. For years the yard, which lies on the Down side of the main line between the station and Grove Park Electric Carriage Sheds, transferred freight to and from the other London yards as part of the process of serving South-East London and the industry and agriculture of Kent. This activity has diminished and changed in recent years as BR's wagonload activity has been replaced by the Speedlink facility but Hither Green got a new function on October 10 1960 when the new Continental traffic depot was opened on the Up side.

Hither Green station follows Parks Bridge Junction and consists of a platform in the vee of the junction, a Down platform for the loop and two more platforms for the fast and Up Slow lines. Lee Spur Junction follows the connection to the Down Yard, is situated at 7 m 44 ch and furnishes a link to the permanent way depot. The Continental Depot complex lies on the Up side, behind the overgrown freight sidings of the Up yard.

Hither Green is served by Orpington and Sevenoaks trains on the main line and by Dartford and Gravesend trains on the Loop.

H.25 Holborn Viaduct

Nearly 200 trains carry more than 22,000 passengers into and out of Holborn Viaduct station every weekday. Not bad for a station described by an eminent writer more than 80 years ago as 'having an ephemeral existence'. None the less, what has been called more accurately 'the Southern's mini terminal' is something of an oddity. It is very close to Blackfriars and was built mostly as a result of a £100,000 deal with the Post Office over telegraphs.

The station opened on March 2 1874 on

Once the latest thing in electric signalling this miniature lever frame has, in turn, become outmoded by the modern panel.

a new street which gave the station its name and with the main object of relieving congestion on the two island platforms at Ludgate Hill on the adjacent line through to Farringdon. Despite the fact that it had only four short platforms, able to accommodate only the half trains which resulted from the splitting of City and West End portions at Herne Hill, within three years Holborn Viaduct had acquired the inevitable hotel across its frontage. This survived to be requisitioned in the First World War, became the offices of a telegraph company between the wars and then be gutted by the great fire bomb raid on the City of London in May 1941.

The 'split' main line services made up most of Holborn's traffic for many years and even included the City portion of boat trains—to Calais and Ostend via Dover and to Flushing via Queenborough. Electric services to Shortlands and Orpington began using the station in 1925 and the Gillingham trains 14 years later, Holborn Viaduct becoming the first SR terminal to bid a complete farewell to steam passenger services.

The old LC&D station was the subject of complete rebuilding between 1960 and 1963. The scheme included a ten-storey office block and, at street level, a low-ceilinged concourse with ticket office and buffet-cum-waiting room. The front of the station is finished in Portland stone and through the plate glass doors passers by can see the trains, something of a novelty for London stations these days. The administrative offices and train crew accommodation are located above the concourse. Control of the three-platform terminus is from the Victoria panel and the train service is the same as that at Blackfriars. Ludgate Siding provides stabling for eight cars on the Up side approaches.

Prior to rebuilding a flight of stairs led down to the subterranean Snow Hill station, renamed Holborn Viaduct Low Level in 1912 and closed in 1916. From Ludgate Hill, the line to Farringdon Street in 1866 had been followed by the 'Smithfield Loop' to Aldersgate Street in 1871, allowing LC&D trains to run via Snow Hill Junction to Moorgate Street. The junction area later became Snow Hill Sidings where LSW Ludgate Hill terminating services were reversed and through vehicles for the Midland, Great Northern and via the Tottenham & Hampstead Joint line were exchanged. Now Snow Hill is just a basement garage.

H.26   Hollingbourne

Victoria-Ramsgate line, between Maidstone East and Ashford. 45 m 2 ch from Victoria

Station and line opened in 1884 and Hollingbourne today is much like its neighbours in both its Up side main buildings and the Down side brick shelter plus canopy. The small wood on brick signal box is on the Down side and when switched in controls three conventional semaphore signals on each line plus a repeater on the Down platform. The hourly Ramsgate trains call.

Holmwood—see Dorking-Horsham Line

H.27   Holton Heath

Waterloo-Weymouth line, between Poole and Wareham. 118 m 61 ch from Waterloo

Holton Heath, opened with the line in 1847, lies between the marshy edge of the Wareham Channel and the A35 road. Its former role was to serve the Admiralty depot on the Up side but the extensive sidings (with access at each end) are now rusty, the signal box closed and the station in a run down condition. Trains call only in the morning and evening.

H.28   Honor Oak Park

London Bridge-Windmill Bridge Junction. 4 m 59 ch from London Bridge

Although this London & Croydon route originated in 1839, Honor Oak Park was not opened by the LB&SC until April 1 1886. It lies on the four-track main line, its outer slow line platforms are reached by stairs from the overbridge ticket office and the service is provided by the London Bridge-Sutton trains.

H.29   Hoo Junction-Grain Line

Branch from North Kent Line. 11 m 3 ch

The single, freight-only line which leaves the North Kent Line at Hoo Junction (27 m 19 ch) began life as the Hundred of Hoo Railway, promoted by the independent company, but taken over by the SER before opening in 1882 and extended to Port Victoria, on the banks of the Medway. With intermediate stations at Cliffe and Sharnal Street (plus six halts) the route was intended to rival the LC&D's port at Queenborough on the Isle of Sheppey, to which there was a ferry connection from the deep water pier built at Port Victoria. Despite the shorter route from London the concept never lived up to the original ambitions, the ferry service being withdrawn in 1901 and the pier gradually falling into disuse.

More ambitions, this time to stimulate a resort to rival the attractions of Southend, led the Southern to become involved in a scheme of development at Allhallows and to build a line from Stoke Junction, 2¾ miles before Port Victoria, to Allhallows-on-sea which was brought into use on May 16 1932. By 1938 the 1¾-mile branch had 11 daily trains to and from Gravesend Central compared with two to Port Victoria but neither route was exactly thriving and the passenger services were finally withdrawn from the latter on June 11 1951 and from Allhallows plus the Hoo Junction-Grain section on December 4 1961.

The original railway installation at Port Victoria became swallowed up in the BP oil refinery complex at Grain and oil traffic has become the mainstay of the surviving railway. Other traffic includes sea-dredged aggregates from the Cliffe private sidings of Brett (Marine Aggregates) Ltd. At Hoo Junction there is an engineers' ballast siding on the Down side and on the Up, reception sidings used by Smeeth Metals and for the assembly of defective wagons. The location has a TOPS office and marshals freight for the Dover, Tonbridge and Maidstone lines.

On the approach to Hoo Junction the Down staff halt platform (27 m 7 ch) stands opposite the ground frame controlling the London end of the Up sidings. It is followed by crossovers at the junction proper (27 m 19 ch) and an Up side trailing link from the yard reception and sorting sidings. Hoo Junction Staff Halt's Up platform (27 m 26 ch) is nearby with the Up line connection to the yard, a further crossover and a Down siding beyond.

On the Grain branch proper the TCB working as far as signal D.12, including the sidings and Cliffe spur, is controlled from Dartford panel. From the signal (28 m 61 ch) No Signalman Key Token Working comes into force based on auxiliary instruments there and at Grain. Cliffe station (29 m 73 ch) is followed by Sharnal Street (33 m 19 ch) and the old Whitehall Siding of Berry Wiggins at Beluncle (34 m 25 ch). After Stoke Junction (37 m 9 ch) and the trackbed of the Allhallows branch come flood gates, the Kent Refinery Siding, Grain Crossing (38 m 22 ch) and then the remains of Grain station and the exchange sidings (38 m 34 ch). BR chargemen deal with the trains from Grain and Yantlett Sidings. There are AOCL crossings at Wybourne (32 m 6 ch) and Stoke (36 m 77 ch) and a maximum line speed of 40 mph applies.

H.30   Hook

Waterloo-Weymouth line, between Farnborough and Basingstoke. 42 m 13 ch from Waterloo

Hook was given a station on July 2 1883. It now consists of a platform plus shelter for the Down Slow line and a platform with simplified brick ticket office buildings for the Up Slow. The Basingstoke trains and the Bournemouth slows call.

H.31   Horley

Victoria-Brighton line, between Redhill and Three Bridges. 25 m 60 ch from London Bridge

Horley was of no great significance until the coming of the railway. Indeed, its 1841 station seems to have had no road to serve it. Remodelled and moved slightly south with the 1905 line widening, Horley now has its single-storey brick ticket office buildings on the overbridge with stairs then leading down to the combination of centre island plus two outer platforms. The Horsham and Bognor Regis trains call.

H.32   Horsham

Victoria-Portsmouth line, junction with route via Leatherhead. 37 m 56 ch from London Bridge

On the main line from Three Bridges, Horsham is preceded by Parsonage Road AHB LC (37 m 14 ch) and on the Leatherhead line by a change of mileage from

35 m 38 ch to 37 m 43 ch. The former route dates from February 14 1848 and was followed by the link to Petworth on October 10 1859. Two years later, on September 16, Horsham got its first link with the coast via Itchingfield Junction and Shoreham, the completion of the gap between Hardham Junction and Arundel Junction to create the new Mid-Sussex route to Portsmouth not coming until August 3 1863. Even then the line to Guildford was to be opened (on October 2 1865) before the Mid-Sussex section north to Dorking was ready on May 1 1868.

With the closure of the Guildford line from Peasmarsh Junction to Stammerham Junction on June 14 1965 and of that from Itchingfield Junction to Shoreham on March 7 1966 Horsham became less of an interchange point and more concerned with its own originating traffic. This is catered for by Victoria-Bognor/Portsmouth and Victoria-Horsham workings using the station's two island platforms created by the existence of Up and Down Passenger Loops in addition to the main lines. The platforms are linked by footbridge to the separate SR station buildings on the Up side, the whole station dating from the rebuilding prior to the 1938 electrification.

The Horsham freight and coal yard, which includes accommodation for Chipman Chemicals and UKF, stands west of the junction with a Cory depot opposite. There are further sidings beyond the Down platform and a single carriage siding either side of the main lines at the country end of the station. Horsham's 1938 signal box remains at work but the roundhouse locomotive depot is now just a memory.

H.33   Horsley

New Guildford Line, between Effingham Junction and Guildford. 22 m 12 ch from Waterloo

Another New Guildford Line station with Down side 1885 main buildings in the Claygate style, well shrubbed, in a delightful woodland setting and with half-hourly trains in each direction.

H.34   Hounslow Loop

Waterloo-Reading line, loop from Barnes to Whitton Junction/Feltham Junction. 7 m 31 ch

This line was authorised to the Windsor, Staines & South Western Railway by an

Act of 1847 and serving Hounslow was one of its primary objectives. It is double track from the junction west of Barnes to Hounslow Junction and from there has connections back to the Reading line west via Feltham Junction and east via Whitton Junction. The half-hourly off-peak service runs via the loop stations to Twickenham, earlier and later services continuing on to return to Waterloo via Richmond. The section to Isleworth was opened on August 22 1849 and the portion on to Feltham Junction on February 1 1850. The completion of the triangle to Whitton Junction was not brought into use until January 1 1883.

Following the junction and CCTV crossing at Barnes (7 m 7 ch) the first station on the loop is Barnes Bridge (7 m 54 ch) which dates from March 12 1916 and enjoys many extra passengers on Boat Race days. From an ornate entrance arch fronting the river, stairs rise to the Barnes Bridge platforms, each of which has a modest shelter plus integral canopy. The line then crosses the river by means of Barnes Bridge, a structure of three bowstring spans carrying the two railway tracks and a footpath.

After a modest climb and descent the route comes to Chiswick (8 m 47 ch), one of the original locations and now comprising Up and Down platforms with the main buildings on the former. Of brick and mildly Georgian these are two-storey and well dressed with stone. There is a bus type shelter on the Down platform and the old station signal box at the London end. Before the point at which the route is crossed by the NL/LT Richmond line comes Grove Park CCTV crossing (8 m 75 ch) with double barriers and adjacent buildings braced by supports across the railway.

The section through Kew Bridge to Brentford includes the triangular junction with the link from the North London-Richmond route at Bollo Lane Junction. The original North & South Western Junction line from Willesden to Old Kew Junction, west of Kew Bridge station, was authorised in 1851 and opened two years later. NLR passenger services ran this way to Twickenham and Kingston and later LMS services operated between Broad Street/Willesden and Kew Bridge using the platforms (still visible) on the curve to New Kew Junction. These were closed on September 12 1940, leaving the route to its freight traffic also much reduced since the closure of Feltham Yard.

From New Kew Junction (9 m 34 ch) the first leg of the triangle runs via the boundary with the LMR (9 m 66 ch/3 m 39 ch) to Kew East Junction (3 m 32 ch). The second leg runs from there, again via a regional boundary point (3 m 61 ch/9 m 68 ch), to Old Kew Junction (10 m 1 ch). The Hounslow Loop leg runs via the station at Kew Bridge (9 m 53 ch) which serves Kew Gardens and has Up and Down platforms with covered stairs and walkway to the street level offices. The goods and coal depots on the west curve are now closed.

Boston Manor Road crosses over Brentford station (10 m 52 ch), one of the original locations and the station for Brentford Town's football ground. The approach is in a shallow cutting previously carrying additional tracks (to allow for the extra freight traffic) on the Up side. The station's goods yard closed in 1965 leaving just the Up and Down passenger platforms, linked by footbridge and with the main buildings on the Down side.

Towards Syon Lane the Hounslow Loop first crosses over the Grand Union Canal and then beneath the route of the former GWR branch from Southall to Brentford Town and Dock. The gradient then rises at 1 in 314 and 1 in 191 to Syon Lane itself (11 m 34 ch) which dates from July 5 1931 and is the station for Syon Park. The ticket office and other facilities are in the Up side single-storey block and the Down side has just a wooden shelter and stairs leading up to the overbridge carrying Syon Lane across the railway at the London end of the platforms.

Isleworth (12 m 10 ch), another of the original locations but formerly called Hounslow (Smallberry Green) has a double barrier CCTV LC at Wood Lane (11 m 69 ch) and then platforms following the bridge over London Road. This brings the upper storey of the Up side building to platform level with access to the Down platform by subway.

Hounslow (13 m 40 ch), the last station before the triangular junction which rejoins the Loop and the Reading line, has an Up Loop at the country end and the old goods yard, shed, bay and dock (all closed 1968 and the latter now filled in) at the London end. In between the severe, gabled brick buildings combining station house and offices are quite unlike any others on the line. They are not unattractive, but have such unusual features as steps down to the platform and a projecting bay on the platform side. The single-

storey wooden buildings on the Down side are also unusual, combining waiting areas and a tiny former ticket office. The 13½ MP is on the Down platform and the station has two crossovers, a footbridge and the overbridge carrying Whitton Road with its nearby 'North Star' public house. In addition to passengers Hounslow deals with a fair amount of GPO traffic.

H.35 Hove

Brighton-Littlehampton/Portsmouth line. 1 m 35 ch from Brighton

The original Hove station, opened on May 12 1840 as part of the line to Shoreham, was about a half mile nearer Brighton. It ceased dealing with passengers and became a goods depot in 1880 using the name Holland Road (which was also taken by the halt opened there in 1905 and closed in 1956) from 1895 onwards. In that same year the present station, opened as Cliftonville on October 1 1865, took the Hove name and the job of serving the Hove community.

Hove today comprises an Up island platform with wooden buildings and canopy and with an Up Passenger Loop behind, a subway then leading to the Down platform and the two-storey, original buildings there. Hove signal box lies on the Up side at the Brighton end and the sidings serving PD Fuels coal concentration depot are at the country end. Other features include the former Sackville Road goods yard and shed, a car park and an overbridge across the station and used, together with the Police Charge Room housed on the station, on football match days.

All trains on the Coastway West route

One of the two-tier seating sets tried out by the SR at the end of 1949.

call plus the Victoria-Littlehampton services which pass via Cliftonville Tunnel on the spur from Preston Park, the 220 yard Hove Tunnel (25 ch to 40 ch) lying on the approach from Brighton.

H.36 Hurstbourne

Waterloo-Exeter line, between Basingstoke and Andover. 60 m 76 ch from Waterloo

The station at Hurstbourne closed in 1964 and it had ceased to be a junction when the cut-off line to Fullerton, designed to thwart the ambitions of the Didcot, Newbury & Southampton Railway, had lost its remaining passenger services on July 6 1931. The location is now marked by a viaduct over watercress beds on the tiny Bourne Rivulet, a name as distinctive as the adjoining Dirty Corner, Devils Dyke and Picket Piece along this section of downland chalk cuttings.

H.37 Hurst Green

South Croydon-East Grinstead line, junction of Uckfield Branch. 21 m 20 ch from London Bridge

The descent from Woldingham approaches Hurst Green via the 551 yd Limpsfield Tunnel (20 m 58 ch to 21 m 3 ch), the station itself then comprising Up and Down platforms linked by a concrete footbridge and with modern buildings on the Up side. It is followed by the facing junction where the East Grinstead and Uckfield lines part company and which is controlled by the small wooden signal box (21 m 35 ch) on a brick base.

Both the East Grinstead and Uckfield demus call at Hurst Green which was only a typical LB&SC 'Motor Train Halt' in the years following its 1907 opening until the expansion of the area after the Second World War led to the present 1961 station.

I.1   Ifield

Victoria-Portsmouth line, between Three Bridges and Horsham. 31 m 66 ch from London Bridge

Ifield station, now serving the west side of Crawley New Town, opened on June 1 1907 as Lyons Crossing Halt. It has shelters on each platform, a small ticket office on the Up side and is served by the Victoria-Horsham trains and some of the Bognor Regis and Portsmouth services.

Isle of Grain Branch—see Hoo Junction-Grain Line

Isle of Wight—see Ryde Pier Head-Shanklin Line

Isleworth—see Hounslow Loop

K.1   Kearsney

Victoria-Dover line, between Canterbury East and Buckland Junction. 75 m 9 ch from Victoria

Opened as Ewell on August 1 1862, Kearsney is approached by a substantial viaduct which helps to even out the valley descent from Lydden Tunnel and the site of Stonehall & Lydden Halt, closed April 5 1954. The station itself has Up and Down platforms in a pleasant setting, the former, once an island used by trains from Deal via the Kearsney Loop, housing the signal box and with just a wooden framed shelter. There is a footbridge of unusual design to the Down side where the traditional buildings include both the station house plus ticket office and the old brick goods shed, still lettered 'Kearsney for River and Ewell'. The basic service is hourly to Victoria and to Dover.

Kempton Park—see Shepperton Branch

K.2   Kemsing

Victoria-Ramsgate line, between Otford Junction and Maidstone East. 26 m 79 ch from Victoria

The simple, single-storey main buildings

on the Up side are difficult to date and may have been modified more than once. A concrete footbridge provides the link to the Down platform with its traditional wooden shelter and the 27 MP on the platform. The slower Victoria-Maidstone East trains call.

Kemsley—see Sheerness Branch

Kenley—see Caterham Branch

K.3   Kent House

Victoria-Ramsgate line, between Brixton and Beckenham Junction. 7 m 66 ch from Victoria

Kent House was opened by the LC&D on October 1 1884, although this section of the main line from Herne Hill had come into being 21 years before. Today the station comprises Up and Down island platforms reached by subway and stairs from the street level below and provided with wooden accommodation and canopies. In addition to the Up and Down Passenger Loops there is a facing cross-over linking the main lines and the station originates and terminates trains during the peak. At other times the Victoria-Orpington services call.

Traces remain of an embankment towards Birkbeck.

Kew Bridge—see Hounslow Loop

Kew Gardens—see Richmond

Keymer Junction—see Wivelsfield

Kidbrooke—see Bexleyheath Line

K.4   Kingston

New Maldon-Twickenham line. 12 m 9 ch from Waterloo

The present station, which gives its name to the Kingston Loop, dates from a major reconstruction in 1934-5. It comprises Up and Down platforms with a bridge to carry them over Richmond Road and a bay towards Twickenham linked to both lines by a facing crossover. The straight course of the bay line is a legacy from the previous layout. This comprised a terminal at street level (variously called Kingston New or Kingston Town to distinguish it from the Kingston on the main line) opened when the line from Twickenham arrived on July 1 1863 and high level through platforms dating from the link to the Surbiton line on January 1 1869.

Kingston's SR-style entrance, complete with flag pole, leads from a busy road intersection to the concourse and ticket office. A tiled subway then links the two sets of stairs to the waiting and staff rooms on the platforms. On the Up side the 1935 passimeter now stands disused and forlorn and the former goods yard, closed in 1966, is now a car park although the elaborate goods shed is still standing.

The loop and Shepperton branch services give Kingston a basic service of four trains an hour each way.

Kingswood—see Tattenham Corner Branch

K.5 Knockholt

Charing Cross-Dover line, between Orpington and Sevenoaks. 16 m 44 ch from Charing Cross

Knockholt lies near the summit of the 12-mile climb from New Cross between the two tunnels (Chelsfield and Polhill) used to pierce the high chalk ridge which precedes the drop into the Darent Valley. The station was opened eight years after the line itself, on May 1 1876, and was known then as Halstead for Knockholt. For a period passengers were invited to 'Alight for Badgers Mount'.

Today Knockholt comprises Up and Down platforms with the original wooden buildings on the former much simplified and with a crossover and Down Refuge Siding at the London end. It derives a basic hourly service from the Charing Cross-Sevenoaks trains.

L.1 Ladywell

Lewisham-Hayes line. 6 m 62 ch from Charing Cross

Ladywell was opened by the Mid-Kent Railway on January 1 1857 and at least part of the Up side, single-storey ticket office building is likely to date from then. The Down side buildings are closed but there is a period 6¾ MP sign on this platform and the valances on both sides are highly ornamented.

The station is served by the Charing Cross/Cannon Street-Hayes trains. To its north lies Ladywell Junction (6 m 41 ch)—see Lewisham map.

L.2 Lancing

Brighton-Littlehampton/Portsmouth line, between Shoreham and Worthing. 8 m 19 ch from Brighton

The double barrier crossing and Up side SR brick signal box stand at the Brighton end of the two-platform station which dates from the opening of the line on November 24 1845. Otherwise the location comprises two small buildings on the Up side and a single-storey gabled building on the Down, the latter with the earlier station house adjacent.

Lancing enjoys a service of three trains hourly in each direction but its importance as a major forwarding point for market garden produce has long passed and the noted carriage works built up by the LB&SC between 1908 and 1912 were closed in 1964-5 and are now marked only by the old Down side ground frame west of the station.

L.3 Leatherhead

Junction of routes to Dorking/Horsham and Effingham Junction from Waterloo via Raynes Park and Victoria via Sutton. 18 m 2 ch from Waterloo

The ornate and attractive station at Leatherhead is the survivor of three stations built to serve the town. The first lay to the north and was opened on February 1 1859 when the joint LSW/LB&SC extension from Epsom reached Leatherhead. With the opening of the penultimate section of the Mid-Sussex route, from Leatherhead to Dorking, on March 11 1867 the present station was built and the joint station closed. The LSW had its own station nearby but this and the separate access on to Epsom formed the basis of a piece of post-Grouping rationalisation when the trains on the 1885 LSW branch from Effingham Junction started using a new junction and the LB&SC station, allowing its LSW neighbour to be closed on July 9 1927 (although it continued in use for carriage stabling). Two tracks still surviving on the Up side mark the link to Leatherhead LSW.

Hardly any part of the main Up side buildings at Leatherhead goes undecorated, special features being the window arches, the doorway to the station house and rising above them all the great tower with its herringbone brickwork patterns. The station has a separate entrance with more modest buildings on the Down side where the signal box is located at the country end. There is also a siding on this side in the dip at the London end while at the country end both routes cross the River Mole before they disappear into the

524 yd Mickleham Tunnel (19 m 55 ch to 19 m 78 ch) on the way to Dorking and into Bookham Tunnel on the Effingham Junction route.

Leatherhead enjoys a good service to Victoria and Waterloo in the Up direction and Effingham Junction and Dorking/Horsham in the Down.

Lee—see Dartford Loop Line

L.4   Leigh

Redhill-Tonbridge line, between Eden-bridge and Tonbridge. 39 m 56 ch from Charing Cross

Opened in 1911, Leigh (at one time spelt Lyghe) is a good example of an SR minimum facilities station. The two platforms are formed from concrete slabs on concrete trestles and each is provided with a wooden shelter. The service is provided by the Tonbridge-Reading dmus.

L.5   Lenham

Victoria-Ramsgate line, between Maidstone East and Ashford. 49 m 11 ch from Victoria

Lenham lies at the summit of a 9-mile climb from Maidstone East and an 11-mile, but gentler, ascent from Ashford. The 1884 LC&D station has substantial Down side buildings in the domestic Gothic style plus a shelter and the large signal box on the Up side, the latter controlling the semaphore signals which include Starters on the Up and Down Passenger Loops. The DPL precedes the platform and has a dock at the London end while the UPL runs behind the Up, island platform. The '1886 Spears English Bacon Factory' remains but no longer has a private siding.

The Victoria-Ashford and Victoria-Ramsgate trains call.

L.6   Lewes

Victoria-Eastbourne/Hastings line, junction with line from Brighton. 49 m 74 ch from London Bridge

From the Keymer Junction direction the approach to Lewes is by way of Hamsey AHB LC (48 m 12 ch)—where the earthworks of the 1858-68 junction for Uckfield are still traceable—and the 396 yd Lewes Tunnel (49 m 49 ch to 49 m 67 ch), with a 10 mph speed restriction applying from the tunnel curve, through the station and on to the junction with the Brighton line. The latter approaches via the 107 yd Kingston Tunnel (7 m 13 ch to 7 m 18 ch) and also has a 10 mph speed restriction through the station and over the junction at the country end. On this route the station stands at 7 m 77 ch from Brighton, the Brighton mileages superseding the London Bridge ones at Southerham Junction (51 m 11 ch/9 m 14 ch) where the Seaford branch departs.

The first station at Lewes, called Friar's Walk, dates from June 8 1846 and the opening of the Brighton, Lewes & Hastings Railway's double track from Brighton. This was extended as a single track to Bulverhythe (2¼ m west of Hastings) 19 days later and from a junction on the Brighton side of the station, new platforms being built to serve the junction. With the opening of a line from Keymer to Lewes on October 1 1847 another platform was brought into use at Lewes and this remained the situation until 1857 when a new station took over. That too was replaced by the present station, on June 17 1889, to complete a remodelling scheme which provided easier curves and better links between the routes (which had been joined by the new line to Uckfield,

The pleasant 1887 station at Lewes.

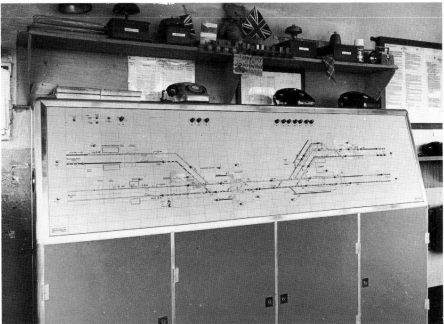

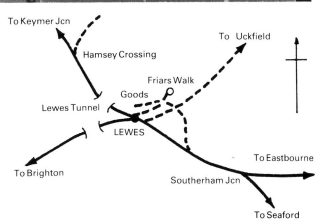

Above *Typical of many smaller control panels is this one at Lewes covering the area out to Glynde, Newhaven Town, Cooksbridge and Falmer.*

Top *A view of Lewes station from the country end. The line to Brighton is on the left and that to Keymer Junction on the right.*

To Keymer Jcn

Hamsey Crossing

To Uckfield

Friars Walk

Goods

Lewes Tunnel

LEWES

To Eastbourne

To Brighton

Southerham Jcn

To Seaford

and then Tunbridge Wells, in 1868). The
remodelling included a new alignment for
the line to Eastbourne, leaving the old
route to be used for access to the Friar's
Walk goods depot.

Passenger access to Lewes station is via
impressive 1887-9 buildings at street level.
The frontage is highly-ornamented and a
high lantern surmounts the booking hall
from which stairs and ramp lead down to
five platforms (Nos 2, 3, 6, 7 and 8). Platforms 2 and 3 are used by main line services and 6, 7 and 8 by trains to and from
Brighton; the old No 1 Platform line has
been shortened and made into an
engineers' siding and platforms 4 and 5
are out of use and the single line between
them lifted. There are buffet and other
station facilities at platform level and a
bookstall above. An 1888 coat of arms
and some vintage clocks are also to be
found.

The former yard area is still apparent
on the Down side, together with the goods
access that took over the old Lewes-
Bulverhythe line's alignment and the
route of the Tunbridge Wells line (closed
May 4 1969). On the Up side stands the
signal box, with a modern push-button
panel.

The basic train service pattern provides
one main line, one Brighton-Seaford, one
Brighton-Eastbourne and one Brighton-
Ore train (and vice versa) in each hour.

L.7 Lewisham

North Kent Line, loop from Charing Cross-Dover line and junction for Hayes line. 6 m 4 ch from Charing Cross

Lewisham's railway importance dates
back to the opening of the North Kent line
on July 30 1849, with the Mid-Kent route
making it a junction from January 1 1857.
The present layout derives largely from
the introduction of the flyover and loop in
1929 to enable cross-London freight
traffic to be routed via Loughborough
Junction and a portion of what had been
the old LC&D Greenwich Park branch
(which had included a station at Lewisham
Road).

From the 87 yd Tanners Hill Tunnel
(5 m 22 ch to 5 m 26 ch) the main line
separates from the North Kent Line in
physical terms at St Johns, with a
reversible line linking Tanners Hill
Junction (5 m 29 ch) with the flyover from
Nunhead. Crossovers between the North
Kent line and the route from Nunhead
precede Lewisham station, the Mid-Kent
line then continuing, to pass beneath the
main line and to link with it via the
Lewisham Loop. The mileages via
Lewisham are St Johns 5 m 47 ch,
Lewisham 6 m 4 ch and Parks Bridge
Junction 6 m 43 ch (6 m 36 ch direct).

Lewisham station is a busy one, mainly
with trains on the Mid-Kent and via Dart-

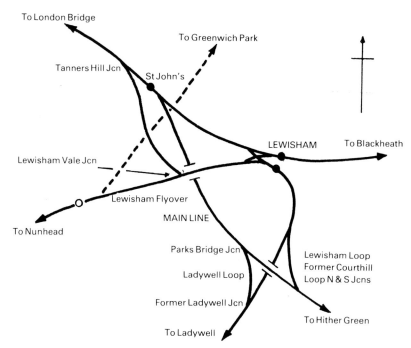

To London Bridge

Tanners Hill Jcn

St John's

To Greenwich Park

Lewisham Vale Jcn

LEWISHAM

To Blackheath

Lewisham Flyover

MAIN LINE

To Nunhead

Parks Bridge Jcn

Lewisham Loop
Former Courthill
Loop N & S Jcns

Ladywell Loop

Former Ladywell Jcn

To Hither Green

To Ladywell

ford routes. It comprises four raised platforms with a traditional station building, modernised in 1983, in the angle between No 2 and No 3. No 1 Platform has a wooden shelter and a signal repeater and No 4 the 6 MP sign. There is a large

CM&EE depot on the Down side towards St Johns where the station opened by the SER on June 1 1873 now consists of a single island platform following the loss of the island serving the Parks Bridge Junction tracks.

Lingfield—see East Grinstead Branch

L.8   Liphook

Waterloo-Portsmouth line, between Godalming and Petersfield. 46 m 67 ch from Waterloo

The extension from Godalming to Havant and all its intermediate stations, including the one at Liphook, was opened in 1859. The main buildings are still in use on the Up side and comprise the ticket office with apartments above and single-storey supplementary accommodation either side. There are still remains of the sidings used for Army traffic on this side while the Down side comprises just platform and large wooden shelter. The Waterloo-Portsmouth slows and semi-fasts call.

L.9   Liss

Waterloo-Portsmouth line, between Godalming and Petersfield. 51 m 35 ch

Following Liss Common AHB LC (50 m 75 ch) is the Up side site of the link with

Left *Lewisham control panel 1970.*
Below *SER milepost at Lewisham.*

the former Longmoor Military Railway. This grew from an extension of the Bordon branch to Longmoor and a further extension to Liss, where connection was made with the Portsmouth line in 1942. The system lasted, in various forms, from 1905 to 1971 and provided an extensive passenger and freight service at its peak.

Liss station now has modern Down side buildings of glass and steel but retains a traditional wooden shelter on the Up side where the public house near the double barrier CCTV crossing is appropriately called 'The Crossing Gate'. AHB crossings follow at Princes Bridge (52 m 12 ch) and Sheet (53 m 72 ch).

The Portsmouth slow and semi-fast services call.

L.10   Littlehampton Branch

Branch from Victoria/Brighton-Portsmouth line. 2 m 8 ch

Littlehampton was once an active port with vessels plying from the harbour formed by the mouth of the River Arun. It remains a pleasant town served by the Victoria-Littlehampton-Bognor trains and by the Brighton-Littlehampton workings which reach the branch via the triangular junction with the coast route east of Ford station.

Opened on August 17 1863 and doubled in 1887 the modestly graded route leaves the main line at Arundel Junction (59 m 75 ch) and runs to Littlehampton Junction (60 m 57 ch)—where the 30 ch link from Ford Junction joins—before heading south east to the once-extensive station near Littlehampton town centre.

Two platforms provide four faces for the platform lines, with a signal box on the Down side and carriage shed, washer and sidings on the Up. The end of platforms 2 and 3 accommodates an excellent floral display while the station buildings and ticket office lie on the Down side at the end of platform 4. Faded wooden canopies then cover the concourse area and a walkway to the exit near 'The Locomotive' public house. Public freight facilities were withdrawn in 1970 but the brick goods shed still stands on the Up side near the east bank of the river.

L.11   Littlehaven

Victoria-Portsmouth line, between Three Bridges and Horsham. 36 m 50 ch from London Bridge

Littlehaven was opened, as Rusper Road,

on June 1 1907. Served by the Victoria-Horsham and Victoria-Bognor Regis trains, the station caters for the northern outskirts of Horsham and consists of Up and Down platforms, a level crossing with traditional gates and a Down side signal box ticket office.

L.12   London Bridge

Friday December 15 1978, when the rebuilt London Bridge station was officially opened by Dr Mervyn Stockwood, Bishop of Southwark (the diocese in which it stands), was exactly 142 years and one day from the Wednesday in 1836 when the first London Bridge station opened. The guest celebrity on that occasion was Thomas Kelly, the Lord Mayor of London, accompanied by his Sheriffs and supported by the bands of the Scots and Coldstream Guards. Special grandstands were erected on what had been the old Flemish burial grounds, bought by the London & Greenwich Railway for the opening of this first permanent railway terminal in London.

Prior to the opening of London Bridge the L&G tracks from Deptford came only as far as Spa Road, where a temporary station had been opened on February 8 1836 (and two later stations were to be built). Subsequent to its opening the London & Croydon became a user and after May 10 1842 extension and rearrangement gave the original area to the L&C, L&B and SER companies, with the L&G using the extension area.

A contemporary account of the original station says: 'The new station is approached by a sloping carriage road and a paved footpath, and entered through handsome iron gates. It is 60 ft wide by 400 ft long, with four lines converging to two at 130 yards from the entrance. There are but two platforms [roughly where the ticket office and buffet are today] with access by steps—and more steps to actually get into the trains. The only protection from the elements is an old sail.'

Despite this the new railway handled nearly 1½ m passengers in its first year, among them the very first London season ticket holder, travelling to and from Deptford each day in an open carriage. It did well financially from the tolls charged to the other users and it was the level of these which led to the SER opening a line to a new terminal at Bricklayers Arms on May 1 1844. Of the many changes in the station's scope and operation one of the

A 1970 scene at London Bridge looking from the control office towards the City.

most significant was the 1864 extension to Charing Cross which brought the opening of the high level through platforms and the allocation (until 1902) of the SER low level area to freight and continental traffic. The approaches were widened in 1866 for the route from London Bridge LB&SC to Victoria, and again in 1880.

For much of its first 100 years the London Bridge story was very similar to that of Victoria—disagreement between the rival users (the SER and the LB&SC)—leading to the existence of the two quite separate stations with a wall between them. Also, it is scarcely necessary to add, the buiding of an hotel. A seven-storey, 150-bedroom affair called 'The Terminal', it was designed by the architect for St Thomas' Hospital and suffered precisely the same fate as the one at Blackfriars; turned into offices and then destroyed by bombs during the war. A cellar full of old hotel crockery was unearthed during the rebuilding of the station.

Again as at Victoria, the coming of the Southern Railway saw the breaching of the boundary between the two London Bridge stations. Again it was done by making a hole in the wall and this survived

until the opening of the new station in 1978.

A prelude to the £9 m rebuilding operation, and an even more costly one, was the opening of the new power signal box and the complete resignalling and remodelling of the track and approaches to London Bridge and all the way through to Charing Cross and Cannon Street. The £21 m scheme also saw the removal of the SR's most notorious bottleneck, the Borough Market Junction. All that now remains of this terrible cause of so many delays is its name on the boundary wall alongside Southwark Cathedral.

With the station still carrying the scars of the great fire raid on the City of London in December 1940, its rebuild was certainly overdue. And while it achieved unification, with a large central concourse and a 30 ft wide footbridge serving all 16 platforms, London Bridge continues, as it must, to be both terminus and through station. It is journey's end for travellers from the Sussex Coast and the suburbs, and an exchange station for commuters bound for Charing Cross and Cannon Street. The ticket office and travel centre are now side by side and the appearance of the station has been much enhanced by the use of modern materials. On the concourse are shops, kiosks and other facilities and the naming of the buffet and

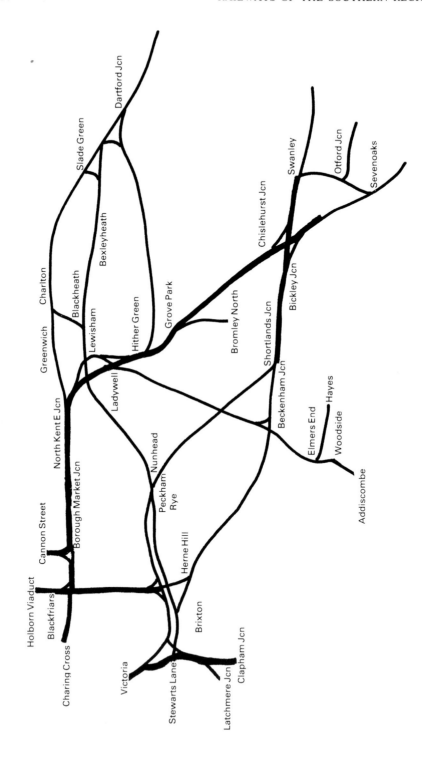

bar as the 'Oast House' was highly appropriate for its location on the site of the old bay platforms once used by the hop pickers' trains. This part of London was the centre of the hop trade, the nearby Borough Market handling most of the hop sales and the local telephone exchange even being HOP at one period. Over the whole London Bridge concourse (and the adjoining bus station) is a space frame roof with 15 miles of steel tubes supporting the covering and pyramid roof lights.

The approach to London Bridge is via Metropolitan Junction (1 m 31 ch from Charing Cross) and Borough Market Junction (1 m 51 ch) where the Up and Down Cannon Street lines join the Charing Cross pair. Of the six platform lines of the through London Bridge portion (1 m 70 ch), three are reversible, allowing No 2 Platform to be used by trains both to and from Cannon Street and Nos 4 and 5 for trains to and from Charing Cross. With some 130 trains to be handled in the 07.00 to 10.00 period this facility is invaluable.

Of the other through platforms No 1 is for Down trains from Cannon Street, No 3 for Up Cannon Street services and No 6 for Waterloo East and Charing Cross. There is also an Up Passenger Loop fulfilling the same function and completing the ex-South Eastern side layout. All tracks then continue to Spa Road (2 m 71 ch) where 1 to 6 are linked by crossovers and the UPL is linked to the Central Division lines. Next comes Blue Anchor (3 m 32 ch) and 5/6—Central links and then the site of Southwark Park (1902-15) where the Bricklayers Arms link still makes rusty connection with the Up side of the four tracks remaining after the loss of the diverging loop to New Cross.

The London Bridge terminal station comprises platforms 7 to 15, used by services to places like Caterham, Crystal Palace, Dorking, Epsom, Tattenham Corner and East and West Croydon, as well as to Brighton and the Sussex coast. Nos 7 and 8 have a loco siding at the country end and 14 and 15 are shorter and have beyond them the remaining No 16 Platform which the South London Line services to and from Victoria use. The total of ten lines reduces to Main and South London pairs with a reversible line between the two from Spa Road (1 m 3 ch) and an additional, Down Slow line from Blue Anchor (1 m 45 ch) and on through South Bermondsey Junction (1 m 49 ch).

The completion of the Victoria signal box will take over the 'showpiece' mantle from London Bridge but not diminish the importance of the latter's role. It was commissioned with two panels, the main 60 ft long South Eastern Division panel controlling 257 signals and 342 sets of points and the smaller Central Division panel 190 signals and 114 sets of points. With visual display units and push button route setting the box controlled 1,600 trains each weekday, over 150 miles, and ensured the safety of 335,000 passengers. Its South Eastern coverage extends as far as Woolwich Arsenal, Eltham Park, New Eltham, Elmstead Woods, the Bromley North branch, the stations between Ladywell and Elmers End and the line out to Hayes.

London Road, Brighton—see Brighton

London Road, Guildford—see Guildford

L.13   Longcross

Waterloo-Reading line, between Virginia Water and Ascot. 25 m 11 ch from Waterloo

Longcross dates from September 21 1942 and one of its main traffics is passengers to and from the REME vehicle testing plant. The station, with shelters on each platform and a small ticket office on the Down side, is set in an area of woodland, heath and heather and enjoys a half-hourly train service on weekdays.

L.14   Longfield

Victoria-Ramsgate line, between Swanley Junction and Rochester Bridge Junction. 23 m 30 ch from Victoria

The station here was opened as Fawkham 12 years after the line, in 1872, and just under a mile west of Fawkham Junction where the branch to Gravesend West Street departed from May 10 1886. There was a Longfield Halt on the latter from 1913 until the withdrawal of passenger services on August 3 1953.

The 1872 station had received a new set of station buildings in the SE&C era and acquired its present name in 1961. It now has Clasp-type station offices on the Down side and a wooden waiting room on the Up. Dover/Ramsgate services call half-hourly and alternately.

At one period there were freight sidings on either side of the line on the 1 in 100 climb up to Meopham.

L.15   Loughborough Junction

Holborn Viaduct-Herne Hill line, junction with the Brixton-Peckham Rye line. 3 m 48 ch from Holborn Viaduct

The LC&D line from Herne Hill across the Thames to the City was opened in 1862-4 and the first station in the Loughborough Junction area was Loughborough Road on the spur towards Brixton and opened in 1864. This was also the first to close, doing so on April 3 1916. The name Loughborough Junction was taken when the main line platforms were opened on December 1 1872, and justified by the opening of platforms on the spur towards Denmark Hill at the same time. The latter closed in 1925 but are still in existence.

Nowadays the former six platforms have shrunk to the two faces of an island with a ticket office access from Coldharbour Lane below. The service comes mainly from the Holborn Viaduct-West Croydon trains.

On the approach to Loughborough Junction there are still vague traces of the former stations and depots at Walworth Road and Camberwell and then come the 20 mph spurs east to Cambria Junction (3 m 37 ch to 3 m 62 ch) and used by Catford Loop and Lewisham trains and west to Canterbury Road Junction (3 m 37 ch to 3 m 79 ch).

L.16   Lower Sydenham

Lewisham-Hayes line. 9 m 2 ch from Charing Cross

The first station here opened with the line on January 1 1857 but the present station was built, on a site slightly to the south, in 1906. It is served by the Charing Cross/Cannon Street-Hayes trains and comprises Up and Down platforms with Clasp-type buildings and linked by an ultra modern concrete footbridge.

L.17   Ludgershall Branch

Waterloo-Exeter line, branch from Andover. 7 m 18 ch

The Swindon, Marlborough & Andover Railway opened its first section from Red Post Junction north to Grafton on May 1 1882. As part of the Midland & South Western Junction Railway this route eventually led through to Cheltenham and carried a substantial volume of military traffic to and from Ludgershall camp. This southern section is now the only portion of the M&SW remaining.

Access to the single line for military traffic is via the Andover ground frame which is released by Annett's Key and this in turn must be carried by any train on the route. The former Red Post Junction is 1 m 34 ch further on and the mileage reverts to zero there as the line turns north west for a further 5 m 64 ch towards the terminal which serves Tidworth Camp.

L.18   Lydden Tunnel

Victoria-Dover line, between Canterbury East and Buckland Junction. 71 m 6 ch from Victoria

The 1 m 609 yd Lydden Tunnel (71 m 66 ch to 73 m 14 ch) lies at the 1 in 132 beginning of the 7-mile descent from Shepherds Well to Dover. Stonehall & Lydden Halt, which lay in the chalk cutting following the tunnel, closed in 1954.

L.19   Lydd Town Branch

Ashford-Hastings line, branch from Appledore. 9 m 30 ch

This lonely line across the Romney Marshes is the survivor of the 1881 Lydd Railway which opened for passengers to Lydd (to Dungeness for goods) on December 7 of that year. Two years later the passenger services were extended to Dungeness and in 1884 a branch was opened to a station at New Romney. This left the original line at a facing junction 1¼ miles beyond Lydd and then ran due north to a station beside the B2071 at New Romney, but a re-routing was brought into use in 1937, leaving the Dungeness line near Halfway Bush crossing and running nearer the coast and the RH&DR route until the two lines approached New Romney together. Dungeness was then closed to passengers and served from Lydd-on-Sea, the route having 11 daily trains from Ashford and a Saturday service doing the journey from Charing Cross in 2 hours 18 minutes and making the total number of trains serving Brookland, Lydd Town, Lydd-on-Sea, Greatstone-on-Sea and New Romney up to 12.

From March 6 1967 the route has remained open solely as a freight-only single line, worked under the One Train system and serving the CEGB power station on Denge Beach behind Dungeness. It leaves Appledore (64 m 50 ch) by a Down side facing connection and runs via four 5 mph open crossings to Brookland AOCL crossing (67 m 20 ch) where the line crosses the A259. Eight more open crossings and several waterway bridges

precede the TMO crossing before the
passing loop and siding area and platforms
at Lydd Town (71 m 51 ch). The line then
continues across Denge Marsh to MP 74
and the CEGB exchange sidings. A key is
taken from Appledore for opening gates
normally locked across the railway.

L.20 Lymington Branch

*Waterloo-Weymouth line, branch from
Brockenhurst. 5 m 29 ch*

This is a single line, worked on the One
Train system by a three-car branch set,
and running via the former Lymington
Junction west of Brockenhurst station to
Lymington Pier at the head of the Lymington River estuary. There the trains connect
with the Sealink passenger and vehicle
ferry to Yarmouth, Isle of Wight.

The original Lymington Railway was
authorised in 1856 and was opened to a
temporary terminus on July 12 1858.
Acquisition of the ferry and a new
Lymington Town station followed. The
route proved popular and by the early
years of this century passengers could
leave Waterloo at 6 am, catch the 10.50 am
sailing from Lymington Pier and alight at
Yarmouth, Totland Bay or Alum Bay (of
coloured sands fame) to spend a few
pleasant hours before returning to the
mainland. Thirty years later, connections
from Yarmouth were by bus instead of
steamer, but Lymington had gained its
own through Restaurant Car service to
and from Waterloo on Saturdays. Today
20 trains are timetabled on the branch
each weekday, with morning and evening
workings between Lymington and East-

*The 5½-mile Lymington branch termi-
nates at Lymington Pier, pictured in 1982
with the Sealink ferry* Cenred *newly-
arrived from Yarmouth.*

leigh and some through Waterloo trains
on summer Saturdays.

Branch services use the outer face of the
Down island platform at Brockenhurst
and travel parallel to the main line for 72 ch
to the former Lymington Junction, where
the old main line route of Castleman's
Corkscrew also diverged. The next stretch
of the Lymington branch is across a flat
plain of heather dotted with tumuli and
followed by a curve round a hill and a
crossing of the A337 road. The latter is
the site of the private Ampress Works
station (96 m 61 ch). Next the line picks up
the course of the river and passes via the
CCTV LC protecting the B3054 into
Lymington Town station (97 m 57 ch),
now minus the overall canopy but with
some of the 1860 buildings backing the
single Up side platform and with the
remains of the goods facilities beyond.

A long bridge takes the branch route to
the east bank of the river, past the old
single-storey signal box and into the Lymington Pier terminus (98 m 15 ch). This
consists of a long wooden platform with
ticket and passenger facilities and direct
access to the ferry vessels. With the latter's
roll-on, roll-off facilities today's railway
timetables need no longer carry the entry:

MOTOR CARS FOR THE
ISLE OF WIGHT
Special arrangements are made at
Lymington Station for this traffic,
including slipways and tugboats which
obviate lifting. Enquiries from Station
Master, Lymington. Tel: No 7.

L.21 Lyndhurst Road

*Waterloo-Weymouth line, between Totton
and Brockenhurst. 85 m 34 ch from
Waterloo*

The station actually lies in the village of
Ashurst on the edge of the New Forest

and is now unstaffed although the truncated station buildings remain on the Up side, with the former dock behind and typical railway housing nearby. Waiting shelters are provided and the hourly Bournemouth line stopping services call.

M.1 Maidstone

Maidstone Barracks and Maidstone West are on the Strood-Paddock Wood line, 42 m and 42 m 36 ch from Charing Cross respectively; Maidstone East is on the Victoria-Ramsgate line, 39 m 76 ch from Victoria

Maidstone became part of the SER network quite early, with the arrival of the branch from Paddock Wood on September 25 1844. The route was extended along the valley of the River Medway to meet the North Kent metals at Strood on June 18 1856. Six years later the Swanley-Bat & Ball section of the Sevenoaks Railway came into use to begin a new route that was to reach Maidstone (East) in 1874, become part of the LC&D in 1879 and be completed to Ashford in 1884.

The two routes approach the town of Maidstone together. On the line from Strood, Maidstone Barracks follows the ARC aggregate terminal at Allington (access controlled by ground frame released from Maidstone West) and is signed 'For Maidstone East, the Barracks and Session House'. The station was opened in 1874, primarily for military use, and comprises Up and Down platforms with modest wooden buildings on the former and carriage sidings behind the Down platform. The line from Swanley passes overhead and Maidstone East is only a short walk away.

Maidstone West follows the 63 yd London Road 'tunnel' and is a substantial station, the main buildings on the Down side probably dating from a reconstruction for the 1856 opening of the line to Strood. The inner face of the Up platform is served by an Up Passenger Loop and there is a Down Bay used for van traffic, the GPO utilising an area nearby. The bay opposite may have been part of the original terminus.

The high, narrow-waisted signal box at Maidstone West stands beside the sharp curve at the Paddock Wood end of the complex, with the freight yard nearby. Beyond it the mileage via Strood (42 m 41 ch) changes to that via Paddock Wood (44 m 56 ch) and the Up and Down directions reverse. The line across the River

Medway to Tovil goods depot closed on October 3 1977 but the bridge and its rusting single line were still there in 1983. Tovil passenger station closed on March 15 1943.

Like the West, Maidstone East station has Up and Down lines plus an Up Passenger Loop. A Down carriage siding precedes the bridge over the Medway and then the signal box overlooks the crossovers and links to the Down side bay and dock. From the platform buildings and their canopies supported by decorated spandrels, ramps lead up to the station entrance over the 98 yd Week Street Tunnel (40 m 1 ch to 40 m 6 ch). This is quickly followed by the 358 yd Wheeler Street Tunnel (40 m 9 ch to 40 m 25 ch).

On the Strood-Paddock Wood route the basic service is half-hourly on the northern portion with alternate trains making the through journey and some services beyond the line. Maidstone East originates and terminates an hourly service with Victoria and links it with the hourly Ramsgate service.

Malden Manor—see Chessington Branch

M.2 Marden

Charing Cross-Dover line, between Paddock Wood and Ashford. 39 m 31 ch from Charing Cross

Marden is a simple station of staggered platforms, linked by a footbridge and with a wooden ticket office on the Up side. It was opened on August 31 1842 and is now served by the Charing Cross-Ashford trains.

M.3 Margate

Victoria-Ramsgate and Charing Cross-Margate lines, 73 m 69 ch from Victoria and also served via Dover

The South Eastern's Ashford-Margate branch reached Margate Sands on December 1 1846, trains reversing at Ramsgate Town. Seventeen years later, on October 5 1863, the Kent Coast protege of the London, Chatham & Dover Railway completed the link between Herne Bay and Ramsgate Harbour to give Margate a second trunk route to London. A terminus planned for Margate was never used, trains using a through station at Margate West which was later linked to the SER's Margate Sands.

A major rationalisation of the Thanet area, placed before the board of the

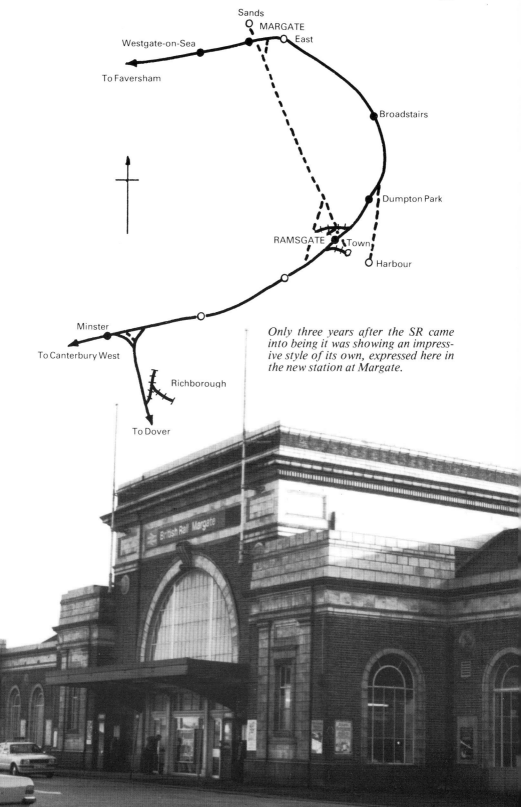

Sands

MARGATE

East

Westgate-on-Sea

To Faversham

Broadstairs

Dumpton Park

RAMSGATE Town

Harbour

Minster

To Canterbury West

Richborough

To Dover

Only three years after the SR came into being it was showing an impressive style of its own, expressed here in the new station at Margate.

newly-formed Southern Railway at the end of 1923, was implemented under a Ministry of Transport Order granted two years later. From July 2 1926 the SER route to Margate Sands was closed and the resort's traffic concentrated on a rebuilt station on the present (former Margate West) site. Through this poured the thousands of day visitors attracted to the sun and sands, their numbers further swollen by the summer Saturday trains to and from such places as Birmingham and Birkenhead.

Margate still enjoys an excellent service on its routes via Chatham, Dover/Canterbury West and Tonbridge, and via Maidstone East. Over a hundred trains call daily with as many again starting or terminating journeys. Externally the station still has a considerable presence, despite the dating of its style, and the trimmings include such touches as wing, locomotive and ship roundels and outsize cherubic figures flanking the clock in the spacious booking hall.

The main administrative offices are also on the Down side with a subway then leading to the two other, staggered platforms. From Down to Up side, the lines are Down Main, Down Platform Loop, Up Main, Up Platform Loop and Up Bay. The parcels bay is at the London end near the high signal box which controls all movements and there are carriage sidings beyond the curve of the two island platforms, access being from the signal box end.

At the Ramsgate end of the station complex the planned LC&D terminus is now an amusement park. Margate East, opened in 1870 on the section towards Ramsgate, closed on May 4 1953. Electrified services were introduced on the ex-LC&D route from June 15 1959.

M4 Martin Mill

Charing Cross-Margate line, between Buckland Junction and Deal. 95 m 5 ch from Charing Cross (via Canterbury West)

Martin Mill, opened with the Dover & Deal joint SER/LC&D line on June 15 1881, lies on the 6-mile descent from Guston Tunnel to the coastal plain at Deal. From the Dover direction it is preceded by the 1,412 yd tunnel (97 m 44 ch to 96 m 60 ch) and paralleled by the earthworks of the former line out to Langdon Bay.

The station buildings are original, and unique in housing not only ticket office

and signal box but also the last remaining post office to be found on a SR provincial station. There is a basic hourly service in each direction.

Maze Hill—see Greenwich Line

M.5 Meopham

Victoria-Ramsgate line, between Swanley and Rochester Bridge Junction. 25 m 76 ch from Victoria

Adjacent to and with the same service as its Sole Street neighbour, Meopham is the busier of the two stations. It has modern Clasp buildings on the Up side but the mean, 1861 station house remains in existence nearby.

M.6 Merstham

Victoria-Brighton line, between Purley and Redhill. 20 m 59 ch from Charing Cross

The original L&B main line was opened along the eastern edge of Gatton Park and the first Merstham station brought into use on December 1 1841 under an agreement with the landowner Lord Monson. That station was subsequently closed and reopened on the present site nearer Merstham proper. Today's station dates from a 1905-6 reconstruction and consists of the main single-storey buildings on the Up side and traditional wooden shelter plus canopy on the Down.

North of the station lies the site of Star Bridge signal box (18 m 39 ch) and then the 1 m 71 yd Merstham Tunnel (19 m 9 ch to 20 m 12 ch). The damp tunnel, approached by a steep cutting and then hewn out of the chalk terrain, is largely level after the long climb from Selhurst. It is followed by a drop at 1 in 264 past the station and its sidings to the small Holmethorpe box (21 m 70 ch) which controls access to the British Industrial Sand siding on the Down side. There was a stone terminal here for the building of the M23 and M25 motorways.

Merstham Tunnel achieved notoriety in 1905 in the 'Did she fall or was she pushed?' case of a young book-keeper aptly named Miss Money who was found in the tunnel with a feather boa stuffed into her mouth. Trouble of a different nature occurred during the building of the tunnel because the site was so far from the nearest pub!

Merton Park—see West Croydon-Wimbledon Line

M.7   Micheldever

Waterloo-Weymouth line, between Worting Junction and Winchester. 58 m 4 ch from Waterloo

From Worting Junction, where the four tracks reduce to two, the approach to Micheldever is via the old Wootton box (51 m 62 ch), Steventon (54 m 2 ch), Waltham box (55 m 38 ch), the 198 yd Litchfield Tunnel (55 m 58 ch to 55 m 67 ch), Roundwood box (56 m 49 ch), the 265 yd Popham No 1 Tunnel (57 m 17 ch to 57 m 29 ch) and the 199 yd Popham No 2 Tunnel (57 m 35 ch to 57 m 44 ch). Micheldever station is then preceded by the Down sidings serving the oil traffic installation and followed by Weston (60 m 13 ch) where the DPL (and UPL) begins.

The 1840 station buildings at Micheldever are probably to William Tite's designs and represent an interesting example of his ability to create a roomy, functional building from economical materials and yet with a touch of distinction derived from the all-round canopy.

The Bournemouth slows call hourly.

M.8   Milford (Surrey)

Waterloo-Portsmouth line, between Godalming and Haslemere. 36 m 21 ch from Waterloo

With its large goods yard area closed since 1961, Milford now consists just of Up and Down platforms plus Down side buildings in the 1859 style of the line and an AHB

crossing at the country end. There is an hourly service in each direction.

Millbrook—see Southampton

M.9   Minster

Charing Cross-Margate line, junction with Dover line. 81 m 64 ch from Charing Cross

Minster station dates from the opening, on April 13 1846, of the SER branch from Ashford to Margate Sands. It became a junction on July 1 of the following year when the branch south along the coast to Sandwich and Deal was brought into use.

In the shadow of Minster's great church, the BR station is preceded by a RG crossing where the old crossing house is still extant. Then come the slightly staggered platforms with the traditional two-storey buildings on the Down side and the second crossover and signal box beyond. The Up platform was formerly an island at which the Sandwich trains reversed until 1981 but it now has just a shelter and the very latest in footbridges. From West Junction a reversible single line, on a new alignment, leads round to Minster South Junction (82 m 21 ch) while the main line continues to East Junction (82 m 17 ch) and then on to AHB crossings at Sevenscore (83 m 10 ch) and Cliffsend (84 m

Minster station, with the re-sited line towards Sandwich veering off right.

4 ch). There is a 32 ch double line section in the coastal route between Minster East and South Junctions, all controlled from the Minster signal box.

Minster has an hourly service to and from both Charing Cross and Victoria (via Maidstone East).

Mitcham—see West Croydon-Wimbledon Line

Mitcham Junction—see West Croydon-Wimbledon Line

Morden Road—see West Croydon-Wimbledon Line

Morden South—see Wimbledon-Sutton Line

M.10   Moreton

Waterloo-Weymouth line, between Wareham and Dorchester South. 130 m 24 ch from Waterloo

This is another 1847 Southampton & Dorchester station and the gabled Up side buildings look their age. The Down side has a bus-type shelter and there is an AHB crossing at the London end. Two more such crossings lie on the rise towards Dorchester, Woodsford No 37 (131 m 17 ch) and Woodsford No 38 (131 m 77 ch).

The hourly Weymouth portions call.

M.11   Mortimer

Reading-Basingstone line. 43 m 14 ch from Paddington

This Berks & Hants line was opened on November 1 1848 with one intermediate station, at Mortimer. Its GWR origins are still evident in the excellent example of the Brunel chalet style of building on the Up platform and in the shelter plus canopy on the Down.

The Southcote Junction end of this double-line, non-electrified section is controlled from the WR panel at Reading. The WR/SR boundary then follows at 37 m 76 ch with control from the Basingstoke box. Local services are in the hands of three-car Class 205 sets, most working through to Portsmouth via Eastleigh and Fareham. A number of services from the Bournemouth line to the North West and North East also use the route.

M.12   Mortlake

Waterloo-Reading line, between Barnes and Richmond. 8 m 21 ch from Waterloo

Served half-hourly by the Kingston Loop trains, Mortlake station dates from the opening of the line to Richmond on July 27 1846. It comprises Up and Down platforms with a ticket office on the Up side and with CCTV crossings at White Hart (7 m 52 ch) and where the line crosses Sheen Lane at the London end of the station.

M.13   Motspur Park

Raynes Park-Leatherhead line, between Raynes Park Junction and Epsom. 9 m 57 ch from Waterloo

Motspur Park was opened when the Raynes Park-Dorking route was electrified on July 12 1925. It became a junction with the opening of the Chessington branch in 1938-9 and the signal box at the country end of the station controls both the junction and the lines beyond (the Chessington route by Signalling Control Panel), together with the adjacent manually-operated crossing barriers.

The island platform station enjoys a half-hourly service on both the Epsom and Chessington routes.

Mottingham—see Dartford Loop Line

M.14   Moulsecoomb

Brighton-Lewes line. 1 m 65 ch from Brighton

Built in seven months prior to opening on May 12 1980, Moulsecoomb was the first new Southern Region station built for 12 years. It owes its existence to the needs of the students at Brighton Polytechnic and of a new housing estate in Hollingdean and it is served by the Brighton-Eastbourne/Ore and Brighton-Seaford trains.

The station lies on the steep climb towards Falmer and has its main buildings on the Up side. These comprise ticket office and heated shelter and there is a similar shelter opposite. The combination of timber and tiled roof in the chalet building style is surmounted by a high clear clock on each side.

M.15   Mountfield

Charing Cross-Hastings line, between Robertsbridge and Battle. 51 m 78 ch from Charing Cross

Mountfield comprises the 526 yd tunnel (51 m 46 ch to 51 m 70 ch), the Mountfield Sidings (51 m 78 ch) serving British Gypsum Ltd and the site of the former Mountfield Halt which lost its suffix just before closure on October 6 1969. Two crossings follow, Riverhall CCTV (52 m 36 ch) and Battle Road AHB (52 m 52 ch), the latter marking the location of the halt.

The tunnel itself is one of the limited width tunnels which have plagued the operation of the Hastings line and the loading gauge problem has been dealt with by operating a Track Circuit Block single line section limited to 55 mph through the bore. On the Up side beyond its southern portal is the exchange siding for the British Gypsum line into Limekiln Wood. The firm have their own motive power which picks up and leaves traffic on the exchange sidings reached from the main line by two ground frame-controlled trailing leads.

N.1 Netley

Southampton-Portsmouth line, between St Denys and Fareham. 6 m 45 ch from Southampton

The Southampton & Netley Railway was built primarily to serve the Victoria Military Hospital on the shores of Southampton Water between the estuaries of the Itchen and the Hamble. It was opened as a single line on March 5 1866 by the LSW which had acquired the local concern two years earlier. Facilities for the hospital traffic were then steadily extended and came to include a short branch and private station. The LSW Working Timetable for 1909 shows two paths in each direction for ambulance trains to and from Southampton.

After the first scheme to extend the route to Fareham had failed, the LSW eventually took powers to fill the gap in 1883 and opened the connecting link on September 2 1889.

Today Netley station comprises an Up platform with two-storey buildings of generous proportions and in the same Italian villa style used at St Denys and Woolston. A footbridge then leads to the Down side with its tiny brick waiting room. There is a rusting Up refuge siding at the Portsmouth end and a ground frame for the emergency crossover at the Southampton end. The basic service is Salisbury/Romsey-Portsmouth hourly.

N.2 New Beckenham

Lewisham-Hayes line. 9 m 44 ch from Charing Cross

The original Mid-Kent line from Lewisham to what is now Beckenham Junction dates from January 1 1857 and New Beckenham from the opening of the extension to what

is now Addiscombe on April 1 1864. This is the year in which the Mid-Kent was absorbed into the SER whose timetabling involved the splitting of trains at New Beckenham, the Addiscombe portions later connecting with Hayes and Selsdon branch trains. New Beckenham was moved to a site slightly nearer London in 1864-8.

Today the station is served by the Charing Cross/Cannon Street-Hayes trains and consists of traditional Down side buildings, with a tall rear wall, windbreaks, canopy and decorative valances on the Up side. There is a period 9½ MP sign on the Down platform.

There is a 40 mph speed restriction through New Beckenham station, a 20 mph limit on the (now freight-only) 10 ch link from New Beckenham Junction (10 m 6 ch) to Beckenham Junction and a 35 mph restraint on the Mid-Kent route as it curves underneath the Chatham main line.

N.3 New Cross

Charing Cross-Dover line, 4 m 68 ch from Charing Cross

The South Eastern Railway opened a station called New Cross & Naval School a year after it had brought its North Kent metals from Gravesend to North Kent East Junction and thence to London Bridge in 1849. It became plain New Cross (SER), until 1923 the same as the 1839 London & Croydon station that was then to become New Cross Gate. New Cross increased in importance from 1876 when it was connected to the East London Line from both the Down and Up sides and the ELR extended its northern end to connect with the GER at Shoreditch.

LT trains on the East London line use a bay on the Down side of the present New Cross station and the main, wooden buildings are also on this side. The second platform is an island with faces to the Up Slow line and to the reversible line which then joins the Up Slow at the country end of the station. Beyond this lie the two Fast lines.

At the London end of New Cross station the LT line drops down to pass the LT depot and then pass beneath the main line. Along its route can be seen the bridge which carried the old Deptford Wharf branch.

New Cross is served by trains on the Hayes, Orpington/Sevenoaks and Dartford lines. On the main line the station is preceded by North Kent East Junction (4 m 25 ch) and followed by the 87 yd

Tanners Hill Tunnel (5 m 22 ch to 5 m 26 ch) and Tanners Hill Junction (5 m 29 ch) which begins the Lewisham complex.

N.4 New Cross Gate

London Bridge-Windmill Bridge Junction line. 2 m 70 ch from London Bridge

Starting life as New Cross, London & Croydon Railway on June 5 1839, the name New Cross Gate came into use in 1923. As with its SER neighbour, the station increased in importance when connected with the East London Line (in 1869). It was also the link, from July 2 1849, with the branch to Deptford Wharf over which the Brighton lines took many thousands of tons of coal and lightered traffic until closure in 1964 (January 1).

Trains for Sutton, Caterham and Tattenham Corner now serve New Cross Gate (plus LT trains and some Brighton services) and the station comprises centre island and two outer platforms with a ticket office on the New Cross Road overbridge at the country end. New Cross Gate also has extensive carriage sidings and servicing facilities with Up side access following the crossovers at Bricklayers Arms Junction (2 m 12 ch), a ground frame prior to the station crossovers and a washer in between. There are more sidings on the Down side.

New Cross Gate formerly had a connection to Old Kent Road Junction as well as East London links on both Up and Down sides, and there was an important LB&SC loco shed which lasted until after the Second World War.

New Eltham—see Dartford Loop Line

N.5 Newhaven

Newhaven Town and Newhaven Harbour are on the Seaford branch from the Victoria-Eastbourne /Hastings line, 56 m 25 ch and 56 m 51 ch from London Bridge repectively.

Despite tidal problems and its poor harbour, Newhaven's early GSN sailings to Dieppe made it one of the L&B's original objectives. Rail facilities became a reality when the Brighton, Lewes & Hastings company obtained powers in 1846 for a 6-mile branch from Southerham Junction, just east of Lewes, to Newhaven and from which great things were expected. The Shoreham packet service was transferred to Newhaven following the opening of the line to what is now Newhaven Town on December 8 1947 and the steamer service

passed into railway hands twenty years later, but the growth of activity was generally slow. The Newhaven Harbour Company came into being in 1878 and Newhaven Harbour station opened on May 17 1886 in place of Newhaven Wharf.

Newhaven Town now comprises Up and Down platforms with the main buildings—single-storey and original—on the Up side and reached by a footpath from the main road. There is a simple shelter on the Down platform and, on the same side at the London end, the signal box with a double barrier crossing nearby. At this end there are sidings on both sides of the line, those on the Up side and former goods yard site serving a car compound and the North Quay aggregate traffic. There is also a Sealink import-export terminal.

Newhaven Harbour station has two small platforms with a ticket office and waiting room on the Up side. There is direct access to this platform from the Marine Terminal. On the Down side, where the access is from Beach Road, there is a large parcels storage shed. The platforms are linked by footbridge, a good viewing point, and the barrier crossing is controlled from the Harbour signal box which stands on the approach to the Marine Terminal. The station, through whose connections a 20 mph restriction applies, is followed by Beach Road LC (56 m 57 ch).

The main service is Brighton-Lewes-Seaford which is hourly off peak but with additional morning and evening trains. Some specials are run in connection with the Dieppe boats and use the harbour station, successor to the route across the Ouse to West Quay which Terriers made their own due to weight restrictions on the bridge.

N.6 New Hythe

Strood-Maidstone West-Paddock Wood line, between Strood and Aylesford. 38 m 3 ch from Charing Cross

The SR-style buildings and signal box on the Up side reflect the origins of this station (opened as a halt in 1929 and accorded full status with 1939 electrification) which lies in the heart of the Reed International paper making complex. At the Strood end is a double barrier crossing and at the Maidstone end both the former Down side Reed Sidings and the Up side Brookgate Sidings which include a fuel discharge point. The short sections here mean that the New Hythe distant signals are on the advance starters of its neighbours and the Aylesford distant is on the New Hythe starter. The Strood-Maidstone West/Paddock Wood trains call half-hourly.

N.7   Newington

Victoria-Ramsgate line, between Chatham and Sittingbourne. 41 m 44 ch from Victoria

Opened four years after the East Kent Railway's line from Chatham to Faversham, on August 1 1862, Newington remains a modest country station at the country end of the Up and Down passenger loops (part of the 1959 electrification alterations) from Rainham. Its platforms serve the loops only and the small 1972 brick ticket office complex on the Up side is open only on weekday mornings. There is a shelter on each platform for passengers using the half-hourly all-stations services.

N.8   New Malden

Waterloo-Weymouth line, between Wimbledon and Surbiton. 9 m 62 ch from Waterloo

The line opened in 1838 with a station, called Malden but renamed several times since, following eight years later. It became a junction when the Kingston Loop was completed on the first day of 1869.

New Malden now comprises a bare, unused central island between the through lines, plus two outer platforms to the local lines, with canopies and simple shelters and connected by a tiled subway which also houses the ticket office. Crossovers link the local and through lines where the Down Kingston line drops below the main line to pass beneath and join the Up Kingston near Malden CCTV LC (10 m 18 ch) which has its former crossing house nearby.

New Malden has a traditional signal box—brick base, wooden upper and gallery around—and is served by the Shepperton, Hampton Court and Kingston Loop trains.

N.9   New Milton

Waterloo-Weymouth line, between Brockenhurst and Bournemouth. 98 m 44 ch from Waterloo

The Up side station buildings, similar to Sway and Hinton Admiral, date from the opening of the line on March 6 1888. The Down side has a sizeable period canopy and the station still has some SR large-wheeled luggage barrows. The Waterloo-Bournemouth slows and semi-fasts call.

N.10   Norbiton

New Malden-Twickenham line, between New Malden and Kingston. 11 m 24 ch from Waterloo

The branch from New Malden to Kingston-on-Thames opened on January 1 1869 and with it the station at Norbiton. The original buildings are still in existence, an impressive two-story block on the Up side.

There is a 50 mph restriction over the curve through the station which is served by Shepperton branch and Kingston Loop trains.

N.11   Norbury

Victoria-Brighton line, between Balham and Gloucester Road Junction. 7 m 36 ch from Victoria

The location dates from January 1878, 16 years after the line opened. It now consists of the standard centre island plus two outer platforms, the one on the Up Fast line being bare and only used in emergencies. From the separate, substantial, but architecturally unco-ordinated ticket office of the Down side the platforms are reached by subway and ramps. Beyond Norbury the fast lines become through lines and the slows become locals. An intermediate station was planned here on a site still marked by a break in the lineside housing.

Epsom Downs, West Croydon and East Croydon trains serve Norbury.

N.12   Normans Bay

Victoria-Eastbourne/Hastings line, between Willingdon Junction and Bexhill. 25 m 77 ch from Brighton

Within sight of the beach, this 1905 station consists of just platforms, corrugated shelters, a minor road crossing with hand-operated gates and a sub-station. Once a halt and now single-manned, the adjacent caravan park keeps it busy in summer, the hourly Brighton/Eastbourne-Ore slows providing the basic service.

N.13   North Camp

Redhill-Reading line, between Guildford and Wokingham. 51 m 18 ch from Charing Cross

The station opened in 1858, three years after the military camp from which it took its name, but the long, low station buildings on the Down side were probably provided a little later. On the Up platform there is just a lapped wooden shelter. Behind this stands a two-siding oil depot

A view of Abbey Wood dated only by the road traffic. Note the decorative canopy valances.

with a ground frame to give access from both lines at the Reading end. There is also a rusting Up siding at this end and a double barrier CCTV crossing.

The Gatwick-Reading trains call as well as the Tonbridge all-stations dmus.

N.14   North Dulwich

South Bermondsey Junction-Leatherhead line, between Peckham Rye and Tulse Hill. 4 m 64 ch from London Bridge

When this line and its North Dulwich station were opened by the LB&SC on October 1 1868 the architect for Dulwich College also designed the station, creating a rectangular block relieved by fretted parapets and arched entrance and surmounted by great chimney clusters. But the platforms are much more severe, lying deep in a cutting with brick retaining walls and served by the Sutton loop trains. A building firm has a siding on the Down side, London end.

Northfleet—see North Kent Line

N.15   North Kent Line

North Kent East Junction to Rochester Bridge Junction. 28 m 58 ch

In 1846 the South Eastern Railway purchased the railway built by the Thames & Medway Canal Company along the route

of its canal linking the Medway estuary and the River Thames near Gravesend. By the following year SER trains were working from Strood to Gravesend and from July 30 1849 were extended to North Kent East Junction and thence to London Bridge.

The North Kent route now leaves the main line loop at Lewisham (6 m 4 ch) and heads for Blackheath (6 m 75 ch) where the 1849/64 ticket office stands on the overbridge above the platforms which precede the separation of the route to Welling and the NK route via the 1,681 yd Blackheath Tunnel (7 m 30 ch to 8 m 26 ch) under Shooters Hill. Beyond the tunnel is the Down side connection for the Angerstein Wharf branch which was opened by John Angerstein in 1852 to bridge the mile gap between the SER and the Thames. Leased by the railway in 1892, the line came to serve several works, the wharf proper and a civil engineers' depot. A 15-ton crane was provided and the route was electrified in 1960. Today it has a private Marcon terminal for Foster Yeoman stone from the Mendips and sidings for sea-dredged aggregates from Cliffe and was also used for the Caldenlow stone used in

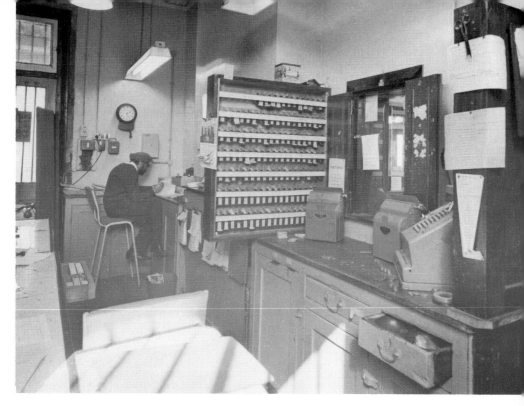

Despite the addition of modern machinery this view of the booking office at Abbey Wood still reveals a traditional ticket rack and cash drawer.

the Thames Flood Barrier Scheme.

The Angerstein Junction connection is followed by the 30 mph junction outside Charlton, where the NK mileage of 8 m 63 ch changes to the Greenwich Line mileage of 7 m 37 ch. Charlton (7 m 44 ch) itself, the station for Charlton Athletic FC, has shelters on each platform and a two-storey Clasp building leading to the overbridge at the country end of the station. It is followed by the double barrier crossing at Charlton Lane (8 m 1 ch) and the 154 yd Charlton Tunnel (8 m 3 ch to 8 m 10 ch), the 121 yd Mount Street Tunnel (8 m 14 ch to 8 m 20 ch) and the 121 yd Dockyard Tunnel (8 m 43 ch to 8 m 50 ch). The latter heralds the cutting whose retaining walls flank the platforms of Woolwich Dockyard (8 m 56 ch) which was opened with the line in 1849, has traditional brick buildings on the Up side and now serves a recent housing development.

Four more tunnels precede Woolwich Arsenal (9 m 32 ch)—the 89 yd Coleman Street Tunnel (8 m 61 ch to 8 m 65 ch), the 238 yd George IV Tunnel (8 m 71 ch to 9 m 2 ch), the 58 yd Calderwood Street

Tunnel (9 m 12 ch to 9 m 15 ch) and the 134 yd Cross Street Tunnel (9 m 21 ch to 9 m 27 ch). The station itself is reached by stairs from the modernised ticket office and has been considerably renovated. Marking its position near the Royal Artillery Barracks the Up side buffet is called 'The Artillery' and sports gunnery scenes on its walls. On the walls of the barrier-controlled car park there are still the rings once used by cavalry from the barracks down Grand Depot Road to tether their horses before taking the train for a night in town. The station was originally in a cutting but was resited and rebuilt in 1905. A 20 mph speed restriction applies through its curves and it still has some of the SR 'armchair/bench' seats. Dartford panel now takes over from London Bridge.

The Royal Arsenal's own railway system connected with the NK line near Plumstead station (10 m 1 ch) where the station buildings, in a gabled style, stand on the overbridge at the country end. There is a 16-car Up siding and further freight, coal and carriage sidings on the Down side as the route starts its straight section, via the short-lived Church Manor Way halt, to Abbey Wood (11 m 43 ch). Here what started life as a quiet country station now serves the Thamesmead housing development and is one of the busiest on the line. Pending a long-planned rebuild Abbey

Wood comprises Up and Down platforms linked by the 1977 overbridge, with a shelter on the Down side and on the Up a single-storey, traditional ticket office which in 1980 booked 2.3 m passengers.

Pending construction of Picardy Manorway road and bridge, Belvedere CCTV barrier crossing (12 m 75 ch) stands at the London end of Belvedere station (1859) and is worked from Crabtree Crossing box (13 m 22 ch) where there are sidings and a double barrier crossing. Belvedere's Up side ticket office buildings are of modular design and date from 1968.

Erith (14 m 18 ch) was another of the 1849 stations and now comprises Up and Down platforms with two-storey traditional buildings on the Down side. It is close to the Thames Riverside Esplanade.

Slade Green station (15 m 30 ch) precedes a triangular junction with the Bexleyheath line, the junction for the Erith Loop towards Bexleyheath following Slade Green station and the line from Bexleyheath towards Dartford joining the North Kent at Crayford Creek Junction (15 m 66 ch). Between the two junctions there are five carriage sidings on each side of the line. Slade Green did not come into use until July 1 1900 but in addition to the subway-linked platforms of the station the location is now important as a carriage-servicing depot for the South Eastern Division, a traincrew signing-on point and a regional maintenance depot.

The servicing activity at Slade Green involves some 900 coaches a week passing through the washer, plus some special interior and exterior cleaning work and 240 vehicles to be stabled and swept out. The CM&EE's repair shed, opened in 1926 and partly an adaption of the old steam loco depot, undertakes the overhaul of the whole of the SR's 2,500-vehicle suburban fleet plus 'heavy collision repairs' on locomotives and rolling stock. In addition to the two groups of five sidings, another 14 are available on the Down side.

Dartford, preceded by the Crayford Spur 'A' Junction (16 m 42 ch) to the Dartford Loop Line and Dartford Junction (17 m 5 ch) from it, sees a change to the via Crayford distances with a consequent 20 ch reduction. The station itself (17 m 12 ch) is dealt with separately although it was an original North Kent location.

Having skirted along the southern edge of Dartford Marshes, the North Kent Line route now heads back for the river, passing the former cement works siding connection and arriving at Stone Crossing (19 m 7 ch).

This was opened in November 1908 and consists of Up and Down platforms with shelters, a small booking hall on the Up side and the gated Cutton Lane level crossing. Then comes Greenhithe (19 m 69 ch), an 1849 station and now with subway-linked platforms and Down side ticket office. The 253 yd Greenhithe Tunnel (20 m 3 ch to 20 m 15 ch) follows.

As the route approaches Swanscombe, Swanscombe Siding Ground Frame (20 m 70 ch) controls access to the two BCI cement works reception sidings on the Down side. Then comes the station (21 m 14 ch), opened on November 2 1908 and rebuilt on its present site in 1930. Each side has a wooden ticket office, waiting accommodation and stairs to the top of the cutting. Neighbouring Northfleet (21 m 69 ch), dating from 1849 or shortly after, has traditional wooden buildings flanked on the Up side by three sidings leading from the connection 19 ch in advance of the station down and under the main line to the BCI complex north of Northfleet. There is inwards coal traffic and gypsum from Mountfield, and outwards cement in train loads.

Gravesend (23 m 75 ch) comprises central through lines, with Up and Down Passenger Loops to serve the platforms, approached by curves, cuttings and overbridges. The original station buildings are attributed to Samuel Beazley but various changes have subsequently taken place and the work of conservation-cum-modernisation is still proceeding. On the approach to Gravesend in the Down direction there are traces of the route opened by the Gravesend Railway from Fawkham Junction on May 10 1886. This route became an LC&D branch and the Gravesend (West Street) terminus had a West Street Pier platform, used for a time for boat trains for the Batavier line vessels and signed in English and Flemish. Gravesend West closed to passengers on August 3 1953 and to freight on March 14 1968 but access to Gravesend is still possible from Fenchurch Street via Tilbury and the ferry. Until 1933 there was a station at Rosherville (for the famous gardens) close to the bridge over the SER.

Once preceded by Milton Road, Denton and Milton Range halts, Hoo Junction (27 m 19 ch), where the Grain branch departs, is the subject of a separate entry, as is Strood. Between the two lies Higham station (28 m 42 ch) comprising Up and Down platforms with modest facilities, a rusting Down siding and the Up side home of the North Downs Railway preservation group. The 1,531 yd Higham Tunnel (28 m 55 ch to 29 m 45 ch) was part of the 1824 canal construction, as was the Strood Tunnel which follows, the gap between the two originally being for barges to pass. Beyond Strood the North Kent route connects at Rochester Bridge Junction (31 m 34 ch) with the Chatham main line and also down the valley of the Medway to its SER homeland at Paddock Wood.

The main service on the North Kent Line is from Charing Cross/Cannon Street to Dartford and Gillingham, with some through Ramsgate services calling.

N.16   North Sheen

Waterloo-Reading line, between Barnes and Richmond. 9 m 3 ch from Waterloo

The island platform at North Sheen was brought into use on July 6 1930. It has a modest canopied shelter and a small ticket office, manned on one turn only and reached by footpath and footbridge. At the country end a CCTV LC spans Manor Road.

The Kingston Loop trains call half-hourly.

N.17   Norwood Junction

London Bridge-Windmill Bridge Junction line, junction with Crystal Palace line. 8 m 55 ch from London Bridge

The LB&SC opened Norwood Junction on June 1 1859, just south of the former Norwood station which, in turn, had been the Jolly Sailor when opened by the pioneer London & Croydon Railway on June 5 1839. Now the station heralds the remodelled Gloucester Road triangle junction with the Victoria-Brighton line to the south and to the north has a 33 ch connection from Bromley Junction to a point 20 ch before Norwood Junction station. A link towards Birkbeck was part of the LB&SC/SER haggling and carried a Beckenham Junction-Norwood Junction service for a time, but the connection was removed in 1966.

From Norwood Junction south there is a Down Relief line in addition to the central Through and outer Local lines. The station itself has six platforms with extensive canopies, linked by subway and with the main buildings on the Up side. London Bridge-Redhill/Sutton, Victoria-West Croydon and Caterham/Tattenham Corner trains call. Norwood was once one of the Southern's major freight transfer yards but only

rusting sidings now mark the area south of the passenger station and opposite the Selhurst depot complex of which it may become part.

N.18   Nunhead

Brixton Junction-Nunhead-Catford Loop line. 5 m 77 ch from Victoria

The route from Canterbury Road Junction through Nunhead to Crystal Palace dates from August 1 1865, with the Catford Loop from Nunhead Junction to Shortlands Junction opening on July 1 1892. By this time the branch from Nunhead Junction to Blackheath Hill and then Greenwich Park was already in use but the 1871 station opened with the former was replaced under the 1925 electrification with a new 520 ft island on the London side of its predecessor. Four years later the re-routing of cross-London freight to Hither Green brought the Nunhead Junction-Lewisham line into use in a piece of rationalisation that closed the link to Blackheath Hill. Passenger services used the new line from 1935 and a few services continue to do so.

The Nunhead station which opened on May 3 1925 has a ticket office in Gibbon Road below the island platform. Nearly 100 trains are dealt with daily, mainly Holborn Viaduct to Sevenoaks but with peak trains to Crayford/Dartford via Lewisham.

N.19   Nutbourne

Victoria-Portsmouth line, between Chichester and Havant. 33 m 14 ch from Brighton

The 1906 station has raised concrete platforms with a corrugated shelter and staff hut on each and outside the peak hours is served by the hourly Brighton-Portsmouth slows. Funtington AHB LC (32 m 19 ch) and Drift Lane LC (32 m 60 ch) come before the station AHB crossing and Inlands Road AHB LC (33 m 70 ch) after it.

N.20 Nutfield

Redhill-Tonbridge line, between Redhill and Edenbridge. 24 m 47 ch from Charing Cross

Nutfield station dates from 1883 and comprises Up and Down platforms with metal shelters and served by the Reading-Tonbridge dmus.

Ockley—see Dorking-Horsham Line

O.1   Ore

Victoria-Eastbourne/Hastings/Ore line and Ashford-Hastings line. 81 m 42 ch from Charing Cross*

Although the South Eastern Railway reached Hastings from Ashford in 1851 (hence the mileage shown above) the station at Ore was not opened until January 1 1888. It became important with the completion of the Hastings electrification scheme in July 1935 when, because of the limited accommodation at Hastings, Ore was used as the terminus for trains from the west and a depot was built behind the Up (inland) platform for servicing the new electric stock. Trains from Victoria and Brighton still turn round at Ore which is also served hourly by the Ashford trains.

The approach to Ore from the Rye direction is over the Tokenless Block single line through the 1,402 yd Ore Tunnel (80 m 26 ch to 81 m 10 ch). An Up siding, crossovers and connection to the four-bay servicing depot are followed by the two platforms, with a wooden ticket office and waiting room on the Up and a foot-bridge link to the waiting shelter on the Down. After a further crossover comes the 230 yd Mount Pleasant Tunnel (81 m 50 ch to 81 m 60 ch).

O.2   Orpington

Charing Cross-Dover line, between Chislehurst and Sevenoaks. 13 m 65 ch from Charing Cross

Orpington is a substantial and busy station comprising centre island and two outer platforms, the latter with bays at the London end. The four tracks from the London direction become two beyond the station and it has an extensive carriage stabling and servicing area on the Down side where the old steam loco depot was.

Orpington first received a station on March 2 1868 when the SER opened the line from Chislehurst to Tonbridge but the present buildings and layout date from the 1901 widening of the line.

In addition to its own services to and from London, Orpington also has calls by the Charing Cross-Sevenoaks, Charing Cross-Hastings and Charing Cross-Tonbridge/Ashford/Dover/Margate services.

Pullman services on the former LSW main line in Devon—an era long vanished. Seen here the Devon Belle leaving Oke-hampton for Plymouth in June 1949 headed by Locomotive 34011.

O.3 Otford

Victoria-Ramsgate line, between Swanley and Otford Junction. 24 m 7 ch from Victoria

The Sevenoaks Railway's line from the LC&D to Bat & Ball dates from June 2 1862 and in this same year the extension to Maidstone East, which was to create the junction at Otford, was authorised. Opening eventually followed on June 1 1874 and ten years later the new route was completed through to Ashford. By then Otford station (opened 1882) had succeeded the earlier junction exchange platform.

Somewhat larger than its contemporaries on the line, Otford follows a cutting and overbridge and has traditional station buildings embodying a station house, now in private hands. The junction (once triangular and used by Maidstone-Bat & Ball trains) and its signal box follow at 24 m 53 ch and there is an Up side engineer's siding between the two.

Otford is served by Holborn Viaduct-Sevenoaks and Victoria-Maidstone East trains, the latter putting London within 40 minutes ride.

A view of Otford in 1922.

O.4 Ouse Valley Viaduct

Victoria-Brighton line, between Balcombe and Haywards Heath

David Mocatta was the L&B's architect for this 1,475 ft long viaduct built by J.U. Rastrick 36 miles along the journey from London to Brighton. Comprising 37 semi-circular arches, each with a span of 30 ft, the viaduct carries the main line across the broad valley of the modest Ouse river at heights varying from 40 ft at the ends to 96 ft at the centre. The river below was the main means of access for the 11 m bricks used in the construction. It is difficult to believe in these days that the contract price, including approaches and the pleasant stone ornamentation at each end of the main structure, was just £38,500. On the Down side of the viaduct, at the south end, can be traced earthworks of the projected line to Uckfield.

O.5 Overton

Waterloo-Exeter line, between Worting Junction and Andover. 55 m 42 ch from Waterloo

Overton station, opened on July 3 1854, now comprises short four-car platforms with bus stop shelters. It was remanned

recently and a shed provided for morning ticket issues. The Waterloo-Salisbury trains call.

A ground frame (55 m 46 ch) gives access to the CCE's siding.

O.6 Oxshott

New Guildford Line, between Hampton Court Junction and Effingham Junction. 16 m 79 ch from Waterloo

Set in the wooded area between Esher Common and Stoke Wood, Oxshott is an original 1885 station to the same pattern as Claygate but with the main buildings on the Up side. It is approached with a bridge carrying the A3 across the line and then a high overbridge just before the station itself, a double barrier crossing following.

Called Oxshott & Fairmile until 1956, the station lost its goods facilities three years later. It has a car park, footbridge, half-hourly trains to Guildford and Waterloo and houses the 17 MP on the Down platform.

O.7 Oxted

South Croydon-East Grinstead line, between Sanderstead and Hurst Green Junction. 20 m 25 ch from London Bridge

Oxted was a joint LB&SC/SER station, opened when the South Croydon to East Grinstead line was opened on March 10 1884. It is now the point at which the units forming the off-peak service on the East Grinstead and Uckfield branches are combined and separated on their way to and from London Bridge. The station also has

Class C2X 0-6-0 32526 takes water near Oxted signal box.

a bay at the country end of the Down platform for the use of branch services. The signal box is nearby and opposite is a siding to the former goods shed and dock. The main buildings are at street level on the Up side with a subway connection to the Down.

On the approach to Oxted the 1 m 501 yd Oxted Tunnel (17 m 66 ch to 19 m 8 ch) lies on the descent at 1 in 132 from Woldingham summit and is followed by the site of the old Oxted Lime Sidings box. After the high underbridge at the country end of the station comes the 551 yd Limpsfield Tunnel (20 m 58 ch to 21 m 3 ch) as the route continues the descent which will go all the way to Lingfield.

P.1 Paddock Wood

Charing Cross-Dover line, junction for Strood. 34 m 65 ch from Charing Cross

A station was opened here on May 31 1842 as part of the SER's route from Redhill to Ashford and Dover. With the opening of that company's first branch, to Maidstone, two years later the station took the name of a local wood in place of its original Maidstone Road title. Between 1892 and 1961 it was also the junction for the branch to Hawkhurst, the 'Hop Pickers' Line'.

In typical SER style, the present station has Up and Down platforms served by passenger loops with 25 mph access and with the Up and Down Main lines running between them. The meandering 11½-mile route to Hawkhurst departed from the country end of the Up side, a location now occupied by the siding of fruit importers Mack & Edwards. On the opposite side the Down Bay is used for the Maidstone West line trains. A footbridge connects the single-storey brick ticket office buildings on the Up side with the Down platform and both sides have decorative canopies.

Behind the Down Bay are six sidings and the Rowntree Mackintosh private siding and, nearer the divergence of the two routes, the Transfesa International Freight Terminal. Opened in 1974, the three-track shed covers 30,000 sq metres, is ¼-mile long and has 106 loading bays. Exit is over the largest weighbridge in Europe. Further along the branch lie traditional gated LCs at Swatlands (35 m 29 ch) and Wagons Lane (35 m 60 ch).

Paddock Wood's former signal boxes have now given way to control from Tonbridge. On the main line Ashford slows and Margate semi-fasts call and there is a basic hourly service via Maidstone West to Strood.

P.2   Parkstone

Waterloo-Weymouth line, between Bournemouth and Poole. 111 m 76 ch from Waterloo

The branch from Broadstone to Poole was extended through Parkstone to Bournemouth West on June 15 1874. The station buildings on the Up side probably date from then and have several decorative features, including the window heads. Beyond the station, which is served by the hourly Bournemouth-Weymouth four-car portions, the line skirts Parkstone Bay with a view of Brownsea Island and the Isle of Purbeck.

Peckham Rye—see South London Line

P.3   Penge

Penge East is on the Victoria-Ramsgate line, 7 m 15 ch from Victoria; Penge West is on the London Bridge-Windmill Bridge Junction line, 7 m 15 ch from London Bridge

The senior of the two Penge stations is the one on the original London & Croydon Railway route which opened with that pioneer line on June 5 1839. Today Penge West is just an ordinary station with a brick ticket office building and platforms

on the slow lines served by the London Bridge-Sutton trains.

There are four tracks through Penge West but only two through Penge East which was opened with the main line on July 1 1863 and has been constrained by the 1 m 381 yd Penge Tunnel (5 m 62 ch to 7 m) ever since. Built to take the LC&D under the heights of Crystal Palace the tunnel involved cutting through a solid wall of London clay although this was then put to good use in manufacturing the 33 m bricks used for the tunnel's lining. The tunnel was subsequently widened and also featured in early experiments with Sykes 'lock and block' signalling. The LB&SC line crosses over the LC&D route immediately after the south portal.

Penge East station has its main buildings, complete with typical LC&D window decoration, on the Up side (where there is also a small station house) and a wooden waiting room plus long canopy on the Down. There is an Up side engineers' siding between the station and the tunnel and the passenger service is provided by the Victoria-Orpington trains.

P.4   Penshurst

Redhill-Tonbridge line, between Edenbridge and Tonbridge. 38 m 3 ch from Charing Cross

Penshurst, in the village of Chiddingstone Causeway, was one of the original 1842 stations but was subsequently rebuilt and now consists of staggered platforms with shelters. It is served by the Reading-Tonbridge dmus. There is a signal box and semaphore signalling and the 78 yd Penshurst Tunnel follows (38 m 13 ch to 38 m 17 ch).

P.5   Petersfield

Waterloo-Portsmouth line, between Haslemere and Havant. 54 m 71 ch from Waterloo

Petersfield lies in the great dip in the Portsmouth Direct line between the Haslemere and Buriton summits. The station, like the line, dates from 1859 and its gabled Down side buildings are in the pattern of its contemporaries, all probably attributable to Tite or at least his ideas. There is a siding behind the Up platform.

The approach to Petersfield is via the AHB crossings at Sheet (53 m 72 ch) and Kings Fernsden (54 m 10 ch). The signal box and the station's own crossing precede the platforms and opposite the former the

Petersfield station with the 1859 station house and ticket office on the right.

route to Petworth can be spotted. This was opened on to Midhurst on September 1 1864, to Petworth on October 15 1866 and closed on February 7 1955, and it had its own bay on the Liss side of Petersfield LC. On the 1 in 100/110 rise which follows the station there are traces of Buriton Siding and a small wooden staff platform. Then comes the 485 yd Buriton Tunnel (57 m 46 ch to 57 m 68 ch).

Petersfield enjoys a basic service of two trains an hour in each direction. 'The Railway' public house, complete with locomotive sign, stands opposite the ticket office.

P.6 Petts Wood

Charing Cross-Dover line, between Chisle-hurst and Orpington. 12 m 55 ch from Charing Cross

Petts Wood, a community which developed from the building of its station, enjoys an excellent train service with calls by the Charing Cross/Cannon Street-Sevenoaks/Orpington trains, by the Victoria-Orping-ton trains and by some additional services

such as the morning Charing Cross-Maidstone West trains. It dates from 1928 and comprises two island platforms between the slow and fast line pairs. At Petts Wood Junction (12 m 25 ch) the Up and Down Tonbridge Loops link the Chatham and South Eastern main lines.

P.7 Pevensey & Westham

Victoria-Eastbourne/Hastings line, between Willingdon Junction and Bexhill. 23 m 7 ch from Brighton

The original station, opened on June 27 1846, was West Ham & Pevensey and the combination has been varied several times since. The location comprises Down side signal box plus double barrier crossing at the Eastbourne end, a modest rendered period building on the Down platform, footbridge, Up refuge siding and sub-station. The former goods yard, closed in 1961, is now occupied by housing.

The station is well served by the trains from Victoria and Brighton to Ore. The ruins of Pevensey Castle can be seen inland.

P.8 Pevensey Bay

Victoria-Eastbourne/Hastings line, between Willingdon Junction and Bexhill. 23 m 68 ch from Brighton

A former halt, now single-manned, this location dates from September 11 1905 and comprises Up and Down platforms, shelters, ticket hut and, operated from Pevensey & Westham box, the Wallsend CCTV barrier crossing (23 m 72 ch). The Brighton-Ore trains call.

P.9   Pirbright Junction

Waterloo-Weymouth line, junction for line to Alton. 29 m 39 ch from Waterloo

This is a junction between the four-track main line and the double line route to Alton, the former dating from 1838 and the latter from 1870 when the direct line via Aldershot was brought into use and began to supersede that via Ash junction. The Up Alton line passes over the main line by a skew bridge.

P.10   Pluckley

Charing Cross-Dover line, between Paddock Wood and Ashford. 50 m 35 ch from Charing Cross

This was one of the original 1842 stations and its single-storey Down side wooden buildings probably date from then. As with Marden and Staplehurst, the Pluckley platforms are partially staggered and there is a crossover, Up siding and Down side coal tenancy. There is an hourly service to Charing Cross and to Ashford.

P.11   Plumpton

Victoria-Eastbourne/Hastings line, between Keymer Jnction and Lewes. 44 m 42 ch from London Bridge

Dating from 1863, Plumpton station has a very long Up platform with direct access to the racecourse and designed with race trains in mind. A footbridge spans the two tracks to the Down side where the pleasant wooden station buildings are situated. At the country end of the station stand the signal box and its gates while towards Keymer Junction is the AHB LC at Spatham Lane (42 m 76 ch). Trains call only in the business periods.

Plumstead—see North Kent Line

P.12   Point Pleasant Junction-Wimbledon Line

Waterloo-Reading line, link to Wimbledon. 3 m 38 ch

This 1889 LSW route with Metropolitan District running powers remains in SR territory from the north side of the Thames to East Putney where the links from Point Pleasant Junction join, and then on to the Up side platforms at Wimbledon. It remains as a SR freight route from Point Pleasant Junction to Wimbledon but the passenger service, which was the LSW's first electric service (1915) and took 23 minutes from Waterloo, ended in 1941 leaving the passenger activity in the hands of the LT District Line trains.

From Point Pleasant Junction (5 m 9 ch) brick arches provide direct and flyover links to join the north-south route at East Putney (5 m 60 ch) where two of the three platforms are still in use. Next comes the 311 yd East Putney Tunnel (6 m 3 ch to 6 m 17 ch) and then Southfields (6 m 57 ch) another busy commuter station and also the station for the All England Lawn Tennis Championships. Wimbledon Park (7 m 50 ch) has an island platform and its signal box controls the movement of empty stock to and from the SR carriage berthing sidings. The main line is joined at Wimbledon 'A' (8 m 37 ch).

P.13   Pokesdown

Waterloo-Weymouth line, between Christchurch and Bournemouth. 106 m 24 ch from Waterloo

The station dates from the 1886 doubling of the line from Christchurch to Bournemouth and now provides the eastern end of the Bournemouth conurbation with an hourly all-stations service. The station lies in a cutting and appears dark and plain beneath its long canopies.

Boscombe, 684 yards further on and now just marked by platform remains, closed to passengers on October 4 1965.

P.14   Polegate

Victoria-Eastbourne/Hastings line, between Southerham Junction and Willingdon Junction. 19 m 60 ch from Brighton

A double barrier crossing (19 m 34 ch) and signal box follow the AHB crossing at Wilmington (17 m 29 ch) and mark the approach to Polegate, once an important junction between the coast route and the route from London via Eridge. Although looking slightly neglected at the beginning of the present decade the station was due to come into its own again when a new railhead was built near the town centre and the signal box site. This would be a return to the position of the first Polegate station for the original 1846 location was displaced on October 3 1881 by the station on the present site some 300 yards nearer Eastbourne. At the same time the Hailsham line became a junction towards Eastbourne instead of towards Lewes. Between these two dates—on May 14 1849—Polegate acquired branches to the coast at Eastbourne and north to Hailsham, the latter eventually becoming a through route to London but lasting only until 1968.

In 1983 Polegate comprised two island platforms with temporary shelters taking over from the traditional wooden buildings, the canopies removed and running lines only to the inner faces. A rusting single line still marked the original direct route to Hastings across the top of the Willingdon Junction triangle to Stone Cross Junction via Stone Cross Halt but it was no longer in use. A subway ran beneath the platforms to the imposing two-storey 1881 Down side station building facing the main road, with its severe frontage relieved by varied and decorated window heads, a hipped roof and tall chimneys.

For many years Polegate was a busy junction, originating its own trains to Eastbourne and Hailsham, splitting trains until 1935, and providing an interchange point for the through services on its routes east, west and to/via Tunbridge Wells. It still has a basic service of three trains an hour, Brighton-Eastbourne and Brighton-Ore with a Victoria-Ore service between.

P.15   Polhill Tunnel

Charing Cross-Dover line, between Orpington and Sevenoaks. 17 m 20 ch from Charing Cross

On the 1 in 143 descent from Knockholt summit, the 1 m 851 yd Polhill Tunnel (17 m 20 ch to 18 m 58 ch) came into use in 1868, at the same time as the 1 m 1,693 yd Sevenoaks Tunnel on a similar slope six miles further on. Polhill was cut through virgin chalk and its roof is brick-lined throughout, with the brick arch resting for the greater part of its length on the chalk which forms the side walls of the tunnel up to 7 ft above rail level.

P.16   Poole

Waterloo-Weymouth line, between Bournemouth and Wareham. 113 m 62 ch from Waterloo

The branch from the Southampton & Dorchester's line at Broadstone reached Poole on December 2 1872 and was extended to Bournemouth West on June 15 1874. The link between Poole and the S&D at Hamworthy, over the Holes Bay causeway,

Poole station looking west and with 33 102 newly arrived. The line continues along the edge of Holes Bay.

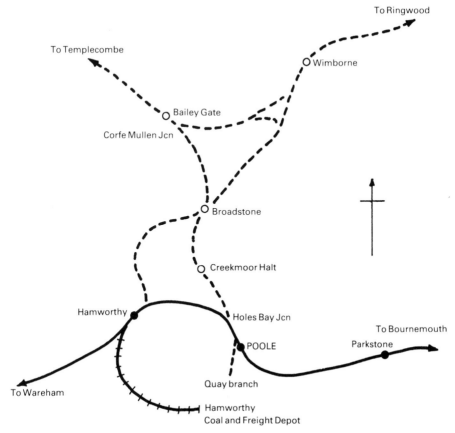

came on June 1 1893. As the direct east-west line grew in importance, the original inland route via Ringwood and Wimborne declined and passenger services eventually ceased in 1964 along with those on the route from Salisbury, the Somerset & Dorset line services via Corfe Mullen Junction ending two years later. The remaining evidence of this once busy link, the trackbed of the line to Broadstone Junction, began to disappear under a building development west of Poole in 1982. There used also to be a one-mile, freight-only Quay Tramway.

Today Poole has a modern station with the ticket office on the Up side. It lies on a sharp curve which starts with the CCTV crossing and requires speed restrictions of 15, 30, 40 mph for about a mile. There are Down sidings for coaching stock near the signal box at the country end of the station and the freight yard opposite includes a Blue Circle cement terminal.

In addition to the four-car Waterloo-Weymouth portions, Poole originates

through services to Liverpool, Leeds/Newcastle, Manchester and Derby, but the Pines Express departure at 10.47 am for Manchester via Bath and its companion services to Sheffield, Lincoln, Birmingham and the West Riding are now just a memory.

P.17   Portchester

Southampton-Portsmouth line, between Fareham and Portcreek Junction. 87 m 35 ch from Waterloo

The station dates from the October 1 1848 LSW link from Fareham to the LB&SC access to Portsmouth. It has footbridge-linked Up and Down platforms with the main, single-storey brick buildings—one of the few examples where the station apartments were provided on the ground floor rather than on the first floor—on the former and just a nondescript wooden shelter on the latter. The hourly Salisbury/Romsey-Portsmouth and Reading/Eastleigh-Portsmouth services call.

P.18   Portslade

*Brighton-Littlehampton/Portsmouth line,
between Brighton and Shoreham. 2 m 73 ch
from Brighton*

The original station, dating from the
opening of the line on May 12 1840, lasted
only seven years. It was re-opened after a
further ten years but the present site may
not correspond to the original one. Today's
station, minus its goods facilities since
1968, has its main two-storey buildings on
the Down side and a small traditional
building on the Up. Both sides have
additional waiting rooms and shelters and
a small signal box on the Up side controls
the double barrier crossing at the country
end.

   All coast line trains call except the
hourly Littlehampton-Victoria semi-fasts
but connection is made with these at Hove.

P.19   Portsmouth

*The routes from Brighton, Victoria,
Waterloo and Southampton merge at
Portcreek Junction (41 m 3 ch from
Brighton) and continue to Hilsea (41 m
41 ch), Fratton (43 m 64 ch), Portsmouth
& Southsea (44 m 50 ch) and Portsmouth
Harbour (45 m 36 ch)*

The first rail travellers from Portsmouth
had to cross the harbour to a station at
Gosport and then travel on the LSW
branch via Fareham to Bishopstoke (Eastleigh). Two years later, in 1844, the LSW

deposited plans for a direct link from
Fareham as a counter to the London &
Brighton scheme to reach Portsmouth
from the east. Other schemes of the period
included a proposed atmospheric line via
Godalming.

   Based on its Act of August 8 1845, the
LB&SC reached Portsmouth via Chichester
on June 14 1847, using the route of the
former Portsmouth & Arundel Canal from
Fratton to the terminus in Commercial
Road. After another 16 months had
elapsed LSW trains reached the town
from Fareham, by which time the Cosham-
Portsmouth section of the route had become a joint LB&SC/LSW enterprise.
Local agitation for a more direct line was
revived in 1852-4, the scheme eventually
being taken over by the LSW which started
serving Portsmouth via Guildford on
January 24 1859 after winning a legal
battle to stop the Brighton from obstruct-
ing the link from Havant to the joint line.

   The route on from Portsmouth & Southsea to Portsmouth Harbour derives from
an Act of 1873 with the line itself being
opened on October 2 1876. It replaced an
earlier tramway and at one period had
wharf and dockyard branches at the
harbour end in addition to the main dockyard connection which was realigned at

Sealink ferry Brading *off to the Isle of
Wight.*

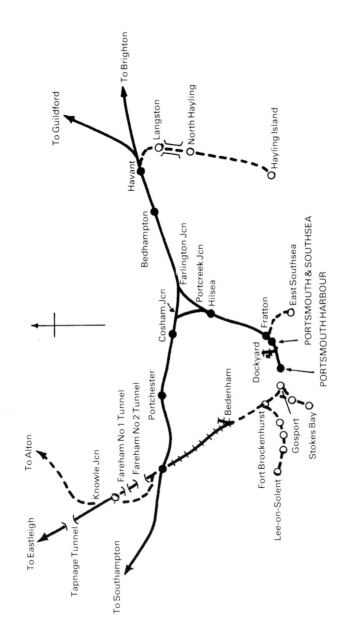

that time. The latter, known as North
Dockyard Line (Admiralty), led from the
high level route to the extensive dockyard
network. Portsmouth's other significant
railway was the privately-originated branch
from an Up facing junction at Fratton to
Southsea, opened on July 1 1885. Under
joint LSW/LB&SC operation the Southsea branch later received a new terminus,
intermediate halts and a railcar service,
but it lasted only until August 6 1914
despite thoughts of linking it with the
Hayling Island branch via a bridge over
the entrance to Langstone Harbour.

The direct line to Portsmouth was
electrified in 1937, the two main Portsmouth stations and Fratton all being
enlarged and new carriage sheds being
provided at the latter where a new goods
depot had just been opened in the previous
year. Electric services reached the town
from the Brighton direction in 1938. Both
Portsmouth stations suffered from war
damage and other changes have included
the loss of the connection for special trains
using the South Jetty and a new signal box
for the area from May 1968. Farlington
Race Station opened in 1891 and became a
halt in 1928, but closed in 1937.

The railway approach to Portsea Island
is by way of Portcreek Junction where the
double lines from Havant and Cosham
combine for the bridge across Broom
Channel. They are linked across the top of

*The through portion of Portsmouth &
Southsea station on December 20 1982
and with a Down train about to leave for
Portsmouth Harbour.*

the triangle by a double line from Farlington Junction to Cosham Junction.

An old overbridge precedes Hilsea, a
modest affair of two platforms, shelters
and staff hut, opened in November 1941
to serve the adjacent factories. There is a
trailing connection from the gas works
controlled by a ground frame (42 m 9 ch)
on the Down side and on the Up side a
ground frame (41 m 45 ch) for the rusting
Hilsea Government Sidings, and the period
Copnor crossing house. Fratton itself,
dating from the opening of the Southsea
branch and with freight facilities, loco
depot and carriage sidings, has a long
group of brick buildings on the Up side
and an island on the Down, extra running
lines linking the carriage sidings and
washer with the cleaning roads and then
with the Down Relief line as far as Portsmouth box (44 m 29 ch).

Portsmouth & Southsea station comprises platforms 6 and 7 of the high level
portion and the terminal platforms of the
lower portion on the shopping centre side.
The former are used by trains rising steeply
from Blackfriars Junction to take the
raised route to Portsmouth Harbour where

connection is made with the ferry vessels to the Isle of Wight. The island platform has a slight double curve and the canopy, still retaining smoke dispersal louvres from the days of steam, is supported by brackets bearing the cipher PJER—Portsmouth Joint Extension Railway.

The terminal portion of Portsmouth & Southsea comprises three active platform faces plus the parcels and office area on the Up side—the site of the original development. The covered concourse has a temporary ticket office and other facilities but the old booking hall remains, some of its nine shuttered windows still carrying their enamel number plates. The 1876 frontage is impressive with much ornamental ironwork above the canopy, fully decorated window arches and doorways and a clock fronting the tower section with decorated parapets. The information office lies beside the approach courtyard.

The Harbour station has a modern approach area including bus interchange facilities and the Gosport ferry adjacent. The brick buildings on the Up side are post-war and include the Look-Out buffet. The rail approach is at high level, past the SR signal box, with three pairs of lines then terminating above the waters of the harbour and ramps leading on to the Sealink vessel berths. Each pair of tracks is supported on piers with beams between the piers forming the foundations for the

The attractive Up side signal box at Pulborough still retains its bell at the head of the steps.

three platforms which serve five of the six lines, the outer Down line being held for stabling.

The routes out of Portsmouth carry about nine trains hourly, three via Chichester (including one to Victoria), three via Guildford and three via Fareham, the latter including the trains to Bristol/South Wales and to Reading. There is a Sealink shipping service to the Channel Islands from the Continental Ferry Post (linked by bus with Harbour station) as well as the service to the Isle of Wight from Portsmouth Harbour.

Preston Park—see Brighton

P.20 Pulborough

Victoria-Portsmouth line, between Horsham and Arundel Junction. 50 m from London Bridge

The Mid-Sussex Railway's line to Petworth brought the railway to Pulborough on October 10 1859 with the link from Hardham Junction, just to the south, creating a new main line to Arundel Junction from August 3 1863. Now the branch trains on from Petworth to Midhurst (and some to

Petersfield) have gone and Pulborough is served just by the Victoria-Littlehampton/Bognor and Bognor/Portsmouth trains.

Pulborough is approached by way of AHB crossings at Adversane (46 m 31 ch) and Cray Lane (48 m 31 ch) and comprises two, subway-connected platforms with drab, two-storey brick buildings on the Down side. The Up platform was formerly an island and its outer face, now with just a siding, was used by the Midhurst line trains. The tall but small signal box stands on this side, by the siding lead and the trailing crossover at the London end.

P.21 Purley

Victoria-Brighton line, between East Croydon and Redhill; Purley Oaks is 12 m 34 ch from London Bridge and Purley, junction for the Caterham and Tattenham Corner branches, is 13 m 29 ch

Purley Oaks station, the northernmost of the two, dates from the 1899 quadrupling and consists of centre island and two outer platforms served by the Caterham and Tattenham Corner trains. The main line is elevated at this point and the Purley Oaks platforms are linked by subway, with the main buildings on the Up side.

The London Bridge-Redhill services give Purley a connection into the Down Brighton trains at Redhill and the station also divides the trains from London to the Caterham and Tattenham Corner branches. For these services it has two islands and two outer platforms, linked by subway and with assorted buildings and canopies.

Halfway up the 1 in 264 bank to Merstham, Purley station opened as Godstone Road—7 miles from the village it served—on July 12 1841. It closed on October 1 1847 and became the centre of a controversy when the Caterham branch opened nine years later. Caught in the rivalry between the SER and LB&SC companies, the Caterham Railway had to sue the latter to get the junction station reopened and matters got even worse when the SER took over the bankrupt local line. Caterham Junction became Purley on October 1 1888 and was reconstructed in the same 1899 period that saw the opening of Purley Oaks. The Tattenham Corner line, also SER, opened between 1897 and 1901 and the layout involves the two branches quitting the main line on the Down side at Caterham Line Junction and separating at Chipstead Line Junction, with the Tattenham Corner route then passing beneath the main to the Up side.

Trains of aggregates from Cliffe are dealt with in Brett Marine's private terminal on the Down side. The engineer also has a siding here and some coal traffic is dealt with.

P.22 Putney

Waterloo-Reading line, between Clapham Junction and Barnes. 5 m 72 ch from Waterloo

Lying at the junction of Putney High Street and Richmond Road, Putney is an 1846 station rebuilt and widened in 1886 to give a long street frontage spanning the four lines and their island plus outer platforms below. An excellent service is provided by trains on the Hounslow and Kingston loops plus stops by the Windsor services.

Q.1 Quarry Line and Tunnel

Victoria-Brighton line, between Coulsdon North and Earlswood. 6 m 64 ch

This 6¾ miles of twin-track railway was opened for goods on November 8 1899 and for passengers on April 1 of the following year. Less than happy with the joint use of Redhill with the SER, the LB&SC decided to avoid that point altogether when extending the four-track capacity southwards. As a result the separate Quarry lines, still used for giving extra capacity on the Brighton route, diverge from the main line on the west side, cross over them 2 miles further on and then rejoin from the east just before Earlswood station.

Part of the cutting south of Coulsdon was artificially covered at first, supposedly at the request of the local mental hospital, but this was later opened out again. The route then rises at 1 in 165, past Star Lane Box and then down again through the 1 m 353 yd Quarry Tunnel (17 m 24 ch to 18 m 40 ch) at 1 in 206, under the Tonbridge line via the 649 yd Redhill Tunnel (20 m 62 ch to 21 m 12 ch) and back into the original main line. Cut through chalk, much of the route is in cuttings but there are glimpses of the older route on the 1 in 200 drop before Redhill. The extensive quarry workings of British Industrial Sand/Standard Brick & Sand Co are east of the Quarry Line but their siding connection is with the Redhill line and their reception lines lie between the two routes.

Right Rainham (Kent) and commuters wait for the arriving train with 2-HAP 6116 at the front end.

Queenborough—see Sheerness Branch

Queens Road, Peckham—see South London line

Q.2   Queenstown Road, Battersea

Waterloo-Weymouth line. 2 m 65 ch from Waterloo

Dating from November 1 1877 (as Queens Road, Battersea) and lying beneath the LB&SC Victoria approach lines, the station comprises outer and island platforms on the Windsor lines and served by the Hounslow and Kingston loop trains.

R.1   Radipole

Waterloo-Weymouth line, between Dorchester South and Weymouth. 167 m 59 ch from Paddington

Serving the approaches to Weymouth, Radipole has two short platforms, plus shelters, at which the Westbury line dmus call. A closure threat was temporarily averted in 1983.

R.2   Rainham

Victoria-Ramsgate line, between Chatham and Sittingbourne. 38 m 74 ch from Victoria

When the station opened on January 25 1858 Rainham was just a small village. Now it is a significant part of the Gillingham suburban complex and the old station buildings have been replaced (in 1972) by a modern ticket office which warranted the station being featured in two major television programmes about commuting. Both platforms have shelters and the Down side, where there is a community centre in the old warehouse nearby, has an additional exit used in the evening peak.

The half-hourly all-stations Dover/ Ramsgate services call at Rainham and are controlled by the country end signal box which also operates the barrier crossing, the trailing crossover and the access to/ from the passenger loops towards Newington.

R.3   Ramsgate

Victoria-Ramsgate line, via Faversham, 79 m 21 ch from Victoria; also on routes via Dover and via Canterbury West

The South Eastern was the first railway to reach Ramsgate, the branch from the main line at Ashford arriving at Ramsgate Town station on April 13 1846 and continuing on to Margate Sands on December 1 of the same year. Ramsgate Town was a terminal station and trains for Margate had to reverse there but although the route from London was a circuitous one the new railway brought many visitors to swell the growing reputation of the resort. For 17 years the SER had only the Thames steamers to compete with but on October 5 1863 the LC&D line from Margate arrived at a Ramsgate Harbour terminus, via a tunnel which took it much nearer to the sea than its rival's station.

Popular and busy, Ramsgate Harbour station suffered from space constraints and from a 1 in 75 approach to take the line down to sea level (and down which a train had gone out of control in 1891). The newly formed Southern Railway soon revived and modified early schemes for altering the Thanet area and on July 2 1926 opened a new line from the vicinity of Ramsgate Town to a point on the LC&D line near Dumpton Park (where a new station was also opened) to create a new, through station at Ramsgate and cut out the line from the Harbour terminus and also the 1846 route across the peninsula to Margate. The old triangular junction at Ramsgate Town disappeared and its place was taken by new locomotive and carriage depots while the station itself was given a dramatic frontage in much the same style as that used in the rebuilding of Margate. The redundant LC&D tunnel was taken over and used by the Ramsgate Tunnel Railway.

The approach to Ramsgate from Margate is via a high bridge and with a 30 mph speed restriction. There are two island platforms served by two through lines and two loops with a layby road, signal box and then the carriage servicing area on the inland side. There are futher sidings at the south end of the station, those on the seaward side occupying the site of the old SER station. The main buildings are also on this side and include the sizeable ticket hall and its coats of arms of the Southern Railway and the town it served.

Margate and Ramsgate no longer have the through services from the GWR and LMS, nor quite the same level of summer Saturday visitors, but both are busy and well served. Ramsgate has about 200 trains daily on the London routes via Chatham and via Dover and Canterbury West. It is also a depot for drivers and guards and the main berthing and carriage servicing

Right *Car loading terminal at Ramsgate.*

Above *The great barn produced by the Southern at Ramsgate.* **Background** *A train at Ramsgate Harbour station with the tunnel and 1 in 75 climb ahead of it.*

point on the South Eastern Division, handling some 600 coaches every 24 hours.

Ravensbourne—see Catford Loop

R.4   Raynes Park

Waterloo-Weymouth line, junction for Epsom line and Chessington South branch via Motspur Park. 8 m 51 ch from Waterloo

This portion of the main line opened in 1838, with the route to Epsom following in 1859 and Raynes Park station being opened on the site of Epsom Junction on October 30 1871. Today the station comprises a ticket office at road level with subway and stairs then leading to the platforms to the outer, local lines and to the Epsom lines.

The station is served by Epsom, Chessington, Hampton Court and Kingston Loop trains and its signal box also controls the CCTV crossing at West Barnes (9 m 18 ch) just along the route to Motspur Park. The Up line from Motspur Park passes beneath the main line and rises to the Raynes Park Up platform which is curved to accommodate it.

R.5   Redbridge

Waterloo-Weymouth line and junction for Romsey/Salisbury route. 81 m 70 ch from Waterloo

Redbridge lies at the head of Southampton Water where the Blackwater and Test rivers join and where the 1847 main line turns away across their waters from the line to Salisbury. The section of the latter between Romsey and Redbridge might

Traffic keeps moving despite piling work in connection with a new bridge at Raynes Park.

have been part of a broad gauge entry into Southampton if the GWR-backed Andover & Redbridge Railway had not run out of funds and agreement been reached on its take-over by the London & South Western. The opening of the link between Romsey and Redbridge made the latter a junction from March 6 1865.

There is a CCE sleeper depot behind the Down platform at Redbridge and the Down line is reversible for movements to Redbridge yard. In LSW days this was a wagon works and the station buildings on the Up side included the works pay office. Nearby the old signal box remains and there is a double barrier road access to the works at the country end of the station platforms.

Portsmouth-Romsey/Salisbury trains and all-stations Bournemouth trains provide the service.

R.6   Redhill

Victoria-Brighton line, junction for lines to Tonbridge and Reading. 22 m 40 ch from Charing Cross

Redhill is a major interchange point served by the Brighton line semi-fasts, by a London Bridge-Redhill service, by the Bognor Regis trains and by the Reading-Tonbridge/Gatwick workings. It has four tracks (Up and Down Through and Up and Down Local), paired by direction, between the long Down platform and the island on the Up side, the latter with an Up loop serving its outer face. The ticket office is at street level with access to the platforms by stairs and subway.

Redhill station is a busy and cluttered one, not easy to work because trains on the old SER route must reverse and cross all lines at Redhill 'B' box (22 m 53 ch). At the other end the five-line section starts at Redhill 'A' (22 m 30 ch). A GPO letter mail sorting activity is directly connected

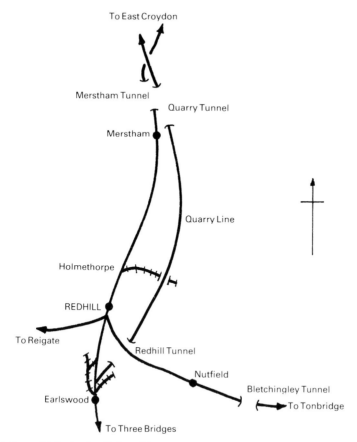

To East Croydon

Merstham Tunnel

Quarry Tunnel

Merstham

Quarry Line

Holmethorpe

REDHILL

To Reigate

Redhill Tunnel

Nutfield

Bletchingley Tunnel

Earlswood

To Tonbridge

To Three Bridges

with the station which also has links with a fully-mechanised parcels sorting office at Salfords.

Such difficulties as today exist at Redhill are nothing compared with those of the past. With Redhill lying on the original SER route to Dover and also on the LB&SC main line to Brighton conflict was inevitable, and frequent. Initially the stations on each of the routes, situated beyond their divergence and highly inconvenient for passengers changing, were named Reigate. This name was still in use when they were replaced by a new station north of the junction that opened on April 15 1844. This station was rebuilt in 1858 when the present buildings on the Down side were constructed, but the SER as owners of the Coulsdon-Redhill section continued to give preference to its own trains and this fact eventually led to the construction of the Quarry Line which enabled the LB&SC to avoid Redhill altogether. It also led to Redhill being known as 'Stopham Junction'!

Reedham—see Tattenham Corner Branch

R.7 Reigate

Redhill-Reading line, between Redhill and Dorking Town. 24 m 27 ch from Charing Cross

Dating from the opening of the line in 1849, Reigate's main buildings on the Down side—tall-chimneyed and multi-gabled—are basically original. On the Up side are more modest brick buildings with a signal box near the double barrier crossing at the country end. At the Redhill end there are sidings on the Down side and the route then drops at 1 in 100 before the final curve into the main line.

Reigate's main service is provided by the Reading-Tonbridge dmus but several Reading-Gatwick trains call and there are some morning/evening electric services to and from Redhill and London, the Redhill-Reigate section having been electrified as part of the 1932/3 Brighton line electrification.

R.8   Richborough Sidings

Charing Cross-Margate line, between Sandwich and Minster South Junction. 82 m 70 ch from Charing Cross (via Canterbury West)

The site of the AD449 Saxon landing has long had aspirations as a port and Richborough was linked to the East Kent Railway at Sandwich Road in 1928 with a view to developing coal exports. The bridge used to carry this route over the main line is still apparent just north of Richborough AHB LC (85 m 24 ch) but the present connection from the Dover-Ramsgate line to the CEGB power station is much nearer Minster. It comprises the signal box, a facing crossover and the lead to the CEGB sidings and is used by oil trains from Grain. Trainmen use a key from the signal box to lock and unlock the access gate to the CEGB reception, oil and cripple siding complex.

There was a Richborough Castle Halt from 1933 to 1939.

R.9   Richmond

Waterloo-Reading line, junction with District/North London routes. 9 m 57 ch from Waterloo

Railways came to Richmond on July 27 1846 with the opening of the Richmond & West End Railway's line from Battersea (now Clapham Junction). In the following year the local company was acquired by the LSW and August 22 1848 brought an extension westwards to Datchet and a new station on the through route, although this was itself replaced a few years later. The opening of the line from Hammersmith gave Richmond a four-platform terminus called Richmond New, operated separately, but finally joined with the main line station with the reconstruction brought into use on August 1 1937.

Today the station precedes the embankment which raises the line for its crossing of the Thames and the street level offices, typical of the SR style of the 1930s, are followed by stairs down to platforms 6 and 7 for Broad Street trains, platforms 4 and 5 for District Line trains and, via the footbridge, to platforms 1 and 2 for services on the Windsor, Reading and Kingston lines. The second face of the Up platform (No 3) is used for parcels van traffic.

The cross-London route via Bollo Lane Junction lies within SR territory for the first 2½ miles and passes via Kew Gardens

(11 m 10 ch), Gunnersbury (10 m 15 ch) and the Regional Boundary, with the LMR, at 9 m 76 ch/3 m 12 ch. The LT trains diverge just beyond Gunnersbury.

R.10   Riddlesdown

South Croydon-East Grinstead line, between South Croydon and Oxted. 13 m 38 ch from London Bridge

Through Riddlesdown's two platforms the line is rising along the eastern side of the valley and at a gradient of 1 in 100. Opened on June 5 1927, the station has pedestrian access paths each side, brick main buildings on the Up side and a basic hourly service from the Uckfield/East Grinstead trains. It is followed by a wooded cutting and the 837 yd Riddlesdown Tunnel (13 m 48 ch to 14 m 6 ch). There is a good milepost example on the Down platform.

R.11   Robertsbridge

Charing Cross-Hastings line, between Tunbridge Wells Central and Battle. 49 m 47 ch from Charing Cross

Robertsbridge, lying in the dip formed by the long descent from Wadhurst Tunnel and the steeper following rise to Mountfield Tunnel, was the terminus of the SER line from Tonbridge from September 1

Above *A mixed train leaving Robertsbridge for the Kent & East Sussex line.* **Below** *Q1 0-6-0 33031 steams through Robertsbridge, which has a full goods yard.*

1851 until the section on to Battle was completed on January 1 1852. The through route to Bopeep Junction was completed a month later. Robertsbridge was also the junction for the Kent & East Sussex Railway which originated as the Rother Valley Light Railway's line to Tenterden, opened in 1900, extended to Tenterden Town in 1903 and then on to Headcorn, as the Kent & East Sussex Railway, in 1905. After a chequered history the route passed to BR in 1948, was finally closed on June 12 1961 but has now been partially revived by the K&ESR preservation project.

The trackbed of the K&ESR route is still visible on the Down side at the London end of the station. The main buildings are also on this side, similar to those at Stonegate and Wadhurst but with extensions added to the original centre section. There is a double barrier crossing at the country end of the station, with the signal box nearby, its semaphore signals regulating the hourly trains to and from Hastings.

R.12   Rochester

Victoria-Ramsgate line and junction with North Kent Line. 33 m 61 ch from Victoria

The Chatham main line approaches Rochester along the bank of the River Medway, some 100 ft higher than the ex-SER route from Maidstone West to Strood. The former bends sharply to cross over the latter with the link between the two, known as the Toomer Loop, joining at Rochester Bridge Junction (33 m 1 ch) and being followed by the bridge itself and then the main station. This is an area of historic significance for the loop was the original connection between the East Kent Railway, which was to grow into the LC&D, and the outside world. It also got its name from the local mayor who had to involve the Railway Commissioners in the LC&D's refusal to allow adequate access via the loop to Chatham.

The present location at Rochester dates from March 1 1892—earlier Strood used the Rochester name and there was a Rochester Bridge LC&D—and comprises two island platforms, complete with decorative LC&D canopy work, served by the two main lines plus two passenger loops and reached by stairs and subway from the ticket office, entrance and forecourt in Rochester High Street. The service is pro-

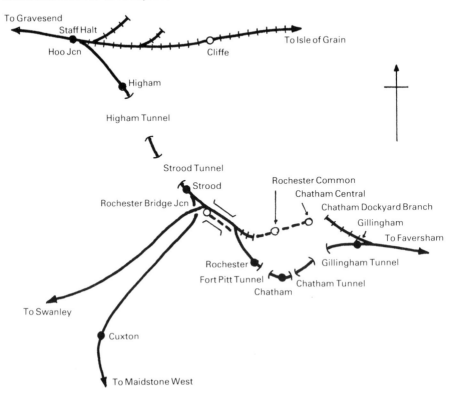

vided by the half-hourly all-stations trains on the Victoria line and via Gravesend with faster services during the peaks which give Rochester a 43-minute journey time to Cannon Street.

Below the Down side signal box and reached from No 1 Down Siding is the Rochester freight depot known as Chatham Goods Sidings plus the abutments of a bridge on the old SER route to Chatham Central. This lasted only from 1891-2 to 1911 (when the main Rochester station was rebuilt) and led from Strood via Rochester Common to the mis-named Chatham Central. Its main value was to contribute a bridge over the river, the previous LC&D one then becoming the road route.

R.13 Romsey

Redbridge Junction-Salisbury line, junction for route from Eastleigh. 80 m 47 ch from Waterloo*

In its heyday Romsey was a very busy station, handling through services from the Salisbury and Andover lines and originating others for Gosport and Portsmouth, Fareham, Eastleigh and the Bournemouth line. Trains from Swindon and Cheltenham called at holiday times and countless freight trains rattled through the station and junction, some detaching at the goods yard or picking up wagons which had been loaded there. Now the service is mainly between Portsmouth and Salisbury with some of the trains originating or terminating at Romsey and some calls by the through Bristol/Cardiff services.

The line from Eastleigh to Salisbury gave Romsey its first rail link and the 1847 station was then used by the 1865 route from Andover to Redbridge which joined the earlier line at Kimbridge Junction and left it again just south of Romsey station. The line from Andover closed on September 7 1964 and the Romsey-Eastleigh link lost its passenger services (but remains open for freight plus one Southampton-Bristol passenger service) on May 5 1969.

From the south the route from Redbridge curves into the station on an embankment where the junction and signal box are situated, the latter now having relinquished its duties to Eastleigh panel. The distances which changed from 81 m 76 ch to 23 m 31 ch at Redbridge Junction now change again from 18 m 16 ch to 80 m 35 ch to recognise the historical routing via Eastleigh. Romsey's old goods shed and dock precede the Down platform where the main period buildings are located, a subway then leading to the Up side where a few little-used sidings remain.

R.14 Rowlands Castle

Waterloo-Portsmouth line, between Petersfield and Havant. 63 m 18 ch from Waterloo

By the time Thomas Brassey's line reaches Rowlands Castle Up trains have been climbing for 3 miles and a steepening 5 miles through rolling, wooded downland lies ahead. Not much trouble for today's three trains an hour on the route, or even for the one train an hour which serves the 1859 station, still with its 1859 main buildings on the Up side. These are very good examples of the style of the line with the planes and gables and single-storey side extensions in pleasant harmony. On the opposite side there is a large shelter, plus the 63¼ milepost and a repeater signal.

R.15 Ryde Pier Head to Shanklin Line

A competitor on the television programme 'Mastermind' was totally stumped by the question 'Where do London Underground trains run over the sea?' The answer was, 'On Ryde Pier' for, since Easter 1967, the service on the Isle of Wight's remaining line to Shanklin has been worked by sets of former LTE stock.

The first railway on the island was the 4½-mile Cowes & Newport line connecting the capital, Newport, with the coast at Cowes from June 16 1862. This was followed on August 23 1864 by the section of today's electrified line from Ryde St John's Road to Shanklin. The company was the Isle of Wight Railway which extended its line to Ventnor on September 10 1866 and also worked (and later took over) the Brading Harbour Branch to Bembridge which came into use on May 27 1882.

In 1875 the Newport & Ryde Railway opened its 8¾-mile line from Smallbrook and the Isle of Wight (Newport Junction) company's route from Sandown reached Shide, on the outskirts of Newport. Extensions of the latter subsequently linked the three Newport lines and led to their amalgamation as the Isle of Wight Central Railway in 1887. A year later an independent line connected Newport with Freshwater.

The remaining two pieces of railway construction on the island affected Ryde and Ventnor. In the case of the former a

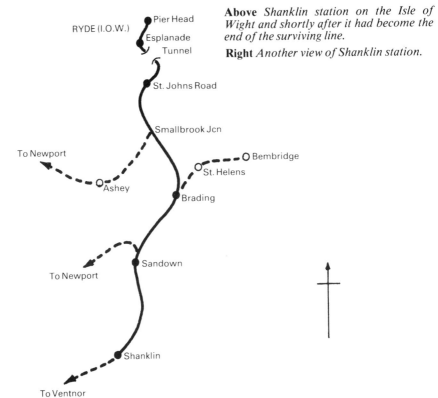

RYDE (I.O.W.)

Pier Head

Esplanade

Tunnel

St. Johns Road

Smallbrook Jcn

To Newport

Bembridge

St. Helens

Ashey

Brading

To Newport

Sandown

Shanklin

To Ventnor

Above *Shanklin station on the Isle of Wight and shortly after it had become the end of the surviving line.*

Right *Another view of Shanklin station.*

line from St John's Road to Ryde Esplanade was opened on April 5 1880 (replacing an 1864 horse tramway) and extended over a ½-mile pier on July 12 of that year. Ventnor got a route from Cowes under an Isle of Wight Central scheme which linked Merstone Junction with St Lawrence on July 26 1897 and finally reached Ventnor on June 1 1900.

As a result of 1923 Grouping the Southern Railway inherited the three island companies, the LB&SC/LSW joint line to St John's Road and the LSW's ferry depot at Yarmouth. For a time, stimulated by the SR's physical improvements and energetic marketing, traffic continued to expand, particularly in the summer when the SR paddle steamers brought thousands across the Solent every Saturday. But closures came soon after nationalisation with the Merstone-Ventnor line going in 1952, the Freshwater and Bembridge branches in the following year and Sandown-Newport in 1956. Ten years later came closure between Ryde and Cowes and beyond Shanklin.

Once the decision had been taken to retain and electrify the line to Shanklin and work it with LT coaches, these were overhauled, converted to run off the SR current system and moved under their own power to Portsmouth for the final road and ferry movement. Painted in BR colours

and with some seats replaced by luggage racks, the four and three-car sub-sets carry the SR stock codes 4-VEC and 3-TIS, Vectis being the Roman name for the Isle of Wight. Power is taken from the Southern Electricity Board 33kV three-phase AC supply.

The Portsmouth steamers dock at Ryde Pier Head, from which point distances on the surviving Isle of Wight line are measured. A few yards across the landing stage is the station, comprising a single-storey building across the end of the single platform and its two platform lines. In addition to displaying the 'Southern Railway Bye-Laws for Steam Vessels' there is a circus train model on the concourse. Then alongside the double line route to dry land runs the road access and the separate pier of the old horse tramway. The original pier Act dates back to 1812 and the tramway to 1864-71, with steam, electric trams, petrol and then diesel traction successively replacing the original horse-drawn vehicles.

Ryde Esplanade (32 ch) has been modernised and is adjacent to the bus depot, but the tram bay is still in evidence at the pier end of the curving main platform. The 391 yd Ryde Esplanade Tunnel (44 ch to 62 ch) precedes Ryde St John's Road (1 m 19 ch) where the old locomotive works has now been superseded by a three-bay shed and stabling sidings on the Down side. The route on to Smallbrook (2 m 14 ch) is double line, having been converted from two single lines in 1926. The Newport route is now marked only by its trackbed and the work of Smallbrook signal box has passed to the power box at St John's Road.

From Smallbrook to Brading (4 m 55 ch) the single line is worked on the Tokenless Block system. The route of the branch to Bembridge can be spotted just before the station which has SR-style buildings plus wooden canopy on the Up side. The Down platform formerly included a bay for branch trains and has a brick signal box plus some vintage gas lighting. The section onwards to Sandown (6 m 42 ch) remains double and the Up island there is flanked by the track of the former Newport branch, now used as engineers' accommodation. The platform also has a modern shelter and a tall brick signal box which can be switched in at peak periods. There is a sub-way link to the Down side where the main buildings and station house are located.

The One Train section to Shanklin (8 m 29 ch) completes the route still open. Trains use the Down platform there, the station buildings overhanging the platform and the IWR monogram still apparent in the ironwork. The half-hourly basic train service connects here with buses for Wrox-hall and Ventnor. Signalling over the route is a mixture of semaphore and colour light and the main gradients are: 1 in 66 Tunnel-St John's Road; 1 in 77 Brading-Sandown; 1 in 80 Sandown-Shanklin.

Rye—see Ashford-Hastings Line

St Denys—see Southampton

St Helier—see Wimbledon-Sutton Line

St Johns—see Lewisham

St Leonards Warrior Square—see Hastings

S.1   St Margarets

Waterloo-Reading line, between Rich-mond and Twickenham. 10 m 66 ch from Waterloo

From a bridge on the Brentford-Tedding-ton road stairs lead down to the Up island and the Down platform of this station opened by the LSW on October 2 1876. The Up Passenger Loop terminates beyond the overbridge at the London end of the station which is served by the Kingston Loop trains.

S.2   St Mary Cray

Victoria-Ramsgate line, between Bickley and Swanley. 14 m 57 ch from Victoria

St Mary Cray was opened on December 3 1860 as a Mid-Kent station served by LC&D trains. It follows St Mary Cray Junction (13 m 17 ch) and comprises island platforms between the fast and slow line pairs and served by the all-stations Dover/ Ramsgate, Maidstone East and Holborn Viaduct-Sevenoaks trains. The station buildings are modern, with a brick ticket office on the Up side and inverted canopies above the additional accommodation on the platforms.

S.3   Salfords

Victoria-Brighton line, between Earlswood and Three Bridges. 23 m 37 ch from London Bridge

Salfords was opened by the SR in 1932 with platforms to the local lines only and with a ticket office on the Up side. Also on this side, at the country end are Salford Oil Sidings, with Up and Down trailing connections, which receive aviation fuel for Gatwick airport. Leading from these is the Marinex siding for aggregate traffic.

The passenger station is open only during the business peaks when the Victoria-Three Bridges trains call.

S.4   Salisbury

Waterloo-Exeter line, junction with West-bury (via Wilton Junction) and Southamp-ton routes. 83 m 43 ch from Waterloo

The original Salisbury station, opened on March 1 1847, took its name from the Mil-ford area in which it was located. The best it could offer was a journey of four hours to London by changing at Eastleigh (then Bishopstoke) but although an affair of only one platform, it became a front line outpost in the battle with the GWR over the territory to the west. While the line from Basingstoke towards Andover was being built the LSW Board was being torn by factions supporting prospective routes to Exeter via Dorchester and via Yeovil, but it had decided in favour of the latter by the time Andover was reached in 1854 and by the time the section on to Salisbury opened on May 1 1857 had agreed to build a new station at the latter point.

Broad gauge metals reach Salisbury via the Wilts, Somerset & Weymouth Rail-way's line from Warminster in 1856, the same year that the Salisbury Railway &

Approaching Salisbury a Class 47 and its load of empty stone wagons passes a Southampton line local set.

Market House Company secured an Act for a short connection to 'the western side of the Market Place'. This connection with the main line had to be replanned when its level was raised in order to make an end-on connection with the Yeovil line, this being opened, along with the new station, on May 2 1859. Milford remained as a goods depot but trains now used the new alignment to reach the through station adjoining the GWR terminus. Another route to Salisbury was that of the Salisbury & Dorset Junction Railway which ran from West Moors, near Wimborne, to Alderbury Junction 1 m 37 ch north of Dean. This single line opened on December 20 1866 and closed two years short of its centenary on May 6 1964.

The present Salisbury station dates from 1900-2 and is slightly to the west of its predecessor, the offices of which lie on the slope up from Fisherton Street. It consists of the main Down platform (No 4) with a full range of passenger and administrative buildings, two reversible lines, the centre island platform, the Up line and a through freight siding and then the outer platform (No 1). Behind this is the old GWR terminus building—closed since September 12 1932 so far as public use is concerned—a Rail Ambassador Exhibition Train depot and the former GWR yard. The East Yard lies on the Up side on the opposite side of Fisherton Street while on the Down side No 6 Bay is used for Romsey line trains. The former No 5 Bay at the country end is now a carriage servicing siding and there is further siding accommodation at both ends.

Outside Salisbury the approach from Grateley is via Laverstock North Junction (82 m 5 ch), recently linked by a single line to Laverstock South Junction (95 m 61 ch) on the line from Romsey. Then comes Salisbury Tunnel Junction (82 m 36 ch/ 96 m 5 ch) where the two join before pass-

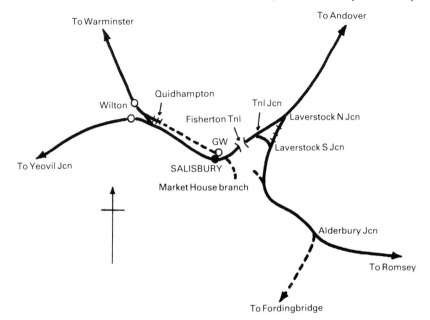

ing through the 443 yd Fisherton Tunnel (82 m 37 ch to 82 m 57 ch) to approach the station. At the other end of the complex the former GWR route trackbed runs parallel as far as Wilton Junction where part of it remains in use to serve ECC's Quidhampton depot. The panel box in the old parcels office area on platform 4 controls the line from Dunbridge and Grateley to the east to Upton Lovell and Wilton Junction on the other side, having replaced the 1904 LSW pneumatic box in 1981.

In 1906 a totally inexplicable lapse by an experienced engine driver brought a devastating crash in Salisbury station. On July 1 of that year, at the height of the competition with the GWR for the Plymouth liner traffic, engine No 421 with

The GWR's station at Salisbury, closed to passengers in 1932.

five eight-wheelers behind ignored the 30 mph speed restriction through the station, became derailed, collided with a passing milk train and ended up as a pile of wreckage in which 24 passengers and 4 railwaymen died. There is a memorial in Salisbury Cathedral.

Salisbury today is served by the Waterloo-Exeter trains, the Portsmouth-Bristol/ South Wales services and by local workings to Portsmouth and Basingstoke/Waterloo.

Rear view of the former GWR station at Salisbury, still retaining its water tower.

S.5 Sanderstead

South Croydon-East Grinstead line, between South Croydon and Oxted. 12 m 23 ch from London Bridge

Sanderstead was opened on March 10 1884 and the single-storey main buildings on the Up side, constructed of brick and wood, are probably original. There is a public right of way over the footbridge to the Down platform where the signal box is no longer manned full time. The station derives a basic hourly service from the Oxted line demu sets but has now lost the weekday peak shuttle along the electrified route to Elmers End.

S.6 Sandhurst

Redhill-Reading line, between Guildford and Wokingham. 57 m 22 ch from Charing Cross

A temporary halt was opened in this vicinity but lasted only a short time, the station being brought into use in 1923. It comprises two raised concrete slab platforms on the curve that precedes the rise to Crowthorne, each with a shelter and reached by stairs from street level. The Tonbridge-Reading dmus call.

S.7 Sandling

Charing Cross-Dover line, between Ashford and Folkestone. 65 m 36 ch from Charing Cross

Approached via the 100 yd Sandling Tunnel (64 m 76 ch to 65 m 1 ch), Sandling station was opened on January 1 1888 at the junction of the branch which had been opened to Sandgate on October 9 1874. The latter had been planned to go through to Folkestone Harbour and to connect with an SER-owned horse tramway at the southern end but nothing happened and the route was cut back to Hythe on April 1 1931 and then closed on December 3 1951.

A rusting siding still lies along the branch platform on the Up side of the station and the single-storey, part-timbered buildings here are original. A footbridge leads to the Down side which has only a shelter. Staffed only for the weekday peaks, Sandling has a basic hourly service in each direction.

Sandown—see Ryde Pier Head-Shanklin Line

S.8 Sandwich

Charing Cross-Margate line, between Deal and Minster South Junction. 86 m 46 ch from Charing Cross via Canterbury West

Having reached Ramsgate from Ashford in 1846, the infant South Eastern Railway lost no time in completing a branch from Minster, via Sandwich and the Lydden Valley to Deal. Opened on July 1 1847, this piece of railway history is still reflected in the milepost distances which are via Minster although the link to Dover has been in existence since 1881.

Sandwich has substantial two-storey period brick buildings on the Up side and a small wooden structure on the Down, ex-island, platform. It has its own LC plus a CCTV crossing at Woodnesborough (86 m 12 ch) monitored from the Sandwich signal box and an AHB LC at Ash Road (85 m 60 ch). There is an hourly service in each direction with some additional morning and evening trains.

S.9 Seaford Branch

Victoria-Eastbourne/Hastings line, branch from Southerham Junction. 7 m 66 ch

Based on powers obtained by the Brighton, Lewes & Hastings Railway in 1846 the line from Southerham Junction along the east bank of the River Ouse to Newhaven was opened on December 8 1847. Today the route, double to Newhaven Harbour and then single on to Seaford, enjoys a basic hourly service to and from Lewes/Brighton connecting at Lewes with services to the east and to Victoria, plus additional morning and evening services and some workings to and from Newhaven in connection with the Sealink sailings.

From Southerham Junction (51 m 11 ch) the line heads through open countryside via Itford RG crossing (53 m 36 ch) to the unstaffed 1906 Southease halt (53 m 40 ch) consisting of just concrete slab platforms with MP 53½ on the Down one, a footbridge and a crossing protecting a private estate road and controlled from a panel by key holders.

A level stretch brings the line to Newhaven Town (56 m 25 ch) at the mouth of the Ouse and described in a separate entry. Single beyond Newhaven Harbour (56 m 51 ch) and dating from June 1 1864, the route then passes Beach Road LC (56 m 57 ch) and the overgrown platforms and concrete nameboards marking Bishopstone Beach Halt which became a summer-only stopping point from 1939 and closed altogether in 1942. Its place was taken by the present Bishopstone station (58 m 3 ch) near the top of the 1 in 100 climb towards Seaford. Opened on September 26 1938, this single-manned station serves the resi-

A view of the docks at Newhaven with a Sealink vessel heading for the harbour entrance.

dent population and holiday caravans from the Up platform. The Down platform, still extant, was abandoned when this portion of the route was singled and further rationalisation has included accommodating the ticket office in the Up waiting room to release the 1938 station building for commercial letting.

Seaford (58 m 77 ch) itself, approached parallel to waves breaking high on the shingle beach, consists of a single platform with a long platform line, adjacent carriage siding and a bay line. The original gabled station buildings, fronting on to the main road, are in brick and include in the ticket hall a vintage barometer bearing a faded enamel invitation to make a donation to the Shipwrecked Mariners' Society. Seaford deals with passenger and parcels traffic and although the goods yard closed in 1964 it still houses the old brick and corrugated shed and a coal yard. Seaford is a train crew depot and has a signal box at the London end of the platform.

S.10   Selhurst

Victoria-Brighton line, between Balham and Gloucester Road Junction. 9 m 31 ch from Victoria

The station, opened by the LB&SC on May 1 1865, is on the familiar centre island plus two outer platforms pattern used at Norbury, with the ticket office at lower street level. Local services to East and West Croydon and Epsom Downs use the Up and Down local lines, grouped together on the Down side. The station also has a guards' depot.

Immediately beyond Selhurst is the remodelled Gloucester Road triangle where the lines from Victoria and London Bridge join and then separate towards East and West Croydon. The adjacent Selhurst group of carriage servicing and CM&EE maintenance facilities is one of the primary locations for rolling stock used on Central Division suburban services. There are three large sheds to undertake routine examinations, general overhaul and exterior painting/interior refurbishing. There is also a train washing plant at the Norwood end of the complex.

S.11   Selling

Victoria-Dover line, between Faversham and Canterbury East. 55 m 18 ch from Victoria

Selling is an attractive little station located deep in the fruit country between Faversham and the valley of the Great Stour. It

Selling station looking towards Faver-sham.

was opened five months after the line itself, on December 3 1860, and consists of Up and Down platforms with an engineers' siding at the country end of the latter. The wooden station buildings on the Up side are probably original and have a typical booking hall with tiny booking office window. When this is closed passengers obtain their tickets from the signalman who has an equally attractive signal box to house the frame controlling the semaphore signals, siding lead and trailing crossover. The station house is also on the Up side, as was the former goods yard.

The station is served hourly by Victoria-Dover Priory trains and it lies on a 2-mile climb at 1 in 100 which ends at the entrance to the 405 yd Selling Tunnel (56 m 33 ch to 56 m 52 ch).

Selsdon—see Addiscombe Branch

S.12 Sevenoaks

Charing Cross-Dover line, between Orpington and Tonbridge. 22 m 9 ch from Charing Cross

The major railway route serving Sevenoaks is the 'cut-off' line built by the South Eastern Railway to shorten its original route to Dover via Redhill. Construction of the 24 miles from St Johns to Tonbridge involved crossing the North Downs with summits and then long tunnels at both Knockholt and Sevenoaks. Having reached Chislehurst in 1865, it then took until 1868 to complete the works, passenger trains reaching Sevenoaks on March 2 of that year and Tonbridge on May 1.

The main line station has now lost its Tub's Hill suffix and has been pleasantly modernised with a clean, attractive and very functional approach bridge housing the ticket office and other station facilities. Stairs then descend to the two island platforms served by the main lines plus Up and Down passenger loops. At the London end the route to Otford Junction veers off after the overbridge and the signal box (21 m 27 ch) stands between the two routes overlooking twin crossovers, the ends of the loops and an Up engineers' siding. At the country end of the station there are 4- and 12-car sidings on the Down side and 10-car accommodation in the Up Sidings South, all contributing to the numerous early and late workings initiated or stabled by Sevenoaks on its routes to Charing Cross and Holborn Viaduct. Main line services to Margate, Ashford and Hastings also call.

Modern functional materials have helped to produce this pleasant station approach area at Sevenoaks.

The other main line feature at Sevenoaks is the 1 m 1,693 yd Sevenoaks Tunnel (22 m 53 ch to 24 m 50 ch), the longest on the Southern Region. The tunnel is brick-lined throughout and is unusual in that, because of the tight clearances and the sheer length of the bore, the 1959 Kent Coast electrification necessitated providing signals in the tunnel itself and mounted at a height of not more than 3 ft above rail level. Because of this the signal aspects are reversed, with the red light at the top, and there are special regulations for trains detained in the tunnel providing for trains to enter an occupied section under a subsidiary signal with the approach automatic signals being held at red until both tunnel sections are clear.

The second route to Sevenoaks originated with the Sevenoaks Railway's single line from Sevenoaks Junction (now Swanley) to Bat & Ball on the outskirts of Sevenoaks. This was opened (with working by the LC&D) on June 2 1862 and, after the opening of the main line of the SER, was extended to Sevenoaks proper on August 1 1869. The portion as far as Otford

Junction (24 m 53 ch) is now part of the main line via Maidstone East with the original route then continuing to Bat & Ball (25 m 51 ch) and then to the junction (26 m 61 ch/22 m 1 ch). Bat & Ball serves the north eastern outskirts of Sevenoaks and has a basic half-hourly service but the station is now rather run-down and its once extensive sidings have gone leaving only a crossover and the nearby Redland private siding.

S.13 Shalford

Redhill-Reading line, between Dorking Town and Guildford. 41 m 2 ch from Charing Cross

Now permanently unstaffed, Shalford consists of two short, staggered and foot-bridge-linked platforms, each with a metal waiting shelter. The station, which lies in the beautiful Tillingbourne Valley, was opened on August 20 1849 and was to have been linked to the Portsmouth line via a connection to Peasmarsh Junction but this never materialised. There was a marshalling area at Shalford during the Second World War and a Down siding remains, opposite the signal box, at the Redhill end.

Tonbridge-Reading dmus provide the service and join the main Waterloo-Ports-

mouth line at Shalford Junction (41 m
60 ch) after crossing a steel girder river
bridge, built in 1912 to replace the original
wooden structure. The conventional
double line junction, with a derelict railway house nearby, is controlled from
Guildford panel.

Shanklin—see Ryde Pier Head-Shanklin
Line

S.14   Shawford

*Waterloo-Weymouth line, between Win-
chester and Eastleigh. 69 m 50 ch from
Waterloo*

Shawford village got its station in 1882
but the name only became important in
terms of railway history nine years later
when the LSW at last permitted the Didcot,
Newbury & Southampton Railway the
connection which would allow it access to
Southampton. The DN&S line from
Winchester Chesil followed the eastern
bank of the River Itchen and the site of
the junction was just before the main line
crosses the present A33 (T), at SU 474 262.

Shawford station is approached via the
62 yd St Cross Tunnel (68 m 31 ch to 68 m
33 ch) and an additional, Down, Slow,
line commences here. The traditional
station buildings are on this side and there
is a wooden goods shed, now in private
hands. The train service is provided by the
hourly Bournemouth slows.

S.15   Sheerness Branch

*Victoria-Ramsgate line, branch from
Sittingbourne. 7 m 29 ch*

Even before the East Kent's line through
Sittingbourne was opened in 1858 the
Sittingbourne & Sheerness Railway had
been authorised to displace the traditional
road and ferry route to the Isle of Sheppey.
It opened its route on July 19 1860, became
part of the LC&D system from 1866 and
had a pier branch at Queenborough added
ten years later with a steamer service
operating from the pier to Flushing.

One of the major features of the 1860
line was its bridge over the River Swale
which separates the Isle of Sheppey from
the mainland. Built to an Admiralty design
it had a central span raised from two towers
to allow passage along the navigable waterway. The SE&C replaced the original
bridge on the night of November 6 1906
with a rolling lift design, originally worked
by hand but later by electricity, and built
by Sir William Arrol & Company, the
people who built the Forth bridges and
also the present Kingsferry Bridge which
took over from the 1906 bridge in October
1959.

*The surviving station at Sheerness with
the branch four-car set waiting to leave
for Sittingbourne and the steelworks
beyond it.*

The present 270-ton bridge, which carries a dual road carriageway and pavement as well as the single line of railway, is 125 ft long and 50 ft wide. Its span is suspended by six sets of wire ropes, connected to 110-ton counterweights rising and falling from four 130 ft towers which dominate the skyline for miles around. Road traffic is controlled by electrically-operated gates with flashing lights and the bridge control room is linked to the signal box at Sittingbourne as well as with the shipping traffic, responsible for over 47,000 lifts by the time the lifting wires were first renewed in 1981.

The line to Sheerness commences at a triangular junction just west of Sittingbourne station. The basic service is an hourly shuttle via the 23 ch link from Eastern Junction (44 m 18 ch) but there are some early through trains from Faversham and one service each way to Victoria and back again in the evening. The latter is routed via Western Junction (43 m 70 ch) to Middle Junction (44 m 13 ch) from whence the route continues to Kemsley (45 m 20 ch), an unstaffed station of bare platforms linked by a footbridge. The double line then continues to the Up side connection from Ridham Sidings from which a long link runs to the Bowaters paper works. Coal is dealt with through the siding plus steel exports when the market is suitable and fragmented scrap from Car Fragmentation Ltd to Sheerness Steel.

Kemsley station was opened to serve the paper mills in 1927 and the next station, Swale (47 m 15 ch), joined it in 1929, having previously been just a platform (Kingsferry Bridge Halt) for workmen. It too is unstaffed and consists of a single Down side platform—the double track becoming single just before the station—labelled 'Swale for Ridham Dock'. There is a Field Station for emergency control here and it is also possible to spot the rail route to the Kingsferry Bridge before re-alignment.

Across sheep marshes the branch now heads for the industrial and shipping area at Queenborough where the pier branch was used by passenger services from 1876 to 1914, re-opening from 1922 to 1923 and then finally closing for freight in 1939. A second branch from Queenborough ran via Sheerness East, East Minster-on-Sea, Minster-on-Sea, Brambledown Halt, Eastchurch, Harty Road Halt to Leysdown with trains taking 36 minutes for the 8¾-mile journey. This was the Sheppey Light

Railway which had opened on August 1 1901 and lasted only until December 4 1950.

Queenborough (49 m 22 ch) now comprises a passing loop with Up and Down platforms with ageing, two-storey gabled buildings on the latter and on the former a traditional wooden shelter with integral canopy. The main sidings are on the Down side leading to the reception yard for Sheerness Steel and providing connections for MCD car traffic and shipbreaking activities. The Sheerness Steel plant has its own locomotive and it is followed by the former link to Sheerness goods-site of the original station, closed to passengers (and by-passed) in 1922 and freight in 1963—and then the Sheerness-on-Sea (51 m 19 ch) terminal station which dates from 1883. Here there are three platform lines although only one is normally used and there is a small, single-storey ticket office building across the end. All signs have gone of the train which ran through the buffers into the street! Traffic for Sheerness Steel is placed in at the Sheerness-on-Sea end with forwarded traffic removed via the ground frame at Westminster Straight at the other end.

S.16 Shepherd's Well

Victoria-Dover line, between Canterbury East and Buckland Junction. 71 m 60 ch from Victoria

The location dates from the LC&D's achievement of a route through to Dover on July 22 1861 and Victoria-Dover trains still serve the station on an hourly basis. The Up side comprises platform plus waiting shelter, with a refuge siding behind and a wooden signal box with a slate roof. Opposite are the station's main buildings, including the station house, and a goods yard with the old goods office still remaining. From the group of three Down sidings which lead into the Long Siding and its headshunt is the surviving connection to the Tilmanstone Colliery line, itself all that is left of the former East Kent Light Railway.

S.17 Shepperton Branch

New Malden-Twickenham line, branch from Shacklegate Junction. 6 m 41 ch

This double line branch has a basic half-hourly service to and from Waterloo via Kingston, Shacklegate Junction and Fulwell Junction plus SX peak hour extras via Twickenham. It originated with the Thames Valley Railway on November 1 1864 and was acquired by the LSW in the following year. Four-car formations are used and the route is controlled from the Feltham panel.

From Shacklegate Junction (14 m 29 ch) the route runs round one side of the Strawberry Hill carriage servicing depot to meet the 34 ch link from Strawberry Hill at Fulwell Junction where the mileage via Kingston (14 m 53 ch) changes to that via Twickenham (12 m 56 ch). Once clear of the second junction the route turns south west through the simple station at Fulwell (12 m 75 ch) for Hampton Hill and the following 62 yd Fulwell Tunnel (13 m 3 ch to 13 m 6 ch), skirting Bushey Park in a slight cutting and coming to Hampton (14 m 47 ch), remarkable for the interesting original buildings on both platforms. The main block is on the Down side and although the brickwork has been painted, the triple windows remain impressive. The station has a double barrier CCTV crossing.

The line now curves in the opposite direction round Kempton Park racecourse and the barest of platforms for this unadvertised station (16 m 28 ch) on the Down side and a stark canopy plus encroaching undergrowth on the Up. The modernised station at Sunbury (16 m 64 ch) precedes a long flat section of the line across Sunbury Common to Upper Halliford (17 m 34 ch) where the two 1944 platforms plus brick shelters and a footbridge nestle under a trunk road near the starting point of the M3 motorway.

Another flat section, drained by the River Ash and skirting the Queen Mary Reservoir, brings the line to the terminus at Shepperton (18 m 73 ch). The two-storey station building, in the same original style as Hampton, houses ticketing and staff accommodation and lies halfway along the single Down side platform. The adjacent dock line becomes the Up line at the approach crossover and there is also a Down carriage siding. The layout appears to reflect thoughts of extending the route to Chertsey.

S.18   Sholing

Southampton-Portsmouth line, between St Denys and Fareham. 4 m 58 ch from Southampton

Sholing opened in 1866 with the line from Southampton to Netley and comprises Up and Down platforms with brick shelters and canopies. Access is by footpath from the overbridge at the Southampton end to the Down platform and then by footbridge

to the Up. Unstaffed, the station is served hourly by the Salisbury/Romsey-Portsmouth trains.

S.19   Shoreham-by-Sea

Brighton-Littlehampton/Portsmouth line, between Hove and Worthing. 5 m 69 ch from Brighton

The port of Shoreham at the mouth of the River Adur figured in the early plans for railways to Brighton and was reached by the London & Brighton's line from that point on May 12 1840, having previously been used as the channel through which materials for the line had been shipped. Five years later the route was extended west to Worthing, in 1846 to Chichester and then on to Havant and Portsmouth to create today's Coastway West route between the two major South Coast centres. Another rail link to Shoreham came into being in 1861 with the opening of the route from Horsham down the valley of the Adur and truncated since 1966 to a single, freight-only line to the Blue Circle cement works at Beeding. There was also a branch to Kingston Wharf to serve Shoreham Harbour which lies close to the route of the main line, and at one time this branch handled considerable volumes of traffic especially coal. It also had its own 6-ton crane.

Today Shoreham's main business is passengers, with all trains on the coast route calling at one or other of the two subway-linked platforms. The main buildings, single-storey with steps and ornamental chimneys, are on the Down side with a brick shelter plus awning opposite. Both platforms have an extension and there is a signal box and gated crossing at either end, Shoreham-by-Sea 'A' (5 m 50 ch) at the Brighton end and 'B' (5 m 74 ch) at the Portsmouth end. There were formerly two other adjacent stations, the 1840 Kingston ¼-mile towards Brighton and the 1910 Bungalow Town Halt ¼-mile in the other direction (and later to serve Shoreham Airport).

Shoreham lost its goods facilities in 1965 but the remains of the route to Kingston Wharf can still be spotted in the goods yard on the Down side. The Beeding Siding junction precedes the bridge carrying the line west over the Adur river.

S.20 Shoreham (Kent)

Victoria-Ramsgate line, between Swanley and Otford. 22 m 52 ch from Victoria

Shoreham is just an ordinary station in a

pretty Darent Valley setting and on the 1862 line of the Sevenoaks Railway now served half-hourly by the Holborn Viaduct-Sevenoaks trains.

S.21 Shortlands

Victoria-Ramsgate line, between Beckenham Junction and Bromley South. 10 m 3 ch from Victoria

Shortlands station is preceded by Shortlands Junction (9 m 57 ch) where the Catford Loop avoiding line joins the Chatham main line and the two tracks on each route combine to become pairs of slow and fast lines. The station itself, comprising two island platforms on an embankment, was opened by the WELCP on May 3 1858 as Bromley, enlarged in 1892-4 and now enjoys a service on both routes to give it four trains an hour to Victoria/Holborn Viaduct.

Sidcup—see Dartford Loop Line

S.22 Sittingbourne

Victoria-Ramsgate line, junction for Sheerness-on-Sea branch. 44 m 59 ch from Victoria

The East Kent Railway, chrysalis of the

Sittingbourne station on January 7 1983 and with the four-car Sheerness branch set awaiting a Down connecting train.

LC&D, opened its line from Chatham through Sittingbourne on January 25 1858. Two years later the Sittingbourne & Sheerness Railway followed with its line on to the Isle of Sheppey.

The approach to Sittingbourne is via the Western Junction (43 m 70 ch) and Eastern Junction (44 m 18 ch) connections with the branch, the four-car branch sets then using the crossovers to work to and from the Down Passenger Loop which runs round the outer face of the island platform. A Down Goods Loop stands beyond the DPL with the Bowaters terminal for train loads of liquid china clay at one end and at the other the Continental Freight Yard leased to A. & R.J. Woods for French and Italian fruit and vegetable imports. There is an Up dock at the London end of the station and an Up siding at the country end, with the signal box standing behind the latter.

Access to Sittingbourne station is on the Up side where parts of the brick building complex probably date back to 1858. The main line service is derived from the half-hourly trains to Dover and to Ramsgate, the branch service leaving for Sheerness after the arrival of the alternate Down semi-fasts and returning to connect with the alternate Up semi-fasts.

Slade Green—see North Kent Line

Smitham—see Tattenham Corner Branch

S.23   Snodland

*Strood-Maidstone West-Paddock Wood
line, between Strood and Aylesford. 36 m
59 ch from Victoria*

Snodland opened with the line on June 18
1856 and comprises an Up platform with
traditional two-storey buildings and a
decorated canopy with a footbridge link
to the Down side which has only a canopy.
The Up side wooden signal box controls
the ground frame at Holborough Sidings
(towards Halling) which gives access to
the large private siding network of the
APCM cement works. Snodland's train
service is half-hourly Strood-Maidstone
West/Paddock Wood.

S.24   Snowdown

*Victoria-Dover line, between Canterbury
East and Buckland Junction. 69 m 60 ch
from Victoria*

Opened as Snowdown Halt in 1914, the
station did not get into Bradshaw until
several years later by which time it was
'Snowdown & Nonington Halt'. Physically
it is a modest affair of Up and Down platforms with a shelter on each and steps up
to the overbridge at the London end. On
the Down side at the country end is Snowdown Colliery signal box with the rusting
exchange sidings and colliery network
behind no longer connected to the main
line and the whole area bearing a mantle
of sad neglect.

Snowdown has an hourly service in
each direction.

S.25   Sole Street

*Victoria-Ramsgate line, between Swanley
and Rochester Bridge Junction. 26 m 71 ch
from Victoria*

Opened shortly after the LC&D extended
the East Kent line towards London in 1860,
Sole Street remains a rural station amid
rolling countryside. The traditional buildings on the Up side are similar to Farningham Road and probably original. The
Down side has a wooden shelter and flat
canopy and there is a single siding trailing
into each of the running lines at the London end plus a crossover at each end.

Sole Street is close to the highest point
on the former LC&D main line and gave
its name to the five mile climb at 1 in 100
from the east. The half-hourly all-stations
Dover/Ramsgate trains call.

S.26   Southampton

*Waterloo-Weymouth line. 79 m 19 ch from
Waterloo*

On the approach to Southampton from
Eastleigh, the course of the BR main line
has the company of the River Itchen, the
main runway of Southampton Airport

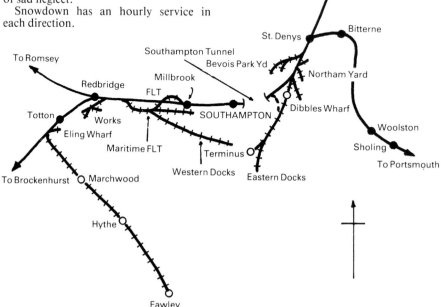

Above *Southampton Airport is one of several Southampton area stations.* **Below** *Southampton Terminus was very close to the original 1843 and 1851 docks and later to the Ocean Dock and Terminal, but closed in September 1966.*

Left *A train heads for Southampton Tunnel, now the subject of a major reconstruction scheme.*
Below left *Southampton.*
Below *Southampton freight depot before the change from the traditional open wagon to the BR Speedlink freight operation.*

and the A335 road. The Airport station (74 m 66 ch) was opened specifically to serve the airport in April 1965 but since then the service of steam trains every second hour has become an hourly electric service with a 72-8 minute journey time from Waterloo. The two platform station can accommodate 12-car trains and there is waiting accommodation at the London end.

The two tracks of the main line continue on to Swaythling (75 m 56 ch) where the station was opened in 1883, a 'revival' period for LSW architecture. It is quite close to the University of Southampton and has an hourly service. St Denys (77 m 10 ch) which follows was opened in 1861 but became a junction five years later with the opening of the Netley line. It has four platforms, impressive villa-type

buildings, hourly services on both routes and is followed by extra Up and Down Slow lines through Mount Pleasant CCTV LC (77 m 54 ch) to Northam Junction (78 m 15 ch).

As the main objective of the London & Southampton Railway, the latter point was a key factor in the evolution of the LSW system. Indeed, Southampton was the birthplace of the idea for the original L&S line which received its Act on July 25 1834 and by June 10 1839 was complete apart from the Basingstoke-Winchester section which was eventually ready on May 11 1840. This original line took the route of the present Canute Road branch from Northam Junction and for nearly a century was to be the port's main rail artery. With the Outer Dock opening three years after the arrival of the L&S line and the Inner Dock following in 1851 this route was eventually to serve the Empress Dock, the Ocean Dock and Ocean Terminal and also the Royal Pier and Town Quay. Its Terminus station eventually closed to passengers on September 5 1966 (although still in existence) and the Town Quay depot closed to freight on May 4 1970.

The freight activity at Southampton is now concentrated in the area between

Mount Pleasant crossing and Northam Junction. This is the location of Bevois Park depot and of the private sidings for MAT and the Rugby Portland and Tunnel cement companies. Blue Circle have a terminal at Mulfords Sidings, Northam and scrap traffic is dealt with in Northam Yard. From a point near the junction and the former Northam station (closed September 5 1966) a branch runs to Dibbles Wharf and the Powell Duffryn mechanised coal depot there. The original main line and route to the Eastern Docks continues via two AOCL crossings, Chapel Road (78 m 52 ch) and Canute Road (79 m 2 ch), the line then passing on to Associated British Ports property.

The main growth in Southampton in the first part of the present century has been in the western part of the port, where the new Southern Railway docks were opened in 1934. The parallel rail route, now the continuation of the Weymouth main line, originated with the Southampton & Dorchester scheme which opened on June 1 1847 from Blechynden westwards, the link through the tunnel to Southampton Terminus being ready on July 29 of that year. Southampton West was opened on the Blechynden site on November 1 1892 and became the present station via a route of enlargement in the 1930s and rebuilding in 1968. The other main rail route, that from St Denys to Netley, and eventually Fareham and Portsmouth, dates from 1866.

The two tracks of the main line from Northam Junction approach Southampton's main station via the 528 yd Southampton Tunnel (78 m 52 ch to 78 m 76 ch). It was the construction of this which had delayed the linking of the Dorchester extension to the London route (in a junction towards the terminus until the triangular junction was completed in 1858), partly because the route used the bed of the old Southampton & Salisbury Canal and suffered subsidence problems. Today the tunnel is again causing problems, distortion due to ground pressures necessitating a programme of works to instal a new concrete base, a process which may occupy up to five years and limit train working to a single line through the tunnel while work takes place on the trackbed of the second line.

Southampton station itself is a modern, functional affair with extensive BR office accommodation above the ticket hall and alongside the Up platform. From the latter stairs lead to the central island and the Down side platform which has its own entrance/exit nearer the docks area. From the London end of the station to Millbrook the fast lines run outside an additional, slow pair. To cope with docks traffic and Freightliner trains there is also a reversible Down Loop and a reversible UGL authorised for permissive working of freight trains.

Millbrook station (80 m 11 ch), renewed with the 1935 quadrupling to help service the new docks, is just a modest island between the slow lines but its access footbridge gives a good view of the adjacent Millbrook Freightliner Terminal.

On the opposite, Down, side is the main BR access to Southampton Western Docks and the Freightliner Maritime Terminal. The former serves the GPO parcels mail terminal and is the route for boat trains and the latter provides highly sophisticated facilities for maritime container traffic moved directly to and from the huge deep sea container vessels by special tug tractors and trailers. The Maritime Terminal is followed by Redbridge (81 m 70 ch) and the parting of the Weymouth and Salisbury routes.

The big change at Southampton in this century, in addition to the eclipse of the ocean liners, has been the virtual disappearance of the traditional wagon load business to and from the docks. It was this, as much as anything, that excited the schemes of the Midland & South Western and the Didcot, Newbury & Southampton backers and the volume of business was phenomenal in the inter-war years with traffic like bananas and meat becoming specialities in their own right, with special wagons, special rates and special train workings. The present container business is equally important and well served but perhaps a shade less spectacular.

Southampton has an excellent train service with three trains an hour each way on the main line, one non-stop and putting Waterloo within 70 minutes journey time. The local service from Salisbury/Romsey to Portsmouth is well patronised and there are links to South Wales via Bristol and to the Midlands and North via the Basingstoke-Reading-Oxford route.

South Bermondsey—see South London Line

Right *The giant Morris crane at Millbrook Freightliner terminal, Southampton.*

184 RAILWAYS OF THE SOUTHERN REGION

S.27 Southbourne

Victoria-Portsmouth line, between Chichester and Havant. 34 m 16 ch from Brighton

Another simple station, dating from 1906 and comprising raised concrete platforms plus shelters, staff accommodation and, at the country end, Down side wooden signal box and traditional gates. Brighton-Portsmouth slow and semi-fast services call, the former providing a Victoria link via Barnham.

S.28 South Croydon

Victoria-Brighton line, between East Croydon and Purley. 11 m 21 ch from London Bridge

Reached by stairs from the ticket office at car park level on the Up side, South Croydon comprises the single face of the Up side platform and two islands in traditional style with wooden buildings and canopies. At the country end the route to Uckfield and East Grinstead veers off behind the SR-style signal box at South Croydon Junction.

South Croydon was opened by the LB&SC on September 1 1865 and the joint route with the SER to Crowhurst East Junction on March 10 1884. Uckfield/East Grinstead line and Caterham/Tattenham Corner trains call.

Southease—see Seaford Branch

S.29 Southerham Junction

Victoria-Eastbourne/Hastings line, junction for Seaford branch. 51 m 11 ch from London Bridge

The 1846 line to Hastings got a branch to Newhaven in 1847 and Southerham Junction dates from December 8 of that year. It is a double line facing junction for Down trains and a change of mileage point—from 51 m 11 ch to 9 m 14 ch, from Brighton—on the coast line.

Access to the Down side cement works, which has its own locomotive, is controlled by the Southerham Ground Frame and is restricted to 10 mph if the movement is from the Up siding.

Southfields—see Point Pleasant Junction-Wimbledon Line

S.30 South London Line

Victoria to London Bridge via Denmark Hill. 8 m 50 ch

This line, today a modest two-car, half-hourly service affair, has a special place in Southern history. To reverse the loss of passengers to London's expanding electric tramways—1¼ m in just six months—the LB&SC chose the South London for the first electrification scheme under powers it had obtained in 1903. On December 1 1909 the line's nine intermediate stations became the pioneers of the vast electric network today operated by BR's Southern Region.

The route was electrified on the overhead system using 6,700-volt alternating current taken from Deptford Power House via a switch cabin at Queen's Road, Peckham. An overhead system of the double catenary type was used, with side poles, centre poles and girders to carry the conductor wires 16 ft above the rails, higher at Victoria where five platforms were equipped and for the six at London Bridge.

For the new service eight three-coach trains were built and alternated with the steam trains for the first three years. The latter—with first, second and third class accommodation—worked from 4.30 am to 7.30 am when the electrics took over and operated a 15-minute interval service until midnight. On Sunday it was electrics all day, from 7.15 am to 11.15 pm, except for a customary 'church interval' break of two hours mid-morning (now lasting all day!). With a reduction in journey time from 36 to 24 minutes the new service was a great success and lifted the line's passenger carryings from 4 m to 7½ m in the first year.

This pioneer electric route, converted to third rail on June 17 1928, owed its existence to the LB&SC's South London Act of 1862, the LC&D becoming involved in the project by another statute two years later. This added another pair of tracks to the existing Wandsworth Road-East Brixton section, the LB&SC opening the London Bridge-East Brixton portion in 1866. The Brighton used the southern tracks west of Peckham Rye, the LC&D the others; several stations were composite.

Today the 22-minute journey begins with a call at Battersea Park (7 m 27 ch from London Bridge) where the platforms and their canopied wooden buildings are well above street level and the stately three-storey 1867 station buildings stand between the two bridges which carry the separating main and South London (or Atlantic) lines over Battersea Park Road.

Wandsworth Road (6 m 52 ch) comes 6 ch after Factory Junction where the Up and Down lines via Stewarts Lane (and

South London Line scene with one of the first 2-EPB sets approaching Battersea Park.

their link from Longhedge Junction) rise between the Chatham and Atlantic lines, and after the crossing of the Waterloo lines. Opened in 1863 (LC&D, LB&SC 1867), the station kept its separate LC&D side until 1916 but is now a modest affair of mainly wooden buildings reached from the road which gives the station its name.

At Clapham (6 m 21 ch) the station is preceded by the Voltaire Road Junction (6 m 33 ch) link to the Chatham Reversible line. The LC&D side again lasted (from 1862) to 1916, the LB&SC side opening in 1867. The upper storey of the station buildings, now showing their age, are at platform level on one side and the other platform is bare. The route continues at this high level while the Chatham lines pass beneath the tied bowstring bridge which carries the Atlantic route over Brixton station, close to the ornate clock tower of the 'Railway Hotel'.

From Brixton Junction (3 m 7 ch) the Catford Loop takes up the parallel position north of the Atlantic lines and is linked via Canterbury Road Junction (3 m 24 ch) and Cambria Junction (3 m 70 ch) with Loughborough Junction and the LC&D

route to Holborn Viaduct. Between the closed East Brixton and the SLL's crossing of the LC&D was Barrington Road Junction where the LB&SC and LC&D tracks joined. The 63 yd Denmark Hill Tunnel is 4 m 32 ch to 4 m 29 ch on the South London route and 4 m 12 ch to 4 m 15 ch (from Victoria) on its companion. Then comes the great Italianate station at Denmark Hill (4 m 23 ch), exciting much attention in the architectural world but showing its decorative frontage to a modest side road behind Denmark Hill proper. The platforms below are reached by stairs from the covered footbridge and followed by the twin, 132 yd Grove Tunnel (4 m 14 ch to 4 m 9 ch). A fire in the French-style roof at Denmark Hill in March 1980 precipitated action on the grand old station's future and led to a campaign by the Camberwell Society which, with a sizeable contribution from BR, would ensure its continued useful existence, as a real ale pub.

Peckham Rye (3 m 36 ch), like Denmark Hill, dates from August 13 1866 (with the LC&D platforms slightly earlier). The station follows the junction with the route to Tulse Hill (Peckham Rye Junction) and a link between the Atlantic and Catford Loop lines at Crofton Road Junction (3 m 67 ch). The platform for the former is an island, but there are separate Up and Down platforms on the Catford Loop, already diverging as a prelude to crossing over its companion. The substantial station buildings stand between the two lines at Rye Lane level.

Now the South London line starts its half circle to make the approach to London Bridge via South Bermondsey Junction (1 m 49 ch). On the way it serves Queen's Road, Peckham (2 m 58 ch), sited amid an area of modern flats and with stairs rising to the small, tiled ticket office-cum-passenger facilities block on the island above. South Bermondsey (1 m 63 ch), originally Rotherhithe, is also a high level island, but this time of wood and with wooden buildings. The 1866 station near the junction was closed in favour of the present situation in 1928. It is followed by the girder bridge over the rusting line to Bricklayers Arms. Between Queens Road and South Bermondsey was Old Kent Road (closed 1917) with lines to New Cross Gate, Deptford Wharf and the East London line.

South Merton—see Wimbledon-Sutton Line

S.31 Southwick

Brighton-Littlehampton/Portsmouth line, between Hove and Shoreham. 4 m 30 ch from Brighton

The location dates from the opening of the line on May 12 1840 but the small ticket office block at the front of the station is of recent construction. A subway and slopes lead to the raised platforms where there is a brick shelter/store plus awning on the Down side. The Brighton slows and semi-fasts call.

S.32 Staines

Waterloo-Reading line, junction for Windsor branch. 19 m 2 ch from Waterloo

The physical junction between the Waterloo-Reading route and the double line branch to Windsor lies, at the country end of Staines station platforms and is overlooked by the footbridge linking the two. The station also has a service to Weybridge, in addition to the half-hourly Reading and Windsor trains plus additional peak services.

The Windsor line (to Datchet) brought the first trains to Staines on August 22 1848. The extension west followed eight years later and a curve between the two (now closed) in 1877, enabling royal trains to run direct between Windsor and the west. The GWR branch from West Drayton to Staines West lasted from 1885 to 1965, the wartime connection with the Windsor branch becoming a local link to the Cory depot private siding when the WR branch was cut back to Colnbrook.

The period main buildings of the station are on the Up side and comprise a rather solid two-storey block with wooden buildings and a disused bookstall at the London end. There is also a rusting bay line and the old wooden goods shed. The Down side has single-storey brick buildings and both sides have rising canopies. There are also carriage berthing sidings at the London end and a bridge across the Thames at the country end.

A good example of a wooden goods shed, at Staines.

S.33 Staplehurst

Charing Cross-Dover line, between Paddock Wood and Headcorn. 41 m 69 ch from Charing Cross

The 1842 station at Staplehurst now has a modern ticket office building on the Up side where there is also a brick signal box panel room and a London end refuge siding. There is an hourly service in each direction with extra trains in the peaks.

S.34 Stewarts Lane

Original Chatham main line, 1 m 36 ch from Victoria

From Battersea Pier Junction (71 ch) the Up and Down Stewarts Lane lines represent the low level route originally taken by the LC&D main line into Victoria. They have connections to the Battersea Reversible line to Longhedge Junction (1 m 66 ch), Culvert Road Junction (2 m 11 ch) and the LMR via Latchmere Junction, to the carriage servicing and washing area, to Wandsworth Road Goods depot and to carriage berthing sidings, and then rise again to Factory Junction (1 m 61 ch). The name Stewarts Lane was carried by the LC&D station which opened on May 1 1863 and closed on January 1 1867 (although the goods depot remained open until 1970) but is more likely to be remembered as a steam shed of some note. From 1934 this replaced Battersea LB&SC and Longhedge SEC; alongside were Longhedge Works (LC&D).

Stone Crossing—see North Kent Line

S.35 Stonegate

Charing Cross-Hastings line, between Tunbridge Wells Central and Robertsbridge. 43 m 66 ch from Charing Cross

Stonegate started life on September 1 1851 (as Witherenden, and soon Ticehurst Road) and lies halfway down the 92 mile bank from Wadhurst Summit. It is typical of the style William Tress used for the SER on this route, the main buildings being very similar to those at neighbouring Wadhurst and the platforms staggered to facilitate crossing the line on the level. The signal box is sited here, on the Up side, and there is an AHB crossing towards Etchingham, at Crowhurst Bridge (45 m 36 ch). Until quite recently the water supply for this country station had to be hand pumped from the mains supply of a nearby farm. Trains call only in the weekday business periods.

S.36 Stoneleigh

Raynes Park-Leatherhead line, between Motspur Park and Epsom. 11 m 74 ch from Waterloo

A concrete footbridge connects the small ticket office with the island platform served by the half-hourly trains between Waterloo and Dorking/Effingham Junction. The station dates from 1932 and has brick buildings plus a canopy.

S.37 Strawberry Hill

New Malden-Twickenham line, between Twickenham and Shacklegate Junction. 12 m 22 ch from Waterloo

The LSW opened this station on December 1 1873, although the line from Twickenham to Kingston opened in 1863 and the branch to Shepperton a year later. Subsequently a connection from the branch towards Kingston produced the present triangular layout of double line routes and inside which the Strawberry Hill emu maintenance depot (formerly an LSW loco shed) is located.

The direction is Down from Twickenham through Strawberry Hill (12 m 22 ch) and as far as Shacklegate Junction (12 m 58 ch) on the Kingston Loop. Towards Shepperton the route runs via Fulwell Junction (12 m 56 ch) but the Shepperton trains which once ran this way now approach from the Kingston direction except for some peak hour workings, leaving Strawberry Hill station to be served primarily by the Kingston Loop trains only. It is typical of its period, two-storey, gabled and mildly Italianate in style.

S.38 Streatham

Streatham is on the South Bermondsey Junction-Leatherhead line, 7 m 48 ch from London Bridge; Streatham Common is on the Victoria-Brighton line, 6 m 48 ch from Victoria, and Streatham Hill is on the Victoria-Beckenham Junction line, 5 m 57 ch from Victoria

The first station to open was Streatham Hill (opened by the WELCP as plain Streatham) on December 1 1856, with the LB&SC's Streatham Common following exactly six years later and Streatham on October 1 1868. It is served by the Victoria-Beckenham Junction and West Croydon trains and has two platforms with an early, small ticket office on the overbridge at the country end. At the London end there are berthing sidings on the Down side and on the Up a four-bay emu shed and carriage

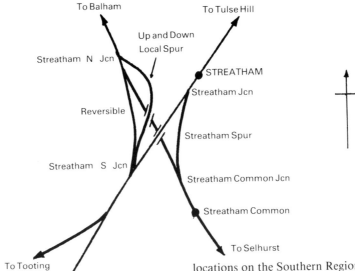

washer. The station is followed by the 443 yd Leigham Court Tunnel (6 m to 6 m 17 ch) and Leigham Junction (6 m 31 ch) where the link towards Tulse Hill departs.

Streatham, served primarily by the Sutton loop and Holborn Viaduct-West Croydon trains, is preceded by the 220 yd Streatham Tunnel (7 m 9 ch to 7 m 19 ch) and followed by the link to Streatham Common and Streatham South Junction (8 m 11 ch) with the main line and the loop to Wimbledon. The two platforms are reached from the ticket office building on the Streatham High Road overbridge at the London end.

Streatham Common is served mainly by Victoria-Epsom Downs and East Croydon and by Holborn-West Croydon trains. Its platforms to the local and through lines follow Streatham North Junction (6 m 14 ch) where spurs from the local lines and a Reversible Fast Spur provide the links with the Mitcham Junction and Wimbledon routes via Streatham South Junction (6 m 43 ch) and the link from Streatham joins the local lines by a trailing junction immediately before the station.

S.39 Strood

North Kent Line, 31 m 11 ch from Charing Cross, and junction with Victoria-Ramsgate and Maidstone West/Paddock Wood lines

Strood is one of the most fascinating locations on the Southern Region. It is an interesting and busy point of interchange between half-hourly services from Charing Cross to Gillingham and those on the Maidstone West line and everywhere around is evidence of its railway history, including roads and pubs with names reflecting its South Eastern Railway origins.

In a way the railway story starts back as far as 1778 when the project for a canal to link the Thames and Medway and save 41 miles around the Isle of Grain was under discussion. Although work on the canal started in 1801 it took 18 years to get to Higham and another five to complete the tunnel through to Strood. The tunnel was 2 m 369 yds long with a 50 yd break and its width of 21 ft 6 ins included a 5 ft towpath. In 1844 the latter was put to use by the Gravesend & Rochester Railway Company which laid a single track, one rail on the towpath and the other on trestles in the water. From February 10 1845 until the November of that year both trains and barges used the tunnel.

The approach to Strood is still via the 1824 canal tunnel which was bought by the SER in 1846, filled where the canal had run and converted to a double line of railway over which North Kent Line trains ran as far as Gravesend from August 23 1847 and over the whole route to London Bridge from 1849. Today the two tunnels—the 1,531 yd Higham Tunnel (28 m 55 ch to 29 m 45 ch) and the 1 m 569 yd Strood Tunnel (29 m 48 ch to 30 m 74 ch)—are much in the same state as when they were originally cut through the raw chalk in 1819. The old canal route can be spotted near Higham station and the Medway end is obvious from the disused deep water dock which continues the line of the tunnel while the railway curves sharply right.

Strood station itself comprises Up and Down platforms with an Up Passenger Loop from the Maidstone West line around the outer face of the Up island. The main buildings, of modern design, are on the Down side and reached via Canal Road, a subway then leading to the Up island. The goods yard is on the Down side at the London end and is leased to Wm Cory Ltd for handling coal and china clay. The Toomer Loop to Rochester Bridge Junction (31 m 34 ch) commences at the country end of the platforms and is controlled from the Rochester signal box.

The present location of Strood station dates from 1856 when the gap to Maidstone West was filled. Two years later, in March 1858 came the bridge across the Medway and the embryo LC&D enterprise which was to grow from the initial East Kent Railway's route to Faversham into the LC&D main line from Victoria to Dover. The SER's route from Strood to Rochester Common of July 20 1891, extended to Chatham Central on March 1 1892 and closed on October 1 1911, has left only its bridge across the Medway. The other important Strood date is that of electrification on July 2 1939 when the station was altered and its platforms extended.

S.40   Sturry

Charing Cross-Margate line, between Canterbury West and Minster. 72 m 58 ch from Charing Cross

Sturry station, dating from two years after the opening of the line in 1846, is approached via the AHB crossing at Broad Oak (71 m 77 ch) and has its own double barrier crossing between the two staggered platforms. In addition to the single-storey Down side building in modern style there is a modern shelter on the Up side and also a small signal cabin, although this is not a block post.

Next on the gentle descent towards the coast comes Chislet Colliery (75 m 16 ch) where the platforms of Chislet Colliery (Halt) were retained after closure on October 4 1971 as a staff halt. The red brick signal box follows on the Up side and then the area of the former colliery connection and exchange sidings. Grove Ferry AHB LC (76 m 62 ch) marks the site of the station closed on January 3 1966.

Sunbury—see Shepperton Branch

Sunridge Park—see Bromley North Branch

S.41   Sunningdale

Waterloo-Reading line, between Virginia Water and Ascot. 26 m 71 ch from Waterloo

The station is situated close to the town and has a double barrier CCTV crossing over the extra wide A30 main road. Its 1856 buildings have been replaced by a modern group on the Down side with waiting accommodation of the same design on the Up. There is a half-hourly basic train service.

Sunnymeads—see Windsor Branch

S.42   Surbiton

Waterloo-Weymouth line, between Wimbledon and Weybridge. 12 m 3 ch from Waterloo

Surbiton opened in 1838 as Kingston, reflecting the ambitions of the L&S to serve the latter point. At later stages it became Kingston Junction and then Surbiton & Kingston. The station was resited in 1845 and reconstructed in the 1936-9 main line electrification period from the then standard pattern of centre island platform to the present layout of an 800 ft island for the two Up lines and another island for the Down Local and Down Loop lines. The latter allow effective handling of the Down service pattern of Guildford, via Cobham, Hampton Court, Alton, Portsmouth trains which recurs every 30 minutes.

Surbiton's station buildings, along the main road which crosses the station at the London end, include a concrete clock tower which dates from the 1937 reconstruction, but the new goods yard provided then lasted only until 1971.

In 1970 the Surbiton signal box replaced 11 traditional boxes to take control of the main line from Berrylands to West Byfleet and of the diverging routes as far as Effingham Junction, Hampton Court and just short of Chertsey. It lies on the Down side before Hampton Court Junction (13 m 27 ch).

The old Surbiton station had a pub called 'The Southampton' attached. This is now part of a new building outside the main entrance. The community itself was at one time known, in mild jest, as Kingston-upon-Railway.

S.43   Sutton

South Bermondsey Junction-Leatherhead line, junction with Norwood Fork Junction-Epsom Downs line, 14 m 75 ch from London Bridge, and with Wimbledon-Sutton line

The line from West Croydon to Epsom brought Sutton its first trains on May 10 1847, with the Epsom Downs branch following on May 22 1865 and the route from Peckham Rye on October 1 1868. Finally came the Southern's line from Wimbledon which was brought into use on January 5 1930.

Together these routes now give Sutton an excellent service with half-hourly intervals on the circular route from/to London Bridge via Mitcham Junction and via Wimbledon and on the Victoria-Epsom Downs and Victoria-Mitcham Junction-Horsham/Effingham Junction lines. There is also a London Bridge-Sutton service via Norwood Junction.

The routes from West Croydon and Mitcham Junction are linked at the London end of the station, which has four platforms in a V configuration. The two tracks from West Croydon curve through platforms 3 and 4 for the Epsom Downs direction and the Mitcham Junction lines pass straight ahead via platforms 1 and 2 to a conventional junction with the route via West Sutton at the country end. The main road passes over the station platforms midway, stairs rising from the platforms to a covered walkway parallel and giving access to the attractive taxi, ticket, parcels and travel centre complex, sporting a nice line in tiles.

There are start back facilities on the Down platforms. A major office development, Quadrant House, now occupies the goods yard, closed in 1968.

Sutton Common—see Wimbledon-Sutton Line

Swale—see Sheerness Branch

S.44   Swanley

Victoria-Ramsgate line, junction for Sevenoaks and Ashford via Maidstone lines. 17 m 31 ch from Victoria

The first station in the area did not come until July 1 1862 when Sevenoaks Junction was brought into use by the Sevenoaks Railway after it had opened its branch from the LC&D main line to Bat & Ball. The name Swanley Junction was taken in

1871 and lasted until April 16 1939 when electrification led to the opening of the present station slightly to the west of its predecessor (still visible in the vee of the junction) in order to facilitate joining/dividing Kent trains.

The four-track section from Shortlands Junction ends at Swanley which has two island platforms reached from the ticket office in Edwards Gardens above. Beyond the platforms there are connections from the fast lines to the slow pair, from there to the Otford lines and direct to the Otford lines. An Up Siding leads from the Up Otford to the Up Fast and there are Up and Down sidings along the secondary route. All are controlled from the signal box at the country end of the Down side island.

Swanley deals with about 180 trains a day, around 80 in the peak. It has services to Dover, Ramsgate, Maidstone East, Ashford and Sevenoaks in the Down direction and to Victoria and Holborn Viaduct in the Up.

Swanscombe—see North Kent Line

S.45 Swanwick

Southampton-Portsmouth line, between St Denys and Fareham. 10 m 50 ch from Southampton

The attractive and original (1889) buildings on the Up side embrace the ticket office and boarded up station house. There is also a small, derelict signal box of wood on a brick base, and opposite, a traditional wooden shelter and canopy. Salisbury/Romsey-Portsmouth trains provide a basic hourly service.

S.46   Sway

Waterloo-Weymouth line, between Brockenhurst and Christchurch. 95 m 45 ch from Waterloo

The direct approach to Bournemouth was completed with the opening of the line from Lymington Junction to Christchurch on March 6 1888. At Sway the Up side combination of single-storey ticket office and gabled station house is original and aesthetically pleasing. Opposite, the Down platform has a sizeable period wooden shelter and the former goods yard, closed April 9 1962, lies behind. The Waterloo-Bournemouth stopping services call hourly.

Swaythling—see Southampton

S.47   Sydenham

Sydenham is on the London Bridge-Wind-mill Bridge Junction line, 6 m 40 ch from London Bridge, and Sydenham Hill is on the Victoria-Ramsgate line, 5 m 57 ch from Victoria

Sydenham, one of the original London & Croydon Railway stations opened on June 5 1839, lies on the four-track main line after the crossovers between the Up and Down line pairs and before the Sydenham Spurs (the Down via a flyover) which curve south west to Crystal Palace (7 m 52 ch). The route here passes over the country end of Penge Tunnel, Sydenham Hill lying at the other end, dating from 1863 and comprising basic Up and Down platforms. Sutton and Orpington trains provide the respective services, with Caterham and Tattenham Corner trains also stopping at Sydenham.

Syon Lane—see Hounslow Loop

Tadworth—see Tattenham Corner Branch

T.1   Tattenham Corner Branch

Victoria-Brighton line, branch from Purley. 8 m 24 ch

The Chipstead Valley Railway, a nominally independent company, left the Caterham line just after the junction with the main line at Purley dipped under the main line and then headed along the valley as a single line. Initially this went as far as Kingswood, with an intermediate station at Chipstead, and opened on November 2 1897. An extension to Tadworth followed on July 1 1900 and another to Tattenham Corner on June 4 1901, by which time the track had doubled.

Today the branch caters for commuters and for Epsom racegoers. On Derby Day Tattenham Corner station plays host to the Queen who arrives by royal train for the classic race but at more normal times the basic weekday service is based on two-car sets detached from the Caterham branch portion at Purley. These run half-hourly to and from Charing Cross (London Bridge in the peak) reflecting the SER ancestry of the two branches, a feature that is also commemorated in the distances. The branch stations are manned up to 20.00; after that and at weekends tickets are issued and collected on the trains.

Having dipped beneath the Brighton main line at 1 in 80/1 in 70, the branch then winds along its Up side through

Reedham (15 m 65 ch) and Smitham (16 m 47 ch) before veering off south west. Opened on March 1 1911, the former is a small, modernised station with a concrete ticket office building on the Down side whereas Smitham, opened on January 1 1904, still displays much traditional woodwork. It has a platform extension at the London end and reverse curves follow the country end subway.

Slowly leaving the area of suburban housing the route now rises via embankment and cutting to its most recent station, Woodmansterne (17 m 40 ch). This was opened on July 17 1932 and differs from the others in having an island platform with a small ticket office at the station end of the footbridge access. The route continues to climb at 1 in 100 and 1 in 300 along the edge of the valley to Chipstead (18 m 41 ch) where the ticket office is below the station apartments in the two-storey, rendered buildings on the Up side. The Down side has only a shelter, the 18½ MP and a footbridge to the car park. Beyond Chipstead's emergency crossover the route continues to climb along Chipstead Bottom, beneath a skew bridge in the deep chalk cutting, levelling out over a viaduct and then resuming the ascent through a mixture of arable, pasture and wooded landscape.

Kingswood (20 m 77 ch) has three-storey part-timbered buildings (at one time including tea rooms) on the Up side and although original, these are decidedly non-standard with a two-storey gabled portion rising above the ticket office and two of the tall chimneys having their own gable between. A concrete footbridge leads to the contrasting shelter on the Down side. Two tunnels come next, the 310 yd Kingswood Tunnel (21 m 36 ch to 21 m 51 ch) which is subject to a 30 mph speed restriction and the tiny, 37 yd Hoppity Tunnel (21 m 61 ch to 21 m 63 ch). Tadworth (22 m 18 ch) lies beyond the summit where the final rise at 1 in 80 has become a descent at 1 in 66 and then 1 in 300. The station has traditional brick buildings on the overbridge at the London end but now has a small ticket office on the Up platform. Prior to electrification services on the branch ran only as far as Tadworth except for race and other 'specials'.

Before Tadworth the route has curved sharply and on the final descent at 1 in 300/100 is heading almost due north. It terminates at Tattenham Corner station (22 m 37 ch) where the signal box and three sidings precede the three platform faces

Terminus at Tattenham Corner with a Class 415 unit in the foreground and a Class 416 set working the branch.

still in use and the original buildings of wood on a brick base. Beyond, the car park must have one of the finest views of any BR car park for it looks out over the racecourse and on for miles over the Epsom plain.

The branch is subject to a maximum line speed of 60 mph but with several lower limitations because of the curves. From October 3 1983, the former Coulsdon North (peak) services were diverted to Smitham.

T.2 Teddington

New Malden-Twickenham line, between New Malden and Shacklegate Junction. 13 m 54 ch from Waterloo

Teddington serves Bushey Park and at one time included the fact in its official naming. The site of the old goods yard still exists on the Up side at the Twickenham end of the station complex which otherwise consists of slightly staggered Up and Down platforms linked by a combined BR and public footbridge. The stately, two-storey main buildings, probably built for the opening in 1863, are on the Down side where the nearby public house is called

'The Railway' and has a brightly coloured emu scene for its sign.

Teddington acts as an interchange point between trains from the Richmond direction and those to Shepperton, deriving from the two routes a combined basic service of eight trains an hour.

T.3 Templecombe

Waterloo-Exeter line, between Gillingham and regional boundary. 112 m 2 ch from Waterloo

Templecombe was opened with the extension of the Salisbury & Yeovil's line from Gillingham to Sherborne on May 7 1860. Then, in February 1862, came the arrival from Cole of a portion of the Dorset Central Railway, which had become part of the Somerset & Dorset by the time the Blandford-Templecombe gap was closed in 1863. The S&D 'Lower Platform' (opened 1887) closed on January 3 1966 with the LSW station following suit on March 7.

Apart from S&D trackbed and derelict LSW platforms and stone goods shed Templecombe now has just a pre-war signal box controlling the end of the Tokenless Block line from Gillingham and its continuation, plus reversible running loop, to Yeovil Junction. It is preceded by Ashford RG crossing (109 m 41 ch) and followed by the site of Milborne Port

(114 m 30 ch) which also closed in 1966. Then comes the regional boundary at MP 117½.

Since closure Templecombe, which was rebuilt by the SR in the 1930s, has still been used on special occasions and was reopened on an experimental basis on October 3 1983.

T.4 Teynham

Victoria-Ramsgate line, between Sitting-bourne and Faversham. 47 m 74 ch from Victoria

The original 1858 station house still exists and the former goods shed stands behind the Up platform but the work of Teynham station is now concentrated on the 1970 ticket office building. The Down platform has a shelter and the two sides are linked by footbridge. Victoria-Dover/Ramsgate stopping services call.

West of Teynham, Buckland LC (49 m 16 ch) has a crossing house, hut and traditional gates and is followed by the AHB crossing at Stone (49 m 40 ch).

Thames Ditton—see Hampton Court Branch

T.5 Thornton Heath

Victoria-Brighton line, between Balham and East Croydon. 8 m 54 ch from Victoria

The location dates from the opening of the line in 1862 but the stylish station buildings on the main road above were built just after the turn of the century. The line, platform and service pattern is the same as at Norbury.

T.6 Three Bridges

Victoria-Brighton line, junction with Portsmouth line. 29 m 21 ch from London Bridge

The Down side house and buildings retain the station's connection with the original opening on July 12 1841, and are one of the few surviving works of David Mocatta, but the main entrance is now on the Up side where a covered way leads from the ticket office to the two island platforms which serve the trains on the Lewes, Brighton and via Horsham routes. The latter was opened as an early LB&SC branch on February 14 1848 and turns west at the country end of the station. In the opposite direction a single line to East Grinstead came into service on July 9 1855 but this was closed in 1967.

The civil engineer has a sizeable complex at the country end of the station where the new panel box has been built on the Down side opposite the SR one it replaces. It takes over from the Victoria Panel north of Croydon and covers the whole of the remaining route to Brighton. On the Up

Three Bridges station in 1982.

side north of the station is the Crawley New Yard freight siding area including a distribution warehouse, an NCB coal concentration depot and a stone terminal.

Three Oaks—see Ashford-Hastings line

T.7   Tilmanstone Colliery Branch

Victoria-Dover line, branch from Shepherds Well. 1 m 73 ch

This modest freight-only single line serving the hot damp workings of the East Kent coalfield at Tilmanstone Colliery is the one surviving fragment of the old East Kent Light Railway. Opened 1912-6 this Colonel Stephens line had once stretched from a junction at Shepherds Well to Sandwich Road, with a branch from Eastry to the colliery (and beyond) at Wingham. It became part of the nationalised railway system at the beginning of 1948 but lost its passenger service on October 30 of that year and was then cut back to its present form.

Today's line, worked on the One Train basis and subject to a maximum speed of 20 mph, leaves the Down side sidings at Shepherds Well (71 m 60 ch) and passes via the open LC (71 m 75 ch) to the 477 yd Golgotha Tunnel (72 m 10 ch to 72 m 32 ch), so called because of the human skull found there during the construction. The second open crossing, at Eythorne (73 m 25 ch), also has reflective approach signs and is followed by Tilmanstone Colliery (73 m 53 ch) where arriving locomotives run round and propel their trains on to the loading pad.

Traces of the light railway include part of the East Kent platform at Shepherds Well and, of course, Golgotha Tunnel, curious in having portals wide enough for two lines but with its chalk bore excavated only for one.

T.8   Tisbury

Waterloo-Exeter line, between Wilton Junction and Gillingham. 96 m 14 ch from Waterloo

Tisbury is on the now single line section of this former main line, opened on May 2 1859. Several of the original stations used slate and wood in their buildings and those surviving on the Up platform at Tisbury are good examples.

The station, served by the Waterloo-Exeter trains, is preceded by two RG crossings—Teffont Mill (92 m 39 ch) and Tisbury Quarry (94 m 75 ch). Tisbury Gates LC (97 m 11 ch) follows.

Tolworth—see Chessington Branch

T.9   Tonbridge

Charing Cross-Dover/Hastings lines, junction with line from Redhill. 29 m 42 ch from Charing Cross

The South Eastern Railway's developing main line reached Tunbridge (as it was then) on May 26 1842 and pushed on east to Headcorn on August 31 of that year. Dover was reached in 1844, Tunbridge Wells in the following year and the winding, undulating link to Hastings was brought into use in 1852. The shorter route from London via Chislehurst arrived in 1868 to complete the Tonbridge network and cement its status as a major junction.

The original approach from Redhill and the later cut-off route both cross the waters of the Medway before joining near the Tonbridge signal box and West Yard. The station—an SR rebuilding—comprises long platforms reached from the ticket offices on the London end overbridge and served by Up and Down Platform lines with the Up and Down Main lines passing between them. There is also an Up Platform Loop to the outer face of the Up island platform and a Down Bay on the opposite side. Beyond the station the separation of the Ashford and Hastings routes has the East Yard to the north and further sidings to the south. This was where the old loco shed stood and pre-1857 was the site of the junction which trailed into the main line towards Ashford. The long canopied goods shed, an interesting example of its kind, stands here and there are carriage sidings at the London end of the complex. The 410 yd Somerhill Tunnel (30 m 14 ch to 30 m 32 ch) lies on the climb towards Tunbridge Wells.

Tonbridge is well equipped with station facilities and benefits from an excellent service on all its routes, including the dmu link via Redhill towards Guildford and Reading.

T.10   Tooting

Streatham South Junction-Wimbledon line. 76 ch from Streatham South Junction

The Tooting, Merton & Wimbledon Company became a joint LSW/LB&SC line before opening on October 1 1868. The present station dates from a resiting of 1894 and comprises a modest ticket office building on the main road with stairs down to the canopied platforms. The half-hourly London Bridge-Wimbledon/

Ferry vans hustle through Tonbridge on their way to Dover.

Sutton-London Bridge circular services now call although at one time Holborn Viaduct was the London terminus.

The junction for the closed route to Merton Park lay on the Wimbledon side of the London Road overbridge.

T.11 Totton

Waterloo-Weymouth line, between Redbridge Junction and Brockenhurst. 82 m 43 ch from Waterloo

Totton got its station four years after the Southampton & Dorchester line opened in 1847, and from July 20 1925 to February 14 1966 it was served by morning and evening trains along the branch to Fawley as well as by services on the main line. Now the branch carries only freight traffic and Totton is catered for by the hourly Waterloo slows.

The area is made up of the station with period brick and wooden buildings on the Up side, and then the branch junction and sidings on the Down side—preceded by the ground frame and CCTV crossing and by the yard area and typical wooden goods shed. There is an AHB crossing at Ashurst (83 m 72 ch).

Totton is approached via a long bridge

over the River Test to which the Eling Tramway provided a link for many years from a junction just west of the station.

T.12 Tulse Hill

South Bermondsey Junction-Leatherhead line, with links to Herne Hill and the Balham-Crystal Palace line. 6 m 7 ch from London Bridge

Tulse Hill was opened by the LB&SC on October 1 1868 and is now served by the Holborn Viaduct-West Croydon and London Bridge-Sutton loop services plus some longer distance trains. The station, comprising a centre island and two outer platforms, is preceded by the 331 yd Knights Hill Tunnel (5 m 56 ch to 5 m 71 ch). Between the tunnel's decorated portal and the London end of the platforms the spur from Herne Hill (3 m 76 ch to 5 m 2 ch) makes its junction.

At the country end of the station the connection to West Norwood Junction (6 m 41 ch) veers off east and the Up and Down lines from London Bridge join the Herne Hill pair to pass beneath the Balham-Crystal Palace line and plunge into the 302 yd Leigham Tunnel (6 m 62 ch to 6 m 76 ch). From the Balham direction the 443 yd Leigham Court Tunnel (6 m to 6 m 17 ch) is followed by Leigham Junction (6 m 31 ch) and the north bound spur to Tulse Hill (6 m 7 ch).

Tulse Hill, with Knights Hill Tunnel in the background.

T.13   Tunbridge Wells

Tunbridge Wells Central is on the Charing Cross-Hastings line, 34 m 32 ch from Charing Cross; Tunbridge Wells West is on the line from Grove Junction to Birchden Junction, 49 m 47 ch from London Bridge*

South Eastern trains reached the outskirts of Tunbridge Wells on September 20 1845, using a temporary station at Jackson Springs until the tunnel access to the present Central station site was ready for use, on November 25 1846. More tunnels were needed when the SER route over the High Weald to Hastings was being constructed, the first section to Robertsbridge opening in 1851 and the through route in 1852.

By this time the Brighton, Uckfield & Tunbridge Wells Railway and the East Grinstead, Groombridge & Tunbridge Wells Railway were in being, duly opening their branches under LB&SC auspices, arriving at Tunbridge Wells, the first from East (now West) Grinstead on October 1 1866.

From High Brooms the approach to Tunbridge Wells is a straight climb at 1 in 103 to Tunbridge Wells Central Goods

(33 m 45 ch) where the signal box stands on the Up side and the long yard opposite includes a large double goods shed. This was the site of the original 1845-6 passenger terminal and although closed for freight in 1980 is still in use by CM&EE and S&T staff. The 823 yd Wells Tunnel (33 m 69 ch to 34 m 27 ch) follows and leads to the two platforms of the Central station (34 m 32 ch). The Up side has long brick buildings with central two-storey section squatly topped by its hipped roof and made even more functional in its appearance by the uncompromisingly rectangular window openings. The 1911 Down side building is much more decorative and is surmounted by a bold clock tower.

Immediately following the station the 20 mph speed restriction eases to 45 mph through the 287 yard Grove Hill Tunnel (34 m 38 ch to 34 m 51 ch) with Grove Junction signal box (34 m 53 ch) then marking the southerly departure of the ex-LB&SC single line round to West station. On the Hastings line the climb continues through the 286 yd Strawberry Hill Tunnel (35 m 12 ch to 35 m 25 ch).

The 1866 station at Tunbridge Wells West is now but a shadow of its former self and the days of a substantial quota of

Right *Scene at the imposing LB&SC station at Tunbridge Wells West.*

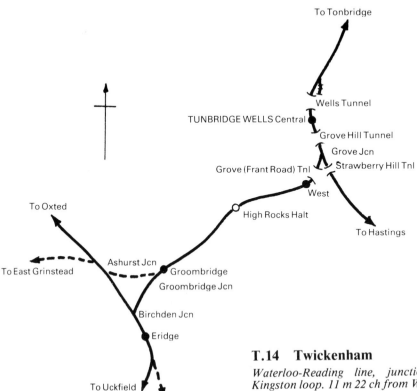

To Tonbridge

Wells Tunnel

TUNBRIDGE WELLS Central

Grove Hill Tunnel

Grove Jcn

Grove (Frant Road) Tnl   Strawberry Hill Tnl

West

To Oxted

High Rocks Halt

To Hastings

Ashurst Jcn

To East Grinstead   Groombridge

Groombridge Jcn

Birchden Jcn

Eridge

To Uckfield

To Polegate

LB&SC trains from London and Brighton, Three Bridges and Eastbourne, and of a busy loco shed and goods yard have contracted to an hourly Tonbridge-Eridge service and this is under threat. The great station building, with huge clock tower and lantern, is grander even than Leatherhead but both it and its two platforms are greatly under-utilised. The station provides siding accommodation and interior cleaning for the Oxted line demu fleet and has trainmens' depots.

The distances from the junction at Groombridge are based on the LB&SC route origins. From West 'A' box (49 m 39 ch), an Up loop runs through the station to West 'B' (49 m 58 ch) where the single line link through the 183 yd Grove (Frant Road) Tunnel (49 m 63 ch to 49 m 72 ch) to Grove Junction (50 m 22 ch) is worked on the Electric Token system.

T.14   Twickenham

Waterloo-Reading line, junction with Kingston loop. 11 m 22 ch from Waterloo

Twickenham's first station, dating from the 1848 opening of the line to Datchet, lasted until the present station was completed in 1954. It lies just before Twickenham Junction where the Up Kingston line passes over the route to Reading and there is a rising connection on the Down side.

Parallel with the concrete raft carrying the main road, the separate bridge from the street entrance and single-storey ticket office leads down to the island used by Up and Down trains (platforms 1 and 2) and the Up side platform (No 3) which also has a double bay (relic of the rugby specials) used for parcels traffic. There are crossovers at each end and the two Up lines are signalled for trains to depart in either direction. In effect the Up Branch continues as an Up loop to St Margarets. On the Down side the former goods yard is still used by a coal merchant and the concrete wall-cum-poster site is an interesting example of its kind.

Twickenham is served half-hourly by the Windsor line trains and those via the Kingston and Hounslow loops.

LB&SC boot scraper and VR letter box at Edenbridge Town.

U.1   Uckfield Branch

Hurst Green Junction to Uckfield. 24 m 56 ch

This double line, non-electrified route crossing the Weald through pleasant Sussex countryside was once a through route to Brighton and Eastbourne. Across country it was linked to East Grinstead and Tunbridge Wells and carried services from Victoria/Oxted to the latter direct and via East Grinstead and from Tonbridge via Tunbridge Wells to Brighton. Now the line is truncated at Uckfield and the basic service consists of hourly three-car Class 207 sets which combine wih East Grinstead portions at Oxted for the journey onward to London Bridge.

Lying on the eastern boundary of the LB&SC empire, the area was also one the SER needed to penetrate if it was to tap Brighton or Eastbourne. Little wonder then that the Brighton should snap up the independent projects as they appeared, resulting in a highly piecemeal development which started at the southern end with a line from Lewes to Uckfield opened in October 1858. In the next decade Uckfield was linked to Tunbridge Wells on August 3 1868, meeting at Groombridge the 1866 line from East Grinstead and both enterprises being absorbed into the LB&SC. Eridge was linked with Polegate, and thus Eastbourne, in 1880 and the section from Hurst Green to Ashurst Junction, and thus Tunbridge Wells, was opened in stages and using the earthworks of an earlier project in 1888.

From Hurst Green Junction (21 m 35 ch), a conventional junction south of Hurst Green station, the route runs through green fields and woods to pass beneath the Redhill-Tonbridge line through the divided 319 yd Edenbridge Tunnel (24 m 10 ch to 24 m 24 ch) and then curve into Edenbridge Town station (25 m 47 ch). Dating from the opening on January 2 1888 the main buildings on the Up side are typical for the line, of red brick with decorative gable ends and tall chimneys with oversailing. They also boast an LB&SC boot scraper and a VR letter box but the subway to the Down platform is dingy and the signal box there is out of use and has had its windows broken. On the opposite side at the country end stands the former goods shed closed on October 7 1968.

After crossing the modest River Eden the line heads for Hever (27 m 27 ch), the station for Hever Castle which is about a mile away. The main buildings on the Down side, which house both ticket office and signal box, date from 1888 and are in the standard pattern for the line. Behind the simple shelter on the Up platform there is a backcloth of trees, and the old goods yard plus dock, closed in 1955, are on this side.

The route now starts to rise through wooded cuttings to the 1,341 yd Mark Beech Tunnel (28 m 26 ch to 29 m 7 ch), brick lined and with some attempt at decoration of the brick portals. Cowden station (29 m 26 ch) follows, opened on October 1 1888 with the extension of the route from Edenbridge to Ashurst Junction and now comprising a setting similar to Hever with tree-backed Up side shelter and a footbridge link to the main buildings on the Down side where the former goods yard was closed in 1960.

Ashurst (32 m 8 ch), now permanently unstaffed and with only the Down canopy and Up side shelter in use, nevertheless still has its 1888 buildings on he Down side with the former goods yard (closed 1960) behind. With its multiple gables, decorative relief in the window arches and rural setting it is a pleasant station and has both subway and footbridge.

On the undulating section which comes next cutting follows embankment until bare signal posts mark the site of Ashurst Junction where the mileage changes from 33 m 57 ch to 45 m 49 ch. The routes trailing in from East Grinstead and veering east to Groombridge are still marked by their formations. For many years the service here was to and from Tunbridge Wells and the link from Ashurst Junction to Birchden Junction, now taken by the Uckfield branch trains, now lay unused. At the latter point the mileage changes again (46 m 48 ch to 27 m 75 ch) and a white, wooden signal box controls the junction with the line to Tunbridge Wells, under threat of closure at the time of writing.

Forge Farm RG LC (27 m 60 ch) precedes Eridge station (26 m 78 ch) which consists of Up and Down platforms, Up Passenger Loop and signal box. The station was opened on August 3 1868 and from the 1881 single-storey, street-level buildings stairs lead down to the island platforms below, only one of these being in full use. The Down side goods yard is now a car park but the station has a fair amount of track-work, a variety of semaphore signals and some ornamental canopy supports.

Bare signal posts mark the former junction (Redgate Mill Junction) for Polegate as the line climbs through heath, bracken and woodland to Crowborough station (23 m 40 ch) where the station buildings carry the legend Crowborough & Jarvis Brook in a colour portion of the window glass and in two different lettering faces. The station's 1868 name of Rotherfield would have been easier to fit in, one thinks. The main buildings and ticket office are on the Up side and on the Down

a traditional brick and wood signal box plus the sidings surviving the goods yard closure in 1968 and now used for stabling ballast trains. The old goods shed is in private hands.

A level section is followed by a 1 in 80 falling gradient, the 1,022 yd brick-lined Crowborough Tunnel (22 m 71 ch to 22 m 25 ch) and two substantial viaducts.

Buxted (18 m 64 ch) again has footbridge-linked Up and Down platforms, the main buildings on the Down side dating from 1868 and being much as the others on the route except for the ornamental barge boards on the eaves and the decorated window heads. The Up side has a traditional wooden shelter with integral awning.

Finally the route comes to Uckfield (16 m 40 ch) a terminus since 1969 with the two lines finishing a little way beyond the station, and a traditional signal box to control the level crossing at the London end. The station buildings on the Down side date from 1901 and their tall gables are timbered. Trains reversing use the crossover beyond the station and depart from the Up side where shelter is provided. The town and its shops are nearby.

The route is an interesting and pleasant one taking 50 minutes from the junction. Some features have passed without trace, like the Monks Lane Halt at the north end, but much remains to be seen including the intriguing milepost mileages which rise to Eridge and Birchden Junction to reflect the original approach from the Lewes end, then record the former cross-country route and finally fall on the northern section from Ashurst Junction.

Upper Halliford—see Shepperton Branch

U.2   Upper Warlingham

South Croydon-East Grinstead line, between South Croydon and Oxted. 15 m 33 ch from London Bridge

The station, on a short level section on the rise to Woldingham summit, opened with the line on March 10 1884. It was on the joint LB&SC/SER section of the route (as far as Crowhurst Junction) born of the drop in feuding between the two and the main Up side buildings are similar to those at Sanderstead. The signal box is also on this platform.

The setting is rolling green hills and there are substantial underbridges either side of the station. Uckfield/East Grinstead demu sets call.

U.3   Upwey

*Waterloo-Weymouth line between Dor-
chester Junction and Weymouth. 166 m
30 ch from Paddington*

Upwey is preceded by the 819 yd Bincombe
Tunnel (164 m 44 ch to 165 m 2 ch) which
cuts through the top of Ridgeway Hill, an
area of numerous ancient tumuli. Upwey
Wishing Well Halt (165 m 18 ch), closed
on January 1 1957, stood in one of the
cuttings which follows.

Today Upwey station is a simple affair
with the bare platform on the Down side
and little more on the Up. From November
9 1855 until December 1 1952 it was the
junction for the 6 m branch that ran on
the lower slopes of Friar Waddon Hill to
Abbotsbury. It was then Upwey Junction
and it is still possible to spot the start of
the final portion of track to Upwey proper,
retained for freight until 1962, at the
London end of the station.

Upwey is served primarily by the West-
bury line dmus.

V1   Vauxhall

*Waterloo-Weymouth line, 1 m 29 ch from
Waterloo*

The first, timber-built station, then called
Vauxhall Bridge, opened on the same day
as Waterloo. Other than being burnt down
in 1856 and completely rebuilt it has no
dramatic history unless, perhaps, you
count the fact that up to 1910 all trains
coming into Waterloo stopped at Vauxhall
for the tickets to be collected by an army
of railway staff who came to be known as
'The Vauxhall Mob'.

Vauxhall has four island platforms, all
with assorted buildings, canopies and stairs
down to connect with London Transport's
1969 Victoria Line. Platforms 1 and 2 are
for Up Waterloo/Windsor side trains, 3
and 4 are the Down equivalent, 5 and 6
Up and Down Through and 7 and 8 Main
Suburban. Hounslow Loop and Rich-
mond/Kingston locals plus Hampton
Court, Chessington South and some
Shepperton trains call at Vauxhall to cater
for its 7,000 passengers a day.

Vauxhall Bridge is close to the station
which also serves the Oval cricket ground
and the new Covent Garden Market at
Nine Elms. The latter is now a hive of
activity very different from its earlier roles
as a noted melon growing area or a railway
goods and locomotive depot, although the
latter is still remembered by a repair in the
boundary wall where locomotive *Melisande*
ran off the turntable, by the old water

tower and by some arches still bearing
their old railway numbers.

V.2   Victoria

As befits its location within walking distance (or a State procession) of Bucking-
ham Palace, Victoria is the Southern
Region's royal terminal. It is where, on
platform 2, the Queen welcomes on average two visiting Heads of State a year—
usually off a special train from Gatwick
Airport—and leaves from platform 15 by
Royal Train for Tattenham Corner station
on Derby Day. There was a day in 1910
when the crowned heads of Europe were
converging on London for the funeral of
Edward VII and seven Royal Trains arrived
at Victoria in as many hours.

The idea of a West End terminus can be
traced back, as can so many other developments, to the 1851 Exhibition and the
resultant West End of London & Crystal
Palace Railway which attracted the interest
of both the Brighton and Chatham lines.
A consequent joint enterprise was the
Victoria Station & Pimlico Railway which
was incorporated in 1858 to build a line
from Stewarts Lane to a new terminus
across the river. The LB&SC section was
ready on October 1 1860 and was used by
LC&D trains from December 3 until the
latter's own section was opened on August
25 1862. The Brighton station had ten
tracks and six platform faces, an entrance
off Eccleston Bridge and an exit in
Victoria Street. The Chatham station,
with nine tracks, five of them mixed gauge
for use by GWR trains from Southall, also
had nine platform faces and was reached
from Wilton Road. The GWR was joint
owner of the Chatham side until 1932, a
fact still commemorated in faded lettering
high up on the frontage.

Victoria was completely rebuilt in the
first decade of the present century, the work
on the Brighton station being completed
in 1908 and that on its Chatham neighbour
in the following year. For the first time the
station had a decent frontage and forecourt, but it still had two separate station
masters and this was to continue until the
two stations were connected in 1924 and
the platforms numbered as an entity in the
following year. In the 1902-8 changes the
privately-owned Grosvenor Hotel was
also rebuilt; it became a BTH hotel in 1977.

This particular London terminus has
always been highly cosmopolitan and had
strong links with other forms of transport.
A bus station was opened in the forecourt

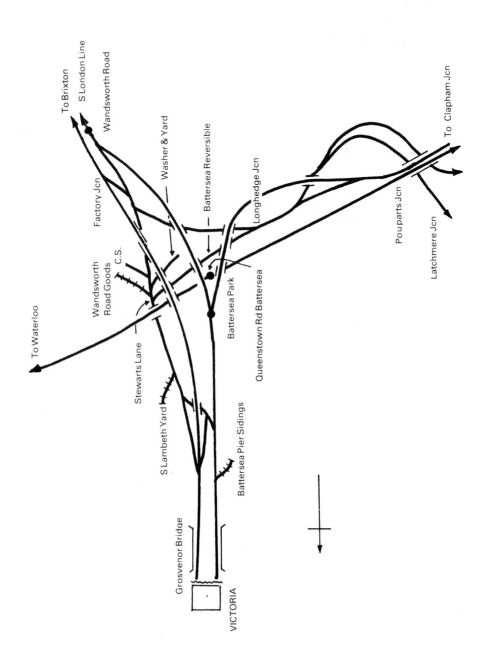

To Brixton
S London Line
Wandsworth Road
Washer & Yard
Battersea Reversible
Longhedge Jcn
To Clapham Jcn
Factory Jcn
Pouparts Jcn
Latchmere Jcn
Wandsworth
Road Goods
C.S.
Battersea Park
Queenstown Rd Battersea
To Waterloo
Stewarts Lane
S Lambeth Yard
Battersea Pier Sidings
Grosvenor Bridge
VICTORIA

Right *Impressive masonry at Victoria.*

in 1926 and is still used by Red Arrow and other services. During the First World War it was the main station for leave trains to and from France and almost as soon as the war was over most of the railway boat train traffic was concentrated at Victoria. A new Continental ticket and enquiry office was opened on June 14 1948, now succeeded by the Sealink travel centre opposite platform 2, and these days nearly half the 4 m people who pass through the station each year are foreign visitors.

The most dramatic recent developments have been in connection with air travel. Since 1961 Victoria has been the London rail terminal for Gatwick Airport and some 2 m passengers a year use the round-the-clock services which include special direct Rapid City Link trains from platform 15. The facility of a special reception lounge has become the basis for a scheme which will give Victoria a rail-air terminal and office block on a raft over platforms 9 to 17 and an extra two platforms for the exclusive use of airport trains. All of this, already being turned into reality in 1983, is a far cry from the modest terminal opened by Imperial Airways in 1939 in connection with its short-lived flying-boat service from Southampton.

As well as these special traffic flows, Victoria also copes with over 200,000 ordinary passengers every day. From the 'Chatham side', platforms 1 to 8, trains go to a vast variety of suburban destinations as well as out to the more distant commuter destinations, to the Medway Towns, the Isle of Thanet and the Kent Coast and ports. The eight platform lines merge into four beyond the platforms, pairing as fast and slow with carriage sidings by the Down Chatham Fast and a link to the Central lines from the Up Chatham Slow. At Battersea Pier Junction (71 ch) the Up and Down Stewarts Lane lines drop below and the previous four lines become three, Down Chatham Main, Up Chatham Fast and Chatham Reversible.

The Central portion of Victoria deals with trains to mid-Sussex and the Sussex Coast, Portsmouth, Bognor Regis and to East and West Croydon. It has its share of commuters and a few boat trains for the Newhaven-Dieppe sailings to match the queues outside platform 8 and the links to the Calais, Boulogne and Ostend steamers. In addition to the Gatwick services, Brighton has an excellent train service even if the Brighton Belle did make its exit in a welter of liquid nostalgia in 1972. The nine tracks reduce to five—local and

The Civil engineer's permanent way staff at work at Victoria.

through pairs plus Carriage Road—before Grosvenor Bridge and there are eight carriage sidings on the Up side. After Battersea Pier Junction and the Chatham lines separating from the Stewarts Lane and Battersea Reversible lines, the Up and Down Atlantic pair separate from the Central route at Battersea Park Junction.

Victoria has just experienced the Southern Region's 'most complicated engineering project' involving the resignalling and modernisation of 267 miles of track leading to the station, and to Holborn Viaduct, and used by more than 1,300 trains a day. Access to the station is now signalled from the Victoria Signalling Centre at Clapham Junction, current is drawn from Lewisham and Selhurst and emu stock from Streatham, Selhurst and Stewarts Lane. The station is controlled by an Area Manager with operating and commercial assistants and with Station Managers operating almost round the clock. They have a control room which also houses the station announcers and there is a train crew signing on point in the same block.

In steam days a heavy train passes the Weybridge line Up platform at Virginia Water.

V.3   Virginia Water

Waterloo-Reading line, junction for Weybridge line. 23 m 15 ch from Waterloo

The line from Staines to Ascot opened on June 4 1856 with the section between Virginia Water and Chertsey completing the link to Weybridge on October 1 ten years later. Today's station has a V platform for Weybridge Up and Reading Down trains, with the junction of the two double track routes at the London end, and outer platforms for Weybridge Down and Reading line Up trains. The main buildings and ticket office are on the latter, the others having shelters. There are little used sidings, headshunt and dock spur at the London end.

The basic service is provided by the half-hourly Reading line trains and the Staines-Weybridge shuttle.

W.1   Waddon

Norwood Fork Junction-Sutton line. 11 m 40 ch from London Bridge

Opened 16 years after the line opened in 1847, Waddon has subsequently been modernised and now comprises Up and Down platforms linked by glass-panelled overbridge from the ticket office. There are tiled waiting rooms and canopies at

platform level and the Sutton and Epsom Downs trains call.

Waddon Marsh—see West Croydon-Wimbledon Line

W.2   Wadhurst

Charing Cross-Hastings line, between Tunbridge Wells Central and Robertsbridge. 39 m 23 ch from Charing Cross

The 1851 station has staggered platforms and Down side main buildings by Tress in the same style as Robertsbridge, Stonegate and St Leonards Warrior Square. The wooden signal box on this side controls the colour light signals, two crossovers and the connection to the Up Refuge Siding. A footbridge leads to the Up platform which has a brick-built waiting room with a decorated canopy.

The station lies in an area of wooded cuttings and is followed by the 1,205 yd Wadhurst Tunnel (39 m 65 ch to 40 m 40 ch). It is served, hourly off-peak, by the Hastings trains.

W.3   Wallington

Norwood Fork Junction-Sutton line. 13 m 5 ch from London Bridge

An 1847 location subsequently reconstructed and now comprising Up and Down platforms with a small modern ticket office at the country end of the former. Called Carshalton until 1868 the station is served by the Epsom Downs and Sutton local services.

W.4   Walmer

Charing Cross-Margate line, between Buckland Junction and Deal. 92 m 27 ch from Charing Cross

The distance from Charing Cross to Walmer is measured via Minster recognising the original approach via the 1847 SER branch to Deal and the Dover & Deal Joint link from Buckland Junction opened on June 15 1881. Walmer lies on the 6-mile descent of the latter from Guston Tunnel to the coast and is approached via an RG crossing at Cold Blow (92 m 54 ch).

With the Down sidings now lifted, the station comprises just the subway-linked platforms with single-storey 1881 buildings on the Up side. There is an hourly service in each direction.

W.5   Walton-on-Thames

Waterloo-Weymouth line, between Surbiton and Weybridge. 17 m 6 ch from Waterloo

The station is about a mile from the river and the centre of the town and consists of a centre island (normally out of use) and outer platforms to the Up and Down Slow lines. It was one of the original 1838 locations and now has a basic half-hourly Waterloo-Guildford/Portsmouth service.

W.6   Wanborough

Redhill-Reading line, between Guildford and Wokingham. 34 m 29 ch from Waterloo

Wanborough was opened on September 1 1891 as a station on the Guildford-Tongham-Alton line and it is now served by the Ascot-Guildford line trains as well as the Tonbridge-Reading dmus. A concrete footbridge links the two platforms, one with an attractive period shelter and the other with an original group of brick buildings including station house and canopy. A coal yard survives from the 1962 goods closure but is not rail connected. Still operative is an agreement from the time of building that the station should not sell platform tickets.

W.7   Wandsworth

Wandsworth Common lies on the Victoria-Brighton line between Clapham Junction and East Croydon and 4 m 5 ch from Victoria; Wandsworth Road is on the South London Line (see that entry) and Wandsworth Town is on the Waterloo-Reading line between Clapham Junction and Barnes and 4 m 60 ch from Waterloo

The West End of London & Crystal Palace Railway opened the first Wandsworth Common on December 1 1856, actually using the name two years later. The present station, slightly to the south, was opened by the LB&SC on November 1 1869 and remodelled in 1906. It comprises a centre island and two outer platforms with the main buildings on the Down side and an elegant, rather unusual, little entrance on the Up. Victoria-West Croydon/Beckenham Junction trains call.

Wandsworth was one of the few towns on the Richmond Railway's line when it opened in 1846 but 40 years later the traffic had expanded sufficiently to warrant reconstruction and widening, an event commemorated in the patterned '1886 LSWR' on the London end of the Up side station buildings.

First called Wandsworth, then Wandsworth Town from 1903, the station now has a canopied central island with subway access and the upper storey of each outer platform building, complete with Dutch gable end, rises to platform level. There are two trains an hour on the Twickenham via Hounslow and Richmond/Kingston circle routes off-peak.

W.8   Warblington

Victoria-Portsmouth line, between Chichester and Havant. 36 m 66 ch from Brighton

On the eastern outskirts of Havant, Warblington got its station in 1907. It comprises platforms, shelters and staff accommodation plus a rusting emergency crossover and a CCTV double barrier crossing at the country end. The hourly Brighton-Portsmouth slows call.

W.9   Wareham

Waterloo-Weymouth line, between Poole and Dorchester South. 120 m 70 ch from Waterloo

Wareham's first station was on the 1847 Southampton & Dorchester line but in the year after the Swanage branch opened on May 2 1885 a new station was built on the present site. The first station, east of the level crossing, then closed in 1887.

Today the 1886 station buildings, with Dutch gable, and weather vane tower, still serve this railhead station for the Isle of Purbeck. They are preceded on the Down side by the old brick goods shed at an angle which suggests a pre-1886 dating and by traditional crossing gates. On the Up side the former island platform has wooden buildings and canopy, with a traditional signal box and three sidings at the London end.

Beyond Wareham and its former Down bay for branch trains comes Worgret Junction (121 m 77 ch) where the Swanage trains once swung off through an area of ancient barrows and tumuli. Now the Swanage end of the line is in the hands of a preservation society and the BR single freight-only line runs for just 2 m 38 ch to Furzebrook Sidings to serve an oil terminal and one of the clay works for which the area was formerly famous. Access is via a ground frame at the junction, One Train Working applies and there is a maximum line speed of 20 mph.

Further on towards Wool come Holme AHB (122 m 78 ch), Rushton No 2 RG (123 m 58 ch) and Stoke (124 m 12 ch) level crossings. The Waterloo-Weymouth push and pull portions serve Wareham hourly.

W.10   Warminster Line

Waterloo-Exeter line, from Wilton Junction to Regional Boundary. 13 m 73 ch

The line between the boundary with the WR at 118½ MP and the junction at Wilton (132 m 33 ch) with the Waterloo-Exeter line was a former GWR route inherited from the Wilts, Somerset & Weymouth Railway. It had stations at Codford, Wylye, Wishford and Wilton until intermediate passenger services were withdrawn on September 19 1955 and the route is still used by the Cardiff-Portsmouth cross-country services.

The Down direction is towards Salisbury and with the distances, reflects the former Paddington influence. The double line route uses the pleasant valley of the River Wylye for its descent through Salisbury Plain and passes by way of Upton Lovell LC (119 m 70 ch) and its crossing box, the crossing at Codford (120 m 45 ch)—the last signal box to survive—and the AHB at Wylye (124 m 41 ch). The goods shed at Wishford was still standing in 1983 plus a few other railway buildings, sidings etc along the route.

Warnham—see Dorking-Horsham Line

W.11   Wateringbury

Strood-Maidstone West-Paddock Wood line, between Paddock Wood and Maidstone West. 39 m 77 ch from Charing Cross

The line opened, with a stop here for the Band of the Lancers to entrain for Maidstone, on September 25 1844. Today the station is notable for its elaborate and interesting buildings in the decorative style of the northern portion of the route (which may date them as 1856) and also for its access to the boating and other leisure opportunities afforded by the adjacent River Medway. Wateringbury has a signal box with traditional wooden crossing gates and an old brick goods shed; there is a CCTV barrier crossing at Teston (41 m 4 ch) site of Teston Crossing Halt from 1909 to 1959. Paddock Wood-Strood trains call.

W.12   Waterloo

Called by the Poet Laureate 'this practical airy place', Waterloo is the Southern Region's busiest station with some 1,250 trains carrying nearly 200,000 passengers to and from London every day. It is the station for the South Bank, County Hall, the Royal Festival Hall and the National

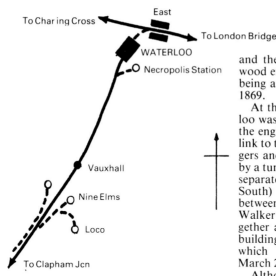

Theatre. It has its own Underground link to the City via the Waterloo & City line and the terminus, which occupies 24½ acres, is the biggest station, not only on the Southern, but on the whole of British Rail.

Waterloo began life on July 11 1848 as the modest metropolitan terminus of the London & South Western Railway, taking over from Nine Elms which had opened ten years earlier and which after years of service as works, locomotive depot and goods depot is now the site of the new Covent Garden Market. The original station was located where platforms 7 to 11 are today. It was opened as a through station with the idea of continuing the tracks to London Bridge and comprised a complex of four platforms and six tracks beneath a roof of iron and glass.

The 1848 station was supplemented by 'Windsor' platforms in 1860 and four years later was given an extension to London Bridge. In contrast to the original plans this took the form of a single line across the concourse and over Waterloo Road to link up with the newly opened SER route from London Bridge to Charing Cross at Waterloo Junction. Traces of the platform are still visible from a spot halfway up the slope to the present Waterloo East.

Many subsequent changes occurred at the LSW's main station, additional platforms being added at frequent intervals and leading to the use of the supplementary labels Windsor, North, Central and South for various sections at varying periods. The first Necropolis station opened in 1854

and the second one in 1902 (see Brookwood entry) and Waterloo East came into being as Waterloo Junction on January 1 1869.

At the beginning of the century Waterloo was something of a busy muddle with the engine shed in an awkward place, the link to the SER lines still impeding passengers and the road approaches constricted by a tunnel. Work began to weld the three separate stations (North, Central and South) into one and continued piecemeal between 1909 and 1918 with Herbert Walker then pulling the whole effort together and helping to create a virtual rebuilding to an efficient, 21-platform station which was officially commissioned on March 21 1922.

Although the 2-acre concourse has changed much since 1922 and there have been major alterations to track layout and signalling—especially in 1935-6—Waterloo still retains the basic features of the 1922 station. Worth study is the Portland stone Victory Arch, the main pedestrian entrance to the station opposite platform 19 and a memorial to the 585 LSW staff who died in the First World War. Along with the whole frontage of the station it was the work of James Robb Scott, the LSW's chief architectural assistant. Left of the Victory Arch is a branch of the National Westminster Bank which, in 1923, became the first bank to open premises on a London railway station. To the right is a small plaque with a likeness of Sir Herbert Walker, the 'Father of the Southern Railway', at the entrance to what are now the headquarters offices of the Southern Region.

Waterloo is unique in having played music over the public address system since 1937 and the two hairdressing salons, opened in 1874, are still in business at either end of the concourse. Another survival of the station opened by Queen Mary in 1922 is the 6 ft wide, four-faced turret clock which hangs over the centre of the concourse. There are still some mermaids in the ornamental ironwork at the Luggage Hall entrance at the Waterloo Road end but the rest of the concourse would surely have given Sir Herbert pause for thought. Gone are the ornamental iron gates to the platforms and the antique train indicator board directing one to the Atlantic Coast Express or the Bournemouth Belle. In their place is a new barrier line interspersed with a range of sales kiosks providing anything from an aspirin to new shoe heels and in place of the old indicator are the giant pieces of electronic wizardry which now detail the train arrivals and departures.

Instead of three ticket offices, all in different parts of the station, Waterloo now has one combined office with 16 working windows and a travel centre next door. Platforms 1-4, the newest part of the station, are used for the inner suburban services to Wimbledon, Hampton Court, Chessington, Kingston and Shepperton. Services from platforms 5 and 6 go further afield to Woking and Guildford via Cobham and platform 7 is for Portsmouth via Guildford. Weymouth and Exeter main line services use platforms 8-10 while the 946 ft No 11, formerly used for boat trains and adjacent to the cab road, is now the departure point for royal journeys and other VIP occasions.

The four platforms on the other side of the cab road, numbers 12-15, are the arrival platforms for many main line trains. Between them and the rest of the station is the two-storey office block built in 1920 and known as 'The Village'. This houses the administrative and lost property offices and at the concourse end are two escalators

Station and Regional SR Headquarters at Waterloo.

and a fixed stairway, dating from 1919, to link with the subway to the Waterloo & City line. Platforms 16-21 on the 'Windsor side' are under the pre-1922 roof and used for the Windsor, Reading, Hounslow and Teddington trains.

Approached by eight lines, Up and Down suburban, two Up and one Down Through and one Up and two Down Windsor, Waterloo is a busy and fascinating station. Its operation is concentrated on the signal box and the combination of Solari Control, train announcers and supervisors on the raft over platforms 7/8, but there are many touches remaining from the era of steam when the working seemed more dramatic and the shortcomings have been forgotten in the passage of time.

One particularly unusual feature lost to Waterloo is the 'Cemetery Station' of the splendidly titled Necropolis & National Mausoleum Company. This was on the Down side of the approach tracks and came to comprise two sidings each with a covered platform, one used by mourners and the other for coffins. Ornamental gates marked the approach from the road and there were stairs from the platforms to the York Street offices. Regular trains ran to the cemetery at Brookwood.

The station opened by the SER as Waterloo Junction took the title Waterloo East officially on May 2 1977 although that name had been in use unofficially for years. It lies 61 ch from Charing Cross

and comprises centre island and two outer platforms to serve the paired fast and slow lines. These four platforms, lettered A to D are used by some 30,000 passengers a day to and from Dartford, Dover and the Medway Towns.

The third surviving station at Waterloo is that of the Waterloo & City line, or 'The Drain' as it is known to many of the 13,000 commuters it takes into the City each morning. This underground route in deep level 12 ft 1¾ in diameter tunnels to Bank station is double track, 1 m 1,012 yds long and the journey takes five minutes. At the City end BR and LT passengers merge on the 302 ft travelator, a huge moving pavement travelling at 180 ft a minute.

The Waterloo & City line itself was inspired by the City & South London line which opened in 1890. Work on the LSW's underground line began four years later and was completed in time for an August 8 1898 opening. Under the influence of signal engineer W.R. Sykes it incorporated many of the earliest forms of modern signalling practices and proved a highly successful counter to the fleet of two-horse omnibuses which had previously carried passengers from Waterloo to the City.

Operation of the Waterloo & City line is based on Class 487 sliding door stock operating in trains of 1-5 units with a four-minute headway at peak periods. Track Circuit Block was installed in 1940 with two-aspect colour light signals, train movements automatically providing points and signals operation. Despite this modern and sophisticated sequential track circuit control, an Annett's Key is still used to release the points into the Armstrong lift at the Bellmouth within the tunnel so that stock can be transferred to and from the surface line for journeys to shops.

Welling—see Bexleyheath Line

W.13   West Byfleet

Waterloo-Weymouth line, between Weybridge and Woking. 21 m 54 ch from Waterloo

Trains have been calling at West Byfleet since December 1887 although the line dates from 1838. The station comprises an island between the Down Local and Down Through lines with a footbridge to the Up platform where the main buildings of glass and wood are situated. The Esher train service applies.

Westcombe Park—see Greenwich Line

W.14   West Croydon

Norwood Fork Junction to Sutton line, junction for Wimbledon line 10 m 35 ch from London Bridge

The London & Croydon Railway was authorised only two years after the London & Greenwich had been incorporated in 1833 as the pioneer constituent of the Southern system. The route from West Croydon used the bed of the acquired Croydon Canal on the first part of its journey to the junction at Corbetts Lane and today's station is more or less on the site of the old canal basin. The route was opened on June 5 1839, the one on to Sutton on May 10 1847 and the link to Wimbledon on October 22 1855.

Conveniently placed for Croydon's main shopping area the station today is of modern design with an entrance amid the shops at street level and leading by a long slope to the main Down platform and by stairs to the Up. The latter, in addition to its through face, has an inset face at the country end for trains on the separate single line from Wimbledon and the opposite side at the London end is used for starting and terminating London direction services.

West Croydon is an important interchange point in addition to dealing with considerable local traffic. It accommodates permanent way and traction staff as well as station staff and supervisors and there is a buffet. A feature at the London end is an elevated signal box and some of its old semaphore signals are still in position.

W.15   West Croydon-Wimbledon Line

Many passengers using the two-car sets of the half-hourly service on this line will have no idea that it is the modern successor to the pioneer, horse-worked Surrey Iron Railway which opened on July 26 1803. The route is also unusual in being one of the few examples of a single line in the Southern Region's electrified suburban network.

Today there are six intermediate stations but when the line opened on October 22 1855, partly due to the reaction to the 1846 closure of the world's first public horse-drawn railway, there were only two, Beddington Lane and Mitcham. Morden Road was opened two years later and Mitcham Junction, the link with the Peckham Rye-Sutton line, followed the latter's opening in 1868. After another two years came

Merton Park, a joint station, and finally Waddon Marsh in 1930. The line owes its existence to the celebrated local railway contractor G.P. Bidder. Born in Mitcham and dubbed 'The Calculating Boy', Bidder worked the line for a year before leasing it to the LB&SC who took over completely in 1858.

From the bay at West Croydon (6 m 12 ch) the single line follows the main route to Sutton but soon turns sharply north west. Waddon Marsh (4 m 79 ch) consists of a crossing loop, an island platform with a shelter and, at the Wimbledon end, the signal box. This was formerly a block post for the line's electric train staff working and controlled access to the gas works on the Down side. The Up line at Waddon Marsh is no longer used and the only reminders of the private siding activity are the shunters accommodation and traditional siding gates towards Beddington Lane.

Where Purley Way crosses the line it is very near the alignment of the Surrey Iron Railway and this situation continues past the hospital and power station and on through Beddington Lane which consists of a double barrier crossing followed by a single platform and small ticket office (housed in the waiting room since the crossing keeper's box was destroyed by fire). The straight course continues its way across the golf course on Mitcham Common and through Mitcham Junction (3 m 4 ch) where the 1868 line had to do the curving.

The single line changes to double between the sub station and the traditional signal box and reverts to single after the two routes have separated beyond the station. The station itself comprises Up and Down platforms with the original, main buildings on the latter. The Up side has a canopy over the waiting room, toilet area etc and displays the warning reminder 'Down Mitcham Line Reversible'.

'Tramway Path' appears south of the line and then north, marking the route of the Surrey Iron Railway and its Hackbridge spur. There is another 'Tramway Path' near Mitcham station (2 m 24 ch) where both platforms remain but only the Down is used. A footbridge leads to the ticket office, part of the listed building whose exact origins are not clear although SIR connections have been suggested. Mitcham goods yard closed in 1967 but at one time it had a temporary steam-worked connection to the LCC housing estate at St Helier and carried materials for the

development there. The small Mitcham signal box is locked out of use.

On the way to Morden Road (1 m 8 ch) the route passes through Morden Hall Park and crosses the two-stream course of the River Wandle. Workmen were at work on the traditional complex of station house, ticket office and waiting room on the single platform of this unstaffed halt in 1982 for the original workmanship was beginning to show its age. The main Merton to Morden road crosses over the line at the Mitcham end of the station and the Northern Line tunnel passes beneath the route at the other end.

Merton Park (51 ch), opened as Lower Merton, was originally a joint LB&SC/LSW station recognising the opening on October 1 1868 of the joint route from Streatham Junction via Tooting. After closure to passengers on March 3 1929 the line continued to serve the Merton Abbey and Tooting coal depots. Although closed, its route remains obvious from the V shape of the platform remaining in use and the concrete in-filling between the Tooting line platforms to give access to the station buildings—on the Up side and partly original.

The section on to Wimbledon is double line, except for the actual junction there, and the electric train staff instrument for the single line portion is housed in Merton Park ticket office and released by the signal box. On this final section, also formerly joint, are double barrier crossings, first at the main Kingston Road (worked manually from the SB) and then at Dundonald Road (18 ch).

The route is modestly graded with short rises and falls within the 1 in 94 to 1 in 296 range. It was electrified on July 6 1930, the push and pull steam service having been withdrawn the day before.

W.16   West Dulwich

Victoria-Ramsgate line, between Herne Hill and Beckenham Junction. 5 m 2 ch from Victoria

From the single-storey ticket office (probably dating from the 1863 opening of the line) on the road bridge beneath the station stairs lead to the two platforms serving the Up and Down Chatham lines. The North Dulwich-Tulse Hill line crosses by an arched and balustraded overbridge beyond the park on the London side, the bridge decoration deriving from the aesthetic requirements of Dulwich College. The Orpington trains call.

W.17   Westenhanger

Charing Cross-Dover line, between Ash-ford and Folkestone. 64 m 15 ch from Charing Cross

Westenhanger, opened as Westenhanger & Hythe on February 7 1844, is preceded by a climb at 1 in 250/280 from the site of the now closed station at Smeeth and via the location of the old Herringe Box. The summit lies just beyond the station and is followed by a continuous descent of 11 miles to the outskirts of Dover. Westen-hanger is the station for Folkestone Race-course and is manned only on race days. It has two platforms with a waiting shelter on each.

W.18   Westgate-on-Sea

Victoria-Ramsgate line, between Herne Bay and Margate. 72 m 35 ch from Victoria

This small station lies on the coastal approach to Margate and was opened in April 1871. It comprises Up and Down platforms served by the hourly Victoria-Ramsgate slows. The station-house is still in existence on the Down side where the tickets are issued from a small separate wooden office of herringbone construction and probably original. The Up side has only a brick shelter.

W.19   West Malling

Victoria-Margate line, between Borough Green and Maidstone East. 34 m 61 ch from Victoria

The Victoria-Maidstone East trains serve West Malling which lies in a pleasant area of fruit orchards. Although the station comprises only Up and Down platforms, signal box and crossover the Up side buildings, dating partly from the 1874 opening and partly from a reconstruction some 14 years later, are quite imposing with tall chimneys rising above the dormer windows and with the station-house section at one end. The opposite platform has just a shelter, the signal box and the 34¾ mile-post sign.

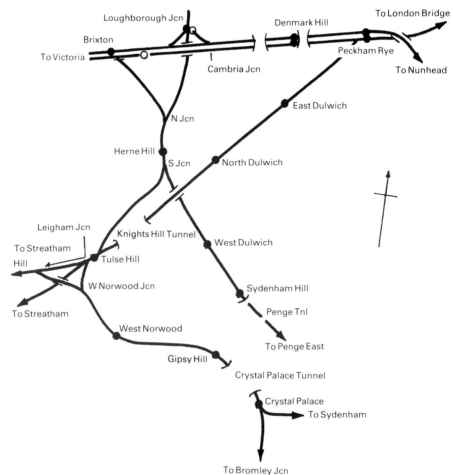

W.20   West Norwood

Victoria-Beckenham Junction line, between West Norwood Junction and Crystal Palace. 7 m 2 ch from Victoria

The rising terrain gives the station an overbridge at the London end and an underbridge at the country end. There are modern shelters on each platform and stairs up to the Clasp-type ticket office on the Down side of the overbridge. West Norwood (as Lower Norwood) was one of the original stations when the Wandsworth Common-Crystal Palace line opened on December 1 1856 and is now served by Victoria-Beckenham Junction/West Croydon and London Bridge-Redhill line trains.

West Norwood is approached in the Down direction via the 443 yd Leigham Court Tunnel (6 m to 6 m 17 ch), Leigham Junction (6 m 31 ch) where the link to Tulse Hill departs, a bridge over the Tulse Hill-Streatham line and West Norwood Junction (6 m 58 ch) where the spur from Tulse Hill joins.

West St Leonards—see Hastings

West Suttun—see Wimbledon-Sutton Line.

W.21   West Wickham

Lewisham-Hayes line. 13 m 19 ch from Charing Cross

Adjacent to the Langley Park estate, West Wickham station lies in a shallow cutting and comprises Up and Down platforms with a modern ticket office building on the Up side. The location dates from 1882 and the SR era is represented by the concrete walls and lamp standards. The Charing Cross/Cannon Street-Hayes trains call every 20 minutes.

W.22   West Worthing

Brighton-Littlehampton/Portsmouth line, between Worthing and Arundel Junction. 11 m 30 ch from Brighton

The main buildings on the Down side date from the opening of the station to serve the growing residential area west of Worthing proper on November 4 1889. They are substantial, two-storey with gable ends, decorative window heads and typical LB&SC cornices and oversailing chimneys. The Up side just has shelters. At the Brighton end is a double barrier crossing and the controlling signal box and at the Portsmouth end an Up side bay leading to the three-berth carriage shed, plus additional loops and sidings. The station is served by the Portsmouth/Littlehampton-Brighton slows and Littlehampton-Victoria semi-fasts and originates some morning Brighton commuter services which return in the evening.

As a Down train draws into Weybridge the Staines set stands in the Up side bay waiting for its next working.

W.23 Weybridge

Waterloo-Weymouth line, between Surbiton and Woking, junction for line to Virginia Water. 19 m 12 ch from Waterloo

This location dates from the opening from Nine Elms to Woking Common in 1838 and its situation, deep in a cutting that caused the London & Southampton Railway many problems, gives the station a sombre air. Up and Down platforms serve the slow lines and are linked by a substantial footbridge with lifts. The main buildings and ticket office are at street level on the Up side and the Down side slope to the overbridge at the London end of the station is now out of use. Fast and slow line pairs are linked at this end with slow and fast and Down Fast to branch links at the other. The branch also connects into the Up Slow and to the Up side bay which most trains use.

Weybridge became a junction with the opening of the line to Chertsey on February 14 1848, the Chertsey-Virginia Water section not following until October 1 1866. This route was electrified on January 3 1937.

Goods traffic at Weybridge ceased in 1964 but the station has a good passenger service—as for Esher on the main line and on the branch half-hourly to Staines with some workings to Chertsey and through to Waterloo.

W.24 Weymouth

Waterloo-Weymouth line. 168 m 63 ch from Paddington

When the broad gauge Wilts, Somerset & Weymouth Railway finally reached the latter point on January 20 1857 the addition

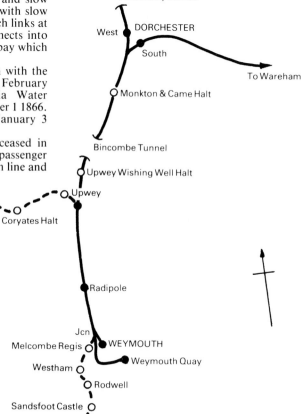

Above *Weymouth station in 1983. The line to the harbour passes to the left of the station and through the town.* **Below** *Under a scheme of modernisation and simplification the Weymouth of 1983 would lose these period timber buildings.*

of extra lines allowed LSW trains to be extended from Dorchester to Weymouth under an agreement made three years earlier. The town and its shipping links to the Channel Islands and France remained GWR/WR oriented until the regional boundary changes and transfer of the boat trains to Waterloo in 1959.

Although the steamers have now relinquished the former fruit and flower business from the Channel Islands, Sealink remains the main commercial operator from the council-owned port. In summer boat trains pass over the Weymouth Quay line to serve the intensified shipping service. This line is operated under the control of the Weymouth supervisor and locomotives carry a warning bell/yellow flashing light unit, two shunters also accompanying the movement to warn road traffic as the train passes along the northern edge of the Wey estuary to the ship berths.

Still busy on summer days, the Weymouth terminal station has been reduced from six running lines to four and from four platform faces to three. The wooden ticket and information offices are on the Up side and the signal box which precedes the station (both due to go under simplification plans) also controls access to the Quay line and carriage sidings. From the same point ran the 4 m single line to Portland via Melcombe Regis and the 3 m 72 ch extension to Easton. The product of four schemes, the first dating back to 1826, this GW/LSW operation produced a service of 22 weekday trains each way between Melcombe Regis and Portland in the '30s with 5-7 extended to/from Easton.

Today Weymouth has a basic hourly service to and from Waterloo using Class 33 locomotives at the country end of four-car sets, a dmu service to Westbury/Bristol, and a number of additional summer services, both scheduled and excursion.

W.25   Whitchurch

Waterloo-Exeter line, between Worting Junction and Andover. 59 m 8 ch from Waterloo

Whitchurch (Hants) was Whitchurch (North) when it was necessary to distinguish it from the station on the Didcot, Newbury & Southampton Railway (later GWR) line which passed beneath the LSW route just west of the station. The former GWR station lost its passenger services on March 7 1960 and when the freight facilities were withdrawn three years later the SR

station was left to provide the town's railway services.

Whitchurch got its first station when the Basingstoke-Andover section was opened on July 3 1854 and it now has two four-car platforms with the ticket office on the Down side and wooden shelter plus canopy on the Up. The Waterloo-Salisbury trains call.

W.26   Whitstable

Victoria-Ramsgate line, between Faversham and Herne Bay. 59 m 6 ch from Victoria

The LC&D line reached Whitstable on August 1 1860 and was then held up while the SER procrastinated over the conditions for crossing beneath the line of the pioneer Canterbury & Whitstable Railway, then 30 years old. Eventually a bridge was built and although the early route lost its passenger services on January 1 1931 and was closed to freight exactly 22 years later, traces of the bridge can still be seen beyond the present BR station. The latter with a half-hourly service to Ramsgate and Victoria, was rebuilt in 1914/15 with its present red brick buildings and 'bracket' canopies.

Graveney AHB LC (54 m 77 ch) lies on the crossing of the coastal plain towards Faversham.

W.27   Whitton

Waterloo-Reading line, between Twickenham and Feltham. 12 m 43 ch from Waterloo

The Richmond-Windsor line opened in 1848/9 and the link from Feltham to the Hounslow loop in the following year. The connection from Whitton Junction (13 m 3 ch) to Hounslow Junction was not made until 1883 and Whitton station was not opened until 1930. It remains a modest affair of Up and Down platforms with canopies, serving the local commuters and the Kneller Hill Army School of Music. The half-hourly trains on the Windsor line and the Hounslow Loop give Whitton an excellent service.

Whyteleafe—see Caterham Branch

Whyteleafe South—see Caterham Branch

W.28   Wilton Junction

Waterloo-Exeter line, junction for Warminster line. 85 m 37 ch from Waterloo

Instead of a separate route to its own

terminus at Salisbury the former GWR route now joins the SR metals at Wilton Junction and the trackbed onwards carries only the siding to the ECC Quidhampton terminal. West of the junction the former LSW main line singles at the closed Wilton station (86 m 25 ch) from which point WR tokenless block applies to Gillingham and Templecombe.

In addition to the signal box there are station remains at the ex-LSW Wilton South, closed March 7 1966 and more at the ex-GWR Wilton North (closed September 19 1955) where the goods shed is also in existence.

W.29   Wimbledon

Wimbledon is on the Waterloo-Weymouth line, 7 m 19 ch from Waterloo; Wimbledon Chase is on the Wimbledon-Sutton line and Wimbledon Park on the Point Pleasant Junction-Wimbledon line (see separate entries)

In addition to its Waterloo-Portsmouth trains Wimbledon has trains on the Alton/Guildford lines, on the Kingston loop, to Chessington/Dorking/Effingham Junction, to Shepperton, to Hampton Court, on the circular route from London Bridge via Tooting/Sutton and to/from West Croydon. The last two routes use the outer island platform (9 and 10) on the Down side while the LT District line trains use platforms 1-4 on the opposite side. Platforms 5 and 6 are for Western Section Up services and 7 and 8 for Down. Some 1,800 trains and 60,000 passengers use the station on a normal day.

Wimbledon was part of the Nine Elms-Woking Common scheme opened on May 21 1838 but did not complete its basic pattern of lines until the Wimbledon & Sutton line was finally completed on January 5 1930. By then both the old (Wimbledon & Merton) stations had gone and the main station had taken the name Wimbledon in 1909. Reconstruction took place in 1929, with further alterations at the time of the Portsmouth electrification.

In addition to the signal box at the London end on the Down side, Wimbledon has a large carriage berthing depot and a CM&EE maintenance depot on which are centred the inspection and maintenance of trains on all local routes as far as Horsham, Guildford and Aldershot. A flyover (carrying the Up local and changing the track pairing from use to direction) links the Up and Down sides north of the station where Wimbledon staff halt (6 m

28 ch) on the Up Through line is also located. The complex includes a carriage washing plant and cleaning platforms, over 100 people being employed on carriage cleaning work.

The station entrance is set back from the busy shopping frontage in Wimbledon Hill Road and a footbridge leads to the canopied platforms. The shell of Wimbledon 'B' box stands south of the station where the branch to West Croydon is followed by the goods depot and then the junction for the Sutton line.

A novel feature at Wimbledon is a glass cased tribute to the dog Laddie who collected £5,000 for the Woking Homes before his death in 1960.

W.30   Wimbledon-Sutton Line

This line had its origins well before World War One when the LSW, LB&SC and District lines all flirted with the proposals. The latter did, in fact, obtain powers to build but, by agreement, the project was shelved. Its revival in 1922 led to more argument and, eventually, a wider SR/Underground agreement under which the former would take over the project. It was opened as far as South Merton on July 7 1929 and on to Sutton on January 5 1930.

From Wimbledon the double line takes a frequently winding course south, skirting between Morden Park and Morden LT and passing through the estate built by the LCC at St Helier. The gradients are modest (1 in 70 to 1 in 733 range) and often only to pass over roads.

All the stations—Wimbledon Chase (8 m 13 ch), South Merton (8 m 61 ch), Morden South (9 m 32 ch), St Helier (9 m 69 ch), Sutton Common (10 m 67 ch) and West Sutton (11 m 47 ch)—are on a similar pattern. West Sutton is typical, wood and concrete buildings beneath a canopy on the island platform with stairs rising to street level where a small passimeter is surrounded by a modest shop development. Other stations have minor variations, eg, the entrance at Wimbledon Chase is below the station and access is by subway. Several have suffered badly from vandals.

The route is double throughout and is worked from the Wimbledon and Sutton panels, although the signal box and frame at St Helier is still intact. Mileposts are on the Down side and there are many bridges but the only notable one is the underbridge between South Merton and Morden South. The line speed is 60 mph but 30/40 mph speed limits result from the curves.

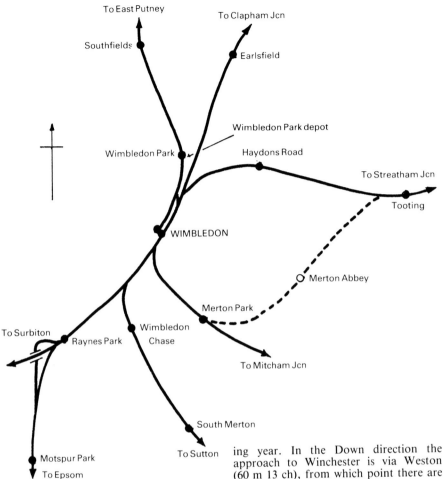

The main service is now half hourly London Bridge-Wimbledon-Sutton-London Bridge (and vice versa) with some Holborn Viaduct-Victoria extensions thereof.

Winchelsea—see Ashford-Hastings line

W.21   Winchester

Waterloo-Weymouth line, between Worting Junction and Eastleigh. 66 m 39 ch from Waterloo

From the summit at Litchfield Tunnel the main line drops at a rolling gradient of 1 in 252 for the remaining 20 miles to the outskirts of Southampton. Halfway down this descent lies Winchester which received its first train in 1839 but was not linked to the Basingstoke direction until the follow-ing year. In the Down direction the approach to Winchester is via Weston (60 m 13 ch), from which point there are Up and Down passenger loops as far as Wallers Ash (61 m 50 ch). Then comes the 501 yd Wallers Ash Tunnel (62 m 22 ch to 62 m 45 ch). Another smaller tunnel, the 62 yd St Cross Tunnel (68 m 31 ch to 68 m 33 ch) follows Winchester Station.

Winchester was once a junction of some note. The Mid-Hants Railway, worked by the LSW, opened a link from Alton to Winchester Junction (64 m 33 ch) on October 2 1865. Twenty years later its position as a gateway to Southampton brought Winchester metals of the Didcot, Newbury & Southampton Railway which arrived at a terminal on the east side of the city on May 4 1885. After a long period of negotiation the independent line was linked to the LSW main line further south at Shawford Junction from October 1 1891 and some traces of both routes are still visible in the Winchester Junction area where a 1939-45 wartime link was put in between the SR and ex-DN&S routes.

Today Winchester derives an excellent service from the slow and semi-fast Bournemouth line trains and the Reading-Portsmouth services also call there. The old GWR Winchester Chesil station had some pretensions of style but the main station has a rather ugly building on the Down side and looks quite as functional as the old brick goods shed beyond the country end of the station.

W.32   Winchfield

Waterloo-Weymouth line, between Farnborough and Basingstoke. 39 m 66 ch from Waterloo

Winchfield, then known as Shapley Heath, was the country terminus of the London & Southampton line for nine months from September 24 1838 to June 10 of the following year when the route was extended on to Basingstoke. It now has platforms to the Up and Down Slow lines with a modest brick office building on the Up side and a gap where the centre island used to be.

There are crossovers between the fast and slow lines and the Basingstoke and Bournemouth slow trains provide the service.

W.33   Windmill Bridge Junction

Victoria-Brighton line, junction with line from London Bridge 10 m 1 ch from Victoria, 9 m 69 ch from London Bridge

One of the best known junctions on the Southern system, Windmill Bridge Junction is where the approach line to Victoria via Balham, opened in 1862, makes junction with the original London & Croydon route to and from London Bridge. It remains an intensely busy junction but the elevated signal box on the Up side has now surrendered its control to the Victoria panel as part of the extensive remodelling of the whole Gloucester Road triangle.

W.34   Windsor & Eton Riverside Branch

Waterloo-Reading line, branch from Staines. 6 m 46 ch

From a double line junction at the country end of Staines station this former L&SW branch heads in a near straight line for Windsor and the three-line terminus at Windsor & Eton Riverside, which is sufficiently near the river and steamer moorings to justify its name. The route was authorised to the Windsor, Staines & South Western Railway in 1847 and opened from Richmond as far as Datchet on August 22 1848. Both the GWR line from Slough and the LSW protege line from Richmond had set their hearts on being the first to serve Windsor and both encountered opposition from Windsor Castle and Eton College interests. In the end the GWR won

Windsor & Eton Riverside with some unusual ornamentation of the station wall.

the race by less than two months, the section from Datchet round Home Park being opened on December 1 1849 after a financial settlement with the Commissioners of Woods & Forests.

On the Down side leaving Staines is the connection to the Cory depot, put in to allow the WR Uxbridge-Staines West branch to be cut back to Colnbrook. This is an area of trunk roads, where the water meadows of the Colne and Wyrardisbury streams have become water leisure areas. The first station, Wraysbury (21 m 40 ch), dates from 1848 and uses the modern name form of Wyrardisbury. It is an unstaffed affair of two platforms and a skew bridge. The style alters at Sunnymeads, (22 m 48 ch) which dates from 1927. Also unstaffed, it consists of a canopied island platform with footbridge access.

Datchet (23 m 63 ch) stands on the opposite side of Home Park from the town of Windsor and is quite near the Thames. It has Up and Down platforms and a ticket office staffed for the morning peak. Two CCTV barrier crossings, one at Datchet itself and then one at Mays (23 m 74 ch), precede the golf course as the line describes a half circle to cross to the south bank of the river and come to the terminus.

Windsor & Eton Riverside, designed by Tite as a royal station and still largely in its original state, is not unimposing despite the brashness of the date, royal initials and other decoration in darker bricks in the outer wall. The frontage has stone facings to enliven the mullioned and transomed main window, the gables and the multi-arch entrance. The main hall with its high ceiling, roof beams and decorative crests still has a period flavour and this is enhanced by the retention of the old ticket office although no longer used. There is a spacious concourse and the overall roof then continues over two of the platform lines, the other having a separate awning.

There is a half-hourly service to and from Waterloo and the route is controlled from the Feltham panel.

W.35   Winnersh

Waterloo-Reading line, between Wokingham and Reading. 64 m 10 ch from Charing Cross

Served by the all-station dmus on the Reading-Tonbridge route and by the emus from Waterloo, Winnersh lies in a shallow cutting bridged at the London end of the station. This dates from 1910 and is a modest affair of Up and Down platforms,

wooden shelters and ticket facilities each side. There is a large comprehensive school nearby and Winnersh can be very busy with its pupils at certain times of the day.

W.36   Witley

Waterloo-Portsmouth line between Godalming and Haslemere. 38 m 36 ch from Waterloo

Served hourly by the Waterloo-Portsmouth all-station trains, Witley is another of the locations opened with the line in 1859. Its main buildings, on the Down side, are original and almost identical to those at Liphook. The Up side has just wooden waiting room, canopy and shelter.

Public rights of way across the railway include a 'horse and hounds' crossing at the south end of the station.

W.37   Wivelsfield

Victoria-Brighton line, between Haywards Heath and Keymer Junction. 40 m 52 ch from London Bridge

The station, comprising Up and Down lines with shelters and a ticket office located midway between platform and street level below, serves the north end of the Burgess Hill area. Between it and Burgess Hill station is Keymer Junction (40 m 69 ch) where, since October 1 1847, Lewes trains have veered off south east.

There was a stopping point near the present barrier crossing and adjacent Keymer Crossing box on the Lewes route until 1883. It was called Keymer Junction and this name was carried by Wivelsfield from its opening in 1886 until the present name was taken ten years later.

Some trains call on both Brighton and Lewes lines.

W.38   Woking

Waterloo-Weymouth line, junction for Portsmouth line. 24 m 27 ch from Waterloo

The London & Southampton line from Nine Elms reached Woking Common, as the station was first called, in 1838, the official opening taking place on May 19 with the public service starting two days later. On September 24 the railway moved forward to Shapley Heath—now Winchfield—and by 1840 had reached Southampton. The Guildford line project was taken over from the original Guildford Railway and opened in 1845, on May 5 of that year Woking becoming known as Woking Junction.

Civil engineer's relaying train at Woking.

Today Woking is served by Waterloo-Portsmouth slow and semi-fast services, by Basingstoke, Southampton and Bournemouth trains and by those running over the truncated main line to Exeter. The present station dates from an SR scheme of 1938 and comprises a central island and outer platforms all with brick buildings and canopies. The former No 1 Platform, the Up bay, has been sacrificed to improve the bus facilities. There are ticket and buffet facilities on both sides of the station but the information office is on the Down side as is the coach link with Heathrow airport.

Woking's original station was one of Britain's earliest provincial terminals although it consisted only of one platform, a house and a goods shed, and its village of Old Woking was 1½ miles away. In some ways the present station is still influenced by the past for the main entrance is not on the same side as the town, this growing up on the Basingstoke Canal side as the local landowner would not permit commercial development to the south. The keen observer might still spot a wall of the old locomotive shed between the station

and Woking Homes and a deep well nearby probably fed many a steam working tender.

The wartime HQ of the SR's London West Division was at Woking and Woking Grange, also on the Down side, started life in July 1909 as the London & South Western Railway Orphanage after a move from the original site at Clapham. Built to accommodate 150 children, the building needed a new wing in 1935 for 90 more but today 'The Southern Railwaymen's Home for Children & Old People' has more elderly retired railway staff than child residents but all expenses are still met by voluntary contributions.

Woking is preceded by carriage sidings on the Down side and followed by the Down Yard and Woking Junction (24 m 62 ch), where the Guildford line departs. Opposite is an extensive permanent way depot.

W.39 Wokingham

Junction of Waterloo-Reading and Redhill-Reading lines. 62 m 8 ch from Charing Cross

The two routes join on the London side of Wokingham station in a conventional, 20 mph, double line junction towards

A branch line scene from the Westerham branch.

Reading. A traditional signal box controls the double barrier crossing which precedes the station and also three AHB crossings on the Bracknell side. There are buildings of modern design on both platforms, with the ticket office among those on the Down side, and a footbridge link to the Up side where the remains of the closed goods yard are still visible.

The former SER route from Ash Junction dates from July 3 1849 and the link from Ascot from July 9 1856. The station is now served by the half-hourly Waterloo trains and the all-stations dmus on the Tonbridge route.

W.40 Woldingham

South Croydon-East Grinstead line, between South Croydon and Oxted. 17 m 15 ch from London Bridge

The station, opened in 1885 a year after the line, lies on the final 1 in 100 rise from South Croydon to the summit amid the Surrey hills. The Up platform has just a wooden waiting room and canopy and the traditional-style signal box; there is a wooden ticket office on the Down side plus a dock siding, used by the civil engineer. Uckfield/East Grinstead demu sets call.

Woodmansterne—see Tattenham Corner Branch

Woodside—see Addiscombe Branch

W.41 Wool

Waterloo-Weymouth line, between Wareham and Dorchester South. 125 m 69 ch from Waterloo

The 1847 Down side buildings have been replaced by a modern ticket office building with just a shelter on the Up side. The small wooden signal box on a brick base also stands on the Up platform and controls the double barrier LC beyond the station. At the London end East Ground Frame and two sidings lie on the Up side with two more terminating in the double end dock opposite. The hourly Weymouth portions call.

The CCTV barrier LC at East Burton (126 m 56 ch) precedes the extensive UKAEA premises at Winfrith and their short private siding trailing into the Down line at the west end.

W.42 Woolston

Southampton-Portsmouth line, between St Denys and Fareham. 4 m 11 ch from Southampton

The approach to Woolston is round the estuary of the River Itchen, the station's hourly trains serving the shipyard there. The main Up side buildings date from the 1866 opening of the route to Netley and are similar to those at St Denys and Netley. There is also an old brick signal box on this platform. Over the footbridge there is only brick waiting accommodation on the Down side, with the former yard behind and where the old brick goods shed is now in the hands of Solent Express.

Woolwich Arsenal—see North Kent Line

Woolwich Dockyard—see North Kent Line

W.43   Worcester Park

Raynes Park-Leatherhead line, between Raynes Park and Epsom. 10 m 53 ch from Waterloo

Originating as Old Malden & Worcester Park with the opening of the line to Leatherhead on April 4 1859, Worcester Park is now the busiest of the stations between Raynes Park and Epsom. It has Up and Down platforms with open plan booking hall and ticket office embodied in the SR-style brick buildings on the former. The Down side has a canopy and there is a footbridge and a car park. The train service is the same as that at Stoneleigh.

W.44   Worplesdon

Waterloo-Portsmouth line, between Woking Junction and Guildford. 26 m 65 ch from Waterloo

The two-platform station at Worplesdon dates from 1883 and has a basic half-hourly service. The main, two-storey buildings are on the Up side with a footbridge spanning the Up and Down tracks to the waiting room on the Down. The combined station house and offices date from opening and embody a variety of features including Dutch gables and dormer windows.

W.45   Worthing

Brighton-Littlehampton/Portsmouth line, between Shoreham and Arundel Junction. 10 m 46 ch from Brighton

With the same service as Shoreham, the main station for this pleasant coastal resort comprises Up and Down platforms, the former an island with the Up Passenger Loop beyond and linked by the subway to the latter on which the main station buildings are housed. The station itself dates from the opening of the line from Shoreham on November 24 1845 but its single storey brick buildings, relieved only by a central gable, date from a 1909 reconstruction. They encompass the ticket office, waiting room, buffet etc and still have an LB&SC clock.

The signal box stands on the Up side

and controls the double barrier crossing at the Portsmouth end of the station.

W.46   Worting Junction

Waterloo-Weymouth line, junction with line to Salisbury. 50 m 21 ch from Waterloo

At Worting Junction the pairs of Up and Down lines from the London direction separate into double tracks towards Southampton and towards Salisbury. The latter route has now lost its West of England traffic making the junction a quieter place on summer Saturdays, but it is still a junction of significance. The Up Southampton line passes over the Salisbury lines and there are railway cottages and a ground frame adjacent.

W.47   Wye

Charing Cross-Margate line, between Ashford and Canterbury West. 60 m 32 ch from Victoria

Wye is the first station out of Ashford on the 1846 line to Ramsgate and the Down line ceases to be reversible from this point onwards. The route here is adjacent to the Great Stour river and the Up side approach to the station is over a pack-horse bridge. On the opposite side of the line there is a small racecourse.

Served by the Victoria-Ramsgate trains, the station comprises a traditional level crossing followed by Up and Down platforms and then a crossover and Down siding. The main red brick buildings, in Tudor style, gabled and well provided with chimneys, are on the Down side and there are various other interesting features including the small signal box controlling semaphore signals, the former private siding, Kellington Gravels and crossing house and adjacent cattle grids.

Y.1   Yalding

Strood-Maidstone West-Paddock Wood line, between Paddock Wood and Maidstone West. 38 m 19 ch from Charing Cross

One of the stations opened with the southern half of the line on September 25 1844, Yalding has staggered platforms with a traditional single-storey brick building plus decorated canopy on the Up side and a wooden shelter on the Down. A small wooden signal box controls semaphore signals and the gated crossing over the road leading to the River Medway and then Yalding village.

Paddock Wood-Strood trains call.

SECTION 4

Route summaries

Waterloo-Weymouth

From the early 1830s interest in linking London and Southampton by rail began to quicken, resulting in the London & Southampton Railway obtaining its Act on July 25 1834, despite opposition from the infant GWR. The section from Nine Elms to Woking Common was opened on May 21 1838 and extended to Shapley Heath on September 24 of that year. Further construction left just the Basingstoke-Winchester gap uncompleted after June 10 1839. The gradients and tunnels necessary to bridge this high chalk plateau were finally ready in time for opening throughout to Southampton on May 11 1840.

Today's main line commences at Waterloo, which took over from Nine Elms on July 11 1848, and passes the site of the latter (now marked by the new Covent Garden Market) on its way beneath the lines from Victoria and along the edge of Battersea Park to Clapham Junction. Here a great carriage servicing area lies in the angle between the 'Windsor Lines' and the main line, the latter also losing its Brighton main line companion on the opposite side. More carriage servicing facilities are located at Wimbledon where the routes from Point Pleasant Junction and Streatham join before the station, with those to West Croydon and Sutton departing after it.

More branches are thrown off as the main line continues its straight, almost level, course down the Thames Valley with the two Through lines between the two Local lines and these becoming Fast and Slow respectively from New Malden. Flyover junctions occur at Raynes Park for the Epsom and Chessington South lines, at New Malden for the Kingston Loop and its Shepperton branch and at Hampton Court Junction beyond Surbiton for the branch to Hampton Court and for the New Guildford Line.

After the cutting at Weybridge comes the triangular junction with the route to Virginia Water and the beginning of a long flirtation with the Basingstoke Canal as the main line takes a higher level course on to the important station at Woking. The main line to Portsmouth departs here, at a junction between the freight yard and the permanent way depot, leaving the Weymouth line to continue to Brookwood which once had Cemetery and Bisley Camp branches.

By now the route is climbing, modestly enough at 1 in 387/326/314, and this process is to continue over the whole 35 miles preceding Litchfield Summit. The Alton line, once on through routes to Winchester and Fareham, leaves at Pirbright Junction and, after crossing the Ascot-Aldershot and Reading-

Bournemouth, where the four-car Weymouth portions are detached from the 12-car trains that have run fast from Waterloo.

Guildford lines before Farnborough, the main line leads straight on for Basing-stoke where the cross-country route from Reading joins and the Basingstoke & Alton Light Railway once departed. Two miles further up the 1 in 249 section the Weymouth and Exeter lines separate into two two-track routes at Worting Junction.

Now comes the remainder of the climb to Litchfield and then a 14-mile descent at 1 in 252, past Micheldever where the opening was celebrated in 1840 and on to Winchester, where the Didcot, Newbury & Southampton Railway had to abandon its dream of a separate access to Southampton and settle for a junction with the LSW at Shawford.

From Eastleigh (originally Bishopstoke) the LSW pushed out its branches to Gosport and Salisbury, the former now used by the Reading-Portsmouth service via Fareham. Although the days of building the great Southern steam locomotive classes have gone, Eastleigh is still busy with its CCE track depot, CM&EE wagon repairs, BREL works, freight yard and depot as well as with its traction and passenger activities.

The making of a railway installation, in this case the Freightliner maritime terminal at Southampton.

Via Southampton Airport station and then St Denys, where the line from Portsmouth joins, the four-track section from the latter continues to Northam Junction. Here the original route lies straight ahead while the present main line turns east, through the ailing tunnel to Southampton's main station and then along behind the docks once built and owned by the SR and once busy with freight vans and boat trains. Today the two Freightliner terminals are the heirs to this business.

The route is now that originated by the Southampton & Dorchester Railway in 1847 but subsequently closed between Lymington Junction and Hamworthy Junction in favour of the present coastal route. The line to Romsey and Salisbury is shed beyond Redbridge station and the main line passes over the River Test to come to Totton and the junction with the line to Fawley's oil installations.

Now comes a long, pleasant, modestly-graded loop through the New Forest with heath, heather, ponies and even wild deer as the railway's companions. After parting with the Lymington branch and the old 'Castleman's Corkscrew' route via Ringwood beyond Brockenhurst the Bournemouth electrics head for the coast, to cross the Avon at Christchurch (which also had a line to Ringwood) and then pass through Bournemouth's suburbs to its spacious station.

The four-car Weymouth portions are detached at Bournemouth for the push and pull operation applying for the remainder of the journey. This passes the line to Bournemouth West, the original access to Bournemouth now truncated and used as a maintenance depot, and soon picks up a holiday atmosphere from the marinas around Poole Bay. Beyond the busy station at Poole comes the causeway line to Hamworthy, the bottom of a triangle which once gave access to the Somerset & Dorset line as well as to the original Southampton & Dorchester route and the rural branch via West Moors to Salisbury. The old main line served Poole via what is now a branch to Hamworthy Goods.

After Wareham the main line heads across rural Dorset, passing the stub of the Swanage branch and climbing steadily to Dorchester South where the old terminal station still exists. The former broad gauge route from Castle Cary and Yeovil joins at Dorchester Junction and then climbs at 1 in 91 to Bincombe Tunnel before the steep drop at 1 in 52/50/74 to Weymouth. Special trains still use the route to the quay and the Weymouth steamers but the lines out to Portland and Easton, like the Abbotsbury branch from Upwey, are long gone.

Although this 142¾-mile main line has seen many changes in the course of its history it is still an important route and one of great variety and character. Electrification, especially when extended through to Bournemouth, brought much alteration but the traffic pattern has also altered greatly with the passage of the years. The Kingston 'Roundabouts' still maintain their long tradition but gone are the Eastleigh horse box trains, the Willesden-Woking goods, the trains to Bulford, Bordon or Brookwood Cemetery, the milk churn trains and the rail motors. The 4.10 pm no longer runs non-stop to Bournemouth to arrive at 6.25 pm but today's 16.35 gets there by 18.13 having called at Winchester and Southampton. And two other services now leave Waterloo for Bournemouth in each hour plus services to Basingstoke and the intensive pattern of suburban plus Portsmouth and Exeter line trains which use the first portion of the route. The Bournemouth fasts carry a Weymouth portion and the route is also served by or linked with the services between Poole and the North East and North West and between Portsmouth and Bristol/South Wales and Reading via Eastleigh and Basingstoke.

W.12	Waterloo	W.31	Winchester (66 m 39 ch)
V.1	Vauxhall (1 m 29 ch)		St Cross Tunnel (68 m 31 ch)
Q.2	Queens Road (2 m 65 ch)	S.14	Shawford (69 m 50 ch)
	West London Junction (3 m 17 ch)	E.9	Eastleigh (73 m 35 ch)
C.24	Clapham Junction (3 m 74 ch)	S.26	Southampton Airport (74 m 66 ch)
E.2	Earlsfield (5 m 46 ch)	S.26	Swaythling (75 m 56 ch)
	Staff Halt (6 m 28 ch)	S.26	St Denys (77 m 10 ch)
P.12	Point Pleasant Junction-		Northam Junction (78 m 15 ch)
	Wimbledon line		Southampton Tunnel (78 m 52 ch)
W.29	Wimbledon (7 m 19 ch)	S.26	Southampton (79 m 19 ch)
W.15	West Croydon-Wimbledon line	S.26	Millbrook (80 m 11 ch)
W.30	Wimbledon-Sutton line	R.5	Redbridge (81 m 70 ch)
R.4	Raynes Park (8 m 51 ch)	T.11	Totton (82 m 43 ch)
N.8	New Malden (9 m 62 ch)	F.8	Fawley Branch
B.14	Berrylands (10 m 78 ch)	L.21	Lyndhurst Road (85 m 34 ch)
S.41	Surbiton (12 m 3 ch)	B.9	Beaulieu Road (88 m 6 ch)
	Hampton Court Junction	B.40	Brockenhurst (92 m 66 ch)
	(13 m 27 ch)	L.20	Lymington Branch
H.5	Hampton Court Branch	S.45	Sway (95 m 45 ch)
E.22	Esher (14 m 31 ch)	N.9	New Milton (98 m 44 ch)
H.19	Hersham (15 m 73 ch)	H.23	Hinton Admiral (101 m 5 ch)
W.5	Walton-on-Thames (17 m 6 ch)	C.21	Christchurch (104 m 28 ch)
W.23	Weybridge (19 m 12 ch)	P.13	Pokesdown (106 m 24 ch)
	Byfleet Junction (20 m 23 ch)	B.32	Bournemouth (108 m 2 ch)
B.47	Byfleet & New Haw (20 m 32 ch)	B.36	Branksome (110 m 51 ch)
W.13	West Byfleet (21 m 54 ch)	P.2	Parkstone (111 m 76 ch)
W.38	Woking (24 m 27 ch)	P.16	Poole (113 m 62 ch)
	Woking Junction (24 m 62 ch)	H.7	Hamworthy (115 m 77 ch)
B.44	Brookwood (27 m 79 ch)	H.27	Holton Heath (118 m 61 ch)
P.9	Pirbright Junction (29 m 39 ch)	W.9	Wareham (120 m 70 ch)
F.3	Farnborough (Main) (33 m 17 ch)		Worgret Junction (121 m 77 ch)
F.13	Fleet (36 m 38 ch)	W.41	Wool (125 m 69 ch)
W.32	Winchfield (39 m 66 ch)	M.10	Moreton (130 m 24 ch)
H.30	Hook (42 m 13 ch)	D.7	Dorchester South (135 m 70 ch)
B.6	Basingstoke (47 m 61 ch)		Dorchester Junction (136 m 15 ch)
	Worting Junction (50 m 21 ch)		Change of mileage to 162 m 14 ch from
	Litchfield Tunnel (55 m 58 ch)		Paddington
	Popham No 1 Tunnel (57 m 17 ch)		Bincombe Tunnel (164 m 44 ch)
	Popham No 2 Tunnel (57 m 35 ch)	U.3	Upwey (166 m 30 ch)
M.7	Micheldever (58 m 4 ch)	R.1	Radipole (167 m 59 ch)
	Wallers Ash Tunnel (62 m 22 ch)	W.24	Weymouth (168 m 63 ch)

Woking-Portsmouth

The Portsmouth Direct line had its beginnings in 1844 when the Guildford Junction Railway was authorised a route from Woking to the market town of Guildford. This was opened on May 5 1845. Four years later, on October 15 1849, a line was in use from Guildford on to Godalming and ten years later still the 'Portsmouth Direct' route was opened from a junction outside the Godalming terminus to another with the LB&SC at Havant. The line had been built thanks to the efforts of Thomas Brassey and was leased by the LSW under threat of a link with the SER at Shalford but it took confrontation and a lawsuit to overcome LB&SC obstruction and permit through services from January 24 1859.

After leaving the Southampton line immediately after Woking station the route heads directly for Guildford and the Wey gap, meeting the Reading and New Guildford lines north of the station and then leaving it via the two short tunnels. At Shalford Junction the SER route to Redhill heads off east and the

On the Portsmouth Direct line a fast service flashes past the traditional footbridge, barrier crossing and signal box at Petersfield.

main line continues, via the site of Peasmarsh Junction and the former LB&SC line to Horsham, to Farncombe which took over the role of the original Godalming station and left it to finish life as a goods depot. The junction curve now eased, the route sets about climbing the steps to the wooded Hampshire plateau, initially at 1 in 82 to Witley and then for over three miles of winding 1 in 80 to Haslemere—the once feared Haslemere Bank.

From Haslemere the route descends towards Liss, where the Longmoor Military Railway made its connection, and then rises again to Petersfield, formerly linked to Midhurst and the LB&SC lines there. The climbing steepens to 1 in 100/110 through Buriton Tunnel to the route's second summit but then begins the final continuous descent to the junction at Havant.

The route is a pleasant one and has a common style, probably Tite's, for its stations. Electrified in 1937, it now has a pattern of three trains an hour with the fasts taking 90 minutes for the 74½-mile journey.

W.38	Woking Junction (24 m 62 ch)	H.9	Haslemere (42 m 79 ch)
W.44	Worplesdon (26 m 65 ch)	L.8	Liphook (46 m 67 ch)
G.15	Guildford (30 m 27 ch)	L.9	Liss (51 m 35 ch)
	Chalk Tunnel (30 m 43 ch)	P.5	Petersfield (54 m 71 ch)
	St Catherine's Tunnel (31 m 13 ch)		Buriton Tunnel (57 m 46 ch)
	Shalford Junction (31 m 42 ch)	R.14	Rowlands Castle (63 m 18 ch)
F.4	Farncombe (33 m 40 ch)	Change of mileage 66 m 18 ch to	
G.7	Godalming (34 m 37 ch)	37 m 24 ch from Brighton	
M.8	Milford (36 m 21 ch)	H.12	Havant (37 m 41 ch)
W.36	Witley (38 m 36 ch)	P.19	Portsmouth Harbour (45 m 36 ch)

Worting Junction-Yeovil

This was the former LSW main line to the Cornish peninsula, born of much complicated intrigue, route of the competition for the Plymouth liner traffic and famous holiday expresses, and now just a secondary route to Exeter in WR hands from Sherborne. Even so the surviving buffet car service fulfils a useful function, running semi-fast to Salisbury in 84 minutes (for 83¾ miles) and interspersed with Waterloo/Basingstoke-Salisbury/Yeovil workings.

The first access from Waterloo to Salisbury was via Eastleigh and Romsey, the LSW requiring considerable pressure to get a single line opened from Basingstoke to Andover on July 3 1854 and complete this through to Salisbury on May 1 1857. A period of internal wrangling and external conflict with the GWR was then to follow before the Salisbury & Yeovil project triumphed over the alternative of extending west from Dorchester and opened its first section on May 2 1859. Trains began running through to Exeter from July 19 1860.

From Worting Junction the route takes an easily-graded course across the Hampshire plain to Andover, crossing at Whitchurch the route of the Didcot, Newbury & Southampton Railway and passing at Hurstbourne the site of the former junction with the Romsey line. At Andover itself (the second link to Romsey) part of the route of the former Midland & South Western Junction company survives as a freight branch to Ludgershall but the line from Grateley/ Amesbury Junction to Bulford Camp out on Salisbury Plain closed back in 1963. This section of the main line involves a 5-mile rise to MP 73¼ and then a steady descent to the junctions with the Romsey/Southampton line, Fisherton Tunnel and then Salisbury.

The old GWR station is still in existence at Salisbury and its once broad-gauge trackbed parallels the SR route as far as Wilton Junction where the Portsmouth-

The Up Exeter-Waterloo has 'got the peg' as a Down train of stone hoppers passes through Salisbury.

Salisbury-Bristol/South Wales trains leave. The main line is now single and rises gently as it passes the sidings at Dinton to a summit at Semley. A steeper drop (1 in 100/114/130) of four miles to Gillingham is followed by a mini-summit at Gillingham Tunnel and another climb to the site of the old junctions with the Somerset & Dorset at Templecombe. There are two single lines for the section on via the regional boundary at MP 117½ to Sherborne and Yeovil Junction.

This route has never been electrified and operation is by dmus for the shorter journeys and locomotive and coaches for the through workings. The scenery is interesting and, west of Salisbury, green and pleasant. The single line sections produce much of operating interest and traffic levels are quite substantial, especially to, from and via Salisbury.

	Worting Junction (50 m 21 ch)		
O.5	Overton (55 m 42 ch)	S.4	Salisbury (83 m 43 ch)
W.25	Whitchurch (59 m 8 ch)	W.28	Wilton Junction (85 m 37 ch)
A.9	Andover (66 m 19 ch)		Wilton (86 m 25 ch)
L.17	Ludgershall Branch	T.8	Tisbury (96 m 14 ch)
G.11	Grateley (72 m 49 ch)	G.2	Gillingham (105 m 23 ch)
	Laverstock North Junction		Gillingham Tunnel (107 m 44 ch)
	(82 m 5 ch)	T.3	Templecombe (112 m 2 ch)
	Salisbury Tunnel Junction		Regional boundary (117 m 40 ch)
	(82 m 36 ch)		Sherborne (118 m 4 ch)
	Fisherton Tunnel (82 m 37 ch)		Yeovil Junction (122 m 31 ch)

Waterloo-Reading

The first section of this route owes its existence to the Richmond Railway which was purchased by the LSW in the year following the opening of its line on July 27 1846. The Windsor, Staines & South Western scheme enabled the LSW to extend the route to Staines and Datchet on August 22 1848 (and to Windsor in the following year) and the Staines, Wokingham & Woking Junction Railway was worked by the LSW from the opening of its Staines-Ascot section on June 4 1856 and the link on to Wokingham on July 9 1856. At the latter point junction was made with the SER line initiated by the Reading, Guildford & Reigate company and opened in 1849 (Reading-Farnborough July 4, throughout October 15).

Windsor & Eton Riverside, very much a 'royal' station.

The Through and Local (outside) 'Windsor Lines' part company with the main line at Clapham Junction and then head for Barnes via the Point Pleasant Junction connection to the LT-Wimbledon line, used by SR stock to and from the Wimbledon depot. At Barnes the two routes separate and become two-track, the 1849-50 Hounslow Loop to cross the Thames by means of Barnes Bridge and the Reading line to cross after Richmond and the junction with the LT/North London line. Then comes the flyover junction linking Twickenham with the Kingston Loop and the triangle of Whitton, Feltham and Hounslow Junctions where the Hounslow Loop rejoins. The desolate site of the former Feltham yard then follows.

After the departure of the Windsor lines at Staines and again crossing the Thames, the Reading route loops between Windsor Great Park and Chobham Common losing the Weybridge line at Virginia Water and the Ash Vale line at Ascot. The latter is no longer the station it was but the wooded countryside hereabouts is delightful. At Wokingham a trailing junction is made with the route from Guildford and beyond the curious buildings of Earley station comes the regional boundary and then Reading station.

The basic Waterloo-Reading service is half-hourly, following the Windsor services, the former connecting into the Ascot-Guildford trains and the latter shedding a Staines-Weybridge portion. The inner pattern is of half-hourly Hounslow Loop trains in front of the Windsors to Barnes and Kingston Loop trains in front of the Readings. The latter connect into the Twickenham-Whitton-Brentford-Waterloo trains. Peak periods produce more through Waterloo services, Waterloo loop running via Richmond/Brentford and other permutations.

C.24	Clapham Junction (3 m 74 ch)	A.18	Ashford (17 m 40 ch)
W.7	Wandsworth Town (4 m 60 ch)	S.32	Staines (19 m 2 ch)
	Point Pleasant Junction (5 m 9 ch)	W.34	Windsor Branch
P.12	Point Pleasant Junction-	E.15	Egham (21 m 2 ch)
	Wimbledon line	V.3	Virginia Water (23 m 15 ch)
P.22	Putney (5 m 72 ch)	L.13	Longcross (25 m 11 ch)
B.4	Barnes (7 m 7 ch)	S.40	Sunningdale (26 m 71 ch)
H.34	Hounslow Loop	A.13	Ascot (28 m 79 ch)
M.12	Mortlake (8 m 21 ch)	A.14	Ascot-Ash Vale Line
N.16	North Sheen (9 m 3 ch)	B.34	Bracknell (32 m 24 ch)
R.9	Richmond (9 m 57 ch)		Change of mileage 36 m 35 ch to
S.1	St Margarets (10 m 66 ch)		61 m 72 ch from Charing Cross
T.14	Twickenham (11 m 22 ch)	W.39	Wokingham (62 m 8 ch)
W.27	Whitton (12 m 43 ch)	W.35	Winnersh (64 m 10 ch)
	Whitton Junction (13 m 3 ch)	E.1	Earley (66 m 1 ch)
	Feltham Junction (13 m 35 ch)		Regional boundary (67 m)
F.10	Feltham (14 m 68 ch)		Reading (68 m 68 ch)

Victoria-Brighton

From the original six schemes for railways to link London and Brighton, the London & Brighton Railway emerged with an Act of July 15 1837 for a line from a junction with the London & Croydon to Brighton, a branch on to Shoreham and another to Newhaven. Work started near Merstham Tunnel on July 12 of the following year. The Brighton-Shoreham section was opened first, on May 12 1840, partly because the construction was relatively simple and partly because materials were being taken via Shoreham Harbour. On the main line a service from London Bridge to Haywards Heath began on July 12 1841, with opening to Brighton following on September 21.

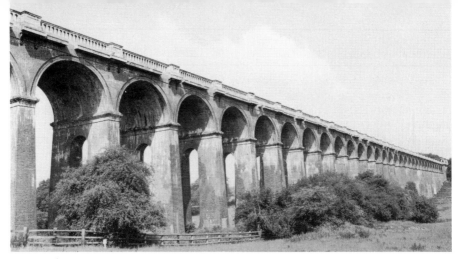

The combined talents of David Mocatta and J.U. Rastrick produced the elegant 37-arch Ouse Valley Viaduct on the Brighton main line.

In 1846 the L&C and L&B amalgamated and the LB&SC came into being on July 27. The line to Victoria via Crystal Palace opened in 1860 (Windmill Bridge-Balham 1862) with track quadrupling gradually extending southwards to cope with increases in traffic. On November 8 1899 (April 1 1900 for passengers) a separate route was provided between Coulsdon North and Earlswood to avoid Redhill and the difficulties of its joint use with the SER. Known as the 'Quarry Line' the new route crossed the old from the west to the east side and rejoined it just north of Earlswood.

There are now three through services from Victoria to Brighton for every one from London Bridge. They pass over the River Thames by Grosvenor Bridge after which the route parts company with the Chatham and South London lines, crosses the LSW main line and then veers away from it after Clapham Junction. At Balham the Crystal Palace lines leave and the four-track main line continues, beneath the Sutton line at Streatham and on to East Croydon via the newly remodelled complex at Gloucester Road where the London Bridge line joins.

The Oxted line quits the Down side after South Croydon as the route starts the first of its 1 in 264 climbs. Then the Caterham line goes at Purley and throws off its Tattenham Corner stem to pass under the main line to the west side and keep it company as far as Smitham. The original pair of lines continue via Coulsdon South, through the level summit portion of Merstham Tunnel and then down, again at 1 in 264, to Redhill and Earlswood. The 'Quarry Line', meantime, has risen through Coulsdon North, passed the site of the former Cane Hill Covered Way artificial tunnel, and climbed to the summit where the old Star Lane signal box heralded the drop through the Quarry Tunnel. The original route again comes into sight before the later route passes under the Tonbridge line via Redhill Tunnel and the two pairs of tracks become four again at Earlswood.

There is now a long straight section dropping at 1 in 264 to Horley and soon rising at the same gradient through busy Gatwick Airport and the Portsmouth line junction at Three Bridges. This is forest land but the next drop at 1 in 264 starts where the four track portion ends at the site of Balcombe Tunnel box and is often in cutting until the crossing of the Great Ouse Viaduct and the link up with the stub of the East Grinstead line (now serving a stone terminal at Ardingly) at Copyhold Junction. There are now four lines again as far as

Haywards Heath which is followed by a small tunnel and then a viaduct near Wivelsfield.

By Keymer Junction and the departure of the Lewes line, the straight main line course is once more rising at 1 in 264 to pass through the South Downs by way of Clayton Tunnel and then drop for 5 miles at the same gradient through Patcham Tunnel to Preston Park on the northern outskirts of Brighton. After the connection to Hove is shed, the old Pullman Works and the huge CM&EE maintenance depot herald the junction with the two coastal routes and then the muted splendour of Brighton station.

In its early years the Brighton main line suffered from Parliament's doubtless well-intentioned decision that the South Eastern and Brighton companies must share the route as far as Redhill. Petty delays and other quarrels were inevitable and led to the quadrupling southwards in the expansion period at the end of the last century turning into the separate LB&SC Quarry Line to avoid the SER influence and bottleneck at Redhill. These historical origins are still reflected in the use of London Bridge distances from Windmill Bridge Junction and Charing Cross distances from Coulsdon South to Redhill and on to the two ex-SER routes east and west from there.

The Brighton was very much a tank engine line (despite its B4s and Atlantics) which earned an affection from its users which continued into Southern days. The character of its main line survived electrification but the end of the Pullman tradition which originated in 1875 completed the transformation to a modern highly efficient piece of railway epitomised by the great signalling schemes which have placed control in the hands of two panels (plus Brighton) and by the major remodelling of the Gloucester Road Triangle.

The line has an excellent basic service of four through trains an hour plus the intermediate workings, services via the Three Bridges and Keymer junctions, the Reading and Victoria links to Gatwick Airport and a cross-country·service to Manchester. Brighton is reached in 58 minutes and the journey contains high railway and scenic interest plus some surviving architecture and civil engineering of note.

V.1	Victoria		P.21	Purley Oaks (12 m 34 ch)
	Battersea Pier Junction (73 ch)		P.21	Purley (13 m 29 ch)
S.30	Battersea Park (1 m 23 ch)		C.5	Caterham Branch
	Pouparts Junction (2 m 4 ch)		T.1	Tattenham Corner Branch
C.24	Clapham Junction (2 m 57 ch)			Stoats Nest Junction (14 m 20 ch)
	New Wandsworth (3 m 19 ch)		C.33	Coulsdon North (14 m 66 ch)
W.7	Wandsworth Common (4 m 5 ch)			*Via Redhill*
B.2	Balham (4 m 52 ch)		Change of mileage 15 m 2 ch to 16 m 66 ch	
	Streatham North Junction		from Charing Cross	
	(6 m 14 ch)		C.33	Coulsdon South (17 m 3 ch)
S.37	Streatham Common (6 m 48 ch)			Merstham Tunnel (19 m 9 ch)
N.11	Norbury (7 m 36 ch)		M.6	Merstham (20 m 59 ch)
T.5	Thornton Heath (8 m 54 ch)		R.6	Redhill (22 m 40 ch)
S.10	Selhurst (9 m 31 ch)			*Via Quarry Line*
G.6	Gloucester Road Junction		Q.1	Quarry Tunnel (17 m 24 ch)
	(9 m 60 ch)			Redhill Tunnel (20 m 62 ch)
W.33	Windmill Bridge Junction		E.3	Earlswood (21 m 50 ch)
	(10 m 1 ch)		S.3	Salfords (23 m 27 ch)
Change of mileage to 9 m 69 ch from			H.31	Horley (25 m 60 ch)
London Bridge			G.1	Gatwick Airport (26 m 47 ch)
E.5	East Croydon (10 m 28 ch)		T.6	Three Bridges (29 m 21 ch)
S.28	South Croydon (11 m 21 ch)		B.1	Balcombe Tunnel (32 m 2 ch)
	South Croydon-East Grinstead Line			

B.1   Balcombe (33 m 64 ch)
O.4   Ouse Viaduct
        Copyhold Junction (37 m)
H.15 Haywards Heath (37 m 59 ch)
        Haywards Heath Tunnel
        (38 m 5 ch)
W.37 Wivelsfield (40 m 52 ch)
        Keymer Junction (40 m 69 ch)
B.45 Burgess Hill (41 m 39 ch)

H.10 Hassocks (43 m 42 ch)
C.26 Clayton Tunnel (44 m 44 ch)
        Patcham Tunnel (47 m 65 ch)
        Preston Park (49 m 21 ch)
B.37 Brighton (50 m 49 ch)

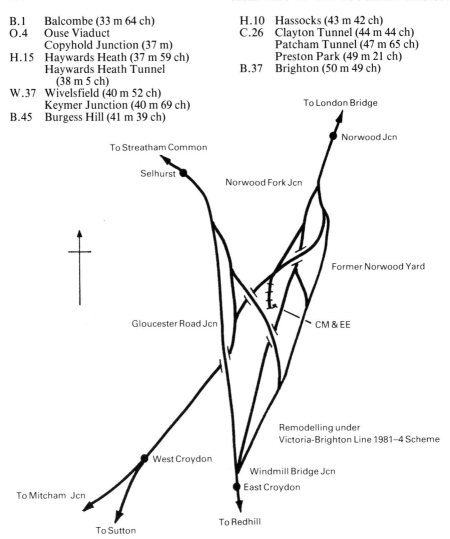

Three Bridges-Bognor Regis

This route is used by Victoria-Bognor Regis stopping trains and by the semifasts which separate/unite Bognor and Portsmouth Harbour portions at Barnham. Its first part, that from Three Bridges to Horsham, was opened as an LB&SC branch on February 14 1848. From Horsham the next section uses the Petworth line of the Mid-Sussex Railway which gave its name to the new route which the LB&SC eventually built up between London and Portsmouth.

The line from Horsham to Petworth was opened on October 10 1859 but despite completion by the LSW of its Portsmouth Direct route in that year the link from Hardham Junction on the Petworth line to Arundel Junction on the LB&SC's coast line was not ready until August 3 1863. The new route was completed by bridging the gap from Horsham to Dorking (and thence to Leatherhead) in May 1 1867 and throughout via Sutton in the following year, but only a few peak hour trains are now routed via Dorking, the remainder using the original 1848 branch between Horsham and Three Bridges. The Bognor Regis branch dates from June 1 1864.

There are 1 in 90 and 1 in 100 sections on the line between Dorking and Horsham but the main route is easily graded, taking advantage of the valley of the River Arun from Billingshurst southwards. It leaves the Brighton main line at the south end of Three Bridges station and passes via the Crawley New Town complex to unite with the Dorking line north of Horsham station. Former lines once departed by facing connections at Stammerham Junction (for Guildford), Itchingfield Junction (for Shoreham) and Hardham Junction (for Petworth, Midhurst and Petersfield). Now, the first junction is with the main Brighton line followed by the triangular one with the Littlehampton branch south of the historic town of Arundel, with a short section of coast line then preceding the departure of the Bognor Regis branch beyond Barnham station platforms.

The route was electrified from July 3 1938, Pullman cars then ceasing.

T.6	Three Bridges (29 m 21 ch)		North Stoke Tunnel (55 m 30 ch)
C.34	Crawley (30 m 49 ch)	A.12	Arundel (58 m 28 ch)
I.1	Ifield (31 m 66 ch)		Arundel Junction (59 m 75 ch)
F.9	Faygate (34 m 28 ch)		Change of mileage to 19 m 1 ch from
L.11	Littlehaven (36 m 50 ch)		Brighton
D.9	Dorking-Horsham Line		Ford Junction (19 m 31 ch)
H.32	Horsham (37 m 56 ch)	L.10	Littlehampton Branch
C.22	Christ's Hospital (40 m 7 ch)	F.15	Ford (19 m 55 ch)
B.21	Billingshurst (44 m 71 ch)	B.5	Barnham (22 m 29 ch)
P.20	Pulborough (50 m)	B.27	Bognor Regis (25 m 75 ch)
A.8	Amberley (54 m 62 ch)		

Brighton-Littlehampton/Portsmouth Harbour

Now labelled the Coastway West route, this line along the South Coast helped to justify those words in the LB&SC's title. The first section, from Brighton to Shoreham, was opened on May 12 1840 before the completion of the London & Brighton's main line and, indeed, helped to move materials from ships arriving in Shoreham Harbour to the final works on the latter. Extension westwards was made to Worthing from November 24 1845, to Arundel & Littlehampton March 16 1846, to Chichester June 8 1846, to Havant March 15 1847, to Portsmouth on June 14 of that year and to Portsmouth Harbour on October 2 1876.

Apart from the 5-mile drop at 1 in 264 at the start of the route there are, as might be expected from a route along the coastal plain, no gradients of significance. There is, though, an excellent service based on an hourly pattern (in the Down direction) of Brighton-Portsmouth semi-fast (with a via Horsham service running behind it to Bognor after reversal at Littlehampton), Victoria-Cliftonville Curve-Littlehampton semi-fast, Victoria-Horsham-Bognor/Portsmouth semi-fast and slows from Brighton to Portsmouth and to Littlehampton. There are some additional or varied early, late and peak trains including commuter services between West Worthing and Brighton.

The route has the use of its own platforms at Brighton and joins the Cliftonville spur between Hove Tunnel and Hove station. At Aldrington the old Dyke Branch used to climb up to the Devil's Dyke beauty spot and before the bridge over the Adur at Shoreham the route to Itchingfield Junction and Horsham survives only as a freight branch up the valley to Beeding Cement Works. Running behind the coastal settlements and their bungalows the route now turns inland slightly to the junction with the Mid-Sussex line and the triangle with the 1863 Littlehampton branch and then to the facing junction with the Bognor Regis branch at Barnham.

The long, straight section continues to Chichester where once an independent light railway ran south to Selsey Bill and another line, still in use for freight as far as Lavant, ran north to Midhurst. Behind the deep inlets of Chichester Harbour and Langstone Harbour the direct westward progress continues to Havant, joining with the Portsmouth Direct line there but no longer with the branch over Langstone bridge to Hayling Island. At Farlington Junction the route turns south for Portsea Island meeting at Portcreek Junction another leg of the triangle leading via Cosham Junction to South Western Division territory. At Fratton the East Southsea branch used to trail in as the main line swings east again for Portsmouth & Southsea where the high level lines lead on to Portsmouth Harbour and the Sealink sailings to the Isle of Wight.

B.37	Brighton		Ford Junction (19 m 31 ch)
	Hove Tunnel (25 ch)	F.15	Ford (19 m 55 ch)
H.35	Hove (1 m 35 ch)	B.5	Barnham (22 m 29 ch)
A.6	Aldrington (1 m 74 ch)	C.17	Chichester (28 m 51 ch)
P.18	Portslade (2 m 73 ch)	F.11	Fishbourne (30 m 12 ch)
F.12	Fishergate (3 m 47 ch)	B.30	Bosham (31 m 43 ch)
S.31	Southwick (4 m 30 ch)	N.19	Nutbourne (33 m 14 ch)
S.20	Shoreham-by-Sea (5 m 69 ch)	S.27	Southbourne (34 m 16 ch)
L.2	Lancing (8 m 19 ch)	E.19	Emsworth (35 m 50 ch)
E.11	East Worthing (9 m 55 ch)	W.8	Warblington (36 m 66 ch)
W.45	Worthing (10 m 46 ch)	H.12	Havant (37 m 41 ch)
W.22	West Worthing (11 m 30 ch)		Bedhampton (38 m 14 ch)
D.14	Durrington-on-Sea (12 m 13 ch)		Farlington Junction (40 m 38 ch)
G.10	Goring-by-Sea (13 m 7 ch)		Portcreek Junction (41 m 3 ch)
A.11	Angmering (15 m 44 ch)		Hilsea (41 m 41 ch)
	Arundel Junction (19 m 1 ch)		Fratton (43 m 64 ch)
Change of mileage to 58 m 75 ch		P.19	Portsmouth & Southsea
	Littlehampton Junction		(44 m 50 ch)
	(60 m 57 ch)		Portsmouth Harbour (45 m 36 ch)
L.10	Littlehampton (62 m 3 ch)		

Brighton/Keymer Junction-Ore

Crossing the South Downs ridge to Lewes to meet the cut-off link from Keymer Junction, the Coastway East route then continues behind the inland side of the Downs ridge until it turns back to the sea at Eastbourne. The section on to Hastings and Ore soon runs much nearer to the coast and from Pevensey Bay eastwards is frequently within sight of the Channel.

The route from Brighton to Bulverhythe, just west of Hastings, was authorised to the Brighton, Lewes & Hastings company which was acquired by the London & Brighton in the year before the line was opened as far as Lewes on June 8 1846. Extension to Bulverhythe followed on June 27 of that year and was followed by the Keymer Junction-Lewes line on October 1 1847 and the branch to Newhaven on December 8 1847. Two years later came developments at Polegate with branches opening on May 14 1849 to Eastbourne and to Hailsham and then a further two years brought the SER/LB&SC clash at Bopeep Junction when the former's line from Ashford was connected to the coastal route at Bulverhythe. Other features of the development period were the 1858 Lewes-Uckfield line (rerouted at Lewes and extended to Tunbridge Wells in 1868) and

Brighton Atlantic and its train at Hamsey Crossing near Lewes.

1864 extension from Newhaven to Seaford, the completion of the triangular junction north of Eastbourne in 1871 and the completion of the Hailsham-Eridge route nine years later.

Physically the route has a dramatic start with the crossing of the London Road Viaduct at Brighton, the old Kemp Town branch junction then preceding the three mile climb to breach the Downs ridge via Falmer Tunnel before another three miles, this time dropping at 1 in 88, to Lewes to meet the link from Keymer Junction. From this delightful and historic town the route crosses the River Ouse before shedding the Seaford branch at Southerham Junction and pushing on behind the South Downs to Polegate, with its former lines to Tunbridge Wells and direct towards Hastings, and then heading into Eastbourne. After reversing out again, trains pass through historic Pevensey and then take a flat course along the beach to Bexhill where one of the major areas of rate, fare and service conflict with the South Eastern began. This fight for traffic continued for the remainder of the journey into Hastings, past the ill-famed Bopeep Junction where the 1852 non-electrified line from Tonbridge joins and through the tunnels to the St Leonards Warrior Square and Hastings stations. Another tunnel is required for the rise inland to Ore and its emu depot, and yet another before the single line route to Appledore can start descending towards the marshes, and eventually, Ashford.

The route carries an hourly buffet car service from London to Eastbourne and Ore via Keymer Junction and, between these, all-stations services from Brighton to Seaford, to Ore and to Eastbourne. It is also used by special boat

An Up train from Eastbourne draws into Lewes over the junction with the Brighton line platforms.

trains to Newhaven. Some train splitting and joining is done at Eastbourne and there is a good interchange pattern at Lewes. The Hastings-Ashford workings make connections at Ashford, with the Tonbridge line and with the Brighton slows.

B.37	Brighton	E.4	Eastbourne (23 m 73 ch)
	London Road (57 ch)	P.7	Pevensey & Westham (23 m 7 ch)
	Ditchling Road Tunnel (63 ch)	P.8	Pevensey Bay (23 m 68 ch)
M.14	Moulsecoomb (1 m 65 ch)	N.12	Normans Bay (25 m 77 ch)
F.1	Falmer (3 m 39 ch)	C.30	Cooden Beach (27 m 53 ch)
	Falmer Tunnel (3 m 62 ch)	C.29	Collington (29 m 4 ch)
	Kingston Tunnel (7 m 13 ch)	B.18	Bexhill (29 m 69 ch)
L.6	Lewes (7 m 77 ch)		Bopeep Junction (32 m 76 ch)
		Change of mileage to 60 m 69 ch from
	Keymer Junction (40 m 69 ch)	Charing Cross
P.11	Plumpton (44 m 42 ch)		Bopeep Tunnel (60 m 71 ch)
C.31	Cooksbridge (47 m 31 ch)		St Leonards Warrior Square (61 m
	Lewes Tunnel (49 m 49 ch)		55 ch)
L.6	Lewes (49 m 74 ch)		Hastings Tunnel (61 m 59 ch)
S.29	Southerham Junction (51 m 11 ch)	H.11	Hastings (62 m 33 ch)
S.9	Seaford Branch	Change of mileage to 82 m 34 ch via
Change of mileage to 9 m 14 ch		Ashford
G.5	Glynde (11 m 14 ch)		Mount Pleasant Tunnel (81 m 60 ch)
B.15	Berwick (15 m 50 ch)	O.1	Ore (81 m 42 ch)
P.14	Polegate (19 m 60 ch)	A.17	Ashford-Hastings Line
	Willingdon Junction (21 m 38 ch)		
H.4	Hampden Park (21 m 75 ch)		

Redhill-Tonbridge and Reading

The 65¾-mile route from the WR at Reading to the South Eastern main line at Tonbridge reflects both the geological nature of the southern counties through which it runs and some of the early railway history of the 'Southern' territory. The line lies south of the east-west ridge which stretches from Hampshire into

Kent and which Parliament decreed should be breached at Redhill for the South Eastern's original main line to Dover as well as the L&B's line to Brighton. The sale outright to the SER of the joint Coulsdon-Redhill portion of the main line is still reflected on today's Reading-Tonbridge line by the Charing Cross-based distances radiating east and west from Redhill.

The South Eastern opened its new railway as far as Tonbridge on May 26 1842, reaching Dover two years later. In the opposite direction the route to Reading originated with the Reading, Guildford & Reigate Railway, supported by the SER and acquired by that company in 1852. Opening was from the two ends inwards, from Reading to Farnborough and Redhill to Dorking on July 4 1849 and further to Ash Junction and Shalford Junction on August 20. Through running began when the Guildford-Shalford Junction link was ready on October 15 of the same year.

The line has carried a variety of services over the years including trains from the GWR to the Kent Resorts and London Bridge-Aldershot workings. It was an important wartime route for freight and troop trains. Now it carries the Tonbridge-Reading all-stations dmus and the fast service of dmus which link Gatwick Airport with the WR lines at Reading. Double line throughout, there are electrified sections from Redhill to Reigate, Shalford Junction to Aldershot South Junction and Wokingham to Reading and signalling is a mixture of semaphore and colour light. Many of the stations are unmanned, conductor guards issuing tickets on the dmu services.

From Redhill, the eastern portion of the route takes a straight course to Tonbridge, descending moderately nearly all the way and with Bletchingley Tunnel the main physical feature. The East Grinstead and Uckfield lines are crossed between Godstone and Edenbridge although the spur from the former has now gone and the latter is hidden in the tunnel which the Tonbridge line bridge divides in two. Most of the stations have been simplified although their South Eastern origins are still apparent in the platform staggering.

The Redhill-Reading section is much more steeply graded and curved. Its route west skirts the National Trust beauty spot at Box Hill to historic Deepdene and then rises at 1 in 100/96 after crossing the Mid-Sussex route. From the summit at MP 35 the route descends from its North Downs views to cross the River Wey and join the Portsmouth line at Shalford Junction. Access to Guildford station is by way of the St Catherine's Tunnel—which twice collapsed in its earlier years—and the longer Chalk Tunnel, with the routes separating again for Reading trains to climb the 1 in 100 section on the way to Ash Junction. Here the Waterloo mileage which has applied from Shalford Junction again becomes Charing Cross based. The route parts with the Guildford-Aldershot-Ascot services at Aldershot South Junction and passes under the Southampton main line before taking up a more level course through an area of gravel pits and military establishments. Wooded and residential countryside then precedes the junction with the Staines route at Wokingham.

R.6	Redhill (22 m 40 ch)		T.9	Tonbridge (42 m 16 ch)
N.20	Nutfield (24 m 47 ch)			
	Bletchingley Tunnel (26 m 25 ch)		R.6	Redhill (22 m 40 ch)
G.8	Godstone (28 m 13 ch)		R.7	Reigate (24 m 27 ch)
E.12	Edenbridge (33 m 3 ch)		B.16	Betchworth (27 m 17 ch)
P.4	Penshurst (38 m 3 ch)		D.5	Deepdene (29 m 65 ch)
	Penshurst Tunnel (38 m 13 ch)		D.8	Dorking Town (30 m 42 ch)
L.4	Leigh (39 m 56 ch)		G.9	Gomshall (35 m 21 ch)

C.19   Chilworth (39 m 15 ch)
S.13   Shalford (41 m 2 ch)
       Shalford Junction (41 m 60 ch)

Change of mileage to 31 m 42 ch from
  Waterloo

       St Catherine's Tunnel (31 m 19 ch)
       Chalk Tunnel (31 m 1 ch)
G.15   Guildford (30 m 27 ch)
W.6   Wanborough (34 m 29 ch)
       Ash Junction (35 m 50 ch)

Change of mileage to 48 m 34 ch
A.15   Ash (49 m 18 ch)
       Aldershot South Junction (50 m
         1 ch)
N.13   North Camp (51 m 18 ch)
F.3   Farnborough North (53 m 16 ch)
B.26   Blackwater (55 m 58 ch)
S.6   Sandhurst (57 m 22 ch)
C.36   Crowthorne (58 m 66 ch)
W.39   Wokingham (62 m 8 ch)
       Reading (68 m 68 ch)

Victoria-Ramsgate/Dover

The former London, Chatham & Dover main line, still known as the 'Chatham' lines, originated on August 4 1853 when Royal Assent was accorded the East Kent Railway's Bill for a line eastwards from Strood to Canterbury. This was opened throughout by March 29 1858 and by the time the LC&D title was taken in the following year powers had been obtained for extension to Dover and a link via the Mid-Kent and West End of London & Crystal Palace lines to Victoria. Physical opening eastwards was to Canterbury on July 9 1860 (with the Bickley-Rochester section being brought into use to complete the route to Victoria on December 3 of that year) and to Dover on July 22 1861. In the same month the Margate Railway's Faversham-Whitstable section opened on August 1 1860 was extended to Herne Bay. Worked by the LC&D and absorbed in 1871, the Thanet line reached Ramsgate on October 5 1863.

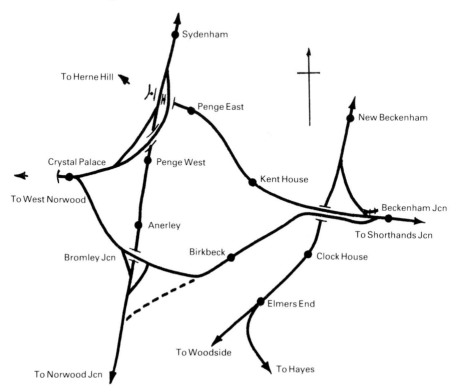

From Victoria the curving bank to Grosvenor Bridge, once needing a banking engine for the heavier trains, is a foretaste of what is to come. Immediately after the City line from Holborn Viaduct joins at Herne Hill there is 1¾ miles of 1 in 101½ to Penge Tunnel. Beckenham Junction and Shortlands Junction, where a pair of Slow lines is added with the arrival of the Catford loop traffic, lead to a 1 in 95 climb to Bickley—something of a test of skill for drivers lifting a steam train from Bromley South—and the links with the South Eastern main line.

Once the River Cray is crossed the countryside becomes more open as the route to Sevenoaks and Maidstone East is shed at Swanley (end of the four-track section) and the main line starts a dip towards Darent Viaduct and up to the site of Fawkham Junction where the Gravesend West Street branch departed. Preceding Rochester Bridge Junction from the North Kent Line and the crossing of the line to Maidstone West/Paddock Wood is the drop of 5 miles at 1 in 100 down Sole Street Bank to the floor of the Medway Valley. Bridging the river is followed by the Medway towns and their tunnels and then a level stretch (with loops from Rainham to Newington) to Sittingbourne and its triangular junction with the Sheerness branch. Then, at Faversham, the Dover and Ramsgate routes divide.

Faversham to Dover, once the senior and most important route, involves two major summits, the first following a 1 in 100 rise to Selling Tunnel after which the line descends at 1 in 132 to accompany the Ashford-Ramsgate line in its use of the Great Stour Valley to approach Canterbury. The LC&D route crosses both to come to Canterbury East and then heads first into fruit country and then the Kent coalfield. The latter is marked by the remains of Snowdown Colliery sidings and then by the portion of the East Kent Light Railway which survives as the Tilmanstone branch from Shepherds Well. From this point, through Lydden Tunnel, the gradient is down, mainly at 1 in 132, all the way to Buckland Junction and the link with the Deal line before the final tunnel approach to Dover Priory and Western Docks.

On the Thanet route the gradients are more modest as the line heads for the coast at Whitstable where the bridge once carrying the historic Canterbury and Whitstable Railway across the LC&D is still evident. A section of 1 in 93 on Blacksole Bank follows Herne Bay as the route crosses Reculver Marshes to Pudding Island. Then come the resort-cum-residential areas which precede Margate, a cut across the peninsula and then the same pattern at Ramsgate, both towns having exchanged their original stations for today's complex of 1926-era buildings and intensive passenger and rolling stock servicing activity.

BR's 1954 Modernisation Plan expanded the 1939 electrification from Gillingham to Ramsgate and Dover in 1959. Where the Granville Express and a selection of Pullman Car services once held sway services are now based on Ramsgate and Dover line trains alternating hourly by destination and by slow and semi-fast running, the latter overtaking and connecting into the former at Faversham. In the peaks some services use Cannon Street and the basic links with the routes via Dartford at Gillingham vary to accommodate some Charing Cross services and a few other variations.

The former LC&D main line is busy and full of contrasts. It has industrial links in the Medway and holiday duties in Thanet. Its buildings range from the outmoded grandeur of Ramsgate and Margate to unimpressive LC&D survivals. Its course curves and undulates and reveals sea, suburbs and scenery in an amazing mixture.

V.2	Victoria	S.22	Sittingbourne (44 m 59 ch)
	Battersea Pier Junction (71 ch)	T.4	Teynham (47 m 74 ch)
	Factory Junction (1 m 61 ch)	F.7	Faversham (51 m 77 ch)
	Voltaire Road Junction (2 m 5 ch)	W.26	Whitstable (59 m 6 ch)
	Brixton Junction (3 m 8 ch)	C.16	Chestfield & Swalecliffe (60 m 45 ch)
B.38	Brixton (3 m 14 ch)		
H.18	Herne Hill (3 m 76 ch)	H.17	Herne Bay (62 m 58 ch)
W.16	West Dulwich (5 m 2 ch)	B.22	Birchington-on-Sea (70 m 56 ch)
S.47	Sydenham Hill (5 m 57 ch)	W.18	Westgate-on-Sea (72 m 35 ch)
	Penge Tunnel (5 m 62 ch)	M.3	Margate (73 m 69 ch)
P.3	Penge East (7 m 15 ch)	B.39	Broadstairs (77 m 9 ch)
K.3	Kent House (7 m 66 ch)	D.11	Dumpton Park (78 m 26 ch)
B.10	Beckenham Junction (8 m 53 ch)	R.3	Ramsgate (79 m 21 ch)
	Shortlands Junction (9 m 57 ch)		
S.21	Shortlands (10 m 3 ch)	S.11	Selling (55 m 18 ch)
B.43	Bromley South (10 m 71 ch)		Selling Tunnel (56 m 33 ch)
B.20	Bickley (11 m 76 ch)	C.2	Canterbury East (61 m 65 ch)
	Bickley Junction (12 m 38 ch)	B.11	Bekesbourne (64 m 58 ch)
	Chislehurst Junction (12 m 62 ch)	A.4	Adisham (67 m 60 ch)
	St Mary Cray Junction (13 m 17 ch)	A.21	Aylesham (68 m 66 ch)
S.2	St Mary Cray (14 m 57 ch)	S.24	Snowdown (69 m 60 ch)
S.44	Swanley (17 m 31 ch)	T.7	Tilmanstone Colliery Branch
F.6	Farningham Road (20 m 41 ch)	S.16	Shepherds Well (71 m 60 ch)
L.14	Longfield (23 m 30 ch)	L.18	Lydden Tunnel (71 m 66 ch)
M.5	Meopham (25 m 76 ch)	K.1	Kearsney (75 m 9 ch)
S.25	Sole Street (26 m 71 ch)		Buckland Junction (76 m 32 ch)
	Rochester Bridge Junction (33 m 1 ch)		Charlton Tunnel (76 m 65 ch)
			Dover Priory Tunnel (77 m 8 ch)
R.12	Rochester (33 m 61 ch)	D.10	Dover Priory (77 m 23 ch)
	Fort Pitt Tunnel (33 m 79 ch)		Dover Harbour Tunnel (77 m 32 ch)
C.11	Chatham (34 m 25 ch)		Hawkesbury Street Junction (77 m 72 ch)
	Chatham Tunnel (34 m 34 ch)		
	Gillingham Tunnel (35 m 7 ch)	D.10	Dover Western Docks (78 m 30 ch)
G.3	Gillingham (35 m 75 ch)		
R.2	Rainham (38 m 74 ch)		
N.7	Newington (41 m 44 ch)		
	Western Junction (43 m 70 ch)		
	Eastern Junction (44 m 18 ch)		
S.15	Sheerness-on-Sea Branch		

The highly popular Thanet resorts produced this sort of scene in the modest confines of Ramsgate Harbour station. This photograph was taken in the summer of 1913.

Charing Cross-Dover/Ramsgate and Hastings

The original South Eastern Railway main line was from London Bridge to Redhill and then east to Dover. It took the arrival of the LC&D at the latter point in 1861 to set the South Eastern seeking powers for a 'cut-off' route from St Johns to Tonbridge. These were granted in 1862 and the line opened six years later (for goods on February 3 and for passengers throughout on May 1) to cut 12½ miles off the via Redhill distances. In the same period the SER had extended from London Bridge to Charing Cross (January 11 1864) and opened its City station at Cannon Street (September 1 1866).

The lines from the two SER London termini come together at Borough Market Junction and then pass through the through platforms of London Bridge. The long, straight complex of South Eastern and Central Division lines reduces to the former's fast and slow pairs as first the latter's lines leave and then the original Greenwich line departs at North Kent East Junction. At St Johns the main line heads straight for Hither Green leaving the North Kent, Bexleyheath, Nunhead and Mid-Kent routes to sort themselves out on the Lewisham Loop.

As the Dartford Loop departs at Hither Green, the main line sets about 10 miles of climbing, mostly at 1 in 140 and 120, to Knockholt Summit. On the way it parts with the Bromley North branch beyond Grove Park, passes through the parallel but separate Chislehurst Tunnels and crosses the Chatham main line to the accompaniment of a variety of spurs and flyovers. Beyond Orpington the four tracks have reduced to two as the final climb through chalk cuttings and Chelsfield Tunnel changes to a 1 in 143 descent through Polhill Tunnel where the locomotive of an express train became derailed on August 24 1927 but continued running over the embankment until it collided with an overbridge in Dunton Green cutting.

From Dunton Green, former junction for the Westerham branch, the route

Early SER junction and now a major interchange station, Ashford is depicted there looking towards London and the junction with the Maidstone East line.

rises at 1 in 160 to a second summit just beyond the modern station at Sevenoaks and its junction with the route from Holborn Viaduct via Otford Junction. Then comes Sevenoaks Tunnel, the longest on the Southern Region, nearly 2 miles cut through the chalk of the North Downs and on a falling gradient of 1 in 144 which then steepens to 1 in 122 to complete the 6-mile descent to the outskirts of Tonbridge.

Tonbridge is an interesting and busy junction where the original line via Redhill now carries a service from Reading and the Hastings line departs beyond the platforms. The straight and easily-graded course of the 1842 main line continues due east to Ashford via the junction at Paddock Wood where the Strood line departs north along the Medway Valley and the Hawkhurst line originally meandered south into hop country. The smaller stations along here have staggered platforms in typical SER fashion although Paddock Wood and Headcorn, like Tonbridge, both have Up and Down loops. Headcorn once represented the northern connection to the Kent & East Sussex Railway.

The SER reached Ashford on December 1 1842 and extended on to Folkestone on June 28 of the following year, eventually running through to Dover from February 7 1844. Ashford soon became highly important, with branches to Margate in 1846 and Hastings in 1851 and the first locomotive emerging from the new locomotive works in 1853. Another major route, that of the LC&D from Maidstone East, arrived in 1884 and although the locomotive works has closed there is a modern emu depot at Chart Leacon to offset the smallness of the surviving BREL activity.

Onwards to Dover the main line climbs at 1 in 260/250/280 to the summit at Westenhanger and then descends through the tunnels at Sandling and Saltwood and past the former junctions for Sandgate and the Elham Valley to make a high level approach to Folkestone. Then, after the trailing junction with the Harbour Branch, comes the coastal approach to Dover where so much explosive and muscle power were needed to create the tunnels and ledges that take the line to its original destination, completely different now but still as busy and important in this age of fast ferries, hovercraft, containers and Ro-Ro operations.

After the triangular link with Western Docks the line now turns inland through Dover Priory to Buckland Junction where the routes from Faversham and Thanet via Deal merge. Deal itself had been reached in 1847 as a branch from Minster on the Margate line but from June 15 1881 it was linked with Dover as one of the pieces of joint SER/LC&D co-operation which preceded their working union. After the Dover tunnels and the great curve which follows Buckland junction the line has to climb at 1 in 60-75 through Guston Tunnel before dropping to the coast at Deal. On the 1847 section across the Lydden Valley and the Minster Marshes the route has freight links with Betteshanger Colliery and Richborough power station, the triangular junction at Minster then bringing the line to Ramsgate and the Thanet complex.

The double-track, non-electrified route from Tonbridge to Hastings was planned by the SER back in its early days. Indeed the section from Tonbridge through Somerhill Tunnel and over Southborough Viaduct to a temporary station outside Tunbridge Wells was opened on September 20 1845, with access through Wells Tunnel to the town following on November 25 1846. Two further tunnels, and the junction with the 1866/7 LB&SC route between them, lead to two modest dips and then the completion of the climb through the High Weald which started back at Tonbridge. This section, opened on September 1 1851, now descends for 9 miles through Wadhurst Tunnel, curving into the valley of the infant River Rother and coming to Robertsbridge where the Kent & East Sussex line continued the exploitation of the waterway. The section on to Battle brings more curves and tunnelling through the pleasantest of wooded country-side, the tunnel at Mountfield now being reduced to a single line as part of the process of coping with the route's limited clearances. From the mini-summit and elaborate station at Battle the route makes its final descent, past the Crow-hurst Junction for the former Bexhill branch, to Bopeep Junction and then Hastings, these last two sections being opened on the first day of January and February 1852 respectively.

The other main line branch, that from Ashford via Canterbury West to Minster and then Ramsgate and Margate, makes use of the valley of the Great Stour and has no gradients to speak of. Opening to Canterbury was on February 6 1846, to Ramsgate on April 13 and Margate on December 1 of the same year. Crossing and recrossing its river companion the route is joined by the trackbed of the old Elham Valley line before it passes under the LC&D line and comes to Canterbury West station. From here the 1830 Canterbury & Whitstable line acquired by the SER ran directly to the coast at Whitstable leaving the main route to continue past the old Chislet Colliery and along the broadening valley of the Stour and its marshes to the triangular junction at Minster and thence to Ramsgate and the Thanet complex, so dramatically altered in 1926.

The fast trains from Charing Cross to Dover, calling just at Waterloo East, Ashford and Folkestone Central, complete their 77¼-mile journey in 88 minutes. Between their departures on the hour are semi-fasts which divide at Ashford for one portion to call at all stations to Margate via Dover and the coast route and the other to take the more direct route via Canterbury West. The Dover fasts connect into the services from Victoria via Maidstone East to give passengers on the former access to the intermediate stations on the via Canterbury route and the Charing Cross-Ashford slower trains link similarly with the combined Dover/Margate trains. Hastings has an hourly service of Class 201-5 demus with some peak trains splitting at Tunbridge Wells Central into 'fast to Battle' and 'all stations' portions.

C.9	Charing Cross	G.14	Grove Park (8 m 78 ch)
W.12	Waterloo East (61 ch)	B.42	Bromley North Branch
	Metropolitan Junction (1 m 31 ch)		Chislehurst Tunnel(s) (9 m 61 ch and 9 m 63 ch)
	Borough Market Junction (1 m 51 ch)	E.18	Elmstead Woods (10 m 21 ch)
L.12	London Bridge (1 m 70 ch)	C.20	Chislehurst (11 m 19 ch)
	North Kent East Junction (4 m 25 ch)		Chislehurst Junction (11 m 55 ch)
			Petts Wood Junction (12 m 25 ch)
G.12	Greenwich Line	P.6	Petts Wood (12 m 55 ch)
N.3	New Cross (4 m 68 ch)	O.2	Orpington (13 m 65 ch)
	Tanners Hill Tunnel (5 m 22 ch)	C.13	Chelsfield (15 m 25 ch)
	Tanners Hill Junction (5 m 29 ch)		Chelsfield Tunnel (15 m 67 ch)
	St Johns (5 m 47 ch)	K.5	Knockholt (16 m 44 ch)
N.15	North Kent Line and, at Blackheath	P.15	Polhill Tunnel (17 m 20 ch)
B.19	Bexleyheath Line	D.13	Dunton Green (20 m 46 ch)
	Parks Bridge Junction(s) (6 m 14 ch and 6 m 36 ch)	S.12	Sevenoaks (22 m 9 ch)
			Sevenoaks Tunnel (22 m 53 ch)
H.24	Hither Green (7 m 16 ch)	H.21	Hildenborough (27 m 2 ch)
D.2	Dartford Loop	T.9	Tonbridge (29 m 42 ch)
	Lee Spur Junction (7 m 44 ch)	P.1	Paddock Wood (34 m 65 ch)

M.2   Marden (39 m 31 ch)
S.33   Staplehurst (41 m 69 ch)
H.16   Headcorn (45 m 20 ch)
P.10   Pluckley (50 m 35 ch)
A.16   Ashford (56 m 9 ch)
W.17   Westenhanger (64 m 15 ch)
       Sandling Tunnel (64 m 76 ch)
S.7   Sandling (65 m 36 ch)
       Saltwood Tunnel (65 m 58 ch)
       Folkestone West (69 m 22 ch)
F.14   Folkestone Central (69 m 73 ch)
       Folkestone East (70 m 79 ch)
       Martello Tunnel (71 m 22 ch)
A.1   Abbotscliffe Tunnel (73 m 23 ch)
       Shakespeare Tunnel (75 m 14 ch)
       Archcliffe Junction (76 m 42 ch)
D.10   Dover Western Docks (76 m 72 ch)
Change of mileage 76 m 53 ch to 77 m
  76 ch from Victoria
       Hawkesbury Street Junction (77 m
         72 ch)
       Dover Harbour Tunnel (77 m 63 ch)
D.10   Dover Priory (77 m 23 ch)
       Dover Priory Tunnel (77 m 16 ch)
       Charlton Tunnel (76 m 77 ch)
       Buckland Junction (76 m 32 ch)
Change of mileage to 99 m 5 ch from
  Charing Cross
       Guston Tunnel (97 m 44 ch)
M.4   Martin Mill (95 m 5 ch)
W.4   Walmer (92 m 27 ch)
D.3   Deal (90 m 56 ch)
B.17   Betteshanger Colliery (89 m 11 ch)
S.8   Sandwich (86 m 46 ch)
R.8   Richborough Sidings (82 m 70 ch)
       Minster South Junction (82 m
         21 ch)

       Minster East Junction (82 m 17 ch)
R.3   Ramsgate (85 m 67 ch)

T.9   Tonbridge (29 m 42 ch)
       Somerhill Tunnel (30 m 14 ch)
H.20   High Brooms (32 m 70 ch)
       Wells Tunnel (33 m 69 ch)
T.13   Tunbridge Wells Central (34 m
         32 ch)
       Grove Hill Tunnel (34 m 38 ch)
       Grove Junction (34 m 53 ch)
       Strawberry Hill Tunnel (35 m 12 ch)
F.17   Frant (36 m 53 ch)
W.2   Wadhurst (39 m 23 ch)
       Wadhurst Tunnel (39 m 65 ch)
S.35   Stonegate (43 m 66 ch)
E.23   Etchingham (47 m 34 ch)
R.11   Robertsbridge (49 m 47 ch)
M.15   Mountfield Tunnel (51 m 46 ch)
B.7   Battle (55 m 46 ch)
C.35   Crowhurst (57 m 50 ch)
       West St Leonards (60 m 59 ch)
       Bopeep Junction (60 m 69 ch)
       Bopeep Tunnel (60 m 71 ch)
       St Leonards Warrior Square (61 m
         55 ch)
       Hastings Tunnel (61 m 59 ch)
H.11   Hastings (62 m 33 ch)

A.16   Ashford (56 m 9 ch)
W.46   Wye (60 m 32 ch)
C.18   Chilham (65 m 9 ch)
C.10   Chartham (67 m 14 ch)
C.2   Canterbury West (70 m 27 ch)
S.40   Sturry (72 m 58 ch)
M.9   Minster (81 m 46 ch)
       Minster East Junction (82 m 17 ch)
R.3   Ramsgate (85 m 67 ch)

Swanley-Ashford

This was the second LC&D probe into SER territory in the southern half of Kent. It started life as the Sevenoaks Railway which opened a modest branch from what is now Swanley to Bat & Ball on the outskirts of Sevenoaks on June 2 1862. Twelve years later came the line from Otford to Maidstone opened on June 1 1874 and just one more aspiring minor railway until the Chatham took over in 1879 and extended the route to a separate station at Ashford on July 1 1884. Now the new route was a major threat to SER traffic but, in 1891, a link was built between the two systems at Ashford and through working and other co-operation became the order of the day as they moved away from competition to the more peaceful existence of the working union era.

The gradient profile of the route is very irregular but its course is generally easier than that of the main line. From the junction at Swanley the line heads for the Darent Valley and only leaves the company of the river at Otford Junction when one of its tributaries provides the opportunity to turn east between the North Downs and the Ragstone Ridge. Beyond Wrotham there is 10 miles of mainly down gradient into the valley of the Medway and a bridge over the Strood-Paddock Wood line as they both arrive at Maidstone. On the final section the route again skirts just south of the North Downs but cannot avoid 9 miles of climbing to Lenham before a comparable descent to the junction west of Ashford.

The hourly Victoria-Ramsgate services on this pleasant route through one of Kent's main fruit and horticultural areas call at Bromley South, Borough Green and all stations from Barming. The intermediate, preceding and slower services to Maidstone East connect there with the Ramsgate trains.

S.44	Swanley (17 m 31 ch)		Preston Hall 'B' Tunnel (37 m 17 ch)
	Eynsford Tunnel (18 m 67 ch)	B.3	Barming (37 m 43 ch)
E.25	Eynsford (20 m 32 ch)	M.1	Maidstone East (39 m 76 ch)
S.19	Shoreham (22 m 52 ch)		West Street Tunnel (40 m 1 ch)
O.3	Otford (24 m 7 ch)		Wheeler Street Tunnel (40 m 9 ch)
	Otford Junction (24 m 53 ch)	B.8	Bearsted (42 m 59 ch)
K.2	Kemsing (26 m 79 ch)	H.26	Hollingbourne (45 m 2 ch)
B.29	Borough Green & Wrotham (29 m 46 ch)	H.8	Harrietsham (47 m 36 ch)
W.19	West Malling (34 m 61 ch)	L.5	Lenham (49 m 11 ch)
E.10	East Malling (35 m 64 ch)	C.8	Charing (53 m 11 ch)
	Preston Hall 'A' Tunnel (37 m 10 ch)		Ashford Junction (58 m 61 ch)

248

SECTION 5

Traffic and operation

The main Southern Region business is, of course, the carriage of passengers. Its commuter traffic is enormous and the region carries over 50 per cent of all the season ticket holders on BR. Nevertheless there is also an immense variety of other movements ranging from Inter-City business travel and journeys to and from the Channel Ports to Awayday leisure business and schoolchildren dawdling their way to school or bursting out of its confines at the end of the day. The commuters may travel all the way from Wareham to London and the schoolchildren just one station from Oxted, but they all add to the wide variety of the demand for conveyance.

After allowing for all the other recognisable flows of traffic, the morning and evening business periods still dominate the region's activity. They represent the main reasons, not only for the existence of stations like Cannon Street, Blackfriars and Holborn Viaduct but also for the retention of some smaller stations which are only open at peak times. Other stations are only staffed at peak times.

Typical of the work of CM&EE maintenance depots, in this case examining a bogie at Bournemouth.

The peak also creates a demand for stabling and routine servicing accommodation near to the stations originating trains. In the London area places like Victoria and Waterloo have some such accommodation but in the main stock has to come in from or be returned to major depots such as the ones at Strawberry Hill (S.37), Clapham Junction (C.24), Wimbledon (W.29), Selhurst (S.10), Streatham Hill (S.38), Stewarts Lane (S.34), New Cross Gate (N.4) and Grove Park (G.14). The picture is repeated in the more distant areas and the range of activities varies from simple stabling to the sort of major overhaul work done at Chart Leacon (A.16).

The peak was and still is responsible for the demand for high density stock, essential to rapid loading and unloading and to conveying the maximum number of people per train. The basic suburban unit has, since the end of the war, been a four-car set capable of carrying 222 people in the two centre trailer vehicles and 82 in each of the Motor Open Brake vehicles. With two-car sets for the lightly used lines and the capability to increase train sizes to 8, 10 or 12 cars these have served the region well. However, many are now getting quite old and a new generation of suburban rolling stock was heralded with the advent of the Class 508 sets in 1979. With a modern design and fitments, and with sliding doors to facilitate rapid access, these units have a lower seating capacity but more standing room and a good circulating area and they are now at work on lines like the Hampton Court branch. The first Class 455s started work in March 1983 but some of the older stock has had to be refurbished to maintain capacity in an era of capital constraint.

The original electrification and its subsequent extension also owes much to the peak demand for transport. It had a hand, too, in producing some of the quadrupling shown on the maps in the early pages. From the flyovers built to improve traffic flow at major junctions, eg, Hampton Court Junction, it has led to the great resignalling and track simplification schemes of recent years, notably the London Bridge and Brighton line schemes.

The modern signal box panel operates through hundreds of miniature relays, here being installed at Guildford.

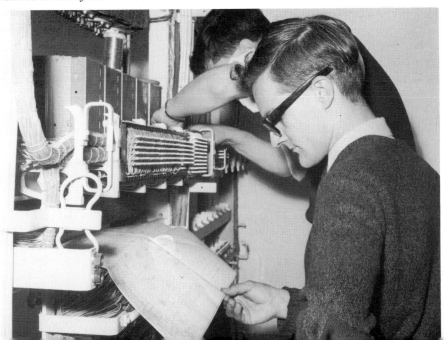

Points machine, an essential feature of modern signalling schemes.

As stock and track capacity yielded their dividends SR attention has turned again to signalling. The first revolution brought in with pneumatic and electric signalling and colour light signals has been succeeded by a second revolution based on the panel signal box of the type now found at Feltham (F.10), Eastleigh (E.9) and other major centres. Based on 'Exit/Entry' control, the operation involves the positive setting of a route by pushing buttons on the panel which correspond to the portion of track being cleared, the clearance then being reproduced, through the motorised points and high density signals, along the track itself via the relays housed near the panel room. A second revolution, in telecommunications, has enabled train announcing and display to be linked with the signalling process and given many other important advantages in such areas as train reporting.

Although a clear distinction between commuter and other passenger business would be difficult, the Southern Region nevertheless has a significant main line activity. This shows up clearly on its longest main line, to Weymouth, where there is a clear basic pattern of a slow, semi-fast and fast train in each hour with the latter conveying a four-car portion then worked on a push-and-pull basis over the non-electrified section of the route west of Bournemouth. For the longer distance services on the main lines the SR uses gangway stock including first class accommodation and, in some cases, buffet facilities.

Despite the extent of SR electrification and the high degree of standardisation in its rolling stock there are quite a few non-standard and special operations. Typical of the latter is the service provided with Class 423/1 stock to Gatwick Airport (G.1) which also has a special service to and from Reading and special

Above *No aspect of the railway scene has altered more than the freight business. The data and multi-language instructions on this hopper testify to the SR's role in ferry traffic movement and to the revolution brought about by the TOPS wagon data system.* **Below** *One of the three-car demu sets formed by using two ex-Hastings units and an emu driving trailer.*

Above *One of the SR's Class 33 fleet used for freight and locomotive-hauled passenger services.* **Below** *Flaw detector in use at Eastleigh maintenance depot.*

facilities at Victoria (V.2). Diesel electric multiple units operate on such non-electrified lines as those to East Grinstead (E.8) and Uckfield (U.1) and are also used on the direct route to Hastings where the difficult terrain led the original builders to keep clearances to the minimum resulting in the need to use narrow-bodied stock and now to start singling through the tunnels. A number of loco-motive and coaches trains work through the region, not only those of the Waterloo-Exeter line but also from the Western Region (and beyond) via Westbury (to Portsmouth), Reading (to Portsmouth and Poole) and Acton (to Brighton).

Not all of the SR's territory is covered by panel boxes. Much of the outer area still has traditional semaphore signalling based on the Absolute Block system, positive track clearance and Distant, Home and Starter signals. The Strood-Paddock Wood line is worth a visit for many reasons, not least for its traditional signalling and examples, as at New Hythe (N.6), where sections are so short that Distants and Starters have to be accommodated on the same post. There are still one or two examples of small signal frames housed in the station buildings, eg, Amberley (A.8) and quite a lot of other period signalling equipment, from finials to Saxby & Farmer ground frames (B.27).

Most of the SR's single lines used for passenger services are panel controlled—an example is the Sheerness Branch (S.15) controlled from the Sittingbourne panel (S.22)—but some Tokenless Block operation is also used. The latter

Points heaters at Slade Green.

Left *Container lifting taking place at Millbrook Freightliner terminal at Southampton.*
Above *The SR has a surprising amount of non-standard equipment, including ex-LT rolling stock seen here at Ryde Pier Head.*

applies on the Appledore-Ore section of the Ashford-Hastings line (A.17), for example.

The single line, freight-only branches to Grain (H.27) and Fawley (F.8) are worked under the 'No Signalman Key Token' system with the trainmen taking the single line authority from an auxiliary instrument and liaising with the private siding operators, in these cases the oil companies. Trainmen also operate train reporting instruments in other single line situations and in cases like the Hampton Court branch (H.5).

In addition to the substantial oil traffic movements from the Grain and Fawley branches the Southern Region has a number of distribution terminals for fuel oil, eg, Bexhill (B.18) for domestic business and Salfords (S.3) for aviation fuel and also several coal concentration depots, eg, Hove (H.35), two on the Chessington branch (C.15), etc. It also has a large volume of inwards aggregates to deal with, the trainloads of Mendip limestone from Foster Yeoman and ARC being increased by the sea dredged aggregates originating in the region (H.29). These traffics are dealt with at special receiving terminals such as those at Basingstoke (B.6), Botley (B.31), Chichester (C.17) and Allington (M.1).

Other important freight traffics are the import/export movements through the ports to such places as the Transfesa International Freight Terminal at

Paddock Wood (P.1), the steel and scrap on the Sheerness branch (S.15), movements to and from various Government/MoD depots, cars through Newhaven (N.5) and the liquid china clay to Sittingbourne (S.22) for the paper industry. Coal is still moved from the Kent coalfield (B.17, S.16) in considerable quantity and North Kent is a major cement producer with BCI Northfleet (N.15) receiving coal plus Mountfield (M.15) gypsum and forwarding cement in high capacity wagons. Some of the silo-equipped terminals for receiving cement are also in the region, eg, at Poole (P.16). The region handles large quantities of GPO mail and parcels plus such specialised traffics as newspapers and trains to the Southampton Freightliner terminals (S.26).

Superficially the Southern Region has an appearance of standardised equipment and routine operation. A more careful look reveals much that is exciting in the apparent standardisation and much that is non-standard. Just two signalling panels to control the Brighton main line is a marvel of modern technology but diagramming trains to leave half a trainload of fertiliser at Andover (A.9) or serve the APCM sidings at Holborough (S.23) also needs a high degree of professionalism, especially if the workings have got to be slotted into a narrow gap in the paths on the main line.

SECTION 6

Civil engineering

No two BR regions are alike and the Southern is no exception to this rule, especially in the civil engineering field. For a start, a high proportion of its 3,000 track miles is electrified and in addition to this the running intensity is 60 per cent higher over much of the system than the BR average. The geological formation of the southern counties produces east-west ridges for the railway routes to cross and these give the SR a heavy burden of tunnels, embankments, cuttings and bridges. The problems increase with so much mileage lying within built up areas with all the attendant complications of maintaining arches, securing access, coping with vandalism and so on.

The main lines of the South Western Division are reasonably graded, except for the Portsmouth Direct line which includes the 3 miles of 1 in 80 up the Haslemere Bank. Nor are the Central Division lines too bad, except between Redhill and Guildford, but the South Eastern has more than its share of long and steep gradients—up to Knockholt, Sevenoaks and Westenhanger on the Dover main line, between Tonbridge and Robertsbridge on the Hastings line, summits at Sole Street, Selling and Shepherds Well on the LC&D route to Dover and more climbing and falling on the Swanley-Ashford and Dover-Minster lines.

The elaborate LB&SC and LSW joint station built in 1866. Known as Portsmouth & Southsea, it includes the platforms on the PJER through line to Portsmouth Harbour— on the right of the picture.

Above *Beyond Fareham station the line to Portsmouth needs this long viaduct to cross two roads and a river.* **Below** *Battersea Bridge renewal in 1969.*

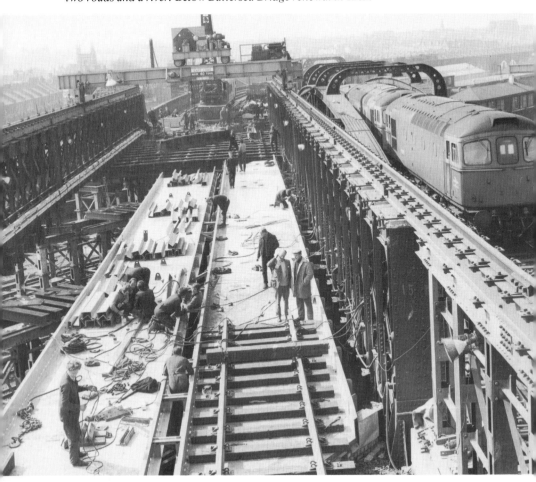

With these track profiles it is not surprising that the SR has so many tunnels and bridges. The former include ten over a mile long—Abbotscliffe (A.1), Clayton (C.26), Lydden (L.18), Merstham (M.6), Quarry (Q.1), Oxted (O.7), Penge (P.3), Polhill (P.15), Strood (S.39) and Sevenoaks (S.12), the latter the longest at 1 mile 1,693 yards long. Many of the tunnels are cut through chalk, and in some cases have water seepage problems, but Penge involved cutting through 1 mile 381 yards of treacherous London clay to carry the LC&D beneath the Crystal Palace heights.

Although the builders of the North Kent line inherited the Higham and Strood tunnels (N.15, S.39) from earlier canal engineers most of the early railway tunnel builders had a major task on their hands. Nowhere was this greater than on the SER's final coastal section into Dover which still taxes the expertise of the successors to those early civil engineers. This was clear in 1978 in the rocky area known as The Warren when it was found that constant pounding from the seas was eroding the base of the cliffs below Abbotscliffe Tunnel. To

CCE department tamping machine at work.

Close up view of expansion joint in modern track.

counteract this the SR spent £250,000 on a 100-metre concrete apron. Working between tides, engineers dug foundations below beach level, cemented in concrete blocks to absorb the initial impact of the seas and then added a special 'wave-back' wall to repel the final surge of the waters.

The same geographical features which produce the gradients and tunnels—helped by the need for rivers to meander—create valleys to be crossed by high bridges or viaducts. There are outstanding examples in the London Road Viaduct at Brighton (B.37) the Foord Viaduct at Folkestone (F.14), the Ouse Valley Viaduct (O.4) and the Southborough Viaduct (H.20) near High Brooms. The London Road Viaduct, for example, is 400 yards long, has 27 arches with spans up to 50 ft and is 67 ft high at the centre. It is also sharply curved, with 11 of the spans at a 10 chains radius.

The southern counties are drained by a host of rivers and smaller waterways so that most railway routes involve significant bridges. Fortunately most of the lifting spans, like those at Deptford and Ford, have now become fixed but this is not so in the case of the Kingsferry Bridge which carries the Sheerness Branch (S.15) on to the Isle of Sheppey. To the traditional waterway bridges such as Barnes Bridge (H.34) modern trends have added motorway bridges involving new construction techniques to contrast with the traditional box and tied girder or bowstring contruction. The bridge over the M25 at Lyne (C.14), for example, was one of the first ever all-concrete, cable-stayed bridges and was designed by the SR for the Department of Transport.

The Southern Region also, of course, has a large number of railway bridges. Many of its major junctions involve flyover bridges—a fact very apparent from

Plenty of examples of decorative valances can still be found on the SR.

a trip along the Southampton main line from Waterloo—and the latest reconstruction in the Gloucester Road triangle (G.6) typifies the major track simplification and resignalling that has been a hallmark of the region in recent years.

Much of the SR track is laid with continuous welded rail and renewed by the latest in tampers, liners and other machines. The same modern image is reflected in many of the region's buildings where trends have included station simplification, joint developments with commercial interests and major new railway schemes—without disregarding the fine architectural traditions to which the region is successor.

Among the smaller stations places like Beltring (B.12) and Chestfield & Swalecliffe (C.10) reflect traditional simplicity with having just sleeper platforms. Simple shelters are adequate for many other stations, especially on lines such as the coastal routes east and west from Brighton and the Tonbridge-Reading line, but many traditional small stations remain, eg, Chartham (C.10) to contrast with imaginative new construction such as that at Moulsecoomb (M.14).

Apart from the simplified stations, the range of small and medium locations still reflects immense variety and a great deal of original architecture. The LC&D lines portray economy with modest decoration to relieve the sombre effects whereas the SER lines do occasionally have flights of fancy—nowhere more apparent than on the Hastings line where the standard approach exemplified by Robertsbridge (R.11) is forgotten in the elaborate Gothic treatment of Battle (B.7). Other lines have standard original approaches, notably the

New Guildford Line and the Portsmouth Direct, but non-standard architecture is everywhere and frequently with some highly decorative Tudor, Italian or French overtones. The Strood-Paddock Wood line is just one worth travelling on for its sheer variety, including Aylesford (A.14) which seems to have been influenced by Aylesford Priory.

Generally speaking the LSW stations were less inclined to grandeur than the Brighton's efforts at Brighton itself (B.37), at Eastbourne (E.4), Leatherhead (L.3) and Tunbridge Wells West (T.13), but notable exceptions include the manor style evident at Hampton Court (H.5), Barnes (B.4), etc, the Dutch gables at places like Brookwood (B.44) and, of course, the special treatment accorded to stations like Windsor & Eton Riverside (W.34). Some styles were, of course, inherited, like the villa examples on the Netley line. Others were hybrid like the joint stations, of which no more interesting example exists than the one at Portsmouth & Southsea (P.19).

Although the SR buildings still reflect much of the work of people like Tite and Tress, and even David Mocatta, a much more obvious impact was made in the era of the Southern Railway. This shows up in countless rebuildings ranging in size from modest Cooden Beach (C.30), through the Kingston (K.4) and Surbiton (S.42) bracket up to the great piles at Hastings (H.11), Margate (M.3) and Ramsgate (R.3). The whole character of the system was changed in this era, frequently as part of the electrification process, and concrete was one of the major instruments of the change. It appeared not only in the station buildings but in all the impedimenta of footbridges, lamp standards, fencing and

Motorised platelayer's trolley.

hoardings and virtually produced a whole railway in the building of the Chessington South branch (C. 15), a sort of 'musique concrete' of the 1930s.

Many rebuildings were delayed by the war and not all post-war construction was as pleasing as that produced at Chichester (C.17). Clasp modular construction buildings (eg, Charlton N.15) do well enough and the D.70 Maze Hill designs (N.15) are economical and efficient but they are not quite in the same class as the achievement at Sevenoaks (S.12) which is light, airy, well-ordered and pleasing to the eye.

Contrasting with the wood and slate of Tisbury (T.8) and the surviving crossing houses like the one at Minster (M.9) are the great London frontages of Waterloo (W.12) and Victoria (V.2). These, in turn, make their own contrast with the rebuildings at London Bridge (L.12) and Blackfriars (B.25) which make extensive use of modern materials, and with the suburban commercial developments at places like Bracknell (B.34) and Crawley (C.34) and the raft extensions at Victoria.

The financial constraints leave many civil engineering problems unsolved but the co-operation with local interests which has redeemed Denmark Hill (S.30) after an arson attack may still help Crystal Palace (C.37), while Gosport is already the subject of rescue plans. On the track cwr and rail lubricators are all increasing track life, but the SR is a busy railway and its civil engineers have a large, complex, and many-faced system to maintain, modernise and renew.

SECTION 7

Early and closed lines

The pioneer Surrey Iron Railway, connecting Croydon with the Thames via the Wandle valley from July 26 1803, is commemorated by the present West Croydon-Wimbledon line which follows the route of its illustrious ancestor near Beddington Lane. Then in July 1805 the Croydon, Merstham & Godstone Railway opened an extension southwards from Croydon and part of this was to be included in the planning of the London & Brighton line some 30 years later. The next pioneer in the Southern area was the Canterbury & Whitstable Railway which opened its 6-mile line on May 3 1830 with a mixture of horse traction, winding engines and the locomotive *Invicta* and survived long enough to become part of the BR network, only finally closing after helping to solve the problems caused by the great floods of 1953. Two other concerns warrant pioneer status. They are the London & Greenwich and London & Croydon enterprises, forerunners of (and now absorbed in) the vital and busy part of the SR network which makes up the approaches to London Bridge.

The high population levels and extensive electrification have reduced the impact upon the SR system of the years of railway rationalisation. There have been few closures in the London area, with the notable exception of the electrified route from Nunhead to Crystal Palace, and most of the provincial closures have affected only rural and branch lines. A few of the latter closed before the Second World War but the major cuts came in the '50s and '60s which saw the loss of the route to Eastbourne via Hailsham, the lines south of East Grinstead and Uckfield and the Southampton & Dorchester line via Ringwood. The network in Hampshire and Dorset lost a number of 'north-south' routes including the links to the Somerset & Dorset and the former Didcot, Newbury & Southampton and Midland & South Western Junction outlets. Another group of lines to go was those around Midhurst and the links from Shoreham and Guildford towards Horsham. Kent fared rather better and lost only branches and light railways.

Not all closures were complete or clear cut. A line might lose its local traffic but retain through passenger services and freight facilities frequently lingered on for the whole or part of a route. Some lines went quietly, others would not die without a fight; and some, happily, have been revived by the preservation activity which produced a new batch of pioneers, notably the Bluebell Railway Preservation Society.

Apart from such examples as the Bricklayers Arms line (1852), the Croydon Central line (1890) and the Hamworthy branch (1896), the closure of lines to passengers is a 20th century phenomenon. And apart from temporary, wartime or emergency situations, the main closures have been:

Line or branch	Closed to passengers	Notes
	1911	
Chatham Central branch	Oct 1	
	1914	
East Southsea branch	Aug 6	
	1915	
Stokes Bay branch	Nov 1	
	1916	
Ludgate Hill-Holborn Viaduct	Jun 1	
	1917	
Greenwich Park branch	Jan 1	
	1926	
Ramsgate Town-Margate Sands	Jul 2	
Broadstairs-Ramsgate Harbour	Jul 2	
	1929	
Merton Park-Tooting Junction	Mar 3	Open for freight until 1972
	1931	
Canterbury-Whitstable	Jan 1	Final closure 1953
Lee-on-Solent branch	Jan 1	Final closure 1935
Hurstbourne-Fullerton	Jul 6	Final closure 1956
	1932	
Basingstoke-Butts Junction	Sep 12	Final closure 1936
	1933	
Bishops Waltham branch	Jan 2	Final closure 1962
Kemp Town branch	Jan 2	Final closure 1971
	1935	
Selsey Tramway	Jan 19	
Midhurst-Chichester	Jul 7	Open to Lavant for freight
Ringwood-Christchurch	Sep 30	
	1937	
Farnham Junction-Tongham-Ash Junction	Jul 4	Final closure 1961
	1938	
Dyke branch	Dec 31	
	1939	
Rye & Camber Tramway	Sep 4	
	1940	
Harbledown Junction-Lyminge	Dec 2	Final closure 1947
	1947	
Cheriton Junction-Lyminge	Jun 16	
	1948	
East Kent Light Railway	Oct 30	Open to Tilmanstone for coal
	1950	
Leysdown branch	Dec 4	
	1951	
Sandgate branch	Dec 3	Closed beyond Hythe April 1 1931

Left *The country end of Alton platform in 1983 with a sleeper across the route that once went on to Winchester with links to Fareham and Basingstoke.*

Right *One of the Wainwright 0-4-4T locomotives taking a breather at Bexhill West.*

Below *High Rocks Halt, closed in 1952.*

Line or branch	Closed to passengers	Notes
	1952	
Weymouth-Portland/Easton	Mar 3	Final closure 1965
Bulford branch	Jun 30	Final closure 1963
Merstone-Ventnor West	Sep 13	
Abbotsbury branch	Dec 1	Final closure 1962
	1953	
Gosport branch	Jun 2	Open to Bedenham for freight
Gravesend West Street Branch	Aug 3	Final closure 1968
Newport-Freshwater	Sep 21	
Bembridge branch	Sep 21	
	1954	
Robertsbridge-Headcorn	Jan 4	Final closure 1961
Nunhead-Crystal Palace	Sep 20	
	1955	
Alton-Knowle Junction	Feb 7	Final closure 1968
Petersfield-Midhurst	Feb 7	
Pulborough-Midhurst	Feb 7	Final closure 1966
	1956	
Newport-Sandown	Feb 6	
	1957	
Bordon branch	Sep 16	Final closure 1966
	1958	
East Grinstead-Barcombe Junction	Mar 17	
	1960	
Didcot, Newbury & Southampton line	Mar 7	Final closure 1966

Above *The pleasant route from Kimbridge Junction to Andover passed through Stocks-bridge but was closed in 1964.* **Below** *No longer can Kent & East Sussex passengers join and leave main line services at Headcorn.*

A preservation group tried to reopen the Westerham line after its closure in 1961 but was thwarted by a road scheme.

Line or branch	Closed to passengers	Notes
	1961	
Hawkhurst branch	Jun 12	
Midland & S W Junction route	Sep 11	Open to Ludgershall for freight
Westerham branch	Oct 30	
Allhallows branch	Dec 4	Port Victoria closed June 11 1951
		Open to Grain for freight
	1963	
Horsted Keynes-Copyhold Junction	Oct 28	Open to Ardingly for freight
Hayling Island branch	Nov 4	
	1964	
Alderbury Junction-West Moors	May 4	
Brockenhurst-Broadstone Junction	May 4	Final closure 1977
Crowhurst-Bexhill	Jun 15	
Andover-Kimbridge Junction	Sep 7	
	1965	
Peasmarsh Junction-Stammerham Junction	Jun 14	
Eridge-Hailsham	Jun 14	Final closure 1968
Bournemouth West branch	Oct 4	Part now used as emu depot

Line or branch	Closed to passengers	Notes
	1966	
Fawley branch	Feb 14	Open for freight
Ryde-Cowes	Feb 21	
Somerset & Dorset line	Mar 7	Final closure 1969
Itchingfield Junction-Shoreham	Mar 7	Open to Beeding for freight
Shanklin-Ventnor	Apl 18	
Southampton Terminus line	Sep 5	Open to Canute Road for freight
	1967	
Three Bridges-Ashurst Junction	Jan 2	
Appledore-Dungeness/New Romney	Mar 6	Dungeness closed to passengers July 4 1937 and completely 1972. Open to Lydd for freight
	1968	
Hailsham-Polegate	Sep 9	
	1969	
Uckfield-Lewes	May 4	
Romsey-Eastleigh	May 5	Remains open for freight (mainly)
	1972	
Swanage branch	Jan 3	Open to Furzebrook for freight
	1973	
Alton-Winchester Junction	Feb 5	
	1983	
Woodside-Selsdon	May 17	

SECTION 8

Preservation and non-BR lines

British Rail is by no means the only railway operator in the counties of the South East. The area embraces five major railway preservation locations with operating lines, including the pioneer Bluebell Railway, and the public passenger lines include such unique systems as the Romney, Hythe & Dymchurch Railway's route across the Romney Marshes, the Volks Electric Railway at Brighton and the line on Hythe Pier which forms a link in the ferry route across from Southampton. There are several static preservation locations of significance and quite a few miniature lines long enough to warrant a visit.

There are still some non-BR freight railway activities in the area but these are now very limited compared with the heyday of industrial railways when saddle tanks of every description could be found shunting wharves all the way from the Thames to the Solent, fussing over wagons of coal won from the hot, damp pits of the Kent coalfield or covered with whitish dust at the CMC and Tunnel cement works. By 1983 only a few remained but the surviving collieries still had a few diesels and there were substantial networks at BP's Isle of Grain installation and at the Esso Refinery at Fawley. At the other end of the Fawley branch diesels hauled the aggregate traffic on the former Eling Tramway and several coal concentrations retained their own power for positioning wagons. In North Kent the industrial railway tradition was being maintained by Wm Cory at Strood and at the steel and ship-breaking plants on the Isle of Sheppey. The RN Dockyard at Chatham also retained its system.

As part of the holiday tradition of the South Coast seaside miniature railways have continued to give pleasure to thousands at places like Littlehampton (12¼ in gauge, 900 yds), Hastings (10¼ in gauge, 600 yds) and East Worthing (Brooklands Miniature Railway, 10¼ in gauge, 1,320 yds). There are similar lines at Chessington Zoo, at Chertsey and even a short, standard gauge line on Alderney. Railed transport also serves the holidaymaker in the form of cliff railways at Bournemouth, Folkestone and Hastings.

The main operating lines and preservation locations are:

Bluebell Railway

Sheffield Park Station, Uckfield, West Sussex TN22 3QL. Along with the Middleton Railway this was the pioneer of standard gauge line preservation. The preservation group now has a 5-mile line between Sheffield Park and Horsted Keynes and operates steam trains at weekends and on weekdays in summer using locomotives and stock from the wide collection housed on the

Above *The 'new' Kent & East Sussex Railway in its early days and with No 10* Sutton *with an NLR coach and SE&C brake near Rolvenden.* **Below** *0-6-2T* Triumph *enjoying a change from its original industrial work on the Sittingbourne & Kemsley Light Railway* (Kent & East Sussex Railway/A.E. Loosley. Sittingbourne & Kemsley Light Railway/ B. Stephenson).

line. As might be expected, this collection has a strong 'Southern' flavour including not only Bulleid and Maunsell designs but also locomotives from the LB&SC and LSW companies and some Wainwright machines from the SE&C.

Isle of Wight Steam Railway

Haven Street Station, near Ryde, Isle of Wight PO33 4DS. The days and character of the Isle of Wight's steam railways are captured at this combination of steam centre and 1¾ miles of railway from Haven Street to Wootton. The railway operates at peak periods in the summer using pre-grouping stock and tank engines, mostly used or of the sort used on the individual Isle of Wight railways.

Kent & East Sussex Railway

Town Station, Tenterden, Kent TN30 6HE. The Kent & East Sussex was one of the light railways of character with which the notable Colonel H.F. Stephens was associated. Twenty years after the line lost its passenger services the preservation group reopened a section on February 3 1974 and since then has continued to extend the route, the activities and the collection of locomotives, stock and other items. On the 4-mile section from Tenterden Town to Wittersham Road, being extended to Hexden Bridge en route for Bodiam, trains are operated at weekends from March to October with additional openings at holiday periods. The location has a very varied collection of locomotives and rolling stock, a feature not at all out of keeping with Colonel Stephens' philosophy.

Mid-Hants Railway

Alresford Station, Alresford, Hants SO24 9JG. Although the original plan to secure the 17-mile line between Alton and Winchester proved too ambitious, the second share issue was a success and the Mid-Hants Railway opened its first

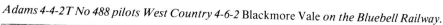
Adams 4-4-2T No 488 pilots West Country 4-6-2 Blackmore Vale *on the Bluebell Railway.*

three miles of line, between Alresford and Ropley, on April 30 1977. Known as the 'Watercress Line', the railway operates at weekends and Bank Holidays from Easter to October and has steadily increased its passenger carryings to the point where Medstead has now been reached and extension to Alton is no longer a pipe dream. The line is operated by the Winchester & Alton Railway Ltd and supported by the Mid-Hants Railway Preservation Society. With a gradient of 1 in 60 to tackle it has a 'big engine' policy and a strong Southern element in its locomotive stud, including four Bulleid Pacifics.

Romney, Hythe & Dymchurch Railway

New Romney, Kent TN28 8JF. This is a 15 in gauge railway operating along the coastal section of the Romney Marshes. It originated in 1927-9 as a private venture endorsed by the Southern Railway and authorised by a Light Railway Order, designed to give an economical transport facility to a remote area and operated, initially, for goods and passengers all the year round. Today the line carries passengers daily from Easter to the end of September and at weekends in March, October and November. A special attraction is the stud of 4-6-2 and 4-8-2 steam locomotives used.

Sittingbourne & Kemsley Light Railway

Sittingbourne, Kent. This 2 ft 6 in gauge line is part of an industrial railway built originally to serve the paper industry. Now 2 miles at the Sittingbourne end of

This scene at Haven Street brings back some of the atmosphere of the Isle of Wight steam lines. LSW 02 No 24 Calbourne *arrives from Wootton with a train of three LB&SC and one SE&C coaches and an SR PMV* (Wright Locomotive Society/P. Relf).

the system survive for the operation of steam passenger services as far as Kemsley Down. Mostly using Bagnall 0-6-2T and Kerr Stuart 0-4-2ST loco-motives which formerly worked on the industrial line, operation is at summer weekends plus Bank Holidays and mid-week in August.

Swanage Railway
Swanage Station, Swanage, Dorset BH19 1HB. At the Swanage terminus of the former SR branch from Wareham this preservation project has restored the station area and now operates trains over a 1½-mile route to Herston. As part of the working railway museum concept the project has accumulated a variety of locomotives and rolling stock and plans to extend its line to Corfe Castle. Operation is on summer Sundays and daily in August but the Swanage site is open every weekend all year round.

Volks Electric Railway
Madeira Drive, Brighton, East Sussex BN2 1EN. It is very gratifying that the first electric railway in Great Britain, opened in 1883, should still be running. Operated by Brighton Borough Council the 2 ft 8½ in gauge line is in use daily from Easter to the end of September and runs from the Aquarium to Black Rock, a distance of 1¼ miles.

In addition to these locations there is a 1½-mile, 2 ft gauge passenger railway in the grounds of Hollycombe House, near Liphook, Hants. This is part of the Woodland Railway and Steam Collection which is open each Sunday and Bank Holiday afternoon from Easter to September. Another mixed interest attraction including a railway line is the Southern Industrial History Centre Trust's Chalk Pits Museum at Amberley, near Arundel. The museum is located in a former chalk quarry and includes a short 2 ft gauge industrial line as part of its repre-sentation of the industrial past of the area. The Brockham Museum Trust also has a large collection of industrial items at its Betchworth site.

The Southern Region since 1984

Electrification on the former L&SW main line has finally been completed through to Weymouth. Public attention was focussed on the event by a record-breaking run on April 14 1988 when one of the new Wessex Electric units achieved an average of 71.7 mph on a special trip over the 142 miles 64 chains from Waterloo to Weymouth. The Class 442 Wessex Electrics were then introduced progressively on the route from May 16.

Two days after the record-breaking effort on the Weymouth line, further records were broken, this time by Thameslink services. An eight-car Class 319 Thameslink set achieved an average speed of 77.5 mph on a Down journey from London Bridge to Brighton and then did even better with 78.4 mph on the return working to Victoria.

The Thameslink saga made its first impact on June 16 1986, the date on which the work on clearing the old Snow Hill Tunnel formally began. The decision to restore the old route from Blackfriars to Farringdon had, of course, been taken much earlier, but the practical task of clearing the debris of years of disuse started in the middle of 1986 and was quickly followed by the laying of 800 yards of new track. At the same time the dual units required to operate from both third rail and overhead current supply were under construction.

The new Thameslink services were introduced on May 16 1988 linking the Bedford line with the SR system and providing an extensive train pattern connecting Bedford with Gatwick Airport and Brighton, Luton with Purley and Cricklewood with Orpington/Sevenoaks. The change from overhead to third rail current collection is made at Farringdon, with the SR boundary then following at the north end of Snow Hill Tunnel. All the Thameslink trains call at Blackfriars where the station reconstruction process was completed with the removal of the redundant LC&D bridge across the Thames.

Although the extension of electrification to Weymouth takes pride of place among the new works on the Southern Region, there have been other major changes in that sphere. The most significant bore fruit on May 12 1986 when the Tonbridge-Hastings route became a normal part of the SR system at last. Shortcomings on the part of the original builders of this line had led to the need to give tunnels an additional lining, reducing the loading gauge profile for the route and necessitating the use of narrow-bodied diesel-electric multiple unit stock. Singling the offending tunnels created room for the power supply equipment and thus permitted the introduction of normal electric operation over the line.

Following completion of the Tonbridge-Hastings scheme, work was started on electrifying the East Grinstead branch. Completed by October 1987, the scheme for

the 18 mile route involved the lengthening of the platforms at East Grinstead, Lingfield and Dormans. There were also alterations at Oxted, including the concentration
of signalling control there with the consequent closure of the signal boxes at East
Grinstead, Lingfield and Hurst Green.

Electrification work then continued on the SR in 1988 following approval for a
£16.4 million expenditure to eliminate the traction gap between Portsmouth,
Southampton and Eastleigh. A formal ceremony on July 28 1988 marked the start
of site work on the 29 route miles involved, completion being due in May 1990.

The BRB's new business sector Network South East was launched on June 10 1986
and has steadily made its impact on passenger services and facilities. The former
gained new through trains via Kensington Olympia to the North West in 1986. A
year later, the Gatwick Express service, now with new, dedicated facilities at Victoria, achieved a cumulative total of 14 million passengers and earned a programme
of renovation for the carriage sets in use.

In the sphere of stations and depots, the contraction of the smaller freight depots
continued with Public Delivery Siding facilities being withdrawn from Basingstoke,
Canterbury, Salisbury, Andover, Newhaven and Guildford. In contrast, there was
a great deal of renovation and improvement to passenger stations, including a num-

*A Class 422 Wessex Electric unit, newly emerged from BREL's Derby Works and in the
Network South East livery.*

The interior of one of the Class 319 units used on the new Thameslink services, showing the decorative panels depicting scenes appropriate to the routes.

ber of sponsorship schemes which involved local firms in these works. Dorchester, for example, got a new set of Up side buildings in a scheme that released land for BR's brewery partners in the station redevelopment scheme. The Waterloo & City line stock got a new livery under a similar commercial arrangement.

Most of the principal London stations have now been involved in some sort of redevelopment. Victoria, in addition to its separate ticketing and handling of Gatwick Express passengers, has special facilities for the users of shipping services and of the Venice Simplon Orient Express. The redevelopment of the station has also created the extensive and attractive Victoria Place shopping complex.

Charing Cross is the latest station to be disrupted by building work, in this instance to provide a 14-storey office block on a raft above the station, which will also receive improvements in the process. At Waterloo a new terminal is being built in readiness for the opening of the Channel Tunnel and the provision of rail services to Paris and Brussels from May 1993. The terminal is expected to handle 6,000 passengers an hour, and a £23 million international station at Ashford is also a possibility under the plans for the tunnel.

The Bill for the Channel Tunnel received the Royal Assent on 29 July 1987. The £6,000 million project provides for 31 miles of twin bore tunnel beneath the Straits of Dover and for a shuttle train service between Cheriton, near Folkestone, and Fréthun on the French side. The Trans Manche Link consortium building the tunnel has established materials depots at Shakespeare Cliff and at Sevington, near Ashford. Tunnel segments pass in trainloads to the latter from the Isle of Grain construction point.

The process of introducing the latest signalling equipment has continued on the Southern Region. Following on from the complete resignalling of the Brighton line, work began on the routes out of Waterloo. Costing £32½ million, the 1985-89 scheme covers the ex-L&SW lines out as far as Berrylands, Boxhill, Bookham, Putney and Chessington. On these the 1936 equipment is being replaced by the latest colour light signalling, with automatic route setting, train describers and other auxiliary systems, all to be controlled from a new signalling centre at Wimbledon.

There have also been a number of more modest improvement schemes. One resignalling scheme has covered the coast line between Portslade and Angmering, while a line and station modernisation scheme has commenced on the riverside route of the Medway Valley line. There six signal boxes have been closed and control centred on Maidstone West. Concurrently Aylesford station has benefitted from a £250,000 renovation and similar work is in hand for other stations.

The widespread programme of station and line improvements has been matched by improvements in the age, condition and comfort of rolling stock. As early as February 1985 the appearance of sliding door Class 455 sets heralded the process of re-equipping the Central lines and improving the services operating out of Victoria and London Bridge. Sliding door stock subsequently appeared on the Waterloo routes. To supplement the benefits conferred by new carriage sets there has also been a programme of stock refurbishment. One scheme affects the 4-VEP Class 423 units, the main vehicles for medium distance routes. Under a £17 million scheme, the seating per four-car set has been increased by 18 as a contribution to the reduction of overcrowding.

The latest route to receive attention is the Waterloo-Exeter line where a package of improvements includes increasing the trains to six-coach sets, adding three locomotives to the Class 50 fleet of 17, and extending refurbishment to some of the smaller stations. There is also the possibility of a new connecting line at Yeovil to allow interchange with the Weymouth trains.

Victoria station is to get a new facility in the form of a dedicated rail link to the leisure park being developed at Battersea Power Station. Two 'bullet'-shaped trains, capable of carrying 363 people, will connect 'The Battersea' with No 1 platform at Victoria.

Gazetteer update

Andover

One of the Southern Region's station sponsorship schemes links Andover with the TSB Trust Company. Under the Andover scheme the station has been repaired, refurbished and repainted using TSB colours. The forecourt has been landscaped and generally improved under a separate scheme.

Ashford

The former BREL workshop site at Ashford was closed in June 1984 but the area has gained a new freight terminal at Sevington to deal with supplies for the Channel Tunnel project. Additionally, consideration is being given to building an international station alongside the present one, provided with full

Below *BR has refurbished a number of stations in the SR Network South East sector in partnership with private commercial concerns, the TSB Trust Company in this Andover example.*

Above *The new Thameslink services were introduced in 1988 providing through workings from the Bedford line to the Southern Region via Blackfriars and using Class 319 stock.*

customs and immigration facilities.

Basingstoke

Basingstoke station has been renovated under an £800,000 scheme of improvement in conjunction with Provident Life Assurance. The scheme, which includes a new car park and up-to-date information systems, was completed in 1987.

Bexleyheath Line

The line has lost one station and gained another in its place. At Eltham Park the last trains prior to closure called on 2 March 1986, with the first trains serving the new Eltham station commencing from the following day.

Blackfriars

Improvements at Blackfriars have given the station a modern approach area and platform furnishings, fitting it for the introduction of Thameslink services from the May 1988 timetables. The frequency of the Thameslink trains have dramatically improved the pattern of journeys which can be made from Blackfriars, and also its level of usage.

One of the last features of the old Blackfriars was the 1864 LC&D railway bridge which was removed between 14 and 21 January 1985 using an 800 tonne floating crane.

Bournemouth

Bournemouth's operational responsibilities have been eased with the introduction of the Wessex Electrics running through to Weymouth. Another effect has been a 500 ft extension to the carriage servicing shed to accommodate the additional sets now requiring attention.

Brighton

There was a fire in the old Brighton signal box at the end of 1984 but this did not delay the programme of equipment renewal and track simplification associated with the concentration of control on the new Three Bridges signalling centre. 1985 brought further changes in the form of a major station remodelling embracing the lengthening of some platforms, new buffer stops, an extension of the concourse, new ticket barriers, and the replacement of the old indicator board by a modern electronically-controlled system.

Bromley South

Under a 1987 renovation scheme, the buildings at Bromley South received extensive interior alterations to improve the station's ticketing, information and parcels facilities.

Charing Cross

Charing Cross has joined the list of London stations undergoing redevelopment. The scheme involves the construction of a 14-storey office block above the station at a cost of £130 million. At the same time, Charing Cross will get a new passenger information system plus a new control office and staff accommodation on a raft above the concourse area.

Physical work began at Charing Cross in 1987 with the initial activity being concentrated on the enlargement of the ticket office and travel centre and improving other passenger facilities. By 1988 the construction works had been extended to the installation of the support columns for the office block building, each column descending through the platforms to the original station foundations and being designed to carry a load of 3,500 tonnes.

Clapham Junction

Under a 1986 development scheme, the station got a new entrance area within a shopping precinct scheme. The alterations also provided new ticket and enquiry offices and the station subway has been retiled in Network South East colours.

The approach to Christmas 1988 was marred by a serious rear-end collision on the LSW route approaches to Clapham Junction.

Crystal Palace

The station was provided with a new ticket office in 1986. Constructed in aluminium and glass, the design reflected the style of the original Crystal Palace.

Deepdene

The former Deepdene station has been renamed Dorking (Deepdene).

Dorchester

Work on new Up side buildings began early in 1986 and was completed in time for a ceremonial opening on 25 November. The scheme involved a partnership with the brewers Eldridge Pope & Co and released the area of the former Up platform and buildings for their expansion. In return, BR got a new main building, constructed in the same style as the adjacent brewery, and a reconstructed Up platform. The opportunity was also taken to provide a landscaped forecourt.

Dorking

The former Dorking Town station has been renamed Dorking West.

Dover

Following the decision to transfer BR train ferry traffic from Harwich to Dover, the latter point has been working on a new train ferry access facility at Western Docks. Operational from 1988, the new facility comprises two approach tracks at the station end, widening to four at the seaward end.

East Croydon

Work began in 1988 on a three-stage £723,000 station improvement scheme. The works will provide an extended ticket office, a new parcels office and new platform buildings.

East Grinstead Branch

The £7 million electrification works for the branch were carried out between May 1986 and October 1987. The process of adding the

18 mile branch to the SR electrified system involved lengthening the platforms at East Grinstead, Lingfield and Dormans to take eight-car trains, and the resignalling of the route to facilitate control from Oxted. The signal boxes at Hurst Green, Lingfield and East Grinstead have been closed.

Epsom Downs

Alterations are planned for Epsom Downs which involve the sale of the area occupied by the 1865 terminus for use as housing land. A new station is to be built at a point near the commencement of the station complex.

Esher

Work began in 1987 on a modernisation and development scheme for Esher. The main feature of this was a new station building in the car park area. The single-storey, flat-roofed building houses the ticket office and ticket hall.

Fareham

At Fareham general station improvements have included extending the ticket office, travel centre and waiting accommodation. The station now deals with the joining and separating of the Portsmouth and Brighton portions of Sprinters on the Bristol/Cardiff route.

Farnborough

There has been a modest refurbishment of the old parcels and information office area to produce a new travel centre and parcels point.

Fleet

A £160,000 improvement scheme has given the station an enlarged booking hall to accommodate a new travel centre, parcels point and bookstall.

Gatwick Airport

The Gatwick Express service for conveying airport passengers non-stop to and from Victoria was introduced on May 14 1984 and by 1987 had carried 14 million passengers. The trains use the Up side platforms at Gatwick Airport while those on the Thameslink terminating services use No 6.

Greenwich

The celebration of the 150th anniversary of the London & Greenwich Railway was rounded off with the unveiling of a commemorative plaque at Greenwich station on November 5 1988.

Guildford

Major reconstruction work began in 1988 to refurbish the main station buildings, forecourt, footbridge and subway. The scheme, which will also cover raising the platform height and new signs and canopies, should be completed in 1989. It will also provide land for a new four-storey office block.

Hastings

Following the conversion of the Tonbridge-Hastings line to conventional emu operation, the St Leonards (West Marina) maintenance depot, which serviced the previous demu fleet, was closed in 1987. The carriage cleaning shed and berthing area remained operational.

Holton Heath

A new, simplified station has been provided and the train service dramatically improved.

Hoo Junction-Grain Line

The commencement of construction work on the Channel Tunnel has produced a new traffic flow for the Isle of Grain line. From March 21 1988, concrete tunnel segments began moving from the construction point on a former refinery site to the new Trans Manche Link terminal at Sevington, near Ashford. The traffic passes in trainloads with two Class 33s providing the traction.

Kensington Olympia

From the May 1986 timetables the spirit of the old 'Sunny South Express' was revived with new through services between the West Coast Main Line and the South Coast via Reading and Kensington Olympia. A new ticket office and departure lounge were provided for passengers using these services, all of which use the Up platform. The Down one is out of use.

Lancing

The resignalling scheme for the Portslade-Angmering section of the coast line resulted in the closure of eight signal boxes and the concentration of their work on the Lancing box.

Littlehampton

A £600,000 station rebuild, using laminated timber and glazing, was completed in 1988.

Martins Heron

Resulting from a £600,000 joint venture by BR and Berkshire County Council, a new station was opened at Martins Heron on 30 September 1988. Lying between Ascot and Bracknell, the new station consists of two platforms, a small Up side building, a foot-bridge, and waiting shelters.

New Cross

The £500,000 spent on improving New Cross station has given it a new ticket hall, improved passenger and staff accommodation, and better information systems. The canopy on the joint BR/LRT platform has also been extended.

North Kent Line

Abbey Wood has benefited from a £700,000 rebuilding scheme which has given the location a new station. Completed in 1987, the works were mainly devoted to a triangular, single-storey main building, slightly east of its predecessor, and including ticket office, shops and waiting area.

Oxted

As part of the electrification scheme for the East Grinstead line, Oxted had its Down side station buildings replaced in 1987 by a new structure housing the ticket, waiting and parcels accommodation. The same year saw completion of the new signal box to control the East Grinstead route, and later that to Uckfield.

Paddock Wood

Paddock Wood has been the subject of a £250,000 modernisation job which included lengthening the platforms to take 12-coach trains.

Polegate

From May 25 1986 the station at Polegate reverted to its original 1846 location, the 1881 station half a mile to the east being closed at the same time.

The scheme for the renovation of Portsmouth & Southsea has included a new three-section roof for the High Level station and general improvements at the Low Level.

Poole

The goods yard at Poole has been closed and the cement traffic it dealt with transferred to Hamworthy. On the passenger station, the former uninspiring buildings have been replaced by a new complex of modern and pleasing design.

Portsmouth

Considerable work has taken place at the two Portsmouth stations. At Portsmouth Harbour, alterations to the 1936 station have enlarged the ticket hall and provided a travel centre. At Portsmouth & Southsea, the through, high-level platform was treated first, giving it a modern three-section vault roof. The low-level concourse was then re-styled, with the addition of retail units.

Radipole

Radipole station was officially closed from February 6 1984 although the actual closure, on safety grounds, was after traffic on December 31 1983.

Redbridge

A 1988 statement indicated that the Regional Civil Engineer's works at Redbridge was to close on March 3 1989.

Redhill

Station improvements have included a new Down side entrance area with refurbishment of the platform buildings following.

Ryde Pier Head-Shanklin Line

The ex-London Transport stock acquired for the surviving Isle of Wight line in 1967 is being replaced by another fleet of tube stock. Eight two-coach units being obtained from London Underground Ltd are due to go into service in May 1989. A new station was opened at Lake, between Sandown and Shanklin, on May 11 1987.

In addition to the advent of the new, ex-LT stock, 1989 changes on the Isle of Wight line include the singling of the route section between Sandown and Brading. These points will lose their signal boxes and the trains will be controlled by Ryde St Johns Road box. The removed track will allow the Isle of Wight Steam Railway to extend 3½ miles to an interchange island platform at Small-brook Junction.

Salisbury

Following the closure of Fisherton (East) Yard at Salisbury, it was taken over by Foster Yeoman as a stone terminal, with the first train from Merehead arriving on July 24 1987. The station has also benefited from a variety of improvements.

Shepperton

New station facilities, including a modern booking office, glazed waiting area, platform canopy and modern signing, were formally opened on November 11 1988. They were part of a development package which included the building of an office block on the old goods yard site.

Sidcup

Starting with the demolition of the Up side buildings, Sidcup has benefited from a £590,000 rebuilding which has provided new ticket, waiting and staff accommodation plus a small travel centre.

Sittingbourne

A 1986 £400,000 scheme of improvements included a new canopy and improved ticket, enquiry and other accommodation.

Slade Green

Repair work at the 1926 repair shed began to run down from 1988 in readiness for the building of a new 'Networker' servicing depot on the site.

Southampton

There has been near-continuous activity in the Southampton area starting with the £4½ million reconstruction of the tunnel west of the station. The work, which included laying a metre thick concrete floor and partial relining, was completed in mid-1985 ahead of schedule.

Subsequently, work was started on a £653,000 improvement scheme for the station. The main feature of this was the complete remodelling of the ticket office and travel centre area. Other changes include a 140 ft mural on the station footbridge and another on the London end crossing. The former, by Sue Ridge, is in semi-1930s style with elements representing the town's past, present and future, while the latter signals 'Welcome to Southampton' with a pattern of nautical flags.

The former Southampton Airport was re-opened on October 15 1986 as Southampton Parkway, with a new ticket office and a 330 vehicle car park.

South London Line

Following fire damage in 1980, the Victorian station buildings at Denmark Hill were restored with the addition of a pub, the 'Pheonix & Furkin'. Further restoration of the 1866 station earned the complex a Civic Trust Award in 1986.

At Peckam Rye a plaque was unveiled on 20 January 1986 to mark a scheme of restoration by BR and environmental groups. In addition to general renewal and redecoration, the ticket office frontage has been rebuilt in oak.

Templecombe

Sixteen years after closure in 1966, excursion trains started to call at Templecombe in 1982, with regular services beginning again in the following year. The success of the reopening was underlined with the provision of additional station facilities in 1988.

Tisbury

A passing loop, installed at a cost of £435,000, became operational from March 24 1986.

Tonbridge-Hastings

Full electric working took over from the previous demu service on May 12 1986 after a formal inauguration by HM the Queen Mother on May 6.

Totton

A new Redland Roof Tiles rail-served depot became operational at Eling Wharf in 1988.

Tunbridge Wells

The last train over the line from Eridge to Tunbridge Wells ran on July 6 1985 and ended the existence of this former LB&SC outpost. Grove Junction, between Tunbridge Wells Central and the now-closed Tunbridge Wells West, was severed on the following day.

Waterloo

The station is to have its own terminal for the Channel Tunnel services to Brussels and Paris in 1993. It is being designed with a capacity of 6,000 passengers per hour.

Weybridge

The station building was badly damaged by fire on January 5 1987.

Wimbledon

The new signalling centre should become operational in 1989 and then control the routes from Waterloo out as far as Berrylands, Boxhill, Bookham, Chessington and Putney.

Winchester

Repainting and roof repairs in 1986 were followed by the 1987 modernisation of the ticketing area and provision of new waiting and staff accommodation. In the second half of 1987 attention turned to extension of the forecourt and approach road area.

Windsor Branch

Following a fire in September 1986, Datchet received a new station building, including shops and office accommodation as well as the ticket office. The platform levels have also been raised.

A 60 ft bridge over a drainage brook collapsed during a midnight storm in 1988, derailing the 00.25 from Windsor and interrupting rail services for 48 hours.

Winnersh

Station improvements, celebrated formally on February 15 1988, include a new street level ticket office and waiting area plus platform shelters. The eight-coach platforms have also been given better signing and lighting.

A new station, named Winnersh Triangle, was opened between Winnersh and Earley on the Reading line on May 16 1986. It consists of a brick main building and eight-coach train timber platforms, and cost £375,000.

Routes, operation, closures and preservation since 1984

The main development affecting the route pattern of the Southern Region has been the reopening of the line through Snow Hill Tunnel. Although involving only a modest 800 yards of double track, it has allowed the introduction of a whole new

A Class 455 four-car emu set in Network South East livery. New sliding door stock of this sort is helping to ease the problems of peak hour congestion.

A scene on the Bluebell Railway, which is now being extended; 80154 heads the 1.30 pm from Sheffield Park through Lindfield Wood on March 27 1988.

pattern of services linking the Bedford line with SR lines to Brighton and Orpington/Sevenoaks. Following a royal opening on April 25 1988, new Class 319 units started operating the full Thameslink workings with the introduction of the May timetables, changing between third rail and overhead current collection just beyond the SR boundary at Farringdon.

The Region has also been affected by some major extensions of its electrified network. The previously restricted route from Tonbridge to Hastings was altered to become part of the normal third rail system in 1986, followed by the electrification of the East Grinstead line in 1987, and the extension of electric trains through to Weymouth in 1988. The next round will electrify the present gap between Portsmouth and Southampton/Eastleigh.

Electrification does, of course, confer a number of operational benefits. The introduction of the 24 100 mph Wessex Electric trains on the LSW main line has enabled 13 minutes to be cut from the journey time as well as providing new standards of passenger comfort. The reduction of station time has been aided by the progressive introduction of sliding door stock and preparations are already in hand for the advent of the new Networker units due in 1990.

To accompany its new and refurbished stock, and a wholesale round of station improvements, the Southern Region has benefited from a steady improvement in the fields of track and signalling. The original London Bridge works were followed by the full modernisation of signalling on the Brighton line and this, in turn, is now being followed by a scheme for the lines out of Waterloo. At the same time a number of smaller improvement schemes have been carried out, like that on the coast route between Portslade and Angmering.

On the debit side, the hurricane conditions of October 1987 brought serious damage to SR buildings and structures, although this was made good in a remarkably short time. The SR was also the scene, on December 12 1988, of Britain's worst rail

Members of Hastings Voluntary Conservation Project start clearing the dense undergrowth on the disused Northiam to Hexden Bridge section of the Kent & East Sussex Steam Railway, ready for reopening in 1990.

crash for 21 years, 34 people losing their lives when the 6.14 from Poole ran into the rear of the 7.18 from Basingstoke near Clapham Junction.

The one contraction on the SR was the withdrawal of services between Tunbridge Wells and Eridge in 1985. In contrast, several of the preserved railways are bent on expansion. The Mid Hants Railway has already completed its extension to the BR station area at Alton and the Swanage Railway has extended its line to Harmans Cross. In 1987 the Kent & East Sussex Railway announced plans to extend from Hexden Bridge to Northiam, and the Bluebell Railway started work on a new section northwards from Horsted Keynes to East Grinstead. More modest developments in the preservation sphere include the leasing of Groombridge station by the Tunbridge Wells & Eridge Railway Preservation Society and of the station site at Shepherdswell by the East Kent Light Railway Society.

The main preservation locations in the area are now:

Amberley Chalk Pits Museum, Amberley, Arundel, West Sussex BN18 9LT. 2 ft gauge passenger and demonstration lines.

Bluebell Railway, Sheffield Park Station, near Uckfield, East Sussex TN22 3QL. Five miles of standard gauge line.

Hollycombe Woodland Railway, Hollycombe House, Liphook, Hants GU30 7LP. Steam collection and 1½ miles of 2 ft gauge line.

Isfield Steam Railway, Isfield Station, Uckfield, East Sussex TN22 5XB. Short operational line.

Isle of Wight Steam Railway, The Station, Havenstreet, Ryde, Isle of Wight PO33

4DS. 1¾ miles of standard gauge line.

Kent & East Sussex Railway, Tenterden Town Station, Tenterden, Kent TN30 6HE. Five miles of standard guage line.

Kew Bridge Engines Trust, Green Dragon Lane, Brentford, Middx TW8 OEN. Pumping engines and 2 ft gauge line.

Mid Hants Railway, Alresford Station, Alresford, Hants SO24 9JG. A standard gauge line of 10½ miles.

North Downs Steam Railway, Cotton Lane, Dartford, Kent. Short standard gauge line, being extended.

Romney, Hythe & Dymchurch Railway, New Romney Station, Kent TN28 8PL. A 15 in gauge line, 13¼ miles long.

Sittingbourne & Kemsley Light Railway, The Walk, Milton Regis, Sittingbourne, Kent. 2 miles of 2 ft 6 ins gauge line.

Swanage Railway, The Station, Swanage, Dorset BH19 1HB. A standard gauge line, 3 miles long and extending.

Volks Electric Railway, Madeira Drive, Brighton, Sussex BN2 1EN. A 2 ft 8½ in gauge tramway of 1¼ miles.

Bibliography

Information on early and minor works relating to the SR area is now readily available again with the 1983 reprint by HMSO of George Otley's mammoth work *A Bibliography of British Railway History*. Two 19th century works are of particular importance, those of G.A. Sekon on the South Eastern Railway in 1895 and on the London & South Western Railway in 1896, while more recent major publications include from Ian Allan *History of the Southern Railway* by C.F. Dendy Marshall and R.W. Kidner (1963), from David & Charles H.P. White's two volumes in the Regional History series *Vol 2 Southern England* (1960/1982) and *Vol 3 Greater London* (1963) and R.A. Williams' two volumes on the *London & South Western Railway*, and from Batsford *The London, Brighton & South Coast Railway* by J.T. Howard Turner and *The Railways of Southern England* by E. Course, both multi-part.

Prime sources of factual information are *A Southern Region Chronology and Record 1803-1965* by R.H. Clark (Oakwood Press 1964), *Clinker's Register of Closed Stations* by the late C.R. Clinker (Avon-AngliA, 1978) and *Chronology of London Railways* by H.V. Borley (R&CHS 1982). In specialist areas the RC&TS has published books by D.L. Bradley on the locomotive history of the LC&D and SE&C concerns and of the railways on the Isle of Wight. Other specialist volumes include from Ian Allan *Southern Electric 1909-78* by G.T. Moody, *Rail Liveries Past and Present: SR* by B. Haresnape and *Sir Herbert Walker's Southern Railway* by C.F. Klapper, from David & Charles *Victorian Stations* by Gordon Biddle (1973) and, also on station subjects, *Railway Stations Southern Region* by Nigel Wikeley and John Middleton (Peco/Patrick Stephens 1971) and *An Historical Survey of Selected Southern Stations* by G. Pryer and G. Bowring (OPC).

The Oakwood Press list includes a number of titles dealing with individual SR lines and the more substantial of these are included in the following list of other relevant titles:
Forgotten Railways: South East England, H.P. White, David & Charles
Portsmouth Railways, E. Course, Portsmouth City Council
Rail Centres: Brighton, B. Cooper, Ian Allan
Southern Railway Handbook, B. Cooper, Ian Allan
SR Branch Lines in the Thirties, R.W. Kidner, Oakwood
The Bexleyheath Line, E. Course, Oakwood
The Brighton Line, John Eddolls, David & Charles
The Brighton-Portsmouth Line, N. Pallant, Oakwood

The Chichester & Midhurst Railway, Paul Clark, Pennine Publications
The Dartford Loop Line, R.W. Kidner, Oakwood
The Guildford-Horsham Line, H.R. Hodd, Oakwood
The Isle of Wight Railways, Michael Robbins, Oakwood
The Kent & East Sussex Railway, S.R. Garrett, Oakwood
The Midland & South Western Junction Railway, T.B. Sands, Oakwood
The North Kent Line, R.W. Kidner, Oakwood
The Oxted Line, R.W. Kidner, Oakwood
The Reading-Tonbridge Line, R.W. Kidner, Oakwood
The South Eastern & Chatham Railway, R.W. Kidner, Oakwood
The Southern Railway, R.W. Kidner, Oakwood
The Waterloo to Southampton Line, R.W. Kidner, Oakwood
This is Southern Region Central Division, C. Heaps, Ian Allan
This is Waterloo, C. Marsden, Ian Allan

Supplementary index

The PSL Field Guide series
by Geoffrey Body

This series, so far covering the entire Western, Southern, Eastern and Anglia regions of British Rail, provides a unique and wide-ranging picture of our railway network, embracing not only the operation and hardware of a modern railway network, but also its origins and special features.

Gazetteer detailing all important locations ● maps and photos ● services and traffic ● civil engineering features ● preservation.

Railways of the Western Region
Railways of the Southern Region
Railways of the Eastern Region
  Vol 1: Southern operating area
  Vol 2: Northern operating area

Also of interest...

Jowett's Railway Atlas of Great Britain and Ireland
by Alan Jowett
Foreword by David Shepherd OBE FRSA

A complete record of all railways in existence during the first two decades of the present century, together with subsequent additions up to the mid 1980s. 150 pages of maps, 7,500-entry index.

'...a great boon for settling arguments' *Sunday Telegraph*

'Such a beautiful atlas...is a work of art in itself' *David Shepherd*

'...a magnificent achievement...I think it's wonderful' *Miles Kington*

Other books on the railways of Southern England

The Waterloo to Weymouth Line
by Michael H.C. Baker

Published to mark the 150th anniversary of the opening of the first section, it is a unique trip down this line of contrasts, exploring its inter-city routes and its sleepy branches through their history and into the future.

London to Brighton
150 years of Britain's premier holiday line
by Michael H.C. Baker.

This book celebrates another 150th anniversary, that of perhaps Britain's best-known railway route which opened throughout in 1841.

A 1970 scene at London Bridge looking from the control office towards the City.